The Heinemann
English Grammar

Edizione Italiana
An Intermediate Reference and Practice Book

Digby Beaumont & Colin Granger

Traduzione di Teresa Tonioli

with answer key

MACMILLAN
HEINEMANN
English Language Teaching

MACMILLAN HEINEMANN ENGLISH LANGUAGE TEACHING, OXFORD
A division of Macmillan Publishers Limited

Companies and representatives
throughout the world

ISBN 0 435 28361 8 (without key)
ISBN 0 435 28362 6 (with progress tests and key)

Designed by Mike Brain

Riconoscimenti

Gli autori desiderano ringraziare tutti coloro che hanno dato il
loro contributo a questo progetto con suggerimenti e commenti.
Un particolare riconoscimento va Gibson Ferguson
dell'Institute of Applied Language Studies della Edinburgh
University, a Hazel Barker dell' English Language Centre, Hove,
Sussex, e a Michèle Cronick della Heinemann International,
Oxford.

Tutti gli autori di testi grammaticali sono in debito verso il
complesso di materiale pubblicato da cui hanno attinto. Al
riguardo vorremmo sottolineare I'importanza che per noi hanno
avuto in particolare i seguenti testi:

A Communicative Grammar of English, G. Leech, J. Svartvik
(Longman, 1975); *Meaning and the English Verb*, G. Leech
(Longman, 1971); *Practical English Usage*, M. Swan (OUP,
1980); *A Basic English Grammar*, J. Eastwood, R. Mackin (OUP,
1982); *Advanced English Practice*, B.D. Graver (OUP, 1963);
Cassell's Students' English Grammar, J. Allsop (Cassell, 1983);
Longman English Grammar, L. G. Alexander (Longman, 1988);
English in Situations, R. O'Neill (OUP, 1970). Infine, English
Grammar in Use, R. Murphy (OUP, 1985) per il trattamento
esemplare del materiale di consultazione ed esercitazione
grammaticale.

Phototypeset by Advanced Filmsetters (Glasgow) Ltd
Printed in Malaysia

98 99 00 01 02 14 13 12 11 10 9 8 7 6 5

Indice

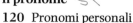

Introduzione

The Heinemann English Grammar è progettata in modo da aiutare gli studenti a capire e mettere in pratica l'inglese. Il livello è intermedio, ma è utile anche per gli studenti che hanno raggiunto uno stadio più avanzato e desiderano rivedere e consolidare quanto già appreso.

SPIEGAZIONI

Le spiegazioni grammaticali sono il più possibile chiare e semplici e l'inglese degli esempi è quello della lingua parlata ogni giorno. Sono stati impiegati alcuni termini grammaticali (per esempio aggettivo, nome, soggetto) quando si è ritenuto necessario. Questi termini sono spiegati nel *Dizionario grammaticale* alle pagine 295–297.

COM' E' STRUTTURATO IL TESTO

- Il testo comprende 190 unità. In generale, ciascuna di queste unità tratta una parte della grammatica (per esempio il presente progressivo, *will*, o gli articoli *a, an* e *the*). Le unità iniziano con spiegazioni ed esempi, cui fanno seguito uno o più esercizi.
- In aggiunta, alcune unità mettono a confronto punti grammaticali di unità precedenti (per esempio l'Unità 2 confronta il presente progressivo con il presente, e l'Unità 18 *will* con *going to*).
- Ci sono poi unità di riepilogo generale che riassumono e raggruppano punti grammaticali di unità precedenti (per esempio l'Unità 28 offre esercizi sul presente e sul passato). Queste unità di riepilogo consistono solo di esercizi e non danno spiegazioni aggiuntive.
- Alcune unità sono semplicemente di consultazione (per esempio le Unità 35, 67 e 75) e non contengono esercizi.
- Alle pagine 305–336 si trovano 88 Progress Tests. I tests trattano ciascuno un solo punto grammaticale e sono mirati sia alla verifica che al consolidamento delle acquisizioni precedenti.
- L' *Indice* è alle pagine iii–v.
- L' *Indice analitico* alle pagine 298–304 elenca dettagliatamente le varie costruzioni grammaticali, i tempi, le parti del discorso e tutti i più importanti termini inglesi. Include inoltre, in italiano, alcune espressioni che indicano il contesto in cui sono usate le varie costruzioni (per esempio abilità, obbligo, richieste, suggerimenti).
- Alle pagine 337–352 ci sono le risposte a tutti gli esercizi e gli Progress Tests.
- L' *Appendice* a pagina 294 dà utili informazioni sull'inglese che si parla negli Stati Uniti.

COME USARE IL TESTO

Alcuni suggerimenti   Usa l' *Indice analitico* o l' *Indice* per trovare le unità che trattano il particolare punto che desideri studiare. Leggi attentamente le spiegazioni e gli esempi, poi fa' gli esercizi. In seguito controlla le risposte alle pagine 337–347. Se, dopo aver controllato le risposte, hai ancora dei problemi, rileggi le spiegazioni e gli esempi.

Abbreviazioni usate nel testo: cfr. = confronta, vedi   ecc. = eccetera
p.es. = per esempio

1 Presente progressivo

1 Forma

Si forma il presente progressivo con il presente di *be* + la forma in *-ing* del verbo.

AFFERMATIVA		
I	am	
you	are	
he she it	is	working
we you they	are	

NEGATIVA		
I	am not	
you	are not	
he she it	is not	working
we you they	are not	

INTERROGATIVA		
am	I	
are	you	
is	he she it	working?
are	we you they	

Questo tempo viene anche chiamato 'presente continuo'.

CONTRAZIONI

'm = am
're = are   aren't = are not
's = is   isn't = is not

Quando si aggiunge *-ing* al verbo, ci possono essere variazioni di ortografia
p.es. *have* → *having*. Cfr. 188.3–6.

2 Uso

a

Si usa il presente progressivo per parlare di qualcosa che si svolge e continua nel momento in cui si parla.

'Where are the children?'   'They**'re playing** in the garden.'
'What **are** you **doing** at the moment?'   'I**'m writing** a letter.'
You can switch off the TV. I**'m not watching** it.
Look, there's Sally. Who **is** she **talking** to?
We**'re leaving** now. Goodbye.

b Si usa il presente progressivo per parlare di qualcosa che si svolge al presente ma non necessariamente nel momento in cui si parla.

You're spending a lot of money these days.
Sue is looking for a job at the moment.

Si usa il presente progressivo per parlare di qualcosa che si svolge al presente per un periodo limitato di tempo.

Robert is on holiday this week. He's staying with his sister in Bournemouth.

Si usa il presente progressivo per parlare di qualcosa che sta cambiando o progredendo al momento presente.

Your children are growing up very quickly.
Computers are becoming more and more important in our lives.

ESERCIZIO 1A

Che cosa stanno facendo i personaggi delle illustrazioni?
Forma delle frasi.

1   2   3   4   5

Esempio:

1 *He's reading a newspaper.*

ESERCIZIO 1B

Completa le frasi usando i verbi fra parentesi al presente progressivo.

Esempio:

'Where are Ken and Kate?'   'They*'re waiting* (wait) outside.'

1 '____ (Sally | have) a shower?'   'No, she ____ (wash) her hair.'
2 You ____ (not | watch) the TV at the moment. Why don't you switch it off?
3 '____ (you | enjoy) yourself?'   'Yes, I ____ (have) a great time.'
4 'What ____ (Maria | do) these days?'   'She ____ (study) English at a school in London.'
5 Ben and Patty are in London on holiday. They ____ (stay) at a small hotel near Hyde Park.
6 Prices ____ (rise) all the time. Everything ____ (get) more and more expensive.

Nota –Cfr. 3 Presente progressivo e presente.
  –Alcuni verbi p.es. *like, know* non vengono normalmente usati nella forma progressiva. Cfr. 27.
  –Si può usare *always* con la forma progressiva per esprimere il concetto di 'troppo spesso', p.es. *He's always saying stupid things.* Cfr. 26.
  –Si usa il presente progressivo anche per parlare del futuro, p.es. *I'm meeting Sue on Saturday evening.* Cfr. 19.

2 Presente

1 Forma

AFFERMATIVA	NEGATIVA	INTERROGATIVA

I you	work
he she it	works
we you they	work

I you	do not work
he she it	does not work
we you they	do not work

do	I you	
does	he she it	work?
do	we you they	

CONTRAZIONI

don't = do not
doesn't = does not

Dopo *he, she, it,* i verbi nella forma affermativa terminano in *-s/-es*
p.es. *I work* → *he works; you play* → *she plays; we finish* → *it finishes.*

Quando si aggiunge *-s/-es* al verbo, ci possono essere variazioni di ortografia
p.es. *study/studies.* Cfr. 188.1,4. Per la pronuncia di *-s/-es,* cfr. 187.1.

2 Uso

a

Si usa il presente per parlare di azioni ripetute o abituali.

*I **have** a shower every morning.*
*Most evenings my parents **stay** at home and **watch** TV.*
***Do** you **go** to the cinema very often?*
*What time **does** Kate **finish** work?*

b

Si usa il presente per parlare di situazioni permanenti (che continuano da un lungo
periodo di tempo).

*Mr and Mrs Shaw **live** in Bristol.* (E' il loro indirizzo permanente.)

c | Si usa il presente per parlare di dati di fatto sempre veri.

*The River Amazon **flows** into the Atlantic Ocean.*
*Vegetarians **don't eat** meat or fish.*

ESERCIZIO 2A

Completa le frasi usando il presente dei verbi tra parentesi.

Esempi:

The President of the USA *lives* (live) in the White House.
I *don't go* (not | go) to the theatre very often.

1 Jet engines ____ (make) a lot of noise.
2 I ____ (not | live) in London. I ____ (live) in Brighton.
3 The sea ____ (cover) two thirds of the world.
4 Loud music ____ (give) me a headache.
5 We ____ (not | come) from Canada. We ____ (come) from the USA.
6 She ____ (work) from Mondays to Fridays. She ____ (not | work) at weekends.

ESERCIZIO 2B

Completa le domande usando il presente.

Esempio:

'What time *do you get up* every morning?'   'I normally get up at 7 o'clock.'

1 '____ to the radio every morning?'   'I listen to it most mornings.'
2 '____ in Manchester?'   'No, he lives in Newcastle.'
3 'What time ____ work every day?'   'She usually finishes at 5.30.'
4 'How often ____ swimming?'   'I go about once a week.'
5 '____ TV every evening?'   'They watch it most evenings.'
6 '____ the guitar?'   'Yes, she plays the guitar and the piano.'

Nota –Cfr. anche 3 Presente progressivo e presente.
–Si usa *'What do you do?'* per chiedere a una persona che lavoro fa, p.es. ***'What do you do?'*** *'I'm a doctor.'*
–Se *who, what* o *which* fungono da soggetto di una frase interrogativa al presente, non si usa *do/does* p.es. **Who lives** in that flat? Cfr. 144.
–Spesso si usano avverbi come *usually, often, every day* con il presente per indicare la frequenza di un'azione, p.es. *I **usually have** a shower every day.* Cfr. 135.
–Si usa il presente anche per riferirsi al futuro, p.es. *The train **leaves** at 7.30 tomorrow morning.* Cfr. 21.
–Per il presente di *be (am, are, is)*, cfr. 31.

3 Presente progressivo e presente

Confronta:

PRESENTE PROGRESSIVO   PRESENTE

Si usa il presente progressivo per parlare di qualcosa che si svolge nel momento o vicino al momento in cui si parla.

Are you working now?
Don't forget your umbrella when you go out. It's raining outside.

Si usa il presente per parlare di azioni ripetute o abituali e di dati di fatto sempre veri.

Do you work every Saturday afternoon?
It rains a lot in Britain in March and April.

Si usa il presente progressivo per riferirsi a situazioni temporanee e il presente per riferirsi invece a situazioni durature. Confronta:

I'm sleeping on a sofa these days because my bed is broken.
I always sleep eight hours every night.

ESERCIZIO 3A

Scegli la forma corretta.

Esempio:

Look outside! *It's snowing!*/~~It snows~~!

1 *It's snowing*/It snows quite often in Britain during the winter.
2 *I'm going*/~~I go~~ to bed now. Goodnight.
3 Normally, *~~I'm going~~*/I go to bed at around 11.30 every night.
4 'Where's Simon?' 'He's cooking/~~He cooks~~ the dinner.'

5 There is something wrong with Lynne's car at the moment so *she's going*/she goes to work by bus this week.
6 The River Thames *is flowing*/flows through London.

Nota –Alcuni verbi p.es. *like, want* non vengono normalmente usati nella forma progressiva. Non si può dire ~~I'm liking this music~~. Cfr. 27.
–Il presente, anche nella sua forma progressiva, può essere usato per riferirsi al futuro. Cfr. 19, 21.

4 Passato remoto

1 Forma

Il passato remoto ha la stessa forma per tutte le persone (*I, you, he, she*, ecc.).

AFFERMATIVA

I you he she it we you they	worked came

NEGATIVA

I you he she it we you they	did not	work come

INTERROGATIVA

did	I you he she it we you they	work? come?

CONTRAZIONE

didn't = did not

Alcuni verbi sono regolari, altri sono irregolari:

■ La forma affermativa del passato remoto dei verbi regolari termina in *-ed* p.es. *work* → *worked*; *play* → *played*; *live* → *lived*. Quando si aggiunge *-ed* al verbo, ci possono essere variazioni di ortografia p.es. *stop* → *stopped*. Cfr. 188.3,4,6. Per la pronuncia di *-ed*, cfr. 187.2.

■ I verbi irregolari hanno forme diverse di passato remoto p.es. *come* → *came*; *see* → *saw*; *go* → *went*. Cfr. 190.

2 Uso

Si usa il passato remoto per parlare di azioni e situazioni accadute nel passato.

*I **played** football yesterday.*
*He **lived** in London from 1970 to 1973. Then he **moved** to Manchester.*
*'**Did** you **see** Sarah yesterday?' 'No, I **didn't**.'*
*We **didn't go** out last night. We **stayed** at home and **watched** TV.*
*They **went** to Italy on holiday last summer.*
*Marie and Pierre Curie **discovered** radium.*

ESERCIZIO 4A

(i) Quali sono le forme del passato remoto dei verbi nel riquadro?

Esempio:

1 paint *painted*

1 paint	2 make	3 end	4 invent
5 discover	6 die	7 win	

(ii) Completa le frasi usando il passato remoto dei verbi nel riquadro (i).

Esempio:

Ferdinand Magellan *made* the first voyage around the world in 1519.

1 The First World War ___ in 1918.
2 Marie and Pierre Curie ___ the Nobel Prize for physics in 1903.
3 Marconi ___ the radio.
4 Elvis Presley was born in 1935 and ___ in 1977.
5 Leonardo da Vinci ___ *The Mona Lisa (La Gioconda)*.
6 Alexander Fleming ___ penicillin in 1928.

ESERCIZIO 4B

Completa le domande al passato remoto.

Esempi:

'I went to the cinema last night.' 'Which film *did you see?*' (see)
'She went to London last weekend.' '*Did she go* on her own?' (go)

1 'What ___ last night?' (do) 'I stayed at home and watched TV.'
2 'Why ___ so early on Saturday morning?' (get up) 'Because she had a lot of things to do.'
3 '___ shopping yesterday?' (go) 'Yes, I bought some new clothes.'
4 'He went to the party on Saturday.' '___ himself?' (enjoy)
5 'They went out a few minutes ago.' 'Where ___? (go)
6 'We stayed at home last night.' '___ TV?' (watch)

ESERCIZIO 4C

Completa le frasi usando il passato remoto dei verbi fra parentesi.

Esempio:

We *didn't play* (not | play) tennis last Monday because it *rained* (rain) all day.

1 I ___ (not | feel) very well last night so I ___ (stay) at home.
2 They ___ (not | go) to Portugal on holiday, they ___ (go) to Spain.
3 He ___ (not | write) to me because he ___ (not | have) my address.
4 I ___ (order) a taxi to take me to the airport, but it ___ (not | come).

Nota –Cfr. anche 5 Passato progressivo; 12 Passato prossimo e passato remoto.
–Se *who, what* o *which* fungono da soggetto di una frase interrogativa al passato, non si usa *did* p.es. **Who discovered** radium? Cfr. 144.
–Per il passato remoto di *be (was, were)*, cfr. 31.

5 Passato progressivo

1 | **Forma**

Si forma il passato progressivo con *was/were* + la forma in *-ing* del verbo.

AFFERMATIVA			NEGATIVA			INTERROGATIVA		
I	*was*		*I*	*was not*		*was*	*I*	
you	*were*		*you*	*were not*		*were*	*you*	
he *she* *it*	*was*	*working*	*he* *she* *it*	*was not*	*working*	*was*	*he* *she* *it*	*working?*
we *you* *they*	*were*		*we* *you* *they*	*were not*		*were*	*we* *you* *they*	

Questo tempo viene anche chiamato 'passato continuo'.

CONTRAZIONI

wasn't = was not
weren't = were not

Quando si aggiunge *-ing* al verbo, ci possono essere variazioni di ortografia
p.es. *write* → *writing*. Cfr. 188.3–6.

2 | **Uso**

a | Si usa il passato progressivo per parlare di qualcosa che era in svolgimento in un
tempo passato. L'azione o situazione era iniziata ma non era ancora terminata in
quel periodo.

*At eight o'clock last night I **was watching** TV.*

Altri esempi:

*I saw you last night. You **were waiting** for a bus.*
***Was** Sue **working** at 10 o'clock yesterday morning?*

Confronta l'uso del passato progressivo con quello del passato remoto:

PASSATO PROGRESSIVO	PASSATO REMOTO
*I **was writing** a letter.* (= La stavo scrivendo.)	*I **wrote** a letter.* (= L'ho cominciata e l'ho finita.)

b | Spesso, nella stessa frase, viene usato sia il passato progressivo che il passato remoto. Osserva cosa succede nelle seguenti frasi:

PASSATO PROGRESSIVO	PASSATO REMOTO
I was driving along	*when suddenly a child ran across the road.*
When Kate was watching TV	*the telephone rang.*
We were walking in the park	*when it started to rain.*

Il passato progressivo descrive un'azione in corso nel passato; il passato remoto descrive un'azione più breve che è avvenuta durante quella più lunga o che l'ha interrotta.

Ma se un'azione si è verificata dopo un'altra, si può usare il passato remoto.

When the telephone rang, Kate answered it.
We sheltered under a tree when it started to rain.

Confronta:

When Kate came home Ken was making some tea. (Ken stava facendo del tè, quando Kate arrivò a casa.)	*When Kate came home, Ken made some tea.* (Kate arrivò a casa, poi Ken fece del tè.)

c | Quando si racconta qualcosa, spesso si usa il passato progressivo per descrivere la scena di sfondo e il passato remoto per gli eventi e le azioni che vi si sovrappongono.

PASSATO PROGRESSIVO	PASSATO REMOTO
I was standing outside the bus station. It was getting late and I was feeling tired. I was waiting for a man called Johnny Mars.	*Suddenly, a woman came round the corner and walked right up to me. 'Are you Mr Marlowe?' she asked.*

ESERCIZIO 5A

Collega una frase di **A** con quella più adatta di **B** usando *when* e il passato progressivo o il passato remoto dei verbi fra parentesi.

Esempio:

1 *I dropped my bag when I was running for a bus.*

A
1 I (drop) my bag
2 I (cut) myself
3 My car (break down)
4 I (see) a shark
5 My clothes (get) dirty
6 I (break) a tooth

B
I (drive) to work
I (eat) a sandwich
I (run) for a bus
I (shave)
I (swim) in the sea
I (clean) the attic

ESERCIZIO 5B

Scegli il tempo giusto dei verbi fra parentesi: passato progressivo o passato remoto.

Esempi:

When she *came* (come) into the room I *was listening* (listen) to the radio.
When my car *broke down* (break down) I *phoned* (phone) a garage.

1 We ____ (go) down in the lift when suddenly it ____ (stop).
2 ____ (they | have) dinner when you ____ (call) to see them?
3 When the doorbell ____ (ring) I ____ (get) up and ____ (answer) it.
4 When I ____ (open) the door, a friend ____ (stand) there.
5 'When I ____ (arrive) back at the car park, my car wasn't there!' 'Oh, no!
   What ____ (you | do)?' 'I ____ (report) it to the police.'

ESERCIZIO 5C

Questi paragrafi danno inizio a tre storie: una storia d'amore, una del Far West e
una dell'orrore.

1 Completa i paragrafi usando il passato progressivo o il passato remoto dei verbi
   fra parentesi.

(i) It was midnight and I was alone in the house. Outside it *was raining* (rain) very
     hard. I __1__ (get) ready to go to bed when I suddenly heard a strange noise
     outside my room in the corridor. Then, when I looked at the door, I noticed
     that someone __2__ (turn) the handle! I __3__ (rush) over to the door and
     quickly __4__ (turn) the key in the lock. Then I __5__ (ask) in a trembling
     voice, 'Who is it?'

(ii) It was early evening and it __1__ (begin) to get dark in the surgery of Doctor
     Nigel Harris. The young, handsome doctor __2__ (stand) looking sadly out of
     the window when there was a quiet knock at the surgery door. The door
     __3__ (open) and Dr Harris __4__ (turn) round to see the young girl who
     had just entered the room. She was very beautiful. With a sad smile the doctor
     __5__ (ask), 'Are you the new nurse?'

(iii) I __1__ (sit) in the big chair in Henry's barber's shop at the time. Henry
      __2__ (cut) my hair with his big pair of scissors when we heard the sound of
      horses outside. The noise was so loud that we __3__ (go) over to the window
      to look. Through the window we could see at least twenty gunmen riding into
      town. Henry immediately __4__ (go) over to his desk and __5__ (put) on his
      gun and Sheriff's badge.

2 Quale paragrafo dà inizio a quale storia?

Nota –Alcuni verbi p.es. *like, own* non vengono di regola usati nella forma progressiva. Non si può
          dire ~~I was liking the film~~. Cfr. 27.
          –Si può usare la forma progressiva con *always* per esprimere il concetto di 'troppo spesso'.
          Cfr. 26.

6 Passato prossimo

1 Forma

Si forma il passato prossimo con *have/has* + il participio passato del verbo.

AFFERMATIVA		
I *you*	*have*	
he *she* *it*	*has*	*worked* *come*
we *you* *they*	*have*	

NEGATIVA		
I *you*	*have not*	
he *she* *it*	*has not*	*worked* *come*
we *you* *they*	*have not*	

INTERROGATIVA		
have	*I* *you*	
has	*he* *she* *it*	*worked?* *come?*
have	*we* *you* *they*	

CONTRAZIONI

've = have   *haven't = have not*
's = has   *hasn't = has not*

Alcuni verbi sono regolari, altri sono irregolari:

■ Il participio passato dei verbi regolari termina in *-ed* p.es. *work* → *worked*; *live* → *lived*. Quando si aggiunge *-ed* al verbo, ci possono essere variazioni di ortografia p.es. *stop* → *stopped*. Cfr. 188.3,4,6. Per la pronuncia di *-ed*, cfr. 187.2.

■ I verbi irregolari hanno forme diverse di participio passato p.es. *come* → *come*; *be* → *been*. Cfr. 190.

2 Uso

Le frasi con il passato prossimo collegano sempre il passato con il presente.

a Si usa il passato prossimo per riferirsi a qualcosa che è iniziato nel passato e continua tuttora nel presente.

I **was** here at 3.00.
Passato ————————————————————

I **am** still here now – at 4.00.
————— **Presente**

Passato prossimo
I've been here for an hour.

Altri esempi:

*She **has worked** in London for six months.* (= Lavora ancora a Londra.)
*How long **have** you **lived** here?* (= Abiti ancora qui.)
*Kate and Ken **have been** married for 20 years.* (= Sono ancora sposati.)

Per *for* e *since*, cfr. 11.

[*]   In italiano, per esprimere questa relazione temporale del passato prossimo inglese, si usa il presente e si può formulare la frase in modo diverso: '*I have known him since we were children*' = '*Lo conosco* da quando eravamo bambini', oppure '*E' da quando eravamo bambini che ci conosciamo*'.

b   Si usa il passato prossimo per parlare di qualcosa che è accaduto durante un arco di tempo che viene considerato non ancora finito.

*I've **been** to Africa and India.* (= in tutta la mia vita, fino a oggi)
*Have you ever **eaten** Chinese food?* (= in tutta la tua vita, fino a oggi)

In questo caso il passato prossimo si usa spesso con gli avverbi di tempo indefinito p.es. *ever* (= in qualsiasi momento fino a oggi), *never* (= in nessun momento fino a oggi), *yet* (cfr. 8) e *before*.

*What's the best film you**'ve ever seen**?*
*I've **never seen** a ghost.*
*She**'s been** there **before**.*

Non si usa il passato prossimo con gli avverbi di tempo passato definito (*yesterday, last night, in 1985* ecc.). Non si può dire *She's been there yesterday*.

Si usa il passato prossimo con *today, this morning, this afternoon* ecc. quando questi periodi di tempo non sono ancora finiti nel momento in cui si parla.

*I've **written** six letters **this morning**.* (E' ancora mattina.)

c   Si usa il passato prossimo anche quando il risultato di un'azione passata è collegato al presente.

*Someone **has broken** the window.*
(= La finestra adesso è rotta.)

Altri esempi:

*The taxi **has arrived**.* (= Il tassì adesso è qui.)
*We**'ve cleaned** the flat.* (= L'appartamento adesso è pulito.)

Spesso si usa il passato prossimo per dare una notizia.

*My brother **has grown** a beard.*
*I've **found** a new job.*

ESERCIZIO 6A

Completa le frasi usando il passato prossimo dei verbi fra parentesi.

My name is Lynne Carter. I work for a travel company called Timeways Travel. I'*ve been* (be) a travel agent for six years now. I'm the manager of Timeways Travel London office. I __1__ (have) this job for three years. I've got a new flat in London. I __2__ (live) there for six months. My boyfriend's name is Bruno. We __3__ (know) each other for two years. Bruno is Italian, but he __4__ (live) in England for over five years. He works for BBC Radio. He __5__ (have) this job for a year.

Lynne Carter

ESERCIZIO 6B

Lynne incontra due clienti, Ben e Patty Crawfors, che sono in vacanza a Londra.
Completa la conversazione usando il passato prossimo dei verbi fra parentesi.

Lynne: How is your hotel?
Ben: Great! It's the best hotel I *'ve ever stayed* (ever | stay) in.
Patty: Yes, Ben is really pleased. He __1__ (never | slept) in such a big bed before.
  But he won't be so pleased when we get the bill. It's also the most expensive
  hotel we __2__ (ever | stay) in!
Lynne: __3__ (you | be) to London before, Ben?
Ben: No, I __4__ (not | be) here before, but Patty __5__ (be) a number of times.
  Haven't you, Patty?
Patty: That's right. But the last time was ten years ago and London __6__
  (change) a lot since then.
Lynne: And what are you going to do this afternoon?
Patty: Well, I __7__ (never | see) Madame Tussaud's. We __8__ (hear) a lot
  about it from friends, so we thought we'd go there.
Lynne: I see. And what about dinner tonight? I know a very good Japanese
  restaurant. __9__ (you | ever | eat) Japanese food, Patty?
Patty: No, I haven't. Is it good?
Lynne: It's delicious.
Ben: I __10__ (not | try) Japanese food before either, so let's go there.
Patty: Yes, why not?

ESERCIZIO 6C

Ogni sabato mattina Simon e
Sally puliscono la cucina. Ecco
quello che fanno:

SIMON E SALLY	SALLY	SIMON
1 do the washing up	2 clean the cooker	3 empty the rubbish bin
4 clean the windows	5 de-frost the fridge	6 clean the floor

Osserva l'illustrazione. Sono le
undici meno dieci di sabato
mattina. Quali lavori hanno già
sbrigato? Quali non ancora?

Esempi:

1 *They've done the washing up.*
2 *Sally hasn't cleaned the cooker yet.*

7 Gone e been

Confronta *gone* con *been*:

*Mr Jones isn't here at the moment. He has **gone** to the hairdresser's.* (= Non è ritornato.)

*Mr Jones is back now. He has **been** to the hairdresser's.* (= E' ritornato.)

ESERCIZIO 7A

Completa le frasi con *gone* o *been*.

'Where's Kate?'   'She's *gone* to the cinema.'

1 I'm sorry I'm late, everyone. I've ____ to the dentist's.
2 There's nobody at home. I think they've ____ away for the weekend.
3 You look very brown. Have you ____ on holiday?
4 Simon isn't here at the moment. He's ____ to a football match.
5 'Have you ever ____ to Scotland?'   'Yes, I've ____ there quite a few times.'

8 Passato prossimo con *just, yet* e *already*

Spesso si usa il passato prossimo con gli avverbi *just, yet* e *already*.

1 Si usa *just* per eventi molto recenti; *just* viene collocato dopo il verbo ausiliare *have*.
   *The taxi **has just** arrived.*
   *They've **just** finished.*

2 Si usa *yet* quando ci si aspetta che avvenga qualcosa; *yet* viene collocato normalmente in fondo alla frase.
   *It's nearly 10 o'clock. Has Andrew woken up **yet?***
   *They haven't finished dinner **yet**.*

   Si usa *yet* in questo modo solo nelle frasi interrogative e negative.

3 Si usa *already* quando qualcosa è accaduto prima del previsto; *already* viene collocato normalmente dopo il verbo ausiliare *have*.

'Where's Kate?' *'She's **already** left.'*
'Could you do the washing up?' *'I've **already** done it.'*

Already può essere collocato in fondo alla frase per dare enfasi.

*She's left **already**.*
*I've done it **already**.*

ESERCIZIO 8A

Metti al posto giusto nelle domande gli avverbi tra parentesi. A volte sono possibili due posizioni diverse.

Esempio:

Has Ken come home from work? (just)   *Has Ken just come home from work?*

1 Have you done your homework? (yet)
2 I haven't worn my new coat. (yet)
3 'Is Sally here?'   'No, she's gone out.' (just)
4 Have you spoken to your parents? (just)
5 It's quite early. Has Jack gone to bed? (already)
6 I've cleaned the windows. (already)

9 Passato prossimo progressivo

1 **Forma**

Si forma il passato prossimo progressivo con *have/has* + la forma in *-ing* del verbo.

AFFERMATIVA			NEGATIVA			INTERROGATIVA		
I *you*	*have*		*I* *you*	*have not*		*have*	*I* *you*	
he *she* *it*	*has*	*been working*	*he* *she* *it*	*has not*	*been working*	*has*	*he* *she* *it*	*been working?*
we *you* *they*	*have*		*we* *you* *they*	*have not*		*have*	*we* *you* *they*	

Questo tempo viene anche chiamato 'passato prossimo continuo'.

CONTRAZIONI

've = have   *haven't = have not*
's = has   *hasn't = has not*

Quando si aggiunge *-ing* al verbo, ci possono essere variazioni di ortografia p.es. *have* → *ha**v**ing*. Cfr. 188.3–6.

2 | **Uso**

Le frasi con il passato prossimo progressivo collegano sempre il presente con il passato.

a | Si usa il passato prossimo progressivo per riferirsi a qualcosa che ha avuto inizio nel passato e dura tuttora.

Passato ————————————————————————— Presente
Passato prossimo progressivo
*She **has been waiting** for an hour.*

Altri esempi:
*I've **been working** all day.*
*How long **have** you **been sitting** there?*
*They've **been listening** to the radio all morning.*

b | Si usa il passato prossimo progressivo quando un'azione è stata in corso fino al passato recente, specialmente se le sue conseguenze si fanno ancora sentire nel presente.

*It's **been snowing**.*

*It's **been snowing**.* (Non nevica più, ma c'è neve in terra.)
***Have** you **been painting**?* (Non stai verniciando adesso, ma hai della vernice nei capelli.)

c | Si può usare il passato prossimo progressivo per indicare il ripetersi di azioni o il perdurare di situazioni in un arco di tempo fino al presente (o al passato recente).

*I've **been having** driving lessons for six months.*
*How long **have** you **been living** in Manchester?*

ESERCIZIO 9A

Completa le frasi usando il passato prossimo progressivo dei verbi fra parentesi.

Esempio:

I'm sorry I'm late. *Have you been waiting* (you | wait) long?

1 She _____ (not | live) in London for very long.
2 How long _____ (you | study) English?
3 Those two men _____ (stand) outside the house for over two hours. Do you think we should call the police?

4 You look tired. I think you _____ (work) too hard lately and you _____ (not | get) enough fresh air and exercise.
5 'Annie's clothes are very dirty. What _____ (she | do)?' 'She _____ (play) in the garden.'

ESERCIZIO 9B

Osserva i personaggi delle illustrazioni.
Che cosa hanno fatto finora?

Esempio:

1 *She's been repairing the car.*

paint	onions
chop	on the beach
repair⌐	some shelves
lie	in the garden
put up	the car
play	the kitchen

Nota   –Alcuni verbi p.es. *know, want* non si usano normalmente nella forma progressiva. Cfr. 27.

10 Passato prossimo progressivo e passato prossimo

1

Confronta:

PASSATO PROSSIMO PROGRESSIVO

I've been cleaning my car.

Se si usa il passato prossimo progressivo, l'azione può essere finita o meno.

Altri esempi:

She's been doing her homework.
(= Forse ha finito i compiti, forse no.)

PASSATO PROSSIMO

I've cleaned my car.

Si usa il passato prossimo quando l'azione è finita.

She's done her homework. (= Li ha finiti.)

2

Si usa il passato prossimo progressivo per dire da quanto tempo è in corso qualcosa.

I've been walking all morning.
How long have you been having driving lessons?

Si usa il passato prossimo per dire quello che è stato realizzato in un arco di tempo.

I've walked six kilometres so far this morning.
How many driving lessons have you had?

3 | Si usa il passato prossimo progressivo per situazioni che sono più temporanee (che durano da poco tempo). | Si usa il passato prossimo per situazioni che sono più durature, (che durano da tanto tempo).

He's been living there for just a few weeks.
I've been working very hard recently.

He's always lived there.

You've worked hard all your life.

4 | La differenza di significato tra le due forme è a volte minima.

I've been living/I've lived in this flat for ten years.
How long *has* she *been working/has* she *worked* for the company?

ESERCIZIO 10A

Scegli la forma corretta.

Esempio:

'Can I have a look at your newspaper?'   'Certainly. You can keep it if you like.
~~I've been reading~~/I've read it.'

1 *They've been repairing/They've repaired* the road all this week, but they haven't finished it yet.
2 I'm very sorry, but *I've been breaking/I've broken* this chair.
3 Sally *has been saving/has saved* nearly two thousand pounds so far this year.
4 What's the matter? *Have you been losing/Have you lost* something?
5 *I've always been working/I've always worked* in the music industry.
6 Someone *has been eating/has eaten* my chocolates. There aren't many left.

Nota   –Alcuni verbi p.es. *know, own* non vengono normalmente usati nella forma progressiva. Non si può dire ~~I've been knowing him for years~~. Cfr. 27.

11   Passato prossimo con *for* e *since*

Spesso si usa *for* e *since* con il passato prossimo per parlare di qualcosa che, avuto inizio tempo addietro, è tuttora in corso (o lo è stato fino al passato recente).
Confronta:

It's been snowing for four days.

MONDAY   TUESDAY   WEDNESDAY   THURSDAY

It's been snowing since Monday.

Si usa *for* quando ci si riferisce alla durata (p.es. *four days*), si usa *since* quando ci si riferisce al momento d'inizio di quel periodo (p.es. *Monday*).

for + durata		*since* + momento d'inizio	
	four hours		*2 o'clock*
	three weeks		*10 April*
for	*nine months*	*since*	*July*
	twelve years		*1961*
	a short time		*I was a child*

| *I've been here for four hours.* | *I've been here since 2 o'clock.* |
| *He's been living in Paris for nine months.* | *He's been living in Paris since July.* |

ESERCIZIO 11A

Completa le frasi usando *for* o *since*.

Esempio:

I've been interested in jazz since I left school.

1 Lynne has been the manager of Timeways Travel in London ⎯ three years.
2 I've lived in Rome ⎯ I was two.
3 Mr Woods hasn't been feeling well ⎯ over a month.
4 Sally and her boyfriend Peter have been going out together ⎯ last winter.
5 I've only been waiting ⎯ a few minutes.
6 He's been in Japan ⎯ 1986.

12 Passato prossimo e passato remoto

1

Il passato prossimo collega sempre il passato con il presente; il passato remoto ci parla solo del passato:

a

Si usa il passato prossimo per parlare di qualcosa che è iniziato nel passato, ma che continua tuttora.

┌⎯ 10 anni ⎯┐
Passato ⎯⎯⎯⎯⎯⎯⎯⎯⎯ Presente

I've lived in London for ten years.
(= Abito tuttora a Londra.)

Altri esempi:

He has worked in a shop for five years.
(= Lavora tuttora in un negozio.)
How long have you been here? (= Sei ancora qui.)

Si usa il passato remoto per parlare di qualcosa che ha avuto inizio nel passato ed è finito nel passato.

┌⎯ 10 anni ⎯┐
Passato ⎯⎯⎯⎯⎯⎯⎯⎯⎯ Presente

I lived in Manchester for ten years.
(= Non abito più a Manchester.)

He worked in a factory for ten years.
(= Non lavora più in fabbrica.)
How long were you there? (= Non sei là adesso.)

b

Si usa il passato prossimo quando il risultato di un'azione passata è collegato al presente.

I've lost my wallet. (= Non ho il portafoglio adesso.)

Spesso si usa il passato prossimo per dare una notizia.

Someone has stolen my motorbike.

Si usa il passato remoto quando il risultato di un'azione passata non è collegato al presente.

I lost my wallet, but I've got it back again now.

Si usa il passato remoto per dare particolari della notizia.

I left the bike outside for a few minutes and when I came back, it wasn't there.

2   Quando si parla di un momento passato ben preciso p.es. *yesterday, last week, six weeks ago*, si usa sempre il passato remoto e mai il passato prossimo.

I lost my wallet yesterday. (Non: ~~I've lost my wallet yesterday~~.)
Someone stole my bicycle last week. (Non: ~~Someone has stolen my bicycle last week~~.)

Si usa il passato prossimo per parlare di un tempo imprecisato fino a coprire il presente p.es. *ever, never, recently.* Confronta:

PASSATO PROSSIMO

Have you ever seen a ghost?
I've never been to New York.
I've started taking driving lessons recently.

PASSATO REMOTO

Did you see your friend yesterday?
I went to London last week.
I started taking driving lessons six weeks ago.

Spesso, durante una conversazione, si comincia parlando del passato in modo generico, usando perciò il passato prossimo; si passa quindi al passato remoto, una volta identificato un momento specifico del passato.

'Have you ever been to the United States?'   'Yes, I went there in 1985.'   'Did you go to New York (= mentre eri là nel 1985)*?'*
I've seen that film. I enjoyed it (= quando l'ho visto) *very much.*

3   Si può usare *today, this morning, this afternoon* ecc.:

con il passato prossimo quando questi periodi di tempo non sono finiti.

I've spoken to Peter this morning. (E'ancora mattina.)

con il passato remoto quando questi periodi di tempo sono finiti.

I spoke to Peter this morning. (Adesso è pomeriggio, sera o notte.)

4   Si usa il passato remoto, e non il passato prossimo, per chiedere quando è successo qualcosa.

When did you arrive home last night? (Non: ~~When have you arrived home last night?~~)

ESERCIZIO 12A

Lynne Carter, direttrice della Società Timeways Travel, sta parlando con un giovane chiamato Paul Norris che ha fatto domanda di lavoro.

Scegli il tempo giusto.

Lynne: Your present company is Sun Travel, isn't it? How long *have you worked/ ~~did you work~~* there?

Paul: (1) *I've worked/I worked* for them for two years.

Lynne: I see. And what were you doing before that?

Paul: (2) *I've worked/I worked* for a student travel company in Spain.

Lynne: Oh, really? How long (3) *have you been/were you* in Spain?

Paul: For nearly a year. (4) *I've moved/ I moved* back to London from Spain two years ago to join Sun Travel.

Lynne: I see. And do you drive, Paul?

Paul: Yes, I do. (5) *I've had/I had* a driving licence for five years.

Lynne: And have you got your own car?

Paul: No, not at the moment. (6) *I've had/I had* a car in Spain, but (7) *I've sold/I sold* it before (8) *I've come/I came* back to Britain.

ESERCIZIO 12B

Completa le conversazioni usando il passato prossimo o il passato remoto del verbo tra parentesi.

1 'I know Sally Robinson.' 'Really? How long *have you known* (you | know) her?' 'Oh, for quite a long time now.' 'When _____ (you | first | meet) her?'

2 _____ (your husband | ever | have) pneumonia?' 'Yes, he _____ (have) it twice. He _____ (had) it ten years ago, and once when he _____ (be) a child.'

3 *(It's 10 o'clock in the morning.)* '_____ (you | see) Mrs Carter this morning?' 'Yes, I _____ (saw) her when I _____ (arrive) in the office, but she _____ (go) out soon afterwards.'

4 *(It's the middle of the afternoon.)* I'm really hungry. I _____ (not | have) any breakfast this morning and I _____ (not | have) time to go out for anything to eat this afternoon.

13 Passato prossimo e presente

Per dire da quanto tempo dura qualcosa, si può usare il passato prossimo, progressivo o meno, ma non il presente, progressivo o meno.

*She **has been waiting** for an hour.* (Non: *~~She is waiting for an hour~~*.)
*I've **lived** here since last year.* (Non: *~~I live here since last year~~*.)

ESERCIZIO 13A

Scegli il tempo giusto.

Esempio:

We've been working/We're working since 9 o'clock.

1 *I've been cleaning/I'm cleaning* my flat for the past two hours.
2 Look. Can you see Simon over there? *He's been sitting/He's sitting* in the corner.
3 'How long *have you been/are you* ill?'   'Since yesterday.'
4 *Have you known/Do you know* Sarah for very long?
5 *I've been learning/I'm learning* English since last year.
6 *They've lived/They live* in London now. *They've been/They're* there for the last six months.

14   Trapassato

1

Forma

Si forma il trapassato con *had* + il participio passato del verbo.

AFFERMATIVA

I you he she it we you they	had	worked come

NEGATIVA

I you he she it we you they	had not	worked come

INTERROGATIVA

had	I you he she it we you they	worked? come?

CONTRAZIONI

'd = had   *hadn't = had not*

Alcuni verbi sono regolari, altri sono irregolari.

- Il participio passato dei verbi regolari termina in *-ed* p.es. *work* → *worked*. Quando si aggiunge *-ed* al verbo, ci possono essere variazioni di ortografia, p.es. *stop* → *stopped*. Cfr. 188.3,4,6. Per la pronuncia di *-ed*, cfr. 187.2.

- I verbi irregolari hanno forme diverse di participio passato p.es. *come* → *come*; *see* → *seen*. Cfr. 190.

2 | **Uso**

a | Quando ci si riferisce al passato, talvolta si intende un passato precedente a un altro passato.

Passato precedente ——————— Passato ——————— Presente

When I telephoned Sue,
*she **had gone** out.*

Si usa il trapassato (p.es. *she had gone out*) per esprimere un'azione avvenuta prima di un'altra, pure passata, che ci interessa (p.es. *when I telephoned*).

Altri esempi:

*We arrived at the cinema at 8.00, but the film **had started** at 7.30.*
*When I spoke to the woman I realized I **had met** her somewhere before.*

b | Il trapassato è la forma passata del passato prossimo. Confronta:

PASSATO PROSSIMO	TRAPASSATO
*I **haven't eaten** all day today, so I'm very hungry now.*	*I **hadn't eaten** all day yesterday, so I was very hungry when I got home.*

c | Confronta l'uso del trapassato con quello del passato remoto:

*We got to the station at 8.00, but the train **had left** at 7.30.*	*We got to the station at 7.20 and the train **left** at 7.30.*
*When Sue arrived, we **had had** dinner.* (Mangiammo, poi Sue arrivò.)	*When Sue arrived, we **had** dinner.* (Sue arrivò, poi mangiammo.)

ESERCIZIO 14A

Completa le frasi usando il trapassato dei verbi tra parentesi.

Esempio:

'Why were you so angry when I saw you yesterday?'   'Oh, I*'d just had* (just | have) a big argument with my parents.'

1 I tried contacting my pen pal when I was in the United States, but she ____ (change) her address and no one knew where she ____ (move) to.

2 He was very nervous when he first drove in Britain because he ____ (not | drive) on the left before.

3 When I heard his voice on the phone, I knew I ____ (speak) to him before. Then I remembered I ____ (already | meet) him. I also remembered that I ____ (not | like) him very much.

ESERCIZIO 14B

Scegli il tempo giusto.

Esempio:

The office was empty when the police arrived. The robbers *had left*/~~left~~.

1 We had just started lunch when the telephone ~~had rung~~/rang.
2 When I opened the safe, the money *had disappeared*/~~disappeared~~.
3 Andrew was late for school yesterday. When he got to the classroom, the lesson *had started*/~~started~~.
4 They waited until everyone was ready and then they ~~had started~~/started the meeting.

ESERCIZIO 14C

Metti un verbo di ogni frase al trapassato e l'altro al passato remoto.

Esempio:

'Did you catch your train yesterday?'   'No, it *had already left* (already | leave) when we *got* (get) to the station.'

1 Andrew _____ (do) the test before, so he _____ (find) it very easy.
2 I _____ (not | laugh) at the joke because I _____ (hear) it before.
3 We _____ (leave) the restaurant when we _____ (have) dinner.
4 When I found my wallet I _____ (discover) that somebody _____ (took) the credit cards out of it.

15   Trapassato progressivo

1 | **Forma**

Si usa il trapassato progressivo con *had been* + la forma in *-ing* del verbo.

AFFERMATIVA		NEGATIVA		INTERROGATIVA		
I you he she it we you they	had been working	I you he she it we you they	had not been working	had	I you he she it we you they	been working?

Questo tempo viene anche chiamato 'trapassato continuo'.

CONTRAZIONI

'd = had   hadn't = had not

Quando si aggiunge *-ing* al verbo, ci possono essere variazioni di ortografia, p.es. *stop* → *stop**ping***. Cfr. 188.3–6.

2

a Quando ci si riferisce al passato, talvolta si intende un passato precedente a un altro passato.

Uso

Passato precedente ——————————— Passato ——————————— Presente

Dave had been driving for an hour when his car broke down.

Si usa il trapassato progressivo (p.es. *Dave had been driving for an hour*) per riferirsi a un'azione in svolgimento fino al verificarsi di un'altra, pure passata, che ci interessa (p.es. *when his car broke down*).

Altri esempi:

I'd been walking for about half an hour when it suddenly started to rain.
Mr Woods had been working for 50 years when he finally retired in 1965.

b Il trapassato progressivo è la forma passata del passato prossimo progressivo. Confronta:

PASSATO PROSSIMO PROGRESSIVO	TRAPASSATO PROGRESSIVO
I've been working hard all day, so I'm very tired now.	*I'd been working hard all day, so I was very tired last night.*

ESERCIZIO 15A

Completa le frasi usando il trapassato progressivo del verbo tra parentesi.

Esempio:

I'd been standing (stand) there for nearly a half an hour when I realized I was at the wrong bus-stop.

1 Maria's sister _____ (study) at university for eight years before she finally passed her exams.
2 'I'm really sorry I was so late last night.' 'That's OK. We _____ (not | wait) long.'
3 The strange thing was that we _____ (just | talk) about ghosts when we heard the noise upstairs.
4 'Robert moved from Manchester to London in 1988.' 'How long _____ (he | live) in Manchester?'

ESERCIZIO 15B

Collega una frase di **A** con un'altra di **B** usando il trapassato progressivo del verbo fra parentesi.

Esempio:

1 *I felt very cold because I had been standing outside for over two hours.*

A	**B**
1 I felt very cold because	they were lost
2 I (play) tennis so	they were very tired
3 The children's hair was wet because	I finally went to see the doctor
4 I (not feel) well for weeks before	I (stand) outside for over two hours
5 They (travel) all day so	they (swim) in the sea
6 They (drive) for about half an hour when they realized	I was feeling hot and sticky

Nota –Alcuni verbi p.es. *know, want* non vengono usati normalmente nella forma progressiva. Cfr. 27.

16 Futuro: *will*

1

a

Forma

will + l'infinito senza *to* del verbo (ma cfr. punto **b**)

AFFERMATIVA		NEGATIVA		INTERROGATIVA		
I you he she it we you they	will work	I you he she it we you they	will not work	will	I you he she it we you they	work?

CONTRAZIONI

'll = *will*   *won't* = *will not*

b Si usa *will* con tutte le persone (*I, you, he, they*, ecc.). Si può anche usare *shall* invece di *will* con *I* e *we*, p.es. *I/we shall work* (ma, nel linguaggio di tutti i giorni, normalmente si usano le contrazioni *I'll* e *we'll*). La forma negativa di *shall* è *shall not* (contrazione: *shan't*).

2 **Uso**

a Si può usare *will* se si prevede il futuro.

*Tomorrow **will be** another cold day in all parts of the country.*

Altri esempi:

*In the future, machines **will do** many of the jobs that people do today.*
*Who do you think **will win** the football match on Sunday?*
*We **won't arrive** home before midnight tonight.*

Quando si prevede il futuro, spesso si usa *will* con i seguenti verbi e espressioni:

think	*expect*	*believe*	*be sure*	*be afraid*

*I **expect** they**'ll be** here at around 10 o'clock tomorrow morning.*
*I**'m sure** you**'ll enjoy** the film if you go and see it.*

Si usa *will* in questo significato anche con gli avverbi di dubbio e valutazione
p.es. *probably, perhaps, certainly.*

*Martin **will probably phone** us this evening.*
***Perhaps** I**'ll see** you tomorrow.*

b Si usa *will* quando si decide di fare qualcosa nel momento in cui si parla.

*'Would you like something to drink?'   'Oh, thank you. I**'ll have** some orange juice.'*

*'There's someone at the door.'   'Is there? Oh, I**'ll see** who it is.'*
*'I'm going out shopping.'   'Oh, are you? I**'ll come** with you, then. I need to get some things myself.'*

ESERCIZIO 16A

Come sarà la vita tra 50 anni? Completa le previsioni usando *will/won't*.

Esempio:

people | eat | more artificial food
People will eat more artificial food.

1 the population of the world | be | much bigger
2 scientists | control | the weather
3 people | take | holidays in space

4 many people | not work | at all during their lives
5 people | live | longer
6 life | not be | better than it is now

Tu sei d'accordo con queste previsioni?

ESERCIZIO 16B

Completa le frasi usando *I'll* o *I won't* e i verbi del riquadro.

> ~~go~~   answer   not go   ~~put on~~   ~~not have~~
> ~~lend~~   wait

Esempio:

I'm tired, I think *I'll go* to bed early tonight.

1 'I haven't got any money.'   'Haven't you?
   Oh, _____ you some if you like.'
2 'The telephone is ringing.'   'Oh, _____ it.'
3 I'm a bit cold. I think _____ on a sweater.
4 'Would you like something to eat?'   '_____
   anything at the moment, thank you. I'm not
   very hungry.'
5 'I'm going out for a walk.'   'It's raining.'
   'Oh, is it? Well, _____ out now, then, _____ until
   it's stopped.'

ESERCIZIO 16C

Completa le frasi usando *will/won't* e i verbi tra parentesi.

Esempio:

You drive very well. I'm sure you*'ll pass* (pass) your driving test tomorrow.

1 Robert has got such a bad memory. Do you
   think he _____ (remember) the appointment?
2 'How long _____ (the meeting | last)?'   'I don't
   know exactly, but I'm sure it _____ (not | finish)
   before lunchtime.'
3 '_____ (you | be) at home this evening?'   'No,
   I'm working tonight and _____ (not | get) home
   until very late.'   'Right. I _____ (phone) you
   tomorrow then.'

Nota   –Cfr. anche 18 Futuro: *will* e *going to.*
   –Si usa *will* anche in questi casi: offerte p.es. *I'll post this letter for you* (cfr. 49.1); richieste
   p.es. **Will** *you post this letter for me?* (cfr. 48.2); rifiuti p.es. *The window* **won't** *open* (cfr. 52);
   promesse p.es. *I* **will** *be careful, I promise* (cfr. 53); minacce p.es. *Stop making that noise or I'll
   scream* (cfr. 53).
   –Si usa *shall?* per chiedere consigli p.es. *What* **shall** *I do?* (cfr. 42.4), per offrirsi di fare
   qualcosa p.es. **Shall** *I help you?* (cfr. 49.2) e per dare suggerimenti o fare proposte p.es.
   Shall *we go out this evening?* (cfr. 50.1).

17 Futuro: *going to*

1 Forma

Presente di *be* + *going to* + l'infinito del verbo

AFFERMATIVA			NEGATIVA			INTERROGATIVA		
I	am		I	am not		am	I	
you	are		you	are not		are	you	
he she it	is	going to work	he she it	is not	going to work	is	he she it	going to work?
we you they	are		we you they	are not		are	we you they	

CONTRAZIONI

'm = am
're = are   *aren't = are not*
's = is   *isn't = is not*

2 Uso

Le frasi con *going to* collegano il futuro con il presente:

a Si usa *going to* per riferirsi a qualcosa nel futuro che può essere visto come risultato di qualcosa nel presente.

Look at those black clouds in the sky. It's going to rain.
Those people are going to get wet.

Altri esempi:

Hurry up! It's getting late. You're going to miss your train.
Look out! That ladder is going to fall!

Per questo motivo, le frasi con *going to* spesso si riferiscono a un futuro immediato.

b Si usa *going to* per parlare di quello che si intende fare nel futuro. Si usa *going to* quando si è già deciso cosa fare.

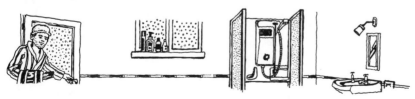

I'm going to have a shower.

Altri esempi:

'Why have you moved all the furniture out of this room?'   '**I'm going to clean** the carpet.'
'Lynne has just sold her car.'   'Is she **going to buy** a new one?'

ESERCIZIO 17A

Che cosa sta per accadere nelle illustrazioni?

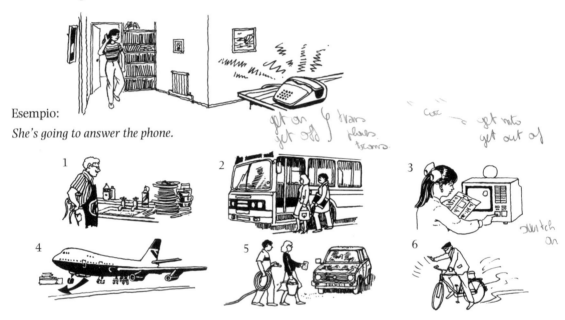

Esempio:
She's going to answer the phone.

ESERCIZIO 17B

Completa le frasi usando *going to* e i verbi fra parentesi.

Esempio:

'I've made up my mind I'*m going to change* (change) my job.'   'What *are you going to do* (you | do)?'   'I'm not sure yet.'

1 'What ____ (you | wear) at the party on Saturday?'   'I haven't decided yet.
   What about you? ____ (you | wear) your new black dress?'
2 'Why have you bought all that wallpaper? What ____ (you | do)?'   'I ____
   (decorate) the living room.'
3 He's decided that he ____ (not | leave) school this summer. He ____ (stay) on for
   another year.
4 'I ____ (buy) a new motorbike.'   'How ____ (you | pay) for it? You haven't got
   enough money.'   'I ____ (ask) my bank to lend me the money.'

Nota   –Cfr. anche 18 Futuro: *will* e *going to*.
   –Si usa la forma del passato *was/were + going to* per riferirsi a un 'futuro nel passato'
   p.es. I **was going to stay** at home last night, but I decided to go out instead. Cfr. 25.

18 Futuro: *will* e *going to*

1 Si usa sia *will* che *going to* per fare delle previsioni future, ma con un diverso significato:

Si usa *will* per parlare di quello che si pensa che avverrà nel futuro.

Si usa *going to* per parlare di un evento futuro che si vede come risultato di un evento presente.

That boat doesn't look very safe. It'll sink in that heavy sea.

Look at that boat! It's going to sink.

Don't climb up that tree. You'll fall and hurt yourself.

Look out! You're going to fall!

2 Si usa sia *will* che *going to* per parlare delle proprie intenzioni, ma anche in questo caso con un diverso significato.

Si usa *will* quando si decide di fare qualcosa nel momento in cui si parla.

'Oh dear! I've spilt some wine on my jacket.' 'Don't worry. I'll clean it for you.'

What shall I do tomorrow? I know! I'll **paint** the kitchen.

Si usa *going to* quando si è già deciso di fare qualcosa nel momento in cui si parla.

'Why have you moved all the furniture out of this room?' 'I'm going to clean the carpet.'

'Why are you putting on those old clothes?' 'I'm going to paint the kitchen.'

ESERCIZIO 18A

Completa le frasi usando *will* o *going to* con i verbi tra parentesi.

Esempio:

What can I do this evening? I know! *I'll go* (go) and see Sue.

1 'Someone told me that you're moving from London.'   'That's right. I ____ (live)
   in Manchester.'
2 'Would you like to come to my house this evening?'   'Yes, all right. I ____
   (come) at 9 o'clock.'
3 I don't feel very well. I think I ____ (faint).
4 'It's Simon's birthday soon. I've decided to buy him the new Blues Brothers
   record.'   'Oh, he doesn't like the Blues Brothers any more.'   'Oh, really? Well,
   I ____ (get) him something to wear.'
5 Oh, no! Look at those cars! They ____ (crash)!
6 'I could lend you some money if you like.'   'Could you? I ____ (pay) you back on
   Friday.'

19   Presente progressivo con valore di futuro

Si usa il presente progressivo per parlare di qualcosa che si è già fissato o
programmato di fare nel futuro.

'*What are you doing on Saturday evening?*'   *I'm meeting Sarah.*'
Sarah is taking an exam on Monday.
We're visiting some friends in Scotland next weekend.

Quando si usa il presente progressivo in simili contesti, spesso si indica il preciso
momento futuro (p.es. *on Saturday evening, on Monday, this afternoon, next weekend*).

ESERCIZIO 19A

Osserva il diario di Sally con i suoi appuntamenti per la prossima settimana. Quindi completa quello che dice al proposito. Usa i verbi del riquadro.

work   meet   do   go   see

On Monday evening I'*m going* to a disco with my friend Louise. On Tuesday evening I __1__ late. __2__ (not) anything on Wednesday evening. On Thursday evening I __3__ my friend Julie at 7 o'clock. I've got an appointment with the doctor on Friday evening. I __4__ him at 6.30. Then on Saturday I __5__ to the cinema with Peter. We __6__ at the Espresso Cafe at 7.30. What about you? What __7__ (you) next week? __8__ (you) anything special?

Nota   –Per la forma del presente progressivo cfr. 1.1.
–Alcuni verbi p.es. *be, like* normalmente non vengono usati nella forma progressiva. Non si può dire ~~I'm being at home tonight~~. Cfr. 27.

20   Futuro: presente progressivo e *going to*

1   Quando si parla di qualcosa che è già fissato o programmato per il futuro, si può usare il presente progressivo (cfr. 19) o *going to* (cfr. 17).
I'm having lunch with Lynne tomorrow.
I'm going to have lunch with Lynne tomorrow.

2   Quando si prevede qualcosa del futuro, si può usare *going to* (o *will*), ma non il presente progressivo.
It's going to rain tomorrow. (Non: ~~It's raining tomorrow~~.)

ESERCIZIO 20A

Completa le frasi usando o il presente progressivo o *going to*. In alcuni casi sono possibili entrambi.

Esempi:

I (see) Sarah this afternoon.   *I'm seeing Sarah this afternoon./I'm going to see Sarah this afternoon.*

Hurry up! We (miss) our bus.   *Hurry up! We're going to miss our bus.*

1 It (snow) later tonight.
2 She (meet) them tomorrow morning.
3 What (you | do) this afternoon?
4 Be careful! You (break) that glass.
5 He (not | come) next Saturday.
6 Look out! You (hurt) yourself with that knife.

Nota   –Alcuni verbi p.es. *be*, *like* non vengono di solito usati nella forma progressiva: si può dire *I'm going to be* in London next Saturday ma non ~~I'm being in London next Saturday~~. Cfr. 27.

21 Presente con valore di futuro

Si usa il presente per parlare di eventi futuri che fanno parte di orari o programmi prefissati.

Ecco alcune trasmissioni televisive in programma per domani sera.

'What time **does** the tennis **start** tomorrow evening?'   'At 6.15.'
The film **starts** at 7.30 and **finishes** at 9.00.

Altri esempi:

What time **does** your plane **leave** tomorrow?
Next summer the school holidays **begin** on July 25th and **end** on September 10th.

Si usa il presente al posto del futuro in casi simili, quando si considera cioè un fatto, un accordo o un programma futuro come qualcosa di non modificabile.

ESERCIZIO 21A

Completa le frasi usando il presente dei verbi tra parentesi.

Esempio:

Our boat *leaves* (leave) Dover at 2.00 on Friday and *arrives* (arrive) in Calais at 6.00.

1 The conference _STARTS_ (start) on June 3rd, and _FINISHES_ (finish) on June 10th.
2 We've got plenty of time. Our plane _DOESN'T TAKE OFF_ (not | take off) until 9 o'clock.
3 Tonight's concert _BEGINS_ (begin) at 8.00 and it _DOESN'T END_ (not | end) until 11.00.
4 When _DOES THE NEXT TRAIN LEAVE_ (the next train | leave) for Bristol?

22 Presente con valore di futuro dopo *when, if,* ecc.

Si usa il presente per riferirsi al futuro in frasi temporali e condizionali dopo *when, while, as soon as, after, before, until, if, unless, as/so long as, provided/providing (that).*

will/won't	presente
I'll buy a newspaper	**when** I **go** out.
We won't go out	**until** it **stops** raining.
We'll go to the beach	**if** the weather **is** nice.
I'll go to the party	**provided** you **go** too.

ESERCIZIO 22A

Metti un verbo di ogni frase al presente e l'altro al futuro usando *will/won't.*

Esempi:

If I *fail* (fail) the exam, I*'ll take* (take) it again.

1 When I _SEE_ (see) him I _'ll GIVE_ (give) him your message.
2 I _'ll BUY_ (buy) a new car as soon as I _HAVE_ (have) enough money.
3 If the weather _IS_ (be) nice tomorrow, we _'ll GO_ (go) sailing.
4 I _'ll LOOK AFTER_ (look after) your cat while you _IS_ (be) on holiday.
5 He _won't DO_ (not | do) anything until he _HEARS_ (hear) from us.
6 The door _won't OPEN_ (not | open) unless you _PUSH_ (push) it hard.
7 We'_ll PLAY_ (play) tennis this evening as long as it _DOESN'T RAIN_ (not | rain).
8 I _'ll LEND_ (lend) you the money provided you _PAY_ (pay) me back tomorrow.

Nota – Si può usare anche il passato prossimo dopo *when, if* ecc. per indicare che l'azione introdotta da *when, if* ecc. finirà prima dell'altra p.es. *I'll lend you the newspaper* **when I've finished** it.

23 Futuro progressivo: *will be* + forma in *-ing*

1

a

Forma

will be + la forma in *-ing* del verbo (ma cfr. punto **b**)

AFFERMATIVA		NEGATIVA		INTERROGATIVA		
I *you* *he* *she* *it* *we* *you* *they*	*will be working*	*I* *you* *he* *she* *it* *we* *you* *they*	*will not be working*	*will*	*I* *you* *he* *she* *it* *we* *you* *they*	*be working?*

Questo tempo viene anche chiamato 'futuro continuo'.

CONTRAZIONI

'll = will   *won't = will not*

Quando si aggiunge *-ing* al verbo, ci possono essere variazioni di ortografia p.es. *live* → *liv**ing***. Cfr. 188.3–6.

b Si può usare *shall* invece di *will* con *I* e *we* p.es. *I/we shall be working* (ma nel linguaggio quotidiano si usano di solito le contrazioni *I'll* e *we'll*). La forma negativa di *shall* è *shall not* (contrazione: *shan't*).

2

a

Uso

Si usa il futuro progressivo per parlare di qualcosa che sarà in svolgimento in un preciso momento futuro.

I'll be having dinner at 7.00.
Don't phone me at 8.00. I'll be doing my homework then.
What **will** you **be doing** this time next week?

b

Si usa il futuro progressivo per parlare di qualcosa già programmato per il futuro, o che fa parte di una routine.

*I'll **be driving** into town later on. Do you want a lift?*

*'Would you like me to give Peter a message for you?' 'Oh, I don't want to trouble you.' 'It's no trouble, really. I'll **be seeing** Peter tomorrow anyway.'*

Spesso si usa il futuro progressivo per chiedere in modo cortese i programmi di una persona, specialmente quando vogliamo che questa persona faccia qualcosa per noi.

*'**Will** you **be going** out this morning?' 'Yes, why?' 'Oh, could you get me a newspaper?'*
*Will you **be using** your camera at the weekend? I wondered if I could borrow it.*

Quando si usa il futuro progressivo in questi casi spesso si vuole dare l'impressione che non si desidera interferire con il programma dell'altra persona.

ESERCIZIO 23A PER AFFARI → ON BUSINESS

Domani Lynne Carter partirà da Londra per andare a Manchester per affari. Ecco il suo programma.

Che cosa starà facendo domani alle seguenti ore?

Esempio:

8.30
At 8.30 tomorrow she'll be flying to Manchester.

8.00 – 8.55	Fly to Manchester.
10.00 – 12.00	Visit the ABC travel company.
13.00 – 14.30	Have lunch with Mary and Ron King.
15.00 – 16.00	Visit Derek Hall.
16.15 – 16.45	Take a taxi to the airport.
17.15 – 18.05	Fly back to London.

1 11.00   2 13.30   3 15.30   4 16.30
5 17.30

ESERCIZIO 23B

Completa le frasi con il futuro progressivo dei verbi fra parentesi.

Esempio:

I'll be going (go) shopping later. Do you want me to get you anything?
1 ____ (you | speak) to Robert in the next few days? I've got a message for him.
2 I ____ (not | use) my car this evening. Do you want to borrow it?
3 We ____ (get) some concert tickets for ourselves. Would you like us to get you one?
4 When ____ (you | visit) your grandparents again?

Nota —Alcuni verbi p.es. *be, know* non vengono usati, di solito, nella forma progressiva: non si può dire *I'll be being at home this evening*. Cfr. 27.

24 Futuro anteriore: *will have* + participio passato

1

a **Forma**

will have + il participio passato del verbo (ma cfr. punto **b**)

AFFERMATIVA			NEGATIVA			INTERROGATIVA			
I you he she it we you they	will have	finished gone	I you he she it we you they	will not have	finished gone	will	I you he she it we you they	have	finished? gone?

CONTRAZIONI

'll = *will*   *won't* = *will not*

Alcuni verbi sono regolari, altri sono irregolari.

- Il participio passato dei verbi regolari termina in *-ed* p.es. *finish* → *finish**ed***. Quando si aggiunge *-ed* al verbo, ci possono essere variazioni di ortografia p.es. *stop* → *stop**ped***. Cfr. 188.3,4,6. Per la pronuncia di *-ed*, cfr. 187.2.

- I verbi irregolari hanno forme diverse di participio passato p.es. *go* → ***gone***; *be* → ***been***. Cfr. 190.

b Si può usare *shall* invece di *will* con *I* e *we* p.es. *I/we shall have finished* (ma nel linguaggio di tutti i giorni normalmente si usano le contrazioni *I'll* e *we'll*). La forma negativa di *shall* è *shall not* (contrazione: *shan't*).

2 **Uso**

Si può usare il futuro anteriore per parlare di qualcosa che sarà completato entro (e non oltre) un preciso momento del futuro.

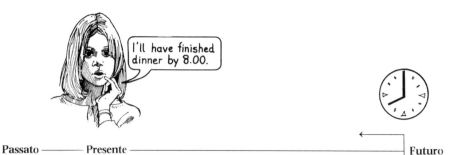

Passato ——— Presente ————————————————————————— Futuro

Quando si usa questa costruzione, si pensa a un periodo futuro entro il quale, nel momento in cui si parla, si ritiene che qualcosa sarà completato.

*I'll **have finished** dinner by 8.00.*

*'I'll phone you at 11.'   'No, I'll **have gone** to bed by then. Can you phone a bit earlier?'*
*I'll **have worked** here for a year next September.*

ESERCIZIO 24A

Completa le frasi usando il futuro anteriore dei verbi fra parentesi.

Esempio:
I need my car first thing tomorrow morning. Do you think *you will have repaired* (you | repair) it by then?

1 By next summer my brother ____ (leave) university.
2 I'll meet you outside your office this evening. ____ (you | finish) work by 6.00?
3 'I'll come round to your house at 7.00.'   'No, that's too late. I ____ (go) out by then.'
4 I'm sure they'll be hungry. When they arrive here, they ____ (not | eat) anything since this morning.

Nota   –E' possibile anche la forma progressiva: *will have been* + . . . *-ing* p.es. *They'll be tired when they arrive. They'll **have been travelling** all day.*

25 Futuro nel passato: *was/were going to*

Si può usare *was/were going to* + l'infinito del verbo per dire che qualcosa era stato programmato per il futuro in un tempo passato.

Futuro ————————→
Passato —————————————————Presente——————————Futuro

*They **were going to get** married, but in the end they changed their minds.*

Nota che quando si usa questa costruzione spesso si vuole dire che l'azione programmata per il futuro non è avvenuta.

*I **was going to stay** at home last night, but I decided to go out instead.*
*We **were going to eat** at the Italian restaurant, but it was full, so we ate somewhere else.*
*I thought you **were going to visit** me yesterday. Why didn't you?*

ESERCIZIO 25A

Collega una frase di **A** con una di **B**, usando *was/were going to* e un verbo tra parentesi.

Esempio:

1 *I was going to take a taxi home last night, but I didn't have enough money, so I had to walk.*

A	**B**
1 I (take) a taxi home last night,	but it rained all afternoon, so we stayed at home.
2 We (write) to them when we were on holiday,	but my boss offered me more money, so I decided to stay.
3 She (drive) to Scotland last weekend,	but I didn't have enough money, so I had to walk.
4 We (play) tennis yesterday afternoon,	but she had seen it before, so she went to bed early.
5 She (watch) the film on TV last night,	but her car broke down, so she went by train.
6 I (change) my job last year.	but we changed our minds and phoned them instead.

Nota –In alcuni casi è possibile esprimere il futuro nel passato con *would* p.es. *I was very surprised you failed the exam. I thought you* **would** *pass easily.*

26   Forma progressiva con *always*

1   Si può usare *always* con la forma progressiva dei vari tempi (p.es. presente progressivo, passato progressivo) per esprimere il concetto di 'troppo spesso'.

He's **always saying** *stupid things.*
Our neighbours **are always having** *arguments.*
She **was always crying** *when she was a baby.*

Questo uso di *always* esprime spesso rabbia o irritazione (per la frequenza con cui accade qualcosa).

2   *Always* di solito significa 'sempre', nel qual caso non viene mai usato con la forma progressiva. Confronta:

always nel significato usuale	*always* con la forma progressiva
She **always comes** *to work at 8.30.*	*She's* **always coming** *to work late.*
I **always pay** *my rent by cheque.*	*I'm* **always paying** *for you when we go out. Why don't you pay sometimes?*
They **always had** *dinner at 8 o'clock.*	*They* **were always having** *arguments.*

Nota che *always* precede il verbo principale (p.es. *she* **always comes**), ma segue il verbo ausiliare *be* (p.es. *she's* **always coming**).

3 Quando si usa la forma progressiva per dire che qualcosa accade troppo spesso, si possono usare avverbi come *forever* o *continually*, invece di *always*.

You're forever losing things.
He's continually saying stupid things.

4 *Always*, usato con la forma progressiva, non vuole sempre e solo dare un tono negativo alla frase (indicando cioè che qualcosa accade troppo spesso); può anche voler dire semplicemente che qualcosa accade più spesso del previsto.

She's always lending people money.
I'm always meeting Maria in the park. (per caso)

ESERCIZIO 26A

Completa le frasi usando *always* e il presente o il passato progressivo dei verbi tra parentesi.

Esempi:

He's a really miserable man. He's *always complaining* (complain) about something.
When I was a child, my sister *was always teasing* (tease) me.

1 Simon is very untidy. He ____ (leave) his clothes lying on the bathroom floor.

2 When we were children, my brother was bigger than me and he ____ (hit) me.

3 My sister really makes me angry. She ____ (borrow) my things without asking me.

4 My memory is getting very bad these days. I ____ (forget) things.

5 Our old car was very unreliable. It ____ (break down).

6 My parents are very lucky. They ____ (win) prizes in competitions.

27 Verbi non usati nella forma progressiva

1 Alcuni verbi (p.es. *like*, *understand*) normalmente non sono usati nella forma progressiva. Si può dire *I like* o *she didn't understand*, ma non ~~I'm liking~~ o ~~she wasn't understanding.~~

Ecco alcuni tra i più importanti di questi verbi:

a **Verbi di facoltà mentali**

think (= ritenere)	*believe*	*understand*	*know*
see (= capire)	*recognize*	*suppose*	*remember*
imagine	*forget*	*mean*	*realize*

*I **think** you're right.* (Non: ~~I'm thinking ...~~)
*Do you **know** Billy Palmer?* (Non: ~~Are you knowing ...?~~)
*She **didn't understand** what you said.* (Non: ~~She wasn't understanding ...~~)

b | **Verbi di sentimento**

> *like   dislike   hate   love   prefer   want   wish*

*I **like** this music.* (Non: ~~I'm liking~~...)
*Do you **want** to go now?* (Non: ~~Are you wanting~~...?)

c | **Verbi di percezione sensoriale**

> *see   hear   smell   taste   feel*

*We **heard** someone outside.* (Non: ~~We were hearing~~...)
*This spaghetti **tastes** delicious.* (Non: ~~This spaghetti is tasting~~...)

d | **Altri verbi**

> *have* (= possedere)   *own*   *belong to*   *owe*   *need*
> *include*   *cost*   *contain*   *weigh*
> *sound*   *be*   *seem*   *deserve*

*How long **has** Sally **had** her motorbike?* (Non: ~~How long has Sally been having~~...?)
*I **weigh** 70 kilos.* (Non: ~~I'm weighing~~...)
*We **were** at home last night.* (Non: ~~We were being~~...)

2 | Nota, però, che alcuni dei verbi sopra elencati hanno più di un significato e, se descrivono attività, possono prendere la forma progressiva. Confronta:

FORMA NORMALE	FORMA PROGRESSIVA
*I **think** you're right.* (think = ritenere)	*Ssh! I'm **thinking**.* (think = riflettere)
*I've **had** my car for six months.* (have = possedere)	*I've **been having** lunch.* (have = mangiare)
*Do you **see** what I mean?* (see = capire)	*Are you **seeing** the doctor tomorrow?* (see = andare dal dottore)

Confronta anche il diverso significato di *be* nelle due forme:

He's stupid. (in genere)	*He's **being** stupid.* (Si sta comportando da stupido ora.)

3 | Spesso si usa *can* o *could* con i verbi di percezione sensoriale *see, hear, smell, taste, feel* e con alcuni verbi di facoltà mentali p.es. *understand, remember.*

*I **can see** you.*
*We **could hear** someone outside.*

4   Confronta *hear* e *see* con *listen, look* e *watch*.

I verbi *hear* e *see*, poiché denotano percezioni per lo più involontarie, non vengono in genere usati nella forma progressiva.

*When I was in the garden I **heard** the telephone ring.*

I verbi *listen, look* e *watch* indicano invece azioni volontarie e possono prendere la forma progressiva.

*Ssh! **I'm listening** to the radio.*
*They **were watching** TV last night.*

5   I verbi che indicano stati fisici p.es. *feel, ache* e *hurt*, possono essere usati in entrambe le forme.

*I **am feeling**/I **feel** ill.*
*My head **is aching**/My head **aches**.*

ESERCIZIO 27A

Scegli la forma corretta.

Esempio:

She says she didn't take the money, but *I don't believe/~~I'm not believing~~* her.

1 You're very quiet. What *~~do you think~~/are you thinking* about?
2 What *do you think/~~are you thinking~~* about my idea?
3 How long *has Simon known/~~has Simon been knowing~~* Maria?
4 What *does this word mean?/is ~~this word meaning~~?*
5 *Did you hear/~~Were you hearing~~* the news?
6 *~~You don't watch~~/You aren't watching* the TV at the moment. Why don't you switch it off?
7 I'm sorry, but *I didn't remember/I ~~wasn't remembering~~* to get your newspaper when I went shopping.
8 *Do you like/~~Are you liking~~* this painting?
9 *She has always wanted/~~She has always been wanting~~* to be a doctor.
10 The man was a stranger to me. *I had never seen/I ~~had never been seeing~~* him before.

Nota   – I verbi che di solito non prendono la forma progressiva possono però assumerla se vengono usati come soggetto p.es. ***Knowing** how to drive is very useful,* o se sono retti da una preposizione p.es. *I'm looking forward to **having** a car of my own.*

28 Riepilogo del presente e del passato

ESERCIZIO 28A

Completa le frasi usando la forma appropriata del presente o del passato dei verbi fra parentesi.

(i) Maria Fernandez is Spanish. She *lives* (live) in Madrid, where she __1__ (work) for an export company. She __2__ (be) with this company for two years now. At the moment she __3__ (study) English on a one-month intensive course in London. She __4__ (be) in London for one week now. She __5__ (arrive) there last Saturday. This is not Maria's first time in Britain. She __6__ (be) there twice before.

(ii) I woke up when I __1__ (hear) a noise downstairs. I __2__ (get) out of bed quietly because my wife __3__ (still | sleep) and __4__ (go) to the top of the stairs. It was dark, but I could see two men downstairs in the living room. They __5__ (try) to open the safe. When I __6__ (switch on) the light, the two men __7__ (run) into the kitchen and __8__ (escape) out of the back door. Then, before I __9__ (have) a chance to do anything, I __10__ (hear) a police car pull up outside the house. A neighbour of mine __11__ (see) the men breaking into my house and __12__ (phone) for the police.

ESERCIZIO 28B

Scegli la forma corretta.

(i) Sono le 6.30 di sera e Sally è appena ritornata a casa. Simon è in cucina.

Sally: Hi, Simon. Something *smells/is smelling* nice. What (1) *do you cook/are you cooking?*

Simon: (2) *I make/I'm making* some onion soup. Would you like some?

Sally: No, thanks. I'm not hungry at the moment. (3) *I've just had/I just have* something to eat in town.

Simon: Oh? What (4) *did you have/do you have?*

Sally: (5) *I've met/I met* Peter at 5.00 and (6) *we were going/we went* to Alfredo's for a pizza. Can I just taste the soup? (7) *It's looking/It looks* delicious. Umm! Very good. I think it's the best onion soup (8) *I've ever tasted/I've ever been tasting*!

(ii) L'amico di Andrew, Les, ha comprato una bicicletta nuova.

Les: Hi, Andrew. (1) *Do you like/Are you liking* my new bike?

Andrew: Yes, very much! I didn't know you'd bought a bike. How long (2) *have you had/did you have* it?

Les: Oh, (3) *I've only had/I've only been having* it for a few days. (4) *I bought/I've bought* it last weekend.

Andrew: How much (5) *did it cost/has it cost*?

Les: £120. (6) *I'd been saving/I'm saving* for over a year to buy it.

(iii) La signora Wood si è fatta male al braccio. E' dal dottore.

Doctor: Does your arm hurt when you move it, Mrs Woods?

Mrs Woods: Yes, a little. (1) *It's hurting/It's been hurting* me for about a week now. (2) *I fell/I was falling* off a ladder when (3) *I cleaned/I was cleaning* the windows at home last Tuesday. (4) *Are you thinking/Do you think* that (5) *I've broken/I've been breaking* my arm, doctor?

Doctor: No, (6) *you aren't breaking/haven't broken* it, Mrs Woods. But I think you should go to hospital for an X-ray.

29 Riepilogo del futuro

ESERCIZIO 29A

Scegli il tempo giusto.

Esempio:

I can't go to the beach this afternoon. *~~I'll play~~/I'm playing* tennis.

1 *It's raining/It's going to rain* tomorrow.
2 *Do you do/Are you doing* anything this evening?
3 I'll write to you when *I arrive/I'll arrive* in Brazil.
4 I feel terrible. I think *I'll be/I'm going to be* sick.
5 'I've got wine or beer. Which would you like?' 'Oh, thank you. *I'll have/I'm going to have* beer, please.'
6 If the weather *is/will be* nice this afternoon, we'll have a picnic.
7 'What are you doing with that ladder?' '*I'll repair/I'm going to repair* the roof.'
8 'It's raining outside. Would you like to borrow an umbrella?' 'Oh, thank you. *I'll bring/I'm going to bring* it back tomorrow.'
9 We're going on holiday next Monday. This time next week *we'll be lying/we'll lie* on a beach in Turkey.
10 Ben and Patty Crawford are on holiday in Europe. *They'll have visited/They'll be visiting* seven countries by the time they get home to Canada at the end of the month.

30 Imperativo e *let's*

1 | **Imperativo**

a | Si usa l'imperativo in diversi casi, per esempio per dare ordini e avvertimenti, per offrire o proporre qualcosa e per fare richieste.

Stop!
Have *some more coffee.*
Tell *your boss you can't work late tonight.*
Help *me with these bags, please.*
Look *out!* **Be** *careful.*

b | L'imperativo ha la stessa forma dell'infinito senza *to*.

Sit *down.*
Open *the window.*

c | Si fa la forma negativa dell'imperativo premettendogli *don't/do not*.

Don't sit *down.*
Don't open *the window.*
Do not feed *the animals.* (p.es. su un cartello dello zoo)

d | Si può premettere *do* all'imperativo per modificarne il tono, cioè per esprimere o cortesia o impazienza, a seconda dei casi.

Do sit *down.*
Do stop *making that noise!*

e | Normalmente l'imperativo non ha soggetto, ma si può usare un nome o un pronome per rendere più chiara l'identità della persona con cui si parla.

Andrew shut *the door, please.*
Have *some more coffee,* **Kate.**
Sit *down,* **everybody.**

f | Dopo l'imperativo si possono fare le domande 'coda' *will/won't/would you?* e *can/can't/could you?*

Shut *the door,* **will you?**
Sit *down,* **won't you?**
Help *me with these bags,* **could you?**

2 | **Let's**

a | Si usa *let's* (= *let us*) + l'infinito senza *to*, come esortativo, una specie di imperativo per la prima persona plurale, per proporre qualcosa.

We're late. **Let's** *hurry.*
'What shall we do this evening?' **'Let's** *stay at home.'*

b | Si possono formare frasi negative con *let's not* o *don't let's*.

Let's not *wait./***Don't let's** *wait.*

Alcuni grammatici considerano *let's not* più corretto.

c Si può usare *do* prima di *let's* per dare enfasi.

    ***Do let's** hurry.*

d Dopo *let's* si può fare la domanda 'coda' *shall we?*

    Let's** go to the cinema, **shall we?

ESERCIZIO 30A

Che cosa dicono i personaggi delle illustrazioni? Cerca la risposta nel riquadro.

Esempio:

Put	that! It's hot.
Take off	me the spanner.
Do turn	your shirt, please.
Please take	that music down, Andrew!
Don't touch	a seat, Mr Woods.
Pass	this in the fridge, could you?

Take off your shirt, please.

ESERCIZIO 30B

Sei con un amico. Fagli delle proposte, in base a quello che dice, usando *Let's* e le parole del riquadro.

Esempio:

Friend: 'I'm hungry.'   You: *'Let's have something to eat.'*

1 'I'd like to see a film.'
2 'I don't feel like waiting for the bus.'
3 'I'm cold.'
4 'It's Sue's birthday soon.'
5 'It's raining hard outside.'

have	a taxi
buy	in this evening
take	something to eat
light	her a present
go	a fire
stay	to the cinema

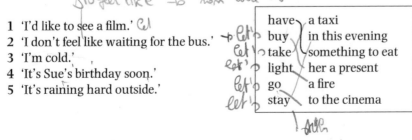

31 Be

1

a

Forma

Presente di *be*

AFFERMATIVA		NEGATIVA		INTERROGATIVA	
I	am	I	am not	am I?	
you	are	you	are not	are you?	
he		he			he?
she	is	she	is not	is	she?
it		it			it?
we		we			we?
you	are	you	are not	are	you?
they		they			they?

CONTRAZIONI

'm = am
're = are   aren't = are not
's = is   isn't = is not

b

Passato remoto di *be*

AFFERMATIVA		NEGATIVA		INTERROGATIVA	
I	was	I	was not	was I?	
you	were	you	were not	were you?	
he		he			he?
she	was	she	was not	was	she?
it		it			it?
we		we			we?
you	were	you	were not	were	you?
they		they			they?

CONTRAZIONI

wasn't = was not
weren't = were not

2

Uso

Si usa *be* per chiedere e dare informazioni sulle persone e sulle cose.

*My name **is** Maria. **I'm** from Spain.*
***Is** Ken ready? No, he **isn't**.*

*'**Were** you at home last night?'   'No, I **wasn't**. I **was** at the cinema.'*
*Anna Pavlova **was** a famous Russian dancer.*

ESERCIZIO 31A

Completa le conversazioni usando le forme di *be* del riquadro.

am ('m)	am not ('m not)
are ('re)	are not (aren't)
is ('s)	is not (isn't)

(i) James è a una festa. Ha appena visto la sua amica Rosie.

James: Hello, Rosie. How *are* you?
Rosie: Oh, hello, James. I ͫͫ1__ fine, thanks. How __2__ you?
James: I __3__ too bad, thank you.
(*alcuni momenti piu' tardi*)
James: Who __4__ that girl over there? Do you know her?
Rosie: Yes, her name __5__ Carla. She __6__ Italian.
James: __7__ she a student at the college?
Rosie: No, she __8__.

(ii) Sally sta aspettando al capolinea dell'autobus. Il suo amico Peter è in ritardo.

Peter: Hello, Sally. Sorry. __1__ I very late?
Sally: Yes, you __2__.
Peter: What __3__ the time?
Sally: It __4__ almost half past seven.
Peter: Really? Oh, I __5__ sorry, Sally. __6__ you angry?
Sally: No, I __7__ angry, but I __8__ very hungry. Let's go for something to eat.

(iii) I signori Ash sono canadesi. Sono appena arrivati in Inghilterra. Stanno
parlando con un doganiere all'aeroporto di Heathrow a Londra.

Officer: Where __1__ you from?
Mrs Ash: We __2__ from Canada.
Officer: __3__ you here on holiday?
Mrs Ash: Yes, we __4__.
Officer: __5__ this your first visit to England?
Mrs Ash: Well, it __6__ my husband's first visit, but I've been here before.
Officer: I see. __7__ these your suitcases?
Mrs Ash: Yes, they __8__.
Officer: And what about this bag? __9__ this yours, too?
Mrs Ash: No, it __10__.

ESERCIZIO 31B

[handwritten: There was a robbery in London at 10:00,]

C'è stata una rapina a Londra alle 10, ieri sera. Un commissario di polizia sta
interrogando Eddie Cooper riguardo alla rapina.

[handwritten: is interrogating]

[handwritten margin: I have my History exam or exam]

Completa la conversazione usando *was* e *were*.

Inspector: *Were* you in London last night, Cooper?
Cooper: Yes, I was 1___.
Inspector: Where were 2___ you at 10 o'clock last night?
Cooper: At 10 o'clock? I was 3___ in a pub called The Bell.
Inspector: And what about your friends Jack Callaghan and Frankie Dobbs?
    Were 4___ they in the pub with you?
Cooper: No, they were 5___n't, Inspector.
Inspector: Where were 6___ they, then?
Cooper: I don't know where they were 7___, but they were 8___n't with me.
Inspector: Were 9___ you on your own in The Bell?
Cooper: No, I was 10___n't. My girlfriend Diana was 11___ with me.
Inspector: And was 12___ she with you all evening?
Cooper: Yes, she was 13___.

Nota   –Per l'uso di *there + be* p.es. **There's a bank in West Street**, cfr. 32.
    –Si usa *be* anche come ausiliare per la forma progressiva p.es. *He's working* (presente
    progressivo), *He was working* (passato progressivo), e con *going to* p.es. *He's going to work*.
    Per la forma progressiva cfr. 1,5,9,15,23; per *going to*, cfr. 17,20. Si usa *be* come ausiliare
    anche per la forma passiva p.es. *It was made in Japan*. Cfr. 59–60.

32   *There is, there are*

1 | Quando si vuole dire che c'è qualcosa, si comincia la frase con *there + be*, poi si fa
seguire il soggetto.

***There is** a bank in West Street*. (Normalmente, non si dice: *A bank is in West Street*).

Si usa questa costruzione con soggetti 'indefiniti' (p.es. *a key, some people, anybody*).

***There's** a key on the floor.*
***There are** some people outside.*
*'**Is there** anybody at home?'*   *'No, **there isn't.**'*

2 Si può usare questa costruzione con i vari tempi di *be*. Per esempio:

There is *a bank in West Street.* (presente)
There was *a telephone call for you last night.* (passato remoto)
There has been *a robbery.* (passato prossimo)
There will be *a lot of people at the party.* (futuro)

Nota che, se il soggetto è plurale, lo deve essere anche *be*. Confronta:

There's *a key on the floor.*	**There are** *some keys on the floor.*
There was *a telephone call for you last night.*	**There were** *two telephone calls for you last night.*
There has been *a robbery.*	**There have been** *a lot of robberies recently.*

3 Confronta *there is/are* con *it is/they are*:

Si usa *there* + *be* per dire che c'è qualcosa; si usa un pronome personale p.es. *it, they* + *be* (o un altro verbo) per dare più particolari.

There's *a letter for you.* **It's** *from Australia.*
'**There's** *someone outside.*'   '**It's** *Mr Davis.*'
There are *some biscuits in the kitchen.* **They're** *in the cupboard.*

ESERCIZIO 32A

Completa le frasi usando *there* e la forma giusta del verbo nel riquadro.

is   are   was   were   has been   will be

Esempio:

There was a terrible accident in Western Road yesterday.

1 Look. ___ *There is* a policeman over there. Can you see him?
2 How many people ___ *were* at the party last night?
3 I think ___ *there will be* some snow later this evening.
4 Excuse me. ___ *is there* a post office near here?
5 ___ *There were* six hotels in this street ten years ago, now ___ *there's* only two.
6 ___ *There has been* a lot of cold weather recently.

ESERCIZIO 32B

Completa le frasi usando le parole del riquadro.

there   it   they   is   are

Esempio:

'*Is there* a police station near here?'   'Yes, *there is. It's* in East Street.'

1 ___ *There is* a good programme on TV this evening. ___ *It is* about the history of pop music.
2 ___ *There are* some envelopes in my bedroom. ___ *They are* on my desk.
3 '___ *Is there* any beer in the kitchen?'   'Yes, ___ *it is* in the fridge.'
4 '___ *There's* a man waiting outside. Who ___ *is it*?'   '___ *It is* Jim Brown.'
5 'Look! ___ *There's* a light on in my bedroom!'   '___ *There's* somebody in there.'

What's on at Marian Cinema?
Cosa danno al
Cinema Marzedni

33 Have e have got

1 | Nell'inglese britannico spesso si usa *have got* invece di *have* quando il significato è 'possedere'.

I've got a new camera.	*I have a new camera.*
I haven't got any paper.	*I don't have any paper.*
Have you got a pen?	*Do you have a pen?*
He's got brown eyes and black hair.	*He has brown eyes and black hair.*

Have got ha esattamente lo stesso significato di *have* negli esempi sopra riportati; *got* qui è una parola 'vuota'. *Have got* è più informale di *have*; si usa molto spesso nelle conversazioni e, per esempio, quando si scrive a un amico.

2 | **Forma**

a | Presente di *have got*

AFFERMATIVA	NEGATIVA	INTERROGATIVA
I you *have got*	I you *have not got*	*have* I you
he she *has got* it	he she *has not got* it	*has* he she *got?* it
we you *have got* they	we you *have not got* they	*have* we you they

CONTRAZIONI

've got = have got	*haven't got = have not got*
's got = has got	*hasn't got = has not got*

b | Presente di *have* (1)

AFFERMATIVA	NEGATIVA	INTERROGATIVA
I you *have*	I you *do not have*	*do* I you
he she *has* it	he she *does not have* it	*does* she *have?* he it
we you *have* they	we you *do not have* they	*do* we you they

CONTRAZIONI

don't = do not
doesn't = does not

c Presente di *have* (2)

Si può usare *have* anche senza *got* e senza *do/does* nella forma negativa e interrogativa:

AFFERMATIVA	NEGATIVA	INTERROGATIVA
I *you* **have**	*I* *you* **have not**	**have** *I?* *you?*
he *she* **has** *it*	*he* *she* **has not** *it*	**has** *he?* *she?* *it?*
we *you* **have** *they*	*we* *you* **have not** *they*	**have** *we?* *you?* *they?*

CONTRAZIONI

've = have *haven't = have not*
's = has *hasn't = has not*

Questo però non è molto comune nell'inglese parlato di tutti i giorni.

3 Quando si parla di qualcosa che accade ripetutamente, di solito si usa *have* (con *do/does* nella forma negativa e interrogativa) e non *have got*. Confronta:

*I often **have** headaches.* | *I **'ve got** a terrible headache at the moment.*
*I **don't** usually **have** much time for lunch.* | *I **haven't got** much time today.*

Non si usa *have (got)* nella forma progressiva quando il significato è 'possedere': non si dice ~~*I'm having got a new camera*~~.

Quando si parla del passato, di solito si usa *had* e non *had got*.

*I **had** a headache last night.* (Non: ~~*I had got a headache…*~~)

Si usa *did* per fare la forma negativa e interrogativa del passato remoto.

*I **didn't** have a pen.*
***Did** you **have** a key?*

Non si usa *got* nelle risposte brevi.

*'**Have** you **got** a pen?'* *'Yes, I **have**.'* (Non: ~~*'Yes, I have got.'*~~)

ESERCIZIO 33A

Completa le frasi usando *have got* se possibile, altrimenti *have*, scegliendo la forma e il tempo giusto.

Esempio:

'Excuse me, *have you got* (you) the time?'   'Yes, it's twenty-five past six.'

1 'Let's have meatballs for supper. ____ (we) any potatoes?' 'No, we ____ but we ____ some rice.'

2 My brother ____ dark hair now, but when he was a child he ____ fair hair.

3 'I'll phone you tomorrow.'   '____ (you) my telephone number?'

4 '____ (we) any aspirins?'   'Yes, there are some in the bathroom cupboard.
Why? ____ (you) a headache?'   'No, I'm fine, but Andrew ____ a terrible toothache.'

5 '____ (your sister) a car at the moment?'   'Yes, she ____.'

6 I couldn't get the concert tickets yesterday because I ____ (not) enough money.

Nota –Si usa *have to* e *have got to* per parlare di necessità e obblighi p.es. *I have to go/have got to go now.* Cfr. 38–39.
      –Si usa *have* (non *have got*) anche come verbo ausiliare del passato prossimo, del trapassato e del futuro anteriore. Per questi tempi, cfr. 6,9,14,15,24.

34 *Have* per indicare azioni

1 | Si usa *have* anche per designare tutta una serie di azioni, per esempio:

> *have breakfast/lunch/dinner/a meal/a drink/a cup of tea/*
>   *some coffee/a beer/a cigarette*
> *have a bath/a shower/a wash/a shave/a sleep/a rest/a dream*
> *have a swim/a walk/a game of tennis, a game of football, etc*
> *have a holiday/a day off work/a party/a good time, a bad time, etc*
> *have a conversation/a talk/a chat/a quarrel/a row/a fight/*
>   *a disagreement/an argument*
> *have a baby*
> *have a look* (= dare un'occhiata)
> *have a try/a go* (= provare)

2 | *Have got* non può essere usato in queste espressioni.

*I usually **have** lunch at around one o'clock.* (Non: ~~I usually **have got** lunch …~~).

3 | Si può usare la forma progressiva dei vari tempi di *have* con queste espressioni (perché descrivono azioni).

*Sally **is having** a shower at the moment.*
*Are you **having** a good time?*
*We **were having** dinner when Peter arrived.*

4 | Si costruisce la forma negativa e interrogativa con *do/does* nel presente e *did* nel passato remoto.

I **don't** normally **have** a bath in the mornings.
When **does** Lynne usually **have** her holiday?
Did you **have** a good time at the zoo yesterday?

5 | Le contrazioni di *have* (*'ve*, *'s*) e *had* (*'d*) normalmente non vengono usate.

I **have** a look at the newspaper every morning. (Non: ~~I've a look ...~~)
They **had** an argument about money. (Non: ~~They'd an argument ...~~)

ESERCIZIO 34A

Completa ogni frase usando il tempo giusto dell'espressione più appropriata nel riquadro. Usa ciascuna espressione una volta sola.

> ~~have a look~~   have a rest   have a shave
> ~~have breakfast~~   have a game of tennis   ~~have a cigarette~~
> have a swim   have a baby   have a good time

Esempio:

'Are you hungry?'   'No, I've just had breakfast (just), thank you.'

1 'Have you stopped smoking?'   'Yes, I ____ (not) since the beginning of the New Year.'
2 Can I ____ at that photo?
3 'Simon and I ____ yesterday.'   'Who won?'
4 She usually ____ in the sea every morning before breakfast.
5 What was the party like last night? ____ (you)?
6 'My sister ____ (just).'   'Is it a girl or a boy?'
7 'I'm tired.'   'Let's ____ for a few minutes, then.'
8 Are you going to ____ today, or are you growing a beard?

35   Verbi modali: schema generale

I 'verbi modali ausiliari' o 'verbi servili' sono *can, could, may, might, will, would, shall, should, ought to, must, need* e *dare*.

1 | **Uso**

Si usano i verbi modali per parlare, per esempio, di possibilità, certezze, abilità, disponibilità, obblighi, permessi.

It **might** rain. (possibilità)
You haven't eaten all day. You **must** be hungry. (certezza)
Can she swim? (abilità)
Will you help me? (disponibilità)
You **must** be home by 11 o'clock. (obbligo)
May I borrow your car? (permesso)

2 | **Forma**

a | Si fa la forma affermativa mettendo il verbo modale tra il soggetto e il verbo principale.

*I **can** swim.*
*We **should** go now.*

I verbi modali hanno la stessa forma per tutte le persone. Non hanno la desinenza -*s* nella terza persona singolare.

*She **can** swim (Non: ~~She cans . . .~~)*
*He **should** go now. (Non: ~~He shoulds . . .~~)*

Dopo tutti i verbi modali (eccetto *ought*) si usa l'infinito senza *to* p.es. *swim, go.*
Dopo *ought* si usa *to* + l'infinito p.es. *to swim, to go.*

*We **ought to** go now.*

b | Si costruisce la forma negativa facendo seguire *n't/not* al verbo modale.

*She **can't** swim.*
*We **shouldn't** go.*
*It **might not** rain.*

Si costruisce la forma interrogativa invertendo la posizione del soggetto con quella del verbo modale. Confronta:

*She can swim. → **Can she** swim?*

*We should go. → **Should we** go?*

Nota che non si usa *do* nella forma interrogativa e negativa: non si dice ~~Does she can swim? She doesn't can swim~~, ecc.

c | Si può usare la costruzione: verbo modale + *be* + . . . -*ing.*

*It's getting late. We really **must be going** now.*
*I **may be working** late tomorrow.*

d | Talvolta si usano espressioni come *be able to, be allowed to* e *have to* invece dei verbi modali. Queste espressioni hanno significati e forme che mancano ai verbi modali.

*I'd like **to be able to** play the piano. (Can non ha l'infinito; non si può dire ~~I'd like to can play . . .~~)*
*She **had to** go to the doctor's yesterday. (Must non viene usato per parlare del passato; non si può dire ~~She must go . . . yesterday~~.)*

e | Quando si parla di fatti passati, si può usare la costruzione: verbo modale + *have* + participio passato. Questo per dire, per esempio, che forse una cosa è accaduta oppure per sottolineare che si è verificato il contrario.

*'Peter is late.'   'He **may have missed** his train.'* (= Forse ha perso il treno.)
*I feel really tired today. I **shouldn't have stayed** up so late last night.* (Ma sono stato alzato fino a tardi ieri sera.)

–Per gli usi particolari dei verbi modali, cfr. 36–55.

36 Abilità: *can, could, be able to*

1 **Can**

Si può usare *can* per indicare abilità. La forma negativa di *can* è *cannot* (contrazione: *can't*).

Can you swim?
He can play the guitar.
I can't open this bottle.
Can you meet me tomorrow evening?

Si può usare *be able to* invece di *can* p.es. *Are you able to swim?* ma *can* è più frequente.

2 **Could e was/were able to**

a Si può usare *could* per dire che qualcuno aveva l'abilità in generale di fare qualcosa nel passato.

I could swim when I was 4 years old.
My sister could talk when she was 15 months old.

Si usa anche *was/were able to* con lo stesso significato.

I was able to swim when I was 4 years old.

b Ma quando si vuole parlare dell'abilità di qualcuno dimostrata nel passato in una particolare circostanza, si deve usare *was/were able to*, non *could*.

Even though I'd hurt my leg, I was able to swim back to the boat. (Non: ... *I could swim back* ....)
The manager wasn't in the office for very long, but we were able to speak to him for a few minutes. (Non: ... *we could speak to him* ....)

In tali casi, si può usare *managed to* (+ l'infinito) o *succeeded in* (+ la forma in *-ing*), invece di *was/were able to*.

Even though I'd hurt my leg, I managed to swim back to the boat/I succeeded in swimming back to the boat.

In genere si usa *managed to* o *succeeded in* quando la riuscita ha comportato il superamento di difficoltà.

c Quanto detto non si applica ai verbi di percezione sensoriale *see, hear, smell, taste, feel* e a certi verbi di facoltà della mente p.es. *understand, remember*. Con questi verbi si può infatti usare *could* proprio riferendosi a una particolare circostanza.

We could see a man in the garden.
I could hear a noise outside my bedroom door.

d Si usa *could not* (contrazione: *couldn't*) per indicare abilità sia in generale che in situazioni particolari.

My grandmother couldn't dance.
He tried very hard, but he couldn't swim back to the boat.

3   *Could have . . .*

Si usa *could have* + il participio passato per dire che qualcuno aveva l'abilità o l'occasione di fare qualcosa, ma non l'ha fatto.

*You **could have helped** me. Why didn't you?*
*I **could have gone** to China on holiday last year, but I decided not to.*

4   Per esprimere abilità in altre forme: *be able to*

Can non ha l'infinito, la forma in *-ing* e il participio. Quindi, se necessario, si ricorre a *be able to*.

*I'd like **to be able to** play the piano.* (Non: *I'd like **to can play** . . .*)
*In the future, people **will be able to** live on other planets.* (Non: *. . . people **will can live** . . .*)
*She enjoys **being able to** speak foreign languages.* (Non: *She enjoys **canning** . . .*)
*I've **been able to** drive since I was 18.* (Non: *I've **could** . . .*)

ESERCIZIO 36A

Completa le frasi usando *can* o *could* tutte le volte che è possibile, altrimenti una forma di *be able to*.

Esempi:

He has been living in France for 6 months. He *can* speak French very well now.
I'll *be able to* go shopping later today.

1 When Robert was younger he _Could_ run quite fast.
2 Look! You _can_ see the mountains from this window.
3 Kate _could_ dance really well when she was a young girl.
4 How long have you _been able to_ play the guitar?
5 Look! I _can_ lift this chair with one hand!
6 I'm sorry, but I won't _be able to_ come to the party on Saturday.

ESERCIZIO 36B

Completa le frasi usando *could* o *was/were able to*. Talvolta, entrambe le forme sono possibili.

Esempio:

Simon *could/was able to* read music when he was 7.
1 We _were able to_ put out the fire before much damage was done.
2 My daughter _could_ walk when she was only 11 months old.
3 I _was able to_ finish all the work you wanted me to do yesterday.
4 _Could_ (you) speak French before you went to live in Paris?' 'I _couldn't_ (not) speak it very well.'
5 They were talking quite loudly. I _could_ hear everything they said.

ESERCIZIO 36C

Robert Wells ha 52 anni. Qualche volta gli sembra di aver sprecato la sua vita.

Leggi di Robert. Sostituisci le parole in corsivo con *could have . . .*, come nell'esempio.

Esempio:

When Robert was 26 *he had the chance to get* married, but he decided not to.
When Robert was 26 *he could have got* married, but he decided not to.

1 *Robert had the ability to go* to university, but he didn't want to go.
2 *He had the intelligence to pass* his final exams at school, but he didn't take them.
3 A lot of people thought *he had the ability to be* a professional footballer when he was younger, but he didn't try.
4 *He had the opportunity to start* his own business once, but he didn't want to.
5 *He had the chance to emigrate* to Australia a few years ago, but he decided not to.

Nota –Per le forme dei verbi modali, come *can* e *could*, cfr. 35.2.
–Si usa *can/could* (= abilità) in richieste, p.es. *Can you help me?* (cfr. 48) e in offerte, p.es. *I could lend you some money* (cfr. 49.3).
–*Could* ha anche un significato condizionale 'would be able to' p.es. *I could repair the car if I had the right tools.* (= Potrei riparare l'auto se . . .) Cfr. 69.3, 71.3.

37 Permesso: *can, could, may, might, be allowed to*

1 | **Chiedere il permesso**

Can I borrow your dictionary?

Si può usare *can, could* e *may* per chiedere il permesso di fare qualcosa.

Can I use your pen for a moment?
Could I ask you a personal question?
May I make a suggestion?

Could è meno diretto e più formale di *can*. *May* è più formale (alcuni grammatici lo considerano più corretto) di *can* o *could*, ma questi due sono più frequenti.

Si può usare anche *might* per chiedere il permesso di fare qualcosa in modo meno diretto e più formale p.es. *Might I make a suggestion?*

2 | **Dare il permesso**

Quando si dà il permesso di fare qualcosa, si usa *can* o *may*, non *could* o *might*.

'Can I use your pen for a moment?'   'Yes, of course you **can***.'*
You **can** *borrow my camera if you want to.*
'Could I make a suggestion?'   'Of course you **may***.'*

3 | **Parlare di cose permesse o meno**

Quando si parla di cose che sono già permesse, o non lo sono affatto (p.es. in conformità a leggi o regolamenti), si usa *can('t)* o *be (not) allowed to*.

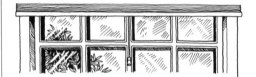 

You **can't** *smoke/***aren't allowed to** *smoke in this room.*

Altri esempi:

You **can** *get married/***are allowed to** *get married in Britain when you are 16.* (E' la legge.)
The children normally go to bed at 9 o'clock, but they **can** *stay up/***are allowed to** *stay up later on Saturdays.* (I loro genitori hanno deciso così.)

4 | *Could* **e** *was/were allowed to*

a | Si usa *could* per dire che si aveva il permesso di fare qualcosa nel passato.

When I was eighteen, I **could** *borrow my parents' car whenever I wanted to.*

Con questo significato si può usare anche *was/were allowed to*.

When I was eighteen, I **was allowed to** *borrow my parents' car whenever I wanted to.*

b | Però, quando si vuole dire che qualcuno aveva il permesso di fare qualcosa in una situazione particolare del passato, si deve usare *was/were allowed to*, non *could*.

I **was allowed to** *borrow my parents' car last night.* (Non: ~~I could borrow …~~)

Si tratta della stessa differenza vista tra *could* e *was/were able to* (cfr. 36.2).

ESERCIZIO 37A

Che domande stanno facendo i personaggi raffigurati? Trovale nel riquadro.

Esempio:

May I sit	in?
Do you think I could close	a look at your magazine?
Could I have	this on?
Can I try	here?
May I come	your bike for half an hour?
Can I borrow	the window?

Could I have a look at your magazine?

ESERCIZIO 37B

Che cosa significano questi cartelli? Da' due spiegazioni per ogni cartello, usando le
frasi del riquadro.

Esempio:

You	can('t)	take — in this street.
	are(n't) allowed to	park — in this room.
		feed — on the grass.
		smoke — photographs.
		turn — the animals.
		walk — left.

You can't take photographs.
You aren't allowed to take photographs.

1 **DO NOT FEED THE ANIMALS**

2 **NO SMOKING**

3

4 **DO NOT WALK ON THE GRASS**

5

ESERCIZIO 37C

Completa le frasi usando *could* o *was/were allowed to*. Talvolta entrambi sono possibili.

Esempio:

I *was allowed to* see him for a few moments yesterday.

1 Andrew ____ leave school early yesterday because he wasn't feeling well.
2 Until the 19th century, people ____ travel freely between most countries without a passport.
3 Sue's children ____ watch the film on TV last night.
4 Her son has to wear a uniform in his new school, but in his old school he ____ wear whatever he liked.

Nota —Per le forme dei verbi modali, come *can, could, may* e *might*, cfr. 35.2.

38 Obbligo e necessità (1): *must, have to, have got to*

1

a

Must e have to

Si usa sia *must* che *have to* per esprimere obbligo o necessità, ma qualche volta c'è differenza tra le due espressioni:

Normalmente si usa *must* quando l'autorità proviene da chi parla.

*You **must** be home by 10 o'clock.* (Insisto io.)

*I've got a terrible pain in my back. I **must** go and see the doctor.* (Sono convinto io di doverci andare.)

*You **must** drive carefully.* (Insisto.)

Normalmente si usa *have to* quando l'autorità non proviene da chi parla.

*I **have to** be home by 10 o'clock.* (I miei genitori me lo impongono.)

*I **have to** go and see the doctor at 9.00 tomorrow morning.* (È un appuntamento a cui devo andare.)

*You **have to** drive on the left in England.* (E' la legge.)

b | Si usa *must* (+ l'infinito) soltanto per riferirsi al presente e al futuro. Quando si parla di obbligo o necessità al passato si usa *had to*.

*I **had to** work late yesterday.* (Non: ~~I must work late yesterday.~~)

c | *Must* non ha l'infinito, la forma in *-ing* e il participio. Quindi, se necessario, si usa al suo posto *have to*.

*I'll **have to** work late tomorrow.* (Non: ~~I'll must ....~~)
*He hates **having to** get up early.* (Non: ~~He hates musting ....~~)
*She's **had to** work hard all her life.* (Non: ~~She's musted ....~~)

Nota che nella forma interrogativa e negativa con *have to* si usa *do/does* al presente e *did* al passato remoto.

*What time **do** you **have to** start work?*
*We **don't have to** hurry. We've got plenty of time.*
*Did you **have to** walk home last night?*

2 | **Have got to**

Spesso si usa *have got to* invece di *have to* per esprimere obbligo e necessità. *Have got to* è più informale.

*I **have to** hurry.*	*I've **got to** hurry.*
*Do you **have to** go?*	*Have you **got to** go?*

In genere si usa *have to*, non *have got to*, per riferirsi a fatti che si ripetono, soprattutto se si usano avverbi di tempo che indicano frequenza e sono composti da una sola parola p.es. *always, often.* Confronta:

*I **always have to** work late on Wednesday evenings.*	*I've **got to** work late this evening.*
*Do you **often have to** get up early?*	*Have you **got to** get up early tomorrow?*

Si usa *got* per lo più nel presente. Riferendosi al passato, si usa di regola *had to*, non *have got to*.

*I **had to** work late last night.* (Non: ~~I had got to work late last night.~~)

Si tratta della stessa differenza già riscontrata tra *have* e *have got* nel significato di 'possedere' (cfr. 33).

ESERCIZIO 38A

(i) La signora Woods non si sente bene. Sta parlando con il medico. Completa il discorso del medico usando *must* e i verbi *drink, take, stay* e *continue*, ciascuno una sola volta.

Doctor: Well, Mrs Woods, your temperature is a little high, so you __1__ in bed for the next few days. You can eat whatever you like, but you __2__ plenty of liquids. And I'll give you some medicine. You __3__ it three times a day after meals. And you __4__ to take it for the next ten days.

(ii) La signora Woods sta riferendo ora a suo marito quello che le ha detto il medico. Completa il suo discorso usando *have to* e i verbi *drink, take, stay* e *continue*, ciascuno una sola volta.

Mrs Woods: The doctor gave me some medicine. I __1__ it three times a day after meals. And I __2__ to take it for the next ten days. I'm not allowed to get up at the moment. I __3__ in bed for the next few days. Oh, and I'm allowed to eat whatever I like, but I __4__ plenty of liquids.

ESERCIZIO 38B

Completa le frasi usando *must* o *have to*. Talvolta sono entrambi possibili.

Esempi:

I couldn't go to the party last night because I *had to* babysit for my sister.
I *have to/must* get up early tomorrow morning.

1 You ____ get a visa to visit the United States.
2 Annie will ____ do her homework tomorrow.
3 It's getting very late. We ____ go now.
4 I ____ stay in bed yesterday because I wasn't very well.
5 Mr Mason ____ wear glasses since he was a child.
6 I don't like ____ work at weekends.

Nota   –Per le forme dei verbi modali, come *must* ecc., cfr. 35.2
–Per le forme negative *mustn't, don't have to, haven't got to, needn't* e *don't need to*, cfr. 39.

39   Obbligo e necessità (2): *mustn't, don't have to, don't need to, haven't got to, needn't*

1

Confronta *mustn't* con *don't have to*:

Annie ha un brutto raffreddore.   Sally è in vacanza.

Si usa *mustn't* quando non si deve fare qualcosa.

*You **mustn't** get up today.* (= Non devi alzarti.)
*You **mustn't** wash that sweater. It has to be dry-cleaned.* (= Non devi lavarlo.)

Si usa *don't have to* quando non è necessario fare qualcosa.

*I **don't have to** get up today.* (= Non è necessario che io mi alzi.)
*You **don't have to** wash that shirt. It isn't* <u>dirty,</u> (= Non è necessario che tu la lavi.)

dirty/is clean.

2   Si può usare anche *don't need to, haven't got to* o *needn't* per dire che non è necessario fare qualcosa.

*I **don't need to** get up today.*
*I **haven't got to** get up today.*
*I **needn't** get up today.*

Nota che spesso si usa *needn't* quando chi parla dispensa qualcuno dal fare qualcosa.

*You **needn't** pay me back the money you owe me until next week.* (= Non mi devi restituire i soldi fino alla prossima settimana.)

ESERCIZIO 39A

Scegli il verbo guisto.

Esempio:

You've been late for work twice this week. You *mustn't*/~~needn't~~ be late again tomorrow.'

1 You *mustn't*/~~don't have~~ to open the door before the train stops. You could fall out.
2 We ~~mustn~~'t/*don't have to* hurry. We've got plenty of time.
3 We *mustn't*/~~haven't got~~ to make any noise going into the house. It's very late and everybody is asleep.
4 You ~~mustn~~'t/*needn't* tell Nicki about the party. I've already told her.
5 You ~~mustn~~'t/*don't need to* phone the station about the time of the trains. I've got a timetable.
6 I *mustn't*/*haven't got to* go now. I can stay a bit longer if you want me to.

Nota   –Per le forme dei verbi modali, come *must*, cfr. 35.2.
–Cfr. anche 41 *Needn't have* e *didn't need to*.

40 Riepilogo dei verbi indicanti permesso e obbligo: *can, can't, must, mustn't, needn't, be allowed to, have to, don't have to*

ESERCIZIO 40A

Completa queste frasi usando i verbi modali del riquadro. Talvolta è possibile usarne due.

must mustn't can can't needn't

Esempi:

You needn't wait any longer, You *can* go now.
We mustn't make a noise. We *must* be quiet.
You must move your car. You *can't/mustn't* park here.

1 You mustn't leave the door unlocked. You ____ lock it.
2 You can only smoke in the canteen. You ____ smoke in this room.
3 We needn't do the washing up now. We ____ do it tomorrow.
4 We can stay a bit longer. We ____ go now.
5 You can't keep on using my tennis shoes. You ____ buy your own.
6 You can keep those magazines. You ____ give them back to me.

ESERCIZIO 40B

Che cosa significano questi cartelli? Cerca le spiegazioni nel riquadro.

Esempio:

		swim here.
You	are allowed to / aren't allowed to	~~stop.~~ overtake. walk here.
	have to / don't have to	be a member to get in. park here. be quiet.

You have to stop.

41 Needn't have e didn't need to

1   *Needn't have* + il participio passato del verbo dice che si è fatto qualcosa senza che ce ne fosse bisogno: è stato uno spreco di tempo.

I **needn't have made** so much food for the party. Nobody was very hungry. (= Non era necessario preparare così tanto da mangiare, ma l'ho fatto.)
I **needn't have told** Kate what happened. She already knew. (= Non era necessario dire a Kate quello che è successo, ma gliel'ho detto lo stesso.)

2   *Didn't need to* + l'infinito del verbo dice che non era necessario fare una determinata cosa (ma non dice se è stata fatta o meno).

She **needn't have waited**. (= Non era necessario che aspettasse, ma ha aspettato.)	She **didn't need to wait**. (= Non era necessario che aspettasse; non sappiamo se ha aspettato o no.)
They **needn't have worried**. (= Non era necessario che si preoccupassero, ma si sono preoccupati.)	They **didn't need to worry**. (= Non era necessario che si preoccupassero; non sappiamo se si sono preoccupati o no.)

3   Spesso, però, quando si usa *didn't need to*, si intende che una persona non ha fatto una determinata cosa (perché non era necessario).

I **didn't need to unlock** the door because it was already unlocked.
I **didn't need to write** to you so I phoned you instead.

Si può usare anche *didn't 'need to* (con l'enfasi su *need*) quando si vuole dire che qualcosa è stato fatto pur non essendo necessario.

I **didn't 'need to write** to you, but I wrote to you anyway.

ESERCIZIO 41A

Completa le frasi usando *needn't have* se possibile, altrimenti *didn't need to*.

Esempi:

'Did you water the garden?'   'Yes, but I *needn't have done* (do) it. Just after I'd finished it started to rain!'
I *didn't need to wake* (wake) her up because she was awake before me.

1 She ____ (get up) early last Saturday, so she stayed in bed until 10 o'clock.
2 I didn't wear my coat when I went out. I ____ (wear) it. It wasn't cold.
3 He was very anxious before the exam, but he ____ (worry). It wasn't as difficult as he'd expected.
4 She ____ (pay) the man, but she gave him some money anyway.
5 She ____ (pay) the man, so she didn't give him any money.
6 Thank you very much for the flowers, but you really ____ (buy) them for me.

42 Obbligo e consigli: *should, ought to, had better, be supposed to, shall*

1	***Should* e *ought to***
a	Si può usare sia *should* che *ought to* per dire quello che una persona dovrebbe fare in base a un obbligo o un dovere, per chiedere o dare consigli e, in generale, per dire quello che è giusto o bene fare.

*You **should** learn to swim./You **ought to** learn to swim.*
*You **shouldn't** tell lies./You **oughtn't to** tell lies.*
*What do you think I **should** do?/What do you think I **ought to** do?*

Should e *ought to* sono molto simili, ma si preferisce *ought to* in casi di autorità esterna a chi parla p.es. quando ci si riferisce a leggi o regolamenti.

Nota che dopo *should* si usa l'infinito senza *to*, p.es. *learn, tell*, mentre dopo *ought* si usa l'infinito con *to*, p.es. *to learn, to tell*.

b	Si usa *should have/ought to have* + il participio passato del verbo per dire che si doveva fare una cosa, ma non si è fatta.

*I **should have posted** this letter yesterday, but I forgot.* (Non l'ho spedita.)
*I'm really tired this morning. I **shouldn't have stayed up** so late last night.* (Sono rimasto alzato fino a tardi.)
*Haven't you finished your homework yet? You **ought to have done** it last night.* (Non l'hai finito.)

2	***Had better***

Had better (+ l'infinito senza *to*) esprime una forte raccomandazione in una particolare circostanza.

*I'm going to an interview tomorrow. I**'d better iron** my shirt.*
*It's going to be cold tonight. We**'d better turn** on the heating.*

(*'d better = had better*)

In questa costruzione si usa sempre *had* (mai *have*) con *better*, ma il significato è presente o futuro, non passato.

Si costruisce la forma negativa con *had better not*.

*We**'d better not be** late.*

Had better è più forte di *should* e di *ought to*, e spesso esprime un avvertimento o una velata minaccia.

3	***Be* + *supposed to***

Si può usare *supposed to* per dire cosa ci si aspetta che una persona faccia, in base a un accordo, un regolamento o un dovere.

*You**'re supposed to start** work at 8.00 every morning.*
*I**'m supposed to see** Maria this afternoon.*

Si usa *not supposed to* per formulare un divieto.

*You know you**'re not supposed to eat** in the classroom.*

Spesso non c'è corrispondenza tra quello che si doveva fare e quello che invece si fa.

I'm supposed to see Maria this afternoon, but I'm not going to have enough time.
Put those sweets away! You know you**'re not supposed to eat** in the classroom.
He **was supposed to phone** me yesterday, but he didn't.

Spesso si usa *supposed to* nel significato di 'si dice che' p.es. *I'd like to read that book. It's supposed to be very good.* Cfr. 64.2.

4   **Shall**

Si può usare *shall I?* quando si desidera avere l'opinione di qualcuno, o un consiglio o istruzioni su cosa fare.

*I've missed my last bus. What **shall I do**?*
*I'm not sure what to do. **Shall I apply** for the job or not?*
*How long **shall I cook** this spaghetti?*

ESERCIZIO 42A

Cerca il consiglio giusto per ogni problema e completane la formulazione usando *should* oppure *ought to*.

Esempio: **1** 'I've lost my credit card.'
'You should report it to the credit card company immediately.'/
'You ought to report it to the credit card company immediately.'

PROBLEMS	ADVICE
1 'I've lost my credit card.'	'I think you | sell it.'
2 'I can't wake up in the mornings.'	'Perhaps you | look for another job.'
3 'I'm bored with my job.'	'Don't you think you | apologize to them?'
4 'I've got a terrible headache.'	'Perhaps you | buy a new alarm clock!'
5 'I was very rude to my parents.'	'You | report it to the credit card company immediately.'
6 'My car keeps on breaking down.'	'Perhaps you | take some aspirin.'

ESERCIZIO 42B

Fa' delle frasi usando *should(n't) ..., ought(n't) to ..., should(n't) have ...* o *ought(n't) to have ...* e le parole fra parentesi.

Esempi: My car is always dirty. (I | clean | it more often.)
I should clean it more often./I ought to clean it more often.

1 You think your friend works too hard. You tell him/her:
   (You | not work | so hard.) (You | relax | more.)
2 Your friend overslept this morning and was late for work. His boss said to him: (You | buy | an alarm clock!)
3 Kate didn't feel well yesterday, but she went to work and now she feels really terrible. (She | not go | to work yesterday.) (She | stay | in bed.)
4 Mr Woods walked straight out into the road without looking. He was nearly killed by a bus. (He | not walk | into the road without looking.) (He | look | first.)

ESERCIZIO 42C

Completa le frasi usando *had better* e i verbi del riquadro.

Esempio: The phone is ringing. I'*d better answer* it.

> park   stay   hurry   ~~answer~~   put out   be   not leave

1 This knife is very sharp. You ___ careful when you use it.
2 Oh no! Look! There's a 'No Parking' sign here. We ___ somewhere else.
3 You're not very well. I think you ___ in bed today.
4 We're late. We ___.
5 There's a lot of crime in this area. We ___ any doors or windows unlocked.
6 The plane is just going to take off. You ___ that cigarette.

ESERCIZIO 42D

Completa le frasi usando il tempo giusto di *be + supposed to* e i verbi del riquadro.

Esempio: I'm on a diet, so I'*m not supposed to eat* cream cakes.

> arrive   ~~not eat~~   go   not open   not park   have

1 What are you doing with your birthday presents? You ___ them until your birthday!
2 I ___ to work yesterday, but I couldn't because I was ill in bed.
3 You ___ your car here at any time.
4 We ___ in Manchester at 6 o'clock this morning, but our plane was delayed.
5 Peter ___ a one-hour lunch break, but he sometimes takes a bit longer.

ESERCIZIO 42E

Completa ogni domanda usando *shall I* e il verbo più appropriato del riquadro.

Esempio: How much money *shall I get* from the bank?

> paint   invite   ~~get~~   tell   put

1 Who ___ to my party, do you think?
2 Where ___ all these dirty plates and glasses?
3 What do you think? ___ my parents what has happened?
4 What colour ___ my bedroom? Have you got any ideas?

Nota   –Per le forme dei verbi modali, come *should, ought to* e *shall*, cfr. 35.2.

43 Possibilità: *may, might, could*

1

a   **Possibilità nel presente o nel futuro**

Si usa *may, might* e *could* per esprimere possibilità nel presente o nel futuro.

'There's someone at the door.'   *'It **may** be Sarah.'* (= Forse è Sara.)
*We aren't sure what we are going to do tomorrow. We **might** go to the beach.* (= Forse andremo alla spiaggia.)
'Where's Simon?'   *'He **could** be in the living room.'* (= Forse è nel salotto.)

Di regola *might* esprime meno certezza di *may*, e *could* meno di *may* e *might*.

$+++may$ $++might$ $+could$

b   Si usano le forme negative *may not* e *might not* (contrazione *mightn't*), ma non *could not*, con questo significato.

*Simon **may not** be in the living room.* (= Forse non è nel salotto.)
*We **might not** go to the beach.* (= Forse non andremo alla spiaggia.)

c   Nota la costruzione: *may/might/could + be + ...-ing.*

*They **may be having** dinner at the moment.* (= Forse stanno pranzando in questo momento.)

2

a   **Possibilità nel passato**

Si può usare *may/might/could + have +* il participio passato per esprimere possibilità nel passato.

'Where was Sally last night?'   *'I think she **may have been** at the cinema.'* (= Forse era al cinema.)
'Peter is late.'   *'He **might have missed** his train.'* (= Forse ha perso il treno.)
'I can't find my wallet anywhere.'   *'You **could have left** it at home.'* (= Forse l'hai lasciato a casa.)
'She walked straight past me without saying hello.'   *'She **might not have seen** you.'* (= Forse non t'ha visto.)

b | Si usa *could* e *might* (non *may*), con *have* + il participio passato anche per dire che qualcosa sarebbe stato possibile nel passato, ma non si è avverato.

'I forgot to lock my car last night.'   'You were very lucky. Someone could have stolen it.'
You were stupid to try to climb that tree. You might have killed yourself.

ESERCIZIO 43A

Riscrivi queste frasi usando i verbi modali fra parentesi.

Esempio:

Perhaps she is ill. (may)   *She may be ill.*
Perhaps they went out. (might)   *They might have gone out.*

1 Perhaps you're right. (could)
2 Perhaps she'll win the race. (might)
3 Perhaps she forgot about the meeting. (may)
4 Perhaps they were asleep. (might)
5 Perhaps he doesn't know the address. (may)
6 Perhaps they left early. (could)
7 Perhaps he isn't coming now. (might)
8 Perhaps I'll see you tomorrow. (may)
9 Perhaps they're going on holiday. (could)
10 Perhaps she didn't catch the bus. (may)

Nota –Per le forme dei verbi modali, come *may*, *might*, *could*, cfr. 35.2.
–Si usa *could* anche per fare una proposta p.es. *We could go out tonight.* Cfr. 50.3.
–*Might* ha anche il significato condizionale di 'forse' p.es. *If I won a lot of money, I might stop working.* (= ... forse smetterei di lavorare). Cfr. 69.3, 71.3.

44   Possibilità: *can*

1 | Si usa *can* per esprimere 'possibilità teorica'.

Anyone can learn to swim. (= Chiunque può imparare a nuotare.)

In questi casi *can* spesso ha un significato simile a 'qualche volta'.

My brother can be very nice. (= Mio fratello è carino qualche volta.)

Si usa *may*, *might* o *could*, ma non *can*, per esprimere una possibilità nel presente o nel futuro (cfr. 43).

It may rain later. (Non: *It can rain later.*)
'Where's Ken?'   'He could be outside.' (Non: *He can be outside.*)

Confronta:

It can be cold in England. (= Qualche volta fa freddo in Inghilterra.)	*It may be cold tomorrow.* (= Forse domani farà freddo.)

2 | Si usa *could* per esprimere possibilità nel passato.

My brother could be really horrible when he was a child.

ESERCIZIO 44A

Completa le frasi usando *can* o *could* e i verbi del riquadro, ciascuno una volta sola.

grow   ~~be~~   make   reach   live   survive   cross

Esempio:

Tigers *can be* dangerous.

1 Elephants ⎯⎯ for up to 70 years.
2 Temperatures near the South Pole ⎯⎯ minus 43 degrees centigrade.
3 A hundred years ago ships ⎯⎯ the Atlantic in 10 days.

4 Camels ⎯⎯ for up to 17 weeks in the desert without water.
5 Dinosaurs ⎯⎯ up to 5 metres long.
6 Anyone ⎯⎯ mistakes.

Nota   –Per le forme dei verbi modali, come *can* ecc., cfr. 35.2.
–Si usa *can* anche per proporre qualcosa, p.es. *We **can** have dinner now if you like.* Cfr. 50.3.

45   Probabilità: *should, ought to*

1   Si può usare *should* o *ought to* per dire della probabilità di qualche cosa nel momento in cui si parla o nel futuro.

*Sally **should** be at work by now. She's normally there at this time.* (= Sally dovrebbe essere al lavoro adesso.)
*I **should** finish work early today. I haven't got much to do.* (= Oggi dovrei finire di lavorare prima.)
*He **ought to** pass his driving test easily. He's a very good driver.* (= Dovrebbe passare l'esame di guida con facilità.)

2 | ### Should have ... e ought to have ...

Si usa *should have/ought to have* + il participio passato per dire che un fatto dovrebbe essere avvenuto, ma non se ne è sicuri.

They **should have arrived** by now. (Non so se sono arrivati.)
'I wonder if he passed his driving test this morning.'   *'He **ought to have passed** it easily.'* (Non so se è passato.)

Si usa questa costruzione anche per dire di fatti che ci si aspettava accadessero, ma che non si sono avverati.

They **should have arrived** by now, but they aren't there yet.
He **ought to have passed** his driving test easily. I was surprised that he failed.

ESERCIZIO 45A

Completa le frasi usando *should* o *ought to* e il tempo giusto dei verbi nel riquadro.
Usa ciascun verbo una volta sola.

pass ~~be~~ win not take
sell arrive receive

Esempio:

I've only got £15, but that *should be/ought to be* enough. We won't need to buy very much.

1 You ____ my letter first thing tomorrow morning. I posted it early today.
2 I was surprised Liverpool lost the football match. They ____ easily.
3 I ____ my car easily. I only want £950 for it and it's in very good condition.
4 Andrew ____ the exams last week. He worked very hard for them.
5 'How long will it take to drive to the park?'   'Well, it ____ long. It isn't very far.'
6 I'm still waiting for the 7 o'clock bus. It ____ half an hour ago.

Nota   –Per le forme dei verbi modali, come *should* e *ought to*, cfr. 35.2.

46 Deduzioni: *must, can't*

1 | *Must, can't*

a Si usa *must* per fare delle deduzioni di cui si è certi.

It's not very warm and you're not wearing a coat. You **must** *be cold.* (= Senz'altro hai freddo.)
Mrs Woods **must** *know London very well. She has lived there all her life.* (Deve conoscere Londra molto bene.)

b In tali casi si usa *can't*, non *mustn't*, come forma negativa, quando cioè si deduce che qualcosa è impossibile.

Peter was here a moment ago, so he **can't** *be far away.* (= Non può essere lontano.)
Annie **can't** *be asleep. There's a light on in her bedroom.* (= E' impossibile che stia dormendo.)

c Nota la forma: *must/can't + be + ...-ing.*

You've been working hard all day. You **must be feeling** *tired.* (= Devi essere stanco.)
Simon has bought two tickets for the concert, so he **can't be going** *on his own.* (= Sono sicuro che non va da solo.)

d Si può usare *can* anche in domande in cui ci si chiede qualcosa.

The telephone is ringing. Who **can** *that be?*
Sally is late. Where **can** *she be?*

2 | *Must have ... e can't have ...*

a Si usa *must/can't + have +* il participio passato per deduzioni riferite al passato.

Those shoes you bought are very nice. They **must have been** *expensive.* (= Sono sicuro che sono costate molto.)
You **can't have been** *at the swimming pool yesterday! The swimming pool was closed all day yesterday!* (= E' impossibile che tu sia stato in piscina.)

Qui si può usare *couldn't have ...* invece di *can't have ....*

You **couldn't have been** *at the swimming pool yesterday! The swimming pool was closed all day yesterday!*

b Si usa *can have ...* e *could have ...* in domande che riguardano possibilità riferite al passato.

Where **can** *they* **have gone***?*
Sally is very late. What **could have happened** *to her?*

ESERCIZIO 46A

Rispondi alle domande di **A** usando *must* o *can't*, dando una motivazione di **B**.

Esempio:

1 They *can't be* Greek. They're speaking Italian.

A	**B**
1 Are they Greek?	It's very cold in here.
2 Is he ill?	He's too young.
3 Is the heating on?	She's just passed her driving test.
4 Are they asleep?	They're speaking Italian.
5 Is she happy?	Their bedroom lights are off.
6 Is he a doctor?	He's got a high temperature.

ESERCIZIO 46B

Ieri, a Londra, c'è stato un furto alla Central Art Gallery. Un detective sta interrogando Billy Palmer.

Il detective sa che Palmer mente. Leggi, a sinistra, quello che Palmer dice, poi confrontalo con gli indizi a destra.

Deduci l'accaduto usando *must have . . .* o *can't/couldn't have . . . .* Motiva poi tutte le tue deduzioni.

Esempio:

1 *Palmer can't/couldn't have stayed in bed all morning yesterday. Someone saw him in town at 10.00 yesterday morning.*

Nota —Per le forme dei verbi modali, come *must, can('t)* e *could(n't)*, cfr. 35.2.

47 Riepilogo dei verbi indicanti possibilità, probabilità e deduzioni: *may, might, could, should, ought to, must, can't*

ESERCIZIO 47A

Osserva questi esempi:

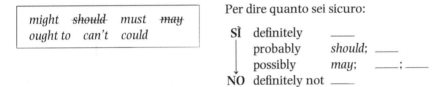

Colloca al posto giusto nella tabella i verbi del riquadro.

might ~~*should*~~ *must* ~~*may*~~
ought to   can't   could

Per dire quanto sei sicuro:

SÌ   definitely   ____
| probably   *should;* ____
| possibly   *may;*   ____ ; ____
NO   definitely not ____

ESERCIZIO 47B

Riscrivi le frasi usando la forma corretta dei verbi fra parentesi.

Esempi:

I'm sure she is in bed. (must)   *She must be in bed.*
We'll probably arrive before 11 o'clock. (should)   *We should arrive before 11 o'clock.*
Perhaps he was ill. (may)   *He may have been ill.*
It's impossible that they missed the plane. (can't)   *They can't have missed the plane.*

1 Perhaps she'll phone later. (might)
2 I'll probably be at home by 6 o'clock. (should)
3 Perhaps they went home. (could)
4 It's impossible that he's telling the truth. (can't)
5 I'm sure you've heard the news. (must)
6 Perhaps I won't go out this evening. (may)
7 It's impossible that she saw us. (can't)
8 I'm sure the bus has left. (must)
9 Perhaps he didn't apply for the job. (might)
10 She'll probably be here soon. (ought to)

48 Richieste: *can, could, may, will, would*

1   **Chiedere qualcosa**

Si può chiedere qualcosa usando *can, could* e *may.*

Can I have a glass of water, please?
Could I have the bill, please? (p.es. al ristorante)
May I have some more coffee?

Could è meno diretto e più formale di *can*; *may* è più formale di *can/could.*

2   **Chiedere il permesso di fare qualcosa**

Si usa *can, could* e *may* anche per chiedere il permesso di fare qualcosa (cfr. 37.1).

Can I borrow your dictionary?
Could I ask you a personal question?
Excuse me. May I have a look at your newspaper?

3   **Chiedere a qualcuno di fare qualcosa**

a   Spesso si usa *can you?* (= puoi?) per chiedere a qualcuno di fare qualcosa per noi.

Can you post this letter for me please?
Can you switch on the light, please?

Could svolge lo stesso ruolo, ma è meno forte e più cortese di *can.*

Could you pass me that newspaper please?
Could you give me some advice?

b   Si usa anche *will you?* (= sei disposto?) per chiedere a qualcuno di fare qualcosa.

Will you switch on the light, please?

Would svolge lo stesso ruolo, ma è meno forte e più cortese di *will.*

Would you post this letter for me?
'The phone is ringing.'   'Would you answer it?'

c   *Would* viene inoltre usato con il verbo *mind* (= avere qualcosa in contrario), per chiedere educatamente qualcosa.

Would you mind switching on the light?

d   Si può usare anche *would like* per dire educatamente quello che si vuole.

I'd like a glass of water, please.
I'd like to ask you a personal question.

ESERCIZIO 48A

Che cosa chiedono i personaggi delle illustrazioni? Trova le domande nel riquadro.

Esempio:

Can I close the window?

Could you tell	the TV for me, please?
Would you mind changing	the window?
Would you answer	the menu, please?
May I have	the phone, please?
Can I close	me where the hospital is, please?
Will you switch on	me the cloth, please?
Can you pass	places with me?

Nota   –Per le forme dei verbi modali, come *can, could, may, will* e *would*, cfr. 35.2.

–Nota il significato di *yes* e *no* dopo una richiesta formulata con *mind* p.es. '**Would you mind** *waiting?*'   '*No, that's all right.*' (= No, non mi dispiace aspettare)/'**Yes, I would!**' (=Sì, mi secca aspettare!)

49 Offerte: *will*, *shall*, *can*, *could*, *would*

1 Si usa *will* per esprimere disponibilità o per offrirsi di fare qualcosa.

I'll help you with your suitcase.
I'll lend you my bicycle if you want.
Are you hungry? I'll make you something to eat.

(*I'll* = *I will*)

Si usa *will you?* anche per offerte o inviti.

*What **will you** have to drink?*
***Will you** have dinner with us?*

2 Si usa *shall I?* (= vuoi che io …?) per offrirsi di fare qualcosa per qualcuno.

***Shall I** help you?*
***Shall I** open the door for you?*
***Shall I** post this letter for you?*

3 Si usa anche *can/could* (= 'abilità') per offrirsi di fare qualcosa per qualcuno.

*I **can** post this letter for you.*
*I **could** lend you some money if you want.*

Talvolta, quando si usa *can* o *could* per chiedere il permesso di fare qualcosa, si intende, di fatto, offrire la propria disponibilità allo scopo.

***Can** I make you something to eat?*
***Could** I carry that bag for you?*

In tali casi, *could* è meno forte e più cortese di *can*.

4 Si usa anche *would* con verbi come *like* e *prefer* e con *rather* per fare un invito o per offrirsi gentilmente di fare qualcosa.

***Would** you **like** to go to a party on Saturday?*
***Would** you **like** me to help you?*
***Would** you **prefer** to stay in or go out this evening?*

ESERCIZIO 49A

Offri la tua disponibilità nelle situazioni raffigurate, usando le frasi del riquadro.

Esempio:

Shall I switch off	something to drink?
I'll help	you an umbrella if you like.
Would you like me to phone	your coat?
Can I take	the light?
Would you like ———	some bags for you?
Could I carry	for the doctor?
I can lend	you do the washing up.

Would you like something to drink?

Nota   –Per le forme dei verbi modali, come *will, shall, can, could* e *would*, cfr. 35.2.

50 Suggerimenti: *shall, let's, why don't we? how/what about? can, could*

1 | Si usa *shall we?* per chiedere e dare suggerimenti.

Where **shall we** *go?*
What time **shall we** *leave?*

Shall we *stay at home?*
Shall we *play tennis tomorrow?*

2 Si può suggerire qualcosa anche in questi modi:

a

> *Let's* (+ l'infinito senza *to*)

Let's watch TV.
Let's go for a swim.

(*Let's* = Let us)

b

> *Why don't we* (+ l'infinito senza *to*)?

Why don't we go for a swim?
Why don't we play tennis?

c

> *How/What about* (+ la forma in *-ing* o un sostantivo)?

How about playing tennis/a game of tennis?

3 Si usa *can* e *could* per proporre qualcosa.

We **can** watch TV if you like.
We **could** go to the cinema tomorrow.

In questi casi *could* è meno forte e più cortese di *can*.

ESERCIZIO 50A

Peter e Sally cercano di decidere cosa fare stasera.

Completa la conversazione usando le espressioni del riquadro, alcune più di una volta.

> Why don't we   Let's   shall we   How about   could

Peter: So, what *shall we* do this evening?
Sally: Well, we haven't got much money. __1__ staying in and watching TV?
Peter: Oh, no! I'm fed up with watching TV.
Sally: __2__ go out for a drink, then. We can afford one drink each.
Peter: All right. Where __3__ go?
Sally: __4__ go to The Tropical Bar? They have really good music there.
Peter: Yes, but the drinks are very expensive.
Sally: That's true. Well, we __5__ go to the pub on the corner.
Peter: Yes. They have very good videos. __6__ go there.
Sally: I thought you said you were fed up with watching TV!

Nota   –Per le forme dei verbi modali, come *shall, can* e *could*, cfr. 35.2.

51 Abitudini: *used to, will, would*

1

a

Used to

Uso

Si usa *used to* + l'infinito per parlare di abitudini che si avevano nel passato.

Robert da giovane   Robert oggi

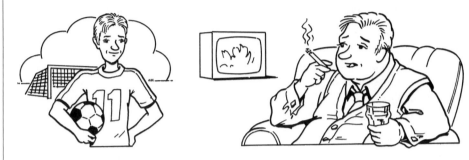

*Robert **used to play** football when he was younger, but he stopped playing 20 years ago.*
(= Robert giocava sempre a pallone da giovane, non più adesso.)

Altri esempi:

*Kate **used to go** swimming a lot, but she never goes swimming now.*
*When I was a child, I **used to suck** my thumb.*

Si usa *used to* anche per stati fisici e situazioni del passato che non sussistono più.

*Robert **used to be** very slim when he was younger.*
*I **used to live** in London, but I moved in 1980.*

Si usa *used to* solo riferendosi al passato. Quando si vuole parlare di abitudini o situazioni attuali si usa il presente.

*Robert never **plays** football now.*
*Kate **goes** sailing quite often nowadays.*
*I **live** in Manchester.*
*Robert **is** quite fat.*

Non si usa *used to* per dire quanto è durato qualcosa.

*I **worked** in Rome for six months.* (Non: ~~I used to work in Rome for six months.~~)

b

Forma

Used to + l'infinito ha la stessa forma per tutte le persone.

I You He She etc	used to	**play** football. **live** in London. **be** very slim.

La forma negativa di *used to* normalmente è *didn't use to* (= *did not use to*).

*I **didn't use to live** in London.*
*You **didn't use to like** classical music.*

Si dice anche *never used to* p.es. *You **never used to like** classical music.*

Si formano le domande con *did . . . use to . . . ?*

*Where **did** you **use to live**?*
***Did** you **use to like** classical music?*

Nota la pronuncia particolare di *used* /juːst/ e *use* /juːz/ di questa costruzione.

2 | **Will e would**

a | Si può usare *will* per parlare del comportamento tipico o delle abitudini di qualcuno.

*Simon loves music. He**'ll** sit for hours listening to his stereo.*
*Kate is very kind. She**'ll** always help people if she can.*

Si usa *would* con lo stesso significato riferendosi però al passato.

*When I was a child my father **would** sometimes take me fishing.*
*My grandmother was very absent-minded. She **would** often buy something and then leave the shop without it.*

Will e *would* in tali casi non sono enfatizzati.

b | Se *will* o *would* sono enfatizzati (ʹ), esprimono una critica.

*He ʹ**will** slam the door when he comes in. It really makes me angry.*
*'She borrowed my camera without asking.'   'She ʹ**would** do a thing like that. She's always borrowing things without asking.'*

3 | **Used to e would**

Quando si parla di abitudini passate, si può usare *used to* o *would*.

*When we were children, we **used to**/**would** play Cowboys and Indians together.*
*When I was a child, my elder brother **used to**/**would** take me to the cinema every Saturday morning.*

Quando si parla di lavori, condizioni o stati fisici passati, si può usare *used to*, ma non *would*.

*My grandfather **used to** be a policeman.* (Non: ~~*My grandfather **would** be . . .*~~)
*I **used to** have a moustache, but I shaved it off.* (Non: ~~*I **would** have . . .*~~)

ESERCIZIO 51A

Metti un verbo di ogni frase alla forma *used to* e l'altro al presente.

Esempi:

When Margot first became a doctor, she *used to work* (work) in a small hospital in Brighton, but now she *works* (work) in a large hospital in London.

1 Robert ____ (be) interested in football, but he ____ (not | be) very interested in it any more.
2 Nowadays Kate ____ (never | go) dancing, but she ____ (go) a lot before she was married.
3 That shop ____ (be) a grocer's when I was a child. Now it ____ (be) a supermarket.
4 Britain ____ (have) military service, but it ____ (not | have) it any more.
5 France ____ (be) a republic now, but it ____ (be) a monarchy.
6 '____ (you | like) history when you were at school?' 'No, I didn't, but now I ____ (find) it quite interesting.'

ESERCIZIO 51B

Completa le frasi usando *will* o *would* e uno dei verbi del riquadro.

Esempio:

Robert has got a very bad memory. He *'ll often forget* (often) where he's parked his car.

> carry on   spend   lend   go   throw   ~~forget~~

1 Kate is very generous. She ____ (always) you money if you need it.
2 Ken's grandfather was very mean. He ____ (never) anything away if he could use it again.
3 Mr Woods is a real chatterbox! He ____ talking for hours and hours if you give him a chance.
4 When Simon was a child, he ____ (often) hours just looking out of the window.
5 'I'm always tired these days.' 'Well, you ____ to bed so late every night, it isn't surprising!'

ESERCIZIO 51C

Quali frasi possono essere completate sia con *used to* che con *would*? Quali solo con *used to*?

Esempi:

We *used to* live in a village in the North of England.
When Robert was younger, he *used to/would* go running every morning.

1 When Andrew was a small baby he ____ cry a lot.
2 When I was little, I ____ be afraid of the dark.

3 When we were children, we ____ visit my grandmother every Sunday afternoon.
4 When Mrs Woods was younger, she ____ play tennis every weekend.
5 Years ago I ____ have a motorbike.
6 There ____ be quite a lot of cinemas in the town, but now there aren't any.

Nota –Per le forme dei verbi modali, come *will* e *would*, cfr. 35.2.
–Non confondere *used to* + l'infinito, p.es. *He **used to get** up very early*, con *be used to* + la forma in *-ing* p.es. *He's **used to getting** up early*. Cfr. 89.

52 Rifiuti: *won't, wouldn't*

> Si usa *won't* (= *will not*) per dire che le persone o le cose si rifiutano di fare qualcosa.
>
> *Annie **won't** do her homework.* (= Si rifiuta di farlo.)
> *This machine **won't** work.* (= Si rifiuta di funzionare.)
>
> Si usa *wouldn't* (*would not*) per dire che le persone o le cose si rifiutavano di fare qualcosa nel passato.
>
> *This machine **wouldn't** work yesterday.* (= Si rifiutava di funzionare.)

ESERCIZIO 52A

Sostituisci le parole in corsivo con ... *won't* ... o ... *wouldn't* ..., come negli esempi.

Esempi:

I asked my father, but *he refused to lend* me the money.
I asked my father, but *he wouldn't lend* me the money.
I've decided to take the job and *I refuse to change* my mind.
I've decided to take the job and *I won't change* my mind.

1 I pushed hard, but *the window refused to open.*
2 He's proposed to her, but *she refuses to marry* him.
3 I switched on the machine, but *it refused to work.*
4 I've warned her several times about leaving the windows unlocked, but *she refuses to listen* to me.
5 We've asked him, but *he refuses to help* us.
6 We couldn't drive to the country last weekend because *my parents refused to let* me use their car.

53 Promesse e minacce: *will*

> Si può usare *will* per indicare un'intenzione ben ferma, esprimendola per esempio in una promessa o in una minaccia.
>
> *I **will** be careful with the car, I promise.*
> *I promise I **won't** be late tomorrow.*
> *Stop making that noise or **I'll** scream!*

ESERCIZIO 53A

Completa ogni frase usando *will* o *won't* e un verbo del riquadro. Poi specifica se si tratta di una promessa o di una minaccia.

leave   do   tell   ~~hit~~   throw   pay   speak

Esempio:

Don't touch my camera or I*'ll hit* you!   a threat

1 Don't worry. I ___ you the money tomorrow.
2 It's getting late. If you don't hurry up, I ___ without you.
3 I ___ anyone what you said. Don't worry.
4 I'm very sorry I shouted at you. I ___ it again.
5 Get out of my room or I ___ you out!
6 If you don't help me, I ___ to you ever again.

54 *May/might as well*

Si usa *may/might as well* (+ l'infinito senza *to*) per dire che si dovrebbe fare qualcosa non essendoci motivo per non farlo.

'*Shall we get a taxi or wait for the bus?*'   '*We* **might as well** *wait for the bus. We're not in a hurry, are we?*'
'*Why don't we go out for a walk?*'   '*We* **may as well**, *I suppose. We haven't got anything else to do.*'

ESERCIZIO 54A

Componi delle frasi dal riquadro che si accordino con quelle a sinistra.

Esempio:

You may as well switch off the TV. Nobody is watching it.

1 ___. It's not very far.
2 ___. I'm too ill to go on holiday.
3 ___. It isn't going to stop raining.
4 ___. No one wants any more to eat.
5 ___. There's a chance I'll get it.

You may as well switch off	to the station.
We might as well stay	the table.
We may as well walk	the hotel bookings.
I might as well apply	the TV.
You might as well cancel	at home today.
I might as well clear	for the job.

55 Altri usi di *should*

1 | **Verbo + *should***

Si può usare *that . . . should* dopo verbi come *suggest, insist, recommend, agree*; spesso si omette *that* nello stile informale.

I suggest (that) he should see the doctor.
She insisted (that) I should take the money.
I agreed (that) we should tell the police.

Dopo questi verbi sono possibili anche altre costruzioni. Per esempio:

I suggest (that) he sees the doctor. (presente)
She insisted (that) I took the money. (passato)

2 | **Aggettivo + *should***

Si può usare *(that) . . . should* dopo aggettivi che esprimono emozioni p.es. *surprised, sorry, shocked, interesting*.

I was surprised (that) she should fail the exam.
I am sorry (that) he should feel so unhappy.
It is interesting (that) you should say that.

Si usa *(that) . . . should* anche dopo aggettivi come *important* e *essential*.

It is important (that) we should arrive on time.

Tali idee possono essere espresse anche senza *should*.

I was surprised (that) she failed the exam.
It is important (that) we arrive on time.

ESERCIZIO 55A

Riscrivi le frasi usando il discorso indiretto e i verbi fra parentesi seguiti da *(that) . . . should*, come nell'esempio.

Esempio:

'You must visit us,' they said to me. (insist)
They insisted (that) I should visit them.

1 'Why don't you apply for the job?' she said to me. (suggest)
2 'Stay in bed for a few days,' the doctor said to him. (recommend)
3 'You must help me,' he said to me. (insist)
4 'Let's go to the cinema,' they said to us. (suggest)

ESERCIZIO 55B

Completa ogni frase usando *should* e il verbo più adatto del riquadro. Usa ciascun verbo una volta sola.

Esempio:

The situation is very difficult, but it is important that everyone *should stay* calm.

| come   give up   pass   ~~stay~~   feel |

1 The doctor suggested that I ___ smoking.
2 It's essential that Sarah ___ the exams if she wants to go to university.
3 It was embarrassing that Simon ___ into the room just as we were talking about him.
4 I'm sorry that you ___ so angry. I didn't mean to upset you.

Nota –Si può usare *should* dopo *if* quando la possibilità è vaga p.es. *If I should see Maria, I'll give her your message.* Si può anche usare *should* invece di *if* p.es. *Should I see Maria, I'll give her your message.* Cfr. 68.3,73.4.
   –Si usa *should* con questo significato anche dopo *in case* p.es. *I'll take an umbrella with me when I go out in case it should rain.* Cfr. 164.4

56 *Wish* e *if only*

1 *Wish* e *if only* + il passato remoto

Si può usare *wish* e *if only* con il passato remoto per esprimere rammarico nel presente (perché vorremmo che qualcosa fosse diverso).

*I **wish** I **had** a car.* (Ma non ho la macchina.)
*I **wish** he **wasn't** so horrible to me.* (Ma mi tratta male.)
*She **wishes** she **could** play the guitar.* (Ma non la sa suonare.)
*If only we **knew** Maria's address.* (Ma non sappiamo il suo indirizzo.)

If only è più enfatico di *wish*.

Spesso si usa *were* invece di *was* dopo *wish* e *if only*, soprattutto nello stile formale.

*I **wish** he **weren't** so horrible to me.*
*If only I **were** better-looking.*

2 | **Wish e *if only* + would**

I **wish** *you* **would** *stop making that noise.*

Si usa *would* dopo *wish* e *if only* quando si desidera che qualcosa finisca o che accada qualcosa di diverso.

I **wish** *you* **wouldn't** *slam the door when you come in. It makes me angry.*
I **wish** *he* **wouldn't** *leave his clothes lying all over the bathroom floor.*
If only you **would** *stop complaining!*

3 | **Wish e *if only* + il trapassato**

Per esprimere rimpianto per qualcosa che è accaduto o non è accaduto nel passato, si può usare *wish* e *if only* con il trapassato (*had* + il participio passato).

Oh, I'm tired. I **wish** *I'* **d gone** *to bed earlier last night.* (Non sono andato a letto molto presto ieri sera.)
I **wish** *I* **hadn't stayed** *out so late.* (Sono rimasto fuori fino a tardi.)
If only you **had explained** *the situation to me.* (Non mi hai spiegato la situazione.)

ESERCIZIO 56A

Leggi quello che questo signore pensa di sé, a sinistra. Completa quello che dice, a destra.

I'm so shy.
I don't know what to say to people.

I wish *I weren't so shy.*
If only *I knew what to say to people.*

1 I get embarrassed so quickly.   I wish ____
2 I can't relax.   I wish ____
3 I find it so difficult to make friends.   I wish ____
4 I'm not good-looking.   I wish ____
5 My ears are so big.   If only ____

ESERCIZIO 56B

Alcune persone si lamentano perché vorrebbero che altre persone facessero o smettessero di fare certe cose. Completa quello che dicono. Usa *would/wouldn't* e le espressioni del riquadro.

Esempio:

A zoo keeper: 'I wish people *wouldn't feed the animals.'*

take their litter home
pick the flowers
clean the bath after they've used it
do their homework on time
~~feed the animals~~
keep together on a tour

1 A teacher: 'I wish my students ____.'
2 A hotel chambermaid: 'If only guests ____.'
3 A park keeper: 'I wish people ____.'
4 A street cleaner: 'If only people ____.'
5 A travel guide: 'I wish people ____.'

ESERCIZIO 56C

Tutte queste persone hanno fatto qualcosa ieri che adesso rimpiangono. Cosa vorrebbe ognuno? Usa *He/She wishes . . .* e le espressioni del riquadro.

Esempio:

(try) to lift a heavy table on her own
~~(go) out in the rain without an umbrella~~
(eat) less
(drive) more carefully
(stay) in the sun so long

Mrs A has caught a bad cold.
She wishes she hadn't gone out in the rain without an umbrella.

1 Miss B has got very bad sunburn.

2 Mr C has got an awful stomachache.

3 Mr D has hurt his leg in a car crash.

4 Mrs E has hurt her back.

57 *Would rather*

1 | *Would rather* è un'espressione che equivale al condizionale di 'preferire'. E' sempre seguita dall'infinito senza *to*.

> would rather + l'infinito senza *to*

'*Would you like to go on holiday in June?*'   '*I'd rather go in July.*'
Would you **rather meet** on Monday or Tuesday?

Si costruisce la forma negativa con *would rather not*.

I'd rather not lend him any money.

Nota anche la costruzione *would rather . . .* (preferirei . . .) *than . . .* (piuttosto che . . .).

I'd rather take a taxi to the station **than go** by bus.

2 | Si può usare *would rather* + il passato remoto anche per dire che si preferirebbe che una persona facesse o non facesse una certa cosa.

> would rather + il soggetto + il passato remoto

I'd rather you **didn't open** that window. I'm cold.
'*Do you want me to go home?*'   '*I'd rather* you **stayed** here.*'
I'd rather John **didn't borrow** my car.

Qui viene usato il passato p.es. *you didn't open, you stayed, John didn't borrow*, ma il significato è presente o futuro, non passato.

ESERCIZIO 57A

Completa le frasi usando *would rather* e i verbi del riquadro, ciascuno una volta sola.

Esempio:

What would you like to drink? *Would you rather have* (you) wine or beer?

> listen   do   go   ~~have~~   stay

1 'Shall we go out this evening?'   'I think I ___ at home.'
2 It's a beautiful day. Shall we go to the beach or ___ (you) to the country?
3 'Would you like to watch TV?'   'I ___ to some music.'
4 We could wait for the next bus or walk home. What ___ (you)?

ESERCIZIO 57B

Stai parlando con un amico. Completa le frasi usando *I'd rather you* e il passato remoto dei verbi nel riquadro. Usa ciascun verbo una volta sola.

> come   not open   ~~stay~~   phone   not turn on

Esempio:

You could go now if you want to, but *I'd rather you stayed* a bit longer.
1 ____ the window. I'm rather cold.
2 I could phone the restaurant if you like, but ____ them.
3 ____ the TV if you don't mind. I've got a terrible headache.
4 'Shall I come and see you tomorrow morning?' '____ in the afternoon. I'll be quite busy in the morning.'

58   *It's time*

1   Si può usare l'infinito con *to* dopo la costruzione *it's time* (*for* qualcuno).

It's time for us to leave.
It's time to go to bed now.

2   Si può usare anche *it's time* + il passato remoto se si pensa che qualcuno avrebbe già dovuto fare qualcosa.

Your bedroom is in a terrible mess. Don't you think it's time you cleaned it?
I'm tired. It's time I went to bed.

Si usa il passato p.es. *you cleaned, I went*, ma il significato qui è presente o futuro.

Si dice anche *it's about time.*
Your bedroom is in a terrible mess. Don't you think it's about time you cleaned it?

ESERCIZIO 58B

Completa le frasi usando *it's time* e il passato remoto.

Esempio:

Andrew's hair looks awful. He hasn't washed it for a long time. He says: *It's time I washed my hair.*

1 Simon received a bill two weeks ago, but he still hasn't paid it. His friend asks him: Don't you think ____?
2 You're taking an important exam next month, but you haven't started studying for it yet. You say: ____.
3 Sally promised to phone a friend, Mike, two weeks ago, but she still hasn't phoned him. Her mother says: Don't you think ____?
4 There is something wrong with your car. You've been thinking of taking it to the garage for weeks now! You say: ____.

59 Il passivo: schema generale

1

a

Forma

Si forma il passivo con i diversi tempi di *be* (p.es. *is, was, is being, have been*) + il participio passato del verbo.

Presente:	*am/are/is* + il participio passato *The office is locked every evening.*
Presente progressivo:	*am/are/is* + *being* + il participio passato *The house is being painted at the moment.*
Passato remoto:	*was/were* + il participio passato *My car was stolen last night.*
Passato progressivo:	*was/were* + *being* + il participio passato *The bridge was being repaired last week.*
Passato prossimo:	*have/has* + *been* + il participio passato *Sarah has been invited to the party.*
Trapassato:	*had* + *been* + il participio passato *I thought that you had been told the news.*

Il passivo con il passato prossimo progressivo (*have/has/had* + *been being* + il participio passato) è molto raro.

Il participio passato dei verbi regolari termina in *-ed* p.es. *locked, painted*. I verbi irregolari hanno forme diverse di participio passato p.es. *steal* → **stolen**, *tell* → **told** (cfr. 190).

Quando si aggiunge *-ed* al verbo, ci possono essere variazioni di ortografia p.es. *stop* → **stopped**. Cfr. 188.3,4,6. Per la pronuncia di *-ed*, cfr. 187.2.

b

Confronta tra di loro queste frasi attive e passive:

Attiva: *Someone locks* the office *every evening.*

Passiva: The office *is locked every evening.*

Attiva: *Someone has invited* Sarah *to the party.*

Passiva: Sarah *has been invited to the party.*

Nota che il complemento oggetto di un verbo attivo (p.es. *the office, Sarah*) diventa il soggetto di un verbo passivo.

c

Le regole per la scelta dei tempi nel passivo sono le stesse di quelle per l'attivo. Per esempio, per dire che qualcosa è in svolgimento adesso si usa il presente progressivo.

The house is being painted at the moment.

2 | **Uso**

a | Spesso si usa il passivo quando non si sa chi o che cosa fa qualcosa.

My car **was stolen** *last night.* (Non so chi l'ha rubata.)

b | Si usa il passivo anche quando non interessa sapere chi o che fa qualcosa.

The factory **was painted** *last month.*
Sarah **has been invited** *to the party.*

In queste frasi ci interessa lo stabilimento e Sarah, non chi ha verniciato lo stabilimento né chi ha invitato Sarah.

c | Si usa la forma passiva anche quando non si vuole dire chi fa qualcosa. Confronta:

Attiva: *I* **made** *a mistake.*
Passiva: *A mistake* **was made.**

ESERCIZIO 59A

Che cosa viene fatto in queste immagini?
Completa le frasi usando la forma passiva del presente progressivo di questi verbi:
paint, feed, milk, count, repair, cut, clean.

Esempio:

1 The road _is being repaired_
2 The fence _is   "   painted_
3 The cows _are   "   milk_
4 The windows "   _cleaned maybe_
5 The cats _are being fed_
6 The money _is being counted_

The grass *is being cut.*

to feed fed fed.

ESERCIZIO 59B

Confronta le due immagini. A raffigura una stanza com'era anni fa. B raffigura la stessa stanza com'è adesso. Che cos'è cambiato? Completa le frasi usando la forma passiva del passato prossimo di questi verbi: *repair, paint, take out, put up, clean.* Usa alcuni verbi più di una volta.

Esempio:

In picture B . . .

The door *has been repaired.*
Some new curtains *have been put up.*

A

1 The window _has been repaired_
2 The carpet _HAS BEEN CLEANED_
3 The walls _HAVE BEEN RE PAINTED_
4 The light _HAS BEEN REPAIRED_
5 Some posters _have been put up._
6 The old fireplace _has been taken out_

B

ESERCIZIO 59C

Completa le frasi.
(i) Usa il presente passivo dei verbi fra parentesi.

Esempio:

Bread *is made* (make) from wheat.

1 Football _IS PLAYED_ (play) all over the world.
2 Millions of cars _ARE EXPORTED_ (export) from Japan every month.
3 A compass _IS USED_ (use) for showing direction.
4 How many languages ____ (speak) in Switzerland?

ARE SPOKEN

active   the
do Swiss speak.

(ii) Usa il passato remoto passivo dei verbi fra parentesi.

Esempio:

President John F. Kennedy *was assassinated* (assassinate) in Dallas in 1963.

1 The Tower of London ____ (build) at the beginning of the eleventh century.
2 The 1986 World Cup for soccer ____ (play) in Mexico.
3 When ____ (television | invent)?
4 The first pyramids of Egypt ____ (build) around 3000 BC.

(iii) Usa il passato progressivo passivo o il trapassato passivo dei verbi fra parentesi.

Esempio:

I couldn't wear my suit last Saturday. It *was being cleaned*. (clean).

1 When I got back to the car park, my car wasn't there. It ____ (steal).
2 We couldn't use the photocopier yesterday morning. It ____ (repair).
3 By the time I arrived at the concert hall, there were no tickets left. They ____ (all | sell).
4 We didn't go to the party on Saturday because we ____ (not | invite).

ESERCIZIO 59D

Scegli la forma corretta: attiva o passiva.

Esempio:

A valuable painting *stole*/*was stolen* from the Central Art Gallery late last night. The thieves *entered*/*were entered* the gallery through a small upstairs window.

1 Walt Disney *created*/*was created* the cartoon character Mickey Mouse.
2 This problem *discussed*/*was discussed* at the last meeting.
3 In 1964 Martin Luther King *won*/*was won* the Nobel Peace Prize. In 1968 he *assassinated*/*was assassinated* in Memphis, Tennessee.
4 The president *arrived*/*was arrived* in Rome yesterday afternoon. Later he *interviewed*/*was interviewed* on Italian TV.
5 Teachers *have given*/*have been given* a new pay rise by the government. The news *announced*/*was announced* earlier today.

Nota   –Per la forma passiva, cfr. anche 60–64.

60 Il passivo: forma con l'infinito e forma con -ing

1 La forma passiva dell'infinito si costruisce con: *be* + il participio passato del verbo.
La si usa dopo i verbi servili (*must, can, will* ecc.) e dopo altre costruzioni (p.es. *going to, have to, want to* e *would like to*).

*This door must **be kept** locked.*
*The job can't **be done**.*
*He's going to **be interviewed** next week.*
*The new motorway will **be opened** next summer.*
*I don't want to **be disturbed**.*

2 La forma passiva dell'infinito passato si costruisce con: *have been* + il participio passato del verbo. La si usa riferendosi al passato.

*The newspaper may **have been thrown** away last night.*
*We should **have been told** about the dangers.*

3 Si può fare la forma passiva dell'infinito anche con *being* + il participio passato del verbo.

*I don't like **being cheated**.*
*He remembers **being given** the book.*

ESERCIZIO 60A

Volgi queste frasi al passivo (omettendo *someone, they, we*).

Esempio:

Someone might steal the car.   *The car might be stolen.*

1 Someone will clean the room.
2 They had to cut down that tree.
3 Someone should tell Sally what happened.
4 They're going to build a new hospital.
5 We can solve the problem.

ESERCIZIO 60B

Completa le frasi usando il passivo dell'infinito passato.

Esempio:

Why doesn't Kate know about the meeting? She should *have been told* (tell) ages ago.

1 'Sally is late this evening.' 'She might ____ (delay) at work.'
2 Why is all this rubbish still here? It ought to ____ (throw away) yesterday.
3 The sweater I wanted to buy isn't in the shop window any more. It must ____ (sell).
4 It was lucky that you didn't fall off the ladder. You might ____ (kill).
5 You shouldn't have left all that money in your hotel room. It could ____ (steal).

ESERCIZIO 60C

Volgi queste frasi al passivo, come nell'esempio.

Esempio:

I don't like people shouting at me.   *I don't like being shouted at.*

1 I don't like people staring at me.
2 I can't stand people telling me what to do.
3 I don't like people interrupting me.
4 I dislike people making jokes about me.
5 I enjoy people praising me.

Pensi che siano vere queste affermazioni?

61 *Get* invece di *be* nel passivo

Talvolta si usa *get* (+ il participio passato) invece di *be* (+ il participio passato) per fare il passivo. Questo, per esempio, quando si parla di cose che accadono per caso o inaspettatamente.

*My flat **got burgled** when I was on holiday.*
*I was surprised that I didn't **get invited** to the party.*
*My parents' fence **got blown** down in the storm.*

Si usa *get* per lo più nello stile informale.

ESERCIZIO 61A

Billy Palmer una volta rubava. Qui sta parlando di una notte, diversi anni fa, quando tutto gli andò male.

Completa il racconto di Palmer facendo il passivo del passato remoto con *get*.

'It was terrible. First of all, my jeans *got ripped* (rip) as I was climbing over the garden wall. Then I __1__ (stick) climbing through the bathroom window. Then I __2__ (bit) by a dog inside the house. The dog made so much noise that everyone in the house woke up and I __3__ (hit) over the head with an umbrella. Then, when I finally got out of the house, there was a police car waiting there. But, to my surprise, I __4__ (not | caught) that night. Although it wouldn't really have mattered if I had. Two weeks later, I __5__ (arrest) burgling another house and I __6__ (sentence) to three years in prison.'

62 Verbi con due complementi nel passivo

Alcuni verbi, p.es, *give*, possono avere due complementi.

*Someone gave **Jimmy the money**.* (I due oggetti sono *Jimmy* e *the money*.)

In questi casi la frase passiva può essere strutturata in due modi diversi.

***Jimmy** was given the money.*   ***The money** was given to Jimmy.*

Di solito, comunque, si comincia la frase passiva con la persona.

Altri verbi che possono avere due complementi sono *send, offer, show, pay, teach, promise, ask* e *tell*.

I was sent *a telegram.*
She will be told *the news.*

ESERCIZIO 62A

Volgi queste frasi al passivo, cominciando con le parole date.

Esempio:

They promised Robert an interview for the job.   Robert *was promised an interview for the job.*

1 They showed Sarah the photographs.
  Sarah ____.
2 Normally, they pay me my salary every month.   Normally, I ____.
3 I think that they have sent us the wrong tickets.   I think that we ____.

4 I hope that someone will give Sally the message.   I hope that Sally ____.
5 They didn't ask me for my address.   I ____.
6 I thought that someone had told you about the meeting.   I thought that you ____.

63 Il passivo con *by* e *with*

1

By + agente

Confronta queste frasi:

Attiva: *Marconi invented the radio.*

Passiva: *The radio was invented by **Marconi**.*

Attiva: *The strong winds blew down a number of trees.*

Passiva: *A number of trees were blown down by **the strong winds**.*

Talvolta si usa il soggetto della frase attiva (p.es. *Marconi, the strong winds*) come agente della stessa frase, volta al passivo. Il complemento d'agente è retto da *by*.

2 │ *With* + **strumento**

With regge il complemento di strumento, che indica il mezzo usato dall'agente per fare qualcosa. Confronta:

*I was hit **with an umbrella**.*   *I was hit **by an old lady**.*

3 │ *With* + **materia**

With regge anche i complementi di abbondanza e di materia.

*The room was filled **with smoke**.*
*Irish coffee is made **with whiskey**.*

ESERCIZIO 63A

Completa le frasi con il passato remoto passivo di questi verbi e *by*.

> paint   ~~write~~   compose and sing
> invent   discover   direct

Esempio:

The Old Man and the Sea was written by Ernest Hemingway.

1 Radium ____ Pierre and Marie Curie.
2 *The Goldrush* ____ Charlie Chaplin.
3 *Imagine* ____ John Lennon.
4 The safety razor ____ King Camp Gillette.
5 *The Chair* ____ Vincent van Gogh.

ESERCIZIO 63B

Completa le frasi con *by* o *with*.

My desk was covered *with* papers.

1 These photos were taken ____ a very cheap camera.
2 These photos were taken ____ my sister.
3 The cake was made ____ dried fruit.
4 The cake was made ____ my aunt.
5 The garage was painted ____ a new kind of paint.
6 The garage was painted ____ a friend of mine.

---

64 *It is said that he . . ./He is said to . . . ecc.*

1 │ Quando si riferisce quello che gli altri dicono, credono ecc., si possono usare due forme di passivo. Confronta:

Attivo: ***People say that Mr Ross is** a millionaire.*

Passivo (1): *It* + passivo + *that* e l'indicativo
***It is said that Mr Ross is** a millionaire.*

Passivo (2): Soggetto + passivo + l'infinito con *to*
***Mr Ross is said to be** a millionaire.*

Spesso si usano queste forme passive nello stile formale e con verbi come:

say	*think*	*believe*	*consider*	*understand*	*know*
report	*expect*	*allege*	*claim*	*acknowledge*	

It is believed that they own *a lot of land in the north.*
They are believed to own *a lot of land in the north.*

It is reported that the president is *seriously ill.*
The president is reported to be *seriously ill.*

It is expected that a new law will be introduced *next year.*
A new law is expected to be introduced *next year.*

Quando quello che si crede ecc. si riferisce a un fatto precedente, si usa l'infinito passato (*to have* + il participio passato). Confronta:

It is believed that the fire started *late last night.*
The fire is believed to have started *late last night.*

It was thought that two prisoners had escaped.
Two prisoners were thought to have escaped.

2 | **Be supposed to**

Si può usare *supposed to* nel significato di 'si dice che'.

I'd like to read that book. It's **supposed to be** *very good.* (= Si dice che sia molto bello.)
He's **supposed to have been** *married before.* (= Si dice che sia già stato sposato.)

Supposed to talvolta implica un dubbio sulla verità o meno di qualcosa.
Nota che si usa *supposed to* anche per esprimere quello che ci si aspetta dalle persone, in seguito a un accordo, un regolamento o un dovere, p.es. *I'm* **supposed to** *see Maria this afternoon.* Cfr. 42.3.

ESERCIZIO 64A

Leggi ogni frase. Poi riscrivi ciascuna al passivo in due modi diversi. Comincia le frasi con le parole date tra parentesi.

Esempio:

People expect that taxes will be reduced soon.
(It)   (Taxes)
It *is expected that taxes will be reduced soon.*
Taxes *are expected to be reduced soon.*

1 People say that the monument is over 2000 years old.
   (It)   (The monument)
2 People expect that the president will resign.
   (It)   (The president)
3 People think the fire started at about 8 o'clock.
   (It)   (The fire)
4 Journalists reported that seven people had been injured in the fire.
   (It)   (Seven people)

ESERCIZIO 64B

Leggi ogni frase. Poi riscrivile tutte usando *be +
supposed to*, come nell'esempio.

Esempio:

People say that Whitby is a very nice town.
Whitby is supposed to be a very nice town.

1 People say that the new film is very violent.
2 People say that those cars are rather
  unreliable.
3 People say that he moved to New York last
  year.
4 People say that the new restaurant is very
  expensive.
5 People say that the concert was very good.

65 *Have something done*

1 | **Forma**

have + complemento + il participio passato del verbo

I am **having**	**a garage**	**built** at the moment.
How often do you **have**	**your hair**	**cut?**
We **had**	**our computer**	**serviced** last week.
Simon has just **had**	**a suit**	**made.**
You should **have**	**your eyes**	**tested.**
Are you going to **have**	**new carpets**	**fitted** in your flat?

Il participio passato dei verbi regolari termina in *-ed* p.es. *serviced, tested.* I verbi
irregolari hanno forme diverse di participio passato p.es. *cut* —> *cut*, *build* —> *built*
(cfr. 190).

Quando si aggiunge *-ed* al verbo, ci possono essere variazioni di ortografia
p.es. *fit* —> *fitted.* Cfr. 188.3,4,6. Per la pronuncia di *-ed*, cfr. 187.2.

2 | **Uso**

a | Si usa la costruzione *have something done* per parlare di qualcosa che facciamo fare
da altri.

I'm having a garage built at the moment.

Confronta:

I'm building a garage at the moment. (Sto costruendo io stesso il garage.)
I'm having a garage built at the moment. (Lo sto facendo costruire da altri.)

Altri esempi:

*We **had the carpet cleaned** by a professional carpet cleaner. We didn't do it ourselves.*
*I usually **have my car serviced** at a garage in East Street.*

b   Si può usare *have something done* anche in altri casi, quando non siamo noi a far fare qualcosa.

I **had my leg broken** *in a football match.*
We **had our fence blown** *down in a storm last week.*

Spesso si usa *have something done* con questo significato quando si verifica qualcosa di inaspettato o spiacevole.
Nota che è frequente l'uso di *get something done* invece di *have something done* soprattutto nello stile informale p.es. *I must* **get this jacket cleaned**.

ESERCIZIO 65A

Che cosa fanno fare queste persone? Forma delle frasi usando le espressioni del riquadro.

Esempio:

1   *They're having their flat decorated.*

> a photograph (take)   ~~their flat (decorate)~~
> a tooth (take out)   her windows (clean)
> a suit (make)   her hair (do)

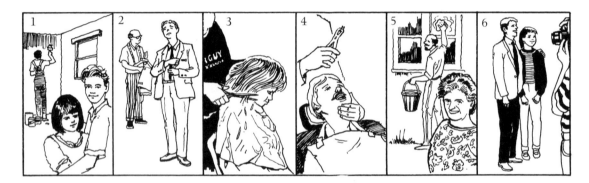

ESERCIZIO 65B

Completa le frasi usando il tempo giusto di *have something done.*

Esempio:

I haven't *had my central heating serviced* (my central heating | service) since last autumn.

1   Are you going to ___ (these shoes | repair) or shall I throw them away?
2   My neighbours are ___ (an extension | build) onto their house at the moment.
3   I must ___ (my glasses | mend). They keep falling off.
4   Where do you ___ (your hair | do)? It always looks very nice.
5   I ___ (four new tyres | fit) on my car last month.
6   I've just ___ (my suit | dry-clean).

ESERCIZIO 65C

La scorsa settimana è accaduto qualcosa di spiacevole a ciascuna di queste persone. Forma delle frasi usando *have something done*.

Esempio:

Kate *had her wallet stolen* (her wallet | steal) from her bag while she was out shopping.

1 Peter ____ (his flat | burgle) while he was out at work.
2 Mr and Mrs Woods ____ (the roof of their house | damage) in a storm.
3 Lynne ____ (the radio | steal) from her car.
4 My brother ____ (his nose | break) in a football match.

66 When e *if*

Confronta:

Si usa *if* se si è incerti che qualcosa accadrà.	Si usa *when* se si è sicuri che qualcosa accadrà.
If I see Sarah, I'll invite her to the party. (Forse la vedrò, forse no.)	*When I see Sally, I'll invite her to the party.* (Sono sicuro che la vedrò.)
I'll visit Martin if I go to Manchester. (Forse andrò a Manchester, o forse no.)	*I'll visit Martin when I go to Manchester.* (Andrò senz' altro a Manchester.)

ESERCIZIO 66A

Completa le frasi usando *if* o *when*.

Esempio:

Perhaps I'll go to the USA next year. *If* I go there, I'll visit a friend of mine in New York.

1 I'll see you ____ I come back from my holiday.
2 I'm going home now. ____ I get home, I'll phone you.
3 We'd like you to come with us on holiday. But ____ you don't want to come, you don't have to.
4 I'll do my homework ____ I finish dinner.
5 ____ it is a nice day tomorrow, I'll go to the beach.
6 ____ Sally wants to come to the concert, I'll get her a ticket.

Nota –Quando si parla di realtà sempre valide, si può usare sia *if* che *when(ever)* senza considerevole differenza di significato p.es. *If/when(ever) I have a big lunch, it makes me sleepy.* Cfr. 72.
–Per le frasi con *if*, cfr. anche 67–74.

67 Condizionale: introduzione

1 Si può usare *if* in varie costruzioni condizionali. Le più comuni riguardano:

a **Ipotesi probabili nel presente o nel futuro** (cfr. 68)

> If + il presente + *will* + l'infinito

*If he **asks** me, **I'll help** him.* (= Se me lo chiede, lo aiuto, *o* Se me lo chiederà, lo aiuterò.)

b **Ipotesi irreali nel presente o nel futuro** (cfr. 69)

> If + il passato remoto + *would* + l'infinito

*If he **asked** me, I **would help** him.* (= Se me lo chiedesse, lo aiuterei.)

c **Ipotesi irreali nel passato** (cfr. 71)

> If + il trapassato + *would have* + il participio passato

*If he **had asked** me, I **would have helped** him.* (= Se me lo avesse chiesto, lo avrei aiutato.)

d **Ipotesi reali generali** (cfr. 72)

> If + il presente + il presente

*If he **asks** me, I always **help** him.* (= Se (tutte le volte che) me lo chiede, lo aiuto sempre.)

2 La frase introdotta da *if*, o frase secondaria, può precedere o seguire quella principale.

If it rains, I'll stay at home.
I'll stay at home if it rains.

Se è la frase secondaria a introdurre il discorso, spesso si mette una virgola prima della frase principale.

3 Si possono formulare delle ipotesi anche senza *if* (cfr. 73).

Unless we hurry, we'll be late.
Suppose you won a lot of money, what would you do?

68 Ipotesi probabili nel presente o nel futuro

1 **Forma base** (Cfr. anche **3**.)

FRASE SECONDARIA	FRASE PRINCIPALE
If I go out,	*I'll buy a newspaper.*
If you don't study,	*you won't pass your exam.*
If they offer you the job,	*what will you do?*

if + il presente + *will* + l'infinito senza *to*

Questa costruzione viene spesso chiamata 'condizionale di 1° grado'.

2 **Uso**

Si usa questa costruzione quando c'è la probabilità che l'ipotesi formulata nella frase secondaria si verifichi nel futuro.

If I go out, I'll buy a newspaper. (Forse comprerò il giornale, forse no.)
If we have enough time, we'll visit Robert. (Forse avremo abbastanza tempo, forse no.)

Si usa questa costruzione anche quando c'è la probabilità che l'ipotesi formulata sia vera nel presente.

If you're hungry, I'll make you something to eat. (Forse hai fame, forse no.)

3 **Altre forme**

a Nella frase principale si può usare *shall* invece di *will* con *I* e *we*.
If I fail the exam, I shall take it again.

b Nella frase principale si può usare un verbo modale p.es. *can, may,* invece di *will.*
If we have enough time, we can visit Robert.

c Nella frase principale si può usare anche l'imperativo.
If you see Maria, give her a message for me, please.

d Nella frase secondaria si può usare il passato prossimo o il presente progressivo invece del presente.
If you have finished the letter, I'll post it for you.
I'll come back later, if you're working now.

e Si può usare *should* dopo *if* quando si è meno sicuri sulla probabilità che qualcosa si avveri. Confronta:

If I see Maria, I'll give her your message. (Forse vedrò Maria.)	*If I should see Maria, I'll give her your message.* (Sono meno sicuro di vederla.)

In casi simili, si può anche cominciare la frase con *should*, omettendo *if*.
Should I see Maria, I'll give her your message.

ESERCIZIO 68A

Metti i verbi al tempo giusto: *will/won't* o il presente.

Esempio:

If I *have* (have) time, I'*ll go* (go) shopping this afternoon.

1 I'm sure you _____ (enjoy) the film if you _____ (see) it.
2 If we _____ (leave) now, we _____ (not be) late.
3 If we _____ (miss) the bus, we _____ (take) a taxi.
4 What _____ (she | do) if she _____ (fail) the exam?
5 If you _____ (need) any help, _____ (you | tell) me?
6 If Simon _____ (not apologize) to me, I _____ (not speak) to him any more.

ESERCIZIO 68B

Completa le frasi usando i verbi del riquadro.

Esempio:

If I don't leave now, I *might be* late.

> have finished can lend ~~might be~~ should need
> are feeling may go should phone

1 If you need any more money I _____ you some.
2 You can go now if you _____.
3 If the weather is fine tomorrow, we _____ for a picnic.
4 Just ask me if you _____ any help.
5 If anyone _____ for me while I am out, tell them I'll be back at 4 o'clock.
6 Go to bed now if you _____ tired.

69 Ipotesi irreali nel presente o nel futuro

1 **Forma base** (Cfr. anche **3.**)

FRASE SECONDARIA	FRASE PRINCIPALE
*If I **had** a lot of money,*	*I'**d travel** round the world.*
*If he **got** up earlier,*	*he **wouldn't be** late for work.*
*If you **didn't pass** the exam,*	***would** you **take** it again?*

if + il passato remoto + *would* + l'infinito senza *to*

Questa costruzione viene spesso chiamata 'condizionale di 2° grado'.

2 **Uso**

Si usa questa costruzione per parlare di situazioni irreali nel presente o nel futuro.

*If I **had** a lot of money, I'**d travel** round the world.* (Ma non ho tanti soldi.)
*If I **didn't feel** so tired, I'**d come** out with you.* (Ma mi sento molto stanco.)
*If the weather **was** nice, I'**d go** to the beach.* (Ma il tempo non è bello.)

Si usa questa costruzione anche per parlare di situazioni improbabili nel presente o nel futuro.

*If she really **loved** you, she **wouldn't be** so horrible to you.*
*If I **won** a lot of money, I'**d take** a long holiday.*

In frasi come queste il passato p.es. *had*, *loved*, non ha significato passato, bensì esprime l'improbabilità o irrealtà dell'ipotesi riferita al presente o al futuro.

3   **Altre forme**

a   Spesso si usa *were* invece di *was* dopo *if*, specialmente nello stile formale.

If the weather **were** *nice, I'd go to the beach.*
I'd come out for a walk with you if I **weren't** *so busy.*
That watch wouldn't be so cheap if it **were** *really made of gold.*

Si usa di frequente la costruzione *if I were you* per dare consigli e *if you were me* per chiedere consigli.

If I were you, *I'd apply for the job.*
What would you do **if you were me?**

b   Nella frase principale si possono usare i verbi modali *might* o *could* invece di *would*.

If I won a lot of money, I **might** *stop working.* (= ... forse smetterei di lavorare.)
I **could** *repair the car, if I had the right tools.* (= Potrei riparare la macchina ...)

ESERCIZIO 69A

Metti i verbi al tempo giusto: passato remoto o *would* ....

Esempio:

Simon would like to buy some new clothes, but he hasn't got much money. He says: 'If I *had* (have) more money, I *would buy* (buy) some new clothes.'

1   Sarah would like to write to her friend, Alan, but she has lost Alan's address. She says: 'If I ____ (know) Alan's address, I ____ (write) to him.'
2   You would like to buy some shoes, but you think they are too expensive. You say: 'I ____ (buy) them if they ____ (not be) so expensive.'
3   Peter is thinking of buying a new record. Sally thinks the record isn't very good. She says: 'I ____ (not buy) it if I ____ (be) you.'
4   Andrew's elder brother, Simon, still lives at home. Andrew says: 'If I ____ (be) Simon's age, I ____ (not live) at home.
5   Mike lives in London, but he doesn't like living there. You ask him: 'Where ____ (you | live) if you ____ (can) live anywhere?'

70   Ipotesi probabili e ipotesi irreali nel presente o nel futuro

Si usa il condizionale di 1° grado (cfr. 68) per parlare di situazioni probabili nel presente o nel futuro.

If you **need** *the money, I'll lend it to you.* (Forse hai bisogno di soldi.)
If we **leave** *at 1.30, we'll arrive at 2.30.* (Forse partiremo all' 1.30.)

Si usa il condizionale di 2° grado (cfr. 69) per parlare di situazioni irreali o improbabili nel presente o nel futuro.

If you **needed** *the money, I'd lend it to you.* (Ma tu non ne hai bisogno, o è improbabile che tu ne abbia bisogno.)
If we **left** *at 2.00, we'd arrive late.* (Ma non partiamo alle 2.00, o è improbabile che partiamo a quell'ora.)

ESERCIZIO 70A

Metti i verbi tra parentesi al tempo giusto.

Esempio:

We'll go out later on if it *stops* (stop) raining.

1 Do you want to watch the TV? I _____ (switch) it on if you do.
2 What _____ (you | do) if you were the President of the USA?
3 If she _____ (have) time, she'll phone me this evening.
4 If I _____ (be) you, I'd go to the doctor.
5 _____ (you | buy) a new car if you could afford one?
6 We'll have a picnic tomorrow if the weather _____ (be) fine.

71   Ipotesi irreali nel passato

1 **Forma base** (Cfr. anche **3.**)

FRASE SECONDARIA	FRASE PRINCIPALE
*If the weather **had been** nice yesterday,*	*I **would have gone** to the beach.*
*If I **had studied** hard,*	*I **would have passed** the exam.*
*If you **hadn't missed** your bus,*	*you **wouldn't have been** late for school.*
*If I **hadn't helped** you,*	*what **would you have done**?*

if + il trapassato + would have + il participio passato

Questa costruzione viene spesso chiamata 'condizionale di 3° grado'.

La contrazione sia di *had* che di *would* è *'d*.

If I'd (= had) studied hard, I'd (= would) have passed the exam.

2 **Uso**

Si usa questa costruzione per parlare di situazioni irreali nel passato.

*If the weather **had been** nice yesterday, I **would have gone** to the beach.* (Ma il tempo è stato brutto.)
*If I'd **studied** hard, I **would have passed** the exam.* (Ma non ho studiato tanto.)
*If you **hadn't missed** your bus, you **wouldn't have been** late for school.* (Ma hai perso l'autobus.)

3 **Altre forme**

Nella frase principale si possono usare i verbi modali *might* o *could* invece di *would*.

*If you had taken the exam, you **might** have passed it.* (= . . . forse saresti passato.)
*I **could** have repaired the car, if I'd had the right tools.* (= Avrei potuto riparare la macchina . . .)

ESERCIZIO 71A

Metti i verbi al tempo giusto: trapassato o *would(n't) have* + il participio passato.

Esempio:

She would have spoken to you if she *had seen* (see) you.

1 If I ___ (not | be) so busy yesterday, I would have visited you.
2 If you had seen the film, you ___ (enjoy) it.
3 She would have gone to university if she ___ (have) the opportunity.
4 If he had been more careful, he ___ (not | have) an accident.

ESERCIZIO 71B

Leggi le frasi, poi collegale formulando delle ipotesi con *if*.

Esempio:

I didn't have time. I didn't go shopping.
If I'd had time, I would have gone shopping.

1 She was ill. She didn't go to work.
2 It rained all morning. We didn't go out.
3 She didn't have enough money. She couldn't buy the shoes.
4 I wasn't hungry. I didn't have breakfast.

72 Ipotesi reali generali

1 | **Forma base** (Cfr. anche **3.**)

FRASE SECONDARIA	FRASE PRINCIPALE
*If I **have** a big lunch,*	*it **makes** me sleepy.*
*If you **mix** yellow and blue,*	*you **get** green.*

if + il presente + il presente

2 | **Uso**

Si usa questa costruzione per parlare di situazioni reali o dati di fatto sempre vedi; qui *if* ha lo stesso significato di *whenever* ('ogni volta che').

*If I **have** a big lunch, it **makes** me sleepy.* (= Ogni volta che mangio molto...)
*If you **mix** yellow and blue, you **get** green.* (= Ogni volta che si mescola giallo e blu...)

ESERCIZIO 72A

Collega una frase di **A** con quella più adatta di **B**.

Esempio:

1 *If I get a headache, I usually take some aspirin.*

A	B
1 If I get a headache,	they die
2 I feel terrible,	it makes me feel nervous
3 If I drink too much coffee,	if you don't get enough exercise
4 If flowers don't get any water,	I usually take some aspirin
5 You put on weight	if I don't get 8 hours' sleep a night

73 Frasi condizionali senza *if*

Per introdurre una frase condizionale si possono usare altre espressioni:

1 *Unless*

Si può usare *unless* nel significato di '*if . . . not*'.

***Unless** you put on some suncream, you'll get sunburnt.* (= Se non ti spalmi della crema solare . . .)
*I won't go to the party **unless** you go too.* (= . . . se non ci vai anche tu.)

Spesso si usa *unless* in minacce p.es. ***Unless** you stop making that noise, I'll scream!* o in avvertimenti p.es. *You'll be hungry later **unless** you eat now.*

Confronta *if* con *unless*:

If you eat now, you won't be hungry later.	*Unless you eat now, you'll be hungry later.*
I'll go to the party if you go too.	*I won't go to the party unless you go too.*

2 *As/So long as, provided/providing (that)*

Si usa *as/so long as* e *provided/providing (that)* nel significato di '*if but only if*'.

*You can borrow my camera **as long as** you're careful with it.* (= . . . a condizione che tu ci stia attento.)
*I'll go to the party **provided** you go too.* (= . . . a condizione che ci vada anche tu.)

3 *And* e *or (else)*

a Talvolta si usa *and* (omettendo *if* nella frase condizionale) per collegare le due frasi.

*Stay in bed for a few days **and** you'll be fine.* (= Stai a letto qualche giorno e starai bene.)

b Si può usare *or (else)* nel significato di '*if not*' o '*otherwise*'.

*Don't try to lift that box **or (else)** you'll hurt yourself.* (= Non cercare di sollevare quella scatola, sennò ti farai male.)

4 *Should*

Si può usare *should* invece di *if* quando si è meno sicuri sulla probabilità che qualcosa si avveri. Confronta:

If we have enough time, we'll visit Robert. (Forse avremo abbastanza tempo.)	*Should we have enough time, we'll visit Robert.* (Non sono molto sicuro che avremo abbastanza tempo.)

In questo caso si può usare anche *should* dopo *if*, p.es. *If we **should have** enough time, we'll visit Robert.* Cfr. 69.3.

5 *Suppose/supposing*

Si può usare anche *suppose* o *supposing* invece di *if*, specialmente in riferimento a ipotesi irreali.

***Suppose/Supposing** you won a lot of money, what would you do?*

ESERCIZIO 73A

Riscrivi le frasi usando *unless*.

Esempio:

If we don't leave now, we'll miss the start of the film.
Unless we leave now, we'll miss the start of the film.

1 If you don't wear your coat, you'll be cold.
2 I'll phone you, if you don't phone me first.
3 He won't receive the letter tomorrow if you don't post it before 1 o'clock today.
4 I won't go to school tomorrow if I don't feel better.
5 I can't write to you if you don't give me your address.
6 Your cough won't get better if you don't stop smoking.

ESERCIZIO 73B

Scegli l'espressione giusta.

Esempio:

We'll have a picnic tomorrow *unless/provided* it rains.

1 *Unless/Provided* you tell the truth, everything will be all right.
2 In Britain you can marry at the age of sixteen *unless/providing* you have your parents' permission.
3 He won't forgive you *unless/as long as* you say you're sorry.
4 *Unless/Providing* you lend me the money, I won't be able to go on holiday.
5 I'll buy the car *unless/as long as* it's not too expensive.

ESERCIZIO 73C

Leggi le frasi. Scrivine altre con lo stesso significato, usando le congiunzioni fra parentesi.

Esempio:

If you don't lend me your map, I'll get lost. (or)
Lend me your map or I'll get lost.
If you do as I say, everything will be all right. (and)
Do as I say and everything will be all right.

1 If you don't stop making that noise, I'll hit you. (or)
2 If you take this umbrella, you won't get wet. (and)
3 If you don't drive more carefully, you'll have an accident. (or else)
4 If you help me, I'll help you. (and)

ESERCIZIO 73D

Completa le frasi usando *should I/he/she* e i verbi del riquadro.

Esempio:

I think I'll arrive at the meeting on time, but *should I be* late, please start without me.

| miss   change   ~~be~~   need   fail |

1 I think I've got enough money, but ____ any more, I'll borrow some.
2 I'm sure he'll pass the exam, but ____, he can always take it again.
3 I don't think I'll go to the party, but ____ my mind, I'll let you know.
4 She expects to catch the last bus, but ____ it, she'll take a taxi.

ESERCIZIO 73E

Scrivi delle nuove frasi, collegandone una di **A** con quella più adatta di **B** e cominciando con *Suppose/Supposing* . . . .

Esempio:

1 *Suppose/Supposing I moved to Scotland, would you come and visit me?*

A

1 I moved to Scotland,
2 someone finds my wallet,
3 they had stayed at our house,
4 they had offered you the job,
5 you had won the competition,

B

would you have taken it?
what would the prize have been?
do you think they will take it to the police?
would you come and visit me?
where would they have slept?

74 Riepilogo del condizionale

ESERCIZIO 74A

Completa le frasi usando il tempo giusto dei verbi tra parentesi: presente, passato remoto, trapassato, *will/won't* . . . , *would(n't)* . . . o *would(n't) have* . . . .

Esempi:

My father would have died if the doctors *hadn't operated* (not | operate) on him straight away.
Don't worry about getting home. If you *miss* (miss) the last bus, I'll give you a lift in my car.
My friend *would get* (get) better marks at school if she did more homework.
If she doesn't have much time, she normally *has* (have) a sandwich for lunch.

1 I ____ (wear) some warm clothes today, if I were you. It's quite cold outside.
2 You ____ (not | have) the accident if you'd been more careful.
3 If I ____ (have) enough money, I'd buy a new car.
4 If you ____ (wait) for a few minutes, I'll come into town with you.
5 I would have told you if I ____ (know).
6 People ____ (like) Robert more if he didn't always talk about himself.
7 I ____ (speak) to my boss about my holidays today if I get the chance.
8 If he ____ (make) a promise, he always keeps it.
9 I'd go to the cinema more often if it ____ (not | be) so expensive.
10 I ____ (not | leave) my last job if the wages had been better.
11 He always ____ (get) angry if you talk to him about politics.
12 If you go out without a coat, you ____ (catch) a cold.
13 If you ____ (ask) me, I would have helped you.
14 What ____ (you | do) if you saw someone drowning in the sea?

75 Discorso diretto e indiretto: introduzione

Quando si vuole riferire quello che una persona ha detto, si può usare o il 'discorso diretto' o il 'discorso indiretto'.

I'm hungry.

Nel discorso diretto si danno le parole esatte che la persona ha pronunciato e si usano le virgolette ('...' o "...").

Discorso diretto: *Annie said, 'I'm hungry.'*

Nel discorso indiretto si cambiano alcune parole che la persona ha detto e non si usano le virgolette.

Discorso indiretto: *Annie said (that) she was hungry.*
       oppure: *Annie says (that) she's hungry.*

Se il verbo dichiarativo è al passato (p.es. *Annie said*), di solito il tempo del discorso indiretto cambia (p.es. *I'm* diventa passato remoto: *she was*).

Ma se il verbo dichiarativo è al presente (p.es. *Annie says*), il tempo non cambia (p.es. *I'm* rimane al presente: *she's*).

Per il discorso indiretto, cfr. 77–80.

76 *Say* e *tell*

1   Dopo *tell* si specifica in genere la persona (p.es. *Sarah, me, us*) a cui si parla, non invece dopo *say*. Confronta:

say + qualcosa	tell + qualcuno + qualcosa

*I **said** I was going home.*   *I **told Sarah** I was going home.*
*He **says** he can speak French.*   *He **tells me** he can speak French.*

2   Se si vuole specificare la persona anche dopo *say*, bisogna premetterle *to*.
*I **said to Sarah** that I was going home.*

3   In alcune espressioni con *tell* si può omettere la persona p.es. *tell a story, tell the time, tell the truth, tell a lie.*

ESERCIZIO 76A

Completa le frasi usando il tempo giusto di *say* o *tell*.

Esempio:

I'll *tell* you all about my holiday when I see you.

1 Could you ____ me how to get to Paris?   4 They ____ the plane was going to be late.
2 Do you think she's ____ us the truth?   5 Did he ____ you that he could play chess?
3 Have you ____ goodbye to everyone?   6 Why didn't you ____ what you wanted?

77   Discorso indiretto

1   **Tempi**

*He said he **was going** home.*

a   Se il verbo dichiarativo è al passato (p.es. *he said*, *you told me*), di solito il tempo del discorso indiretto 'si sposta all'indietro':

■ I verbi al presente cambiano in passato.

DISCORSO DIRETTO	DISCORSO INDIRETTO
'I'm going home.'	*He said he **was going** home.*
'I want to stop.'	*You told me you **wanted** to stop.*
'I don't like tea.'	*She said she **didn't like** tea.*
'Sally has finished.'	*You said that Sally **had finished**.*

■ I verbi già al passato cambiano in trapassato o rimangono invariati.

| *'I spoke to them.'* | *I said I **had spoken** to them./I said I **spoke** to them.* |
| *'We arrived late.'* | *They said they **had arrived** late./They said they **arrived** late.* |

■ I verbi già al trapassato rimangono invariati.

| *'I had seen the film before.'* | *I told you I **had seen** the film before.* |

Verbi modali

Nota la forma del passato di questi verbi modali: *can* —→ *could; will* —→ *would; shall* —→ *should; may* —→ *might.*

DISCORSO DIRETTO	DISCORSO INDIRETTO
*'I **can** swim.'*	*He said he **could** swim.*
*'I **will** be at home.'*	*She said that she **would** be at home.*
*'We **may** go by train.'*	*They told me they **might** go by train.*

I verbi modali al passato *could, would, should* e *might* rimangono invariati nel discorso indiretto.

*'You **could** be right.'*	*I said you **could** be right.*
*'You **should** see the film.'*	*They told me I **should** see the film.*

Must rimane invariato o viene sostituito dal passato di *have to,* cioè *had to.*

*'I **must** go.'*	*He said he **must** go./He said he **had to** go.*

b   Non sempre si cambiano i tempi passando al discorso indiretto se questo viene introdotto da un verbo dichiarativo al passato. Se si riferisce qualcosa che è vero tuttora, talvolta si mantiene il tempo del discorso diretto.

DISCORSO DIRETTO	DISCORSO INDIRETTO
*'The population of London **is** around 9 million.'*	*He said that the population of London **is** around 9 million.*
*'I **live** in Brighton.'*	*She told me that she **lives** in Brighton.*

Tuttavia, anche in questo caso, spesso si cambia il tempo.

*He said that the population of London **was** around 9 million.*

E si cambia sempre se quello che è stato detto non è vero.

*She said that she **was** 18 years old, but in fact she's only 16.*

2   **Pronomi, aggettivi, avverbi ecc.**

a   I pronomi (p.es. *I, me*) e gli aggettivi possessivi (p.es. *my, your*) spesso cambiano nel discorso indiretto. Confronta:

Discorso diretto: *Sue said, 'I'm on holiday with **my** friend'.*
Discorso indiretto: *Sue said (that) **she** was on holiday with **her** friend.*

Parlando di Sue si dice *she,* non *I,* e parlando della sua amica si dice *her* friend, non *my* friend.

b

Nel discorso diretto si usano espressioni come *here, now, today* per indicare il luogo e il tempo in cui si parla. Passando al discorso indiretto, queste espressioni vengono spesso cambiate.

DISCORSO DIRETTO	DISCORSO INDIRETTO
here	*there*
this	*that/the*
now	*then*
today	*that day*
tonight	*that night*
tomorrow	*the next day/the following day*
yesterday	*the day before/the previous day*
next Monday	*the following Monday*
last Monday	*the previous Monday*

Confronta:

*'I'm **here** on holiday.'*   *She said she was **there** on holiday.*
*'I'll see you **tomorrow**.'*   *He said he would see me **the next day**.*

Come cambiano queste espressioni dipende dalla situazione. Per esempio, la frase *'I'll see you **tomorrow**.'*, detta ieri da qualcuno, diventerebbe oggi, nel discorso indiretto, *He said he would see me **today***.

3 | ***That***

Spesso si usa *that* per collegare una frase del discorso indiretto alla frase da cui dipende.

*I said **that** I was feeling tired.*
*You told me **that** you would be careful.*

Dopo *say* e *tell* (+ la persona) spesso si omette *that*, soprattutto nello stile informale.

*I **said** I was feeling tired.*
*You **told me** you would be careful.*

ESERCIZIO 77A

Volgi queste affermazioni al discorso indiretto, come negli esempi.

Esempi:

'I'm tired,' she said. *She said (that) she was tired.*
'I need to borrow some money,' my brother told me. *My brother told me (that) he needed to borrow some money.*

1 'I can't swim very well,' I told her.
2 'Mr Mason has gone out,' the secretary told me.
3 'I don't want to go swimming,' Andrew said.
4 'We're leaving on Friday,' we said.
5 'We had lunch in Luigi's restaurant,' they said.
6 'I'll phone you later,' Sarah told Simon.

ESERCIZIO 77B

Questo è quanto hanno detto oggi a Sally alcune persone:

The manager of the bank where Sally works: 'You'll get a pay rise later in the year.'
An optician: 'There is nothing wrong with your eyes. You don't need to wear glasses.'
Sally's boyfriend, Peter: 'I'd like a big family. I want at least five children.'
Sally's father: 'I've done the shopping. I'll be home at about seven.'
Sally's driving instructor: 'You drove very well. You're making good progress.'
A man who works in a dry-cleaner's: 'Your skirt will be ready on Saturday.'

Adesso è sera e Sally sta dicendo a sua madre com'è andata la giornata. Completa quello che Sally le riferisce con il discorso indiretto.

Sally: I went to the dry-cleaner's at lunchtime. The man there said *my skirt would be ready on Saturday.*
Mother: And what about the optician? What did she say?
Sally: Oh, she told me __1__ eyes and that I __2__ glasses.
Mother: Oh, that's good. And what about your driving lesson? How did that go?
Sally: Oh, fine. My instructor told me that I __3__ and that I __4__ progress.
Mother: That's very good. And what about Peter? Did you see him today?
Sally: No, but he phoned me at work. He made me laugh. He said he __5__ and that he __6__ children.
Mother: Five! Well, I hope you can afford them.
Sally: Oh, yes. That reminds me. I was speaking to the manager at work and she said that I __7__.
Mother: Oh, that's good.
Sally: Yes. Oh, and before I forget. Dad phoned. He said he __8__ and that he __9__ seven.

78   Domande indirette

*The policeman asked the men **what they were doing**.*

1 | Quando si trasforma una domanda da diretta a indiretta, i tempi, gli aggettivi, i pronomi ecc. cambiano seguendo le stesse regole viste per il discorso indiretto (cfr. 77).

DOMANDA DIRETTA	DOMANDA INDIRETTA
'What **are you** doing?'	The policeman asked the men what **they were** doing.
'How **is your** brother?'	She asked how **my** brother **was**.

Nelle domande indirette l'ordine delle parole è come nelle frasi affermative (p.es. *they were doing, my brother was*) e non si usa il punto interrogativo.

2 | Nelle domande indirette non si usa il verbo ausiliare *do* (*do, does* o *did*).

DOMANDA DIRETTA	DOMANDA INDIRETTA
'What **do** you **want**?'	I asked what she **wanted**.
'Where **does** he **live**?'	They asked where he **lived**.
'Why **did** you **say** that?'	He asked why **I'd said** that.

3 | In mancanza di pronomi o avverbi interrogativi (p.es. *what, where, why*) si può introdurre una domanda indiretta con *if* o *whether*.

DOMANDA DIRETTA	DOMANDA INDIRETTA
'Are you cold?'	I asked **if** he was cold.
'Do you want a drink?'	She asked **if** I wanted a drink.
'Can you speak German?'	They wanted to know **whether** I could speak German.

4 | Dopo *ask* si specifica spesso la persona a cui si pone la domanda (p.es. *Ken, me*).

I **asked Ken** if he was cold.
He **asked me** why I'd said that.

ESERCIZIO 78A

A chi faresti queste domande?

1	'Will it take long to repair the car?'	a hotel receptionist
2	'Can I park my car in West Street?'	a doctor
3	'What time does the film finish?'	a policeman
4	'Have you got a double room?'	a mechanic
5	'How many times a day should I take the medicine?'	a waiter
6	'What's the soup of the day?'	a cinema attendant

Ora trasforma le stesse domande da dirette a indirette. Comincia così: *I asked the . . . .*

Esempio:

1 *I asked the mechanic if it would take long to repair the car.*

ESERCIZIO 78B

Andrew, mentre era in vacanza, ha avuto un'esperienza poco piacevole. Stava camminando per la campagna, quando, all'improvviso, è stato circondato da un gruppo di soldati.

Ecco le domande che uno dei soldati ha rivolto a Andrew.

1 'What are you doing here?'
2 'Why are you carrying a camera?'
3 'Did you see the signs warning people not to enter the area?'
4 'Have you been taking photos of the army base?'
5 'What's your name?'
6 'Can I see some proof of your identity?'

Dopo la vacanza, Andrew ha raccontato agli amici quello che gli è successo. Completa il racconto di Andrew usando il discorso indiretto.

'I was about seven miles from the youth hostel in the middle of nowhere when suddenly a jeep roared up to me and I was surrounded by soldiers pointing guns! An officer asked me 1 *what I was doing there*. Then he pointed at my Kodak and asked me __2__. I tried to explain that I was on holiday there, but then he wanted to know __3__. I told him I hadn't. Then he asked me __4__. I said that I didn't even know there was an army base there. Then he wanted to know __5__ and __6__. Then, just because I couldn't prove who I was, they put me in the jeep and drove me to some kind of underground army base. They kept me there while they phoned the youth hostel to check up on me.'

79   Uso dell'infinito con *to* nel discorso indiretto

1 | Spesso, nel discorso indiretto, per riferire di ordini, richieste, avvertimenti, consigli e inviti, si usa la costruzione: verbo + complemento + l'infinito con *to*.

DISCORSO DIRETTO

'Get out of my room.'
'Could you carry some bags, Mike?'
'Stay away from me.'
'You should phone the police.'
'Would you like to have dinner with us?'

DISCORSO INDIRETTO

*She **told the man to get** out of her room.*
*I **asked Mike to carry** some bags.*
*He **warned them to stay** away from him.*
*She **advised him to phone** the police.*
*They **invited me to have** dinner with them.*

2 | Spesso, nel discorso indiretto, per riferire di offerte, promesse e minacce, si usa la costruzione: verbo + l'infinito con *to*.

DISCORSO DIRETTO	DISCORSO INDIRETTO
'Can I help you?'	*The woman **offered to help** me.*
'I'll be careful.'	*You **promised to be** careful.*
'I'll hit you!'	*She **threatened to hit** me.*

3 | Se si tratta di ordini, promesse ecc. in forma negativa, si usa *not to* + l'infinito.

'Don't touch my camera.'	*He told me **not to touch** his camera.*
'I won't be late.'	*You promised **not to be** late.*

ESERCIZIO 79A

Riscrivi queste frasi passando dal discorso diretto a quello indiretto usando la forma dell'infinito con *to*.

Esempi:

'I'll pay back the money.' (she promised)   *She promised to pay back the money.*
'Hurry up.' (he told me)   *He told me to hurry up.*

1 'Can I do the washing up?' (I offered)
2 'I'll phone the police!' (she threatened)
3 'You should stop smoking.' (the doctor advised my brother)
4 'Could you change the light bulb for me?' (he asked me)
5 'Don't be stupid.' (she told me)
6 'Would you like to come to my party?' (he invited her)
7 'I won't forget the shopping.' (I promised)
8 'Don't leave the door unlocked.' (she warned them)

80 Riepilogo del discorso indiretto

ESERCIZIO 80A

Componi delle frasi con il discorso indiretto. Talvolta sono possibili due costruzioni.

Esempi:

'I'm tired,' he said.
He said (that) he was tired.
'Did you enjoy the film?' I asked her.
I asked her if she had enjoyed the film./
I asked her if she enjoyed the film.
'Switch off the TV,' she told me.
She told me to switch off the TV.
'Can you lend me some money?' he asked me.
He asked me if I could lend him some money./
He asked me to lend him some money.

1 'I can't type,' I told them.
2 'Are you English?' they asked me.
3 'Where are you going?' I asked her.
4 'We're going into town,' they said.
5 'I haven't got any money,' he told me.
6 'Could you speak more slowly?' he asked her.
7 'Don't touch the wire,' he warned me.
8 'I was on holiday in July,' he told her.
9 'What time did you get home?' they asked him.

10 'Can you do me a favour?' she asked me.
11 'We won't be home late,' we told them.
12 'I've posted the letters,' I said.
13 'My sister doesn't know,' he said.
14 'My parents had gone to bed,' she said.
15 'You should go to the doctor,' she told him.
16 'We'll do the dishes,' they promised.
17 'Where do you work?' I asked her.
18 'Can you phone the doctor for me?' she asked him.
19 'I passed my driving test in 1986,' he told his boss.
20 'I don't know what to do,' I said.

81 Forma in *-ing*: participio o gerundio

1 Si usa la forma in *-ing* del verbo p.es. *playing, walking, worrying*, nelle forme progressive dei vari tempi.

*'Where's Sally?' 'She's **playing** tennis.'*
*When I was **walking** along Western Road, I saw Maria.*
*He's been **worrying** a lot recently.*

In questo caso la forma in *-ing* viene chiamata 'participio presente'.

Il participio presente funge anche da aggettivo (cfr. 99).

*It's a **worrying** problem.*

Si usa la forma in *-ing* anche per comporre una frase participiale (cfr. 100).

*I hurt my leg **playing** tennis.*
*Who is that girl **walking** towards us?*

2 Si usa la forma in *-ing* anche come sostantivo.

***Playing** tennis isn't expensive in England.*
*I enjoy **walking** in the countryside.*

In quest'ultimo caso la forma in *-ing* viene chiamata 'gerundio' nella lingua inglese. (Per la forma in *-ing* come 'gerundio' cfr. 82–83, 87–90, 92–94, 98.)

3 Quando si aggiunge *-ing* al verbo, ci possono essere variazioni di ortografia p.es. *swim* → *swimming* (cfr. 188.3–6).

82 Verbo + forma in *-ing* o infinito: introduzione

1 | Spesso si usa un verbo dopo un altro verbo.

I enjoy running.   *I hope to run in the marathon next month.*

Dopo alcuni verbi p.es. *enjoy*, il secondo verbo assume la forma in *-ing* p.es. *running* (cfr. 83); dopo altri p.es. *hope*, il secondo verbo è all'infinito con *to* p.es. *to run* (cfr. 84).

2 | Dopo alcuni verbi p.es. *start* si può usare sia la forma in *-ing* che l'infinito con *to*, senza notevoli differenze di significato (cfr. 87).

Look. It's started raining/to rain again.

Ma dopo altri verbi, p.es. *stop*, le due forme hanno significati profondamente diversi (cfr. 88).

I'm a vegetarian. I stopped eating meat 5 years ago. (= Ho mangiato carne fino a 5 anni fa, poi ho smesso).	*After I'd been working for 3 hours, I stopped to eat lunch.* (= Mi sono fermato per pranzare.)

3 | Dopo i verbi modali p.es. *can, must, should* e qualche altro verbo, si usa l'.infinito senza *to* p.es. *play, eat* (cfr. 91).

I can play the guitar.
You must eat something.

83 Verbo + forma in *-ing*

1 | Se un verbo segue i verbi sotto elencati, di solito assume la forma in *-ing*.

admit	*enjoy*	*imagine*	*practise*
avoid	*fancy*	*involve*	*put off* (= rimandare)
consider	*feel like* (= avere voglia)	*keep on* (= continuare)	*risk*
delay	*finish*	*mind*	*stand* (= sopportare)
deny	*give up* (= smettere)	*miss*	*suggest*
dislike	*can't help* (= non poter fare a meno)	*postpone*	

> verbo + la forma in *-ing*

He admitted breaking the window.
I enjoy getting up early in the summer.
Have you finished doing your homework?
They suggested meeting at two o'clock.

Nota la forma negativa *not* + . . . *-ing*.

*He admitted **not paying** for the ticket.*

Mind può esser seguito anche da una frase introdotta da *if* p.es. *Would you **mind** if I closed the window?*

Dopo alcuni dei verbi sopra elencati si può usare anche *that* e l'indicativo.

*He **admitted** (that) he'd broken the window.*
*They **suggested** (that) we met at two o'clock.*

2 Si usa *do* + *the/some/* ecc. + la forma in *-ing* per parlare, per esempio, di occupazioni.

*You **do the cooking**. I'll **do the washing up**.*
*We're going to **do some shopping** this afternoon.*

(Nota che la forma in *-ing* viene usata qui come sostantivo, e come qualsiasi sostantivo può essere preceduta da *the, some* ecc.)

3 Si può usare *go* e *come* con la forma in *-ing* in particolare per parlare di sport e attività del tempo libero.

*I'd like to **go swimming** tomorrow.*

ESERCIZIO 83A

Completa le frasi usando la forma in *-ing* dei verbi del riquadro.

do	have	~~listen~~	play	be	read	go
not make		borrow	swim	rob		

Esempio:

I enjoy *listening* to the radio in the mornings.

1 I'll lend you the book when I've finished ＿＿ it.
2 Do you ever go ＿＿ in the sea?
3 They suggested ＿＿ dinner in an Indian restaurant.
4 Robert gave up ＿＿ football years ago.
5 The men admitted ＿＿ the bank.

6 I really don't mind ＿＿ the housework.
7 I didn't feel like ＿＿ out last night, so I stayed at home.
8 Would you mind ＿＿ so much noise? I'm trying to study.
9 I normally try to avoid ＿＿ money.
10 Since she moved from London, she misses ＿＿ able to see all her friends there.

Nota –Dopo altri verbi si può usare sia la forma in *-ing* che l'infinito con *to*, spesso, però, con significati diversi. Cfr. 87–88.

84 Verbo + infinito con *to*

Se un verbo segue i verbi sotto elencati, di solito assume l'infinito con *to*.

afford	*fail*	*pretend*
agree	*help*	*promise*
appear	*hope*	*refuse*
arrange	*learn* (= imparare a)	*seem*
ask	*manage*	*threaten*
attempt	*mean* (= intendere)	*want*
decide	*offer*	*wish*
expect	*prepare*	

verbo + l'infinito con *to*

*I can't **afford to go** on holiday this summer.*
*The policeman **asked to see** my driving licence.*
*She **decided to stay** at home last night.*
*My brother **expects to find** a job soon.*
*He's going to **learn to drive.***

Nota la forma negativa con *not to* + l'infinito.

*You promised **not to tell** anyone.*
*She seemed **not to notice** me.*

Dopo *help* si può usare l'infinito con o senza *to*.

*I'll **help (to) carry** your bags.*

Nota inoltre che dopo *can't help* (= non poter fare a meno di), si usa la forma in *-ing*
p.es. *I **can't help thinking** we've made a mistake.*

Dopo alcuni dei verbi sopra elencati si può usare anche *that* e l'indicativo.

*She **decided (that)** she would stay at home last night.*
*My brother **expects (that)** he'll find a job soon.*

Dopo alcuni dei verbi sopra elencati si può usare un complemento + l'infinito con *to*
p.es. *He **asked me to help** him.* Cfr. 86.

ESERCIZIO 84A

Robert sta parlando del giorno in cui ha
comprato una macchina usata.

Completa il suo racconto usando l'infinito con *to*
dei verbi nel riquadro.

| buy | be | not like | ~~have~~ | test-drive |

'When I got to the garage, I managed *to have* a quick look at the car before the
salesman came out of his office. It seemed __1__ in very good condition and was
worth about £1000, although the garage was asking £1400 for it. When the
salesman came out, I arranged __2__ the car straight away. The salesman and I
got in and we drove off. I liked the car immediately and I decided that I wanted
__3__ it, but, of course, I didn't say this to the salesman. Instead, I pretended
__4__ the car very much.'

| try | get | accept | pay |

'When we had finished the test-drive and had pulled up outside the garage, I told
the salesman that I couldn't afford __5__ more than £750. The salesman, of
course, refused __6__ such a miserable little offer. He told me that he expected
__7__ at least £1200 for the car. I tried offering £800, £850, £875, but he
wouldn't change his mind. Then I decided __8__ something different.'

| give | be | sell | accept |

'I thanked the salesman politely, said goodbye, got out of the car and started to
walk away. It worked! The salesman got out of the car too and hurried after me.
He told me that he wanted __9__ fair and was prepared __10__ a reasonable
offer for the car. In the end, he agreed __11__ it to me for £1000. He even agreed
__12__ me £200 for my old car!'

Nota –Dopo altri verbi si può usare sia l'infinito con *to* che la forma in *-ing*, spesso però con
significati diversi. Cfr. 97.

–Spesso si usa l'infinito con *to* in questi casi: *ought to* p.es. *You **ought to stop** smoking.*
(Cfr. 42.1); *have (got) to* p.es. *I **have to be** home by 10 o'clock.* (Cfr. 38.2) e *used to* p.es. *I **used
to smoke**, but I stopped 10 years ago.* (Cfr. 51).

–Si usa l'infinito con *to* dopo i verbi passivi p.es. *They **are believed to own** a lot of land in the
north.* Cfr. 64.

–Talvolta si omette il verbo dopo *to* per evitare ripetizioni, se il significato è chiaro p.es. *I
didn't go to the party because I didn't want **to**.* (= because I didn't want **to go to the party**).

85 Verbo + avverbio/pronome interrogativo + infinito con *to*

1 Dopo alcuni verbi si può usare un avverbio o pronome interrogativo p.es. *what, how, where* (ma non *why*) + l'infinito con *to*.

> verbo + avverbio/pronome interrogativo + l'infinito con *to*

I don't know what to say.
Do you know how to play chess?
We can't decide what to buy Sue for her birthday.
I'll explain what to do later on.

2 Spesso si usa la costruzione: complemento + pronome/avverbio interrogativo + l'infinito con *to*.

> verbo + complemento + avverbio/pronome interr. + l'infinito con *to*

I'll show you how to play chess.
Somebody told me where to buy a ticket.

ESERCIZIO 85A

Completa le frasi usando le parole più appropriate del riquadro.

> what | do   how | make   what | wear
> ~~how | get~~   whether | stay   how | spell

Esempio:

'Could you tell me *how to get* to Western Road, please?'   'Yes. Go down this road and it's second on the left.'

1 'Have you decided ____ to the interview?'   'Yes. I'm going to wear my new blue suit.'
2 Could you tell me ____ your name, please?
3 'What are you going to do this evening?'   'I can't decide ____ at home or go out.'
4 Do you know ____ a Spanish omelette?
5 I felt very embarrassed when she started shouting. I didn't know ____, so I just stood there.

86 Verbo + complemento + infinito con *to*

1 Dopo i verbi sotto elencati, di solito si usa un complemento (p.es. *Sue, me, you*)
prima dell'infinito con *to*.

force	*order*	*teach* (how)
get (= persuadere)	*persuade*	*tell*
invite	*remind*	*warn*

verbo + complemento + l'infinito con *to*

*We **invited Sue to have** dinner with us.*
*She **persuaded me to go** to the party.*
*He **warned you not to be** late again.*

Nota che dopo questi verbi, nella forma passiva, si può usare l'infinito con *to* senza
il complemento, p.es. *Sue **was invited to have** dinner with us.*

2 Si può usare la stessa costruzione anche dopo i seguenti verbi:

ask	*help*	*want*
expect	*mean* (= intendere)	

*He **asked me to help** him.*
*I didn't **expect Maria to write** to me.*
*I don't **want you to go**.*

Dopo *help* si può usare il complemento seguito dall'infinito con o senza *to*.

*I'll **help you (to) carry** your bags.*

Dopo tutti i verbi sopra elencati si può usare l'infinito con *to* senza il complemento
p.es. *I **expect to see** Simon tomorrow.* Cfr. 84.

Nota che *want* non può esser seguito da *that* e l'indicativo: non si può dire
~~*I don't **want that you go***~~.

3 Dopo i verbi *advise, allow, encourage, permit* e *recommend*, si può usare la forma in
-ing o un complemento + l'infinito con *to*. Confronta:

verbo + la forma in *-ing*

verbo + complemento + l'infinito con *to*

*I wouldn't **advise going** there.*   *I wouldn't **advise you to go** there.*
*They don't **allow fishing** here.*   *They don't **allow people to fish** here.*

ESERCIZIO 86A

Completa le frasi.

Esempio:

I couldn't do the job on my own, so I | ask | Simon | help me.
I couldn't do the job on my own, so I asked Simon to help me.

1 I was surprised that my brother failed his driving test. I | expect | him | pass | easily.
2 Annie wanted to stay up late, but her parents | tell | her | go to bed at 9 o'clock.
3 Simon phoned Sarah yesterday. He | invite | her | go to a party on Saturday.
4 I was going to buy the car, but a friend of mine | persuade | me | change my mind.
5 Don't tell Sue what I've done. I | not | want | her | know.

ESERCIZIO 86B

Che cosa hanno detto? Completa le frasi con un complemento + l'infinito con *to* . . .

Esempi:

'Remember to phone Chris,' Sue told Peter.
Sue reminded *Peter to phone Chris.*
'Can you lend me some money?' I asked him.
I asked *him to lend me some money.*

1 'Close the door,' Ken told Andrew. Ken told ____.
2 'Can you help me?' I asked her. I asked ____.
3 'Would you like to go to a party?' they asked us. They invited ____.
4 'Please don't be late home,' Kate said to Sally. Kate asked ____.
5 'Get out of your car,' the policeman told the woman. The policeman ordered ____.
6 'Don't be late for work again,' my boss told me. My boss warned ____.

ESERCIZIO 86C

Metti i verbi alla forma corretta: la forma in *-ing* o l'infinito con *to.*

Esempio:

She doesn't allow anyone *to drive* (drive) her car.

1 They don't allow ____ (talk) in the examination.
2 He's always encouraged me ____ (have) confidence in myself.
3 I'd recommend you ____ (see) the film. It's very good.
4 I wouldn't recommend ____ (drive) through the city centre now. The traffic is terrible at this time of the day.
5 What would you advise me ____ (do)?
6 I wouldn't advise ____ (tell) anyone what's happened.

87 Verbo + forma in -ing o infinito con to (1)

1   Dopo i verbi sotto elencati, si può usare la forma in -ing o l'infinito con to per lo più senza differenze di significato.

begin	*can't bear*	*like*	*prefer*
continue	*hate*	*love*	*start*

He **began looking/to look** *for a job 6 months ago.*
I **like swimming/to swim** *in the sea.*
She **prefers working/to work** *at night.*

Ma cfr. 2–4 sotto.

2   *Like*

a   Nell'inglese britannico spesso si usa *like* + la forma in -ing per dire che piace fare qualcosa.

I **like going** *to the cinema.* (= Mi piace andare al cinema.)

Si usa *like* + l'infinito con *to* per dire che si sceglie di fare qualcosa perché si pensa che sia opportuno.

I **like to go** *to the dentist's for a check-up every 6 months.* (= Credo che sia opportuno, sebbene non mi piaccia andarci.)

b   Dopo *would like, would hate, would prefer* e *would love*, si usa l'infinito con *to*.

'**Would** *you* **like to go** *out this evening?*' '*I'd* **prefer to stay** *at home.*'
We'd **love to see** *you at the weekend.*

c   Confronta *like* con *would like*:

Do you **like cooking**? (= Ti piace cucinare, in generale?)	*Would you* **like to cook** *the dinner this evening?* (= Vuoi preparare la cena questa sera?)

3   *Prefer*

Nota queste costruzioni:

> *prefer* + la forma in -ing + *to* + la forma in -ing

I **prefer playing** *football* **to watching** *it.*

> *would prefer* + l'infinito con *to* + *rather than* + l'infinito senza *to*

I **would prefer to drive** *home tonight* **rather than wait** *until tomorrow.*

4 | ***Begin, start, continue***

a | Normalmente non si usa la forma in -*ing* dopo la forma progressiva di *begin, start, continue* (per evitare due verbi consecutivi terminanti in -*ing*).

I'm **beginning to feel** cold. (Normalmente, non si dice: I'm **beginning feeling** cold.)

b | Dopo *begin, continue* e *start*, normalmente si usano l'infinito con *to*, non la forma in -*ing* dei verbi *understand, know* e *realise*.

I **began to realise**. (Normalmente, non si dice: I **began realising**.)

ESERCIZIO 87A

Metti i verbi alla forma corretta. Talvolta ci sono due possibilità.

Esempi:

I quite enjoy *driving* (drive) at night.
Do you like *getting up/to get up* (get up) early?

1 Would you like ___ (listen) to some music?
2 Simon and Sally have started ___ (cook) the dinner.
3 I prefer ___ (windsurf) to ___ (sail).
4 I'd prefer ___ (walk) home rather than ___ (go) by taxi.

5 My sister loves ___ (go) shopping.
6 I'd love ___ (visit) Australia one day.
7 My brother hates ___ (have to) work at weekends.
8 Do you like ___ (play) chess?
9 I try to look after my car. I like ___ (take) it to the garage to be serviced regularly.
10 Shh! The orchestra is starting ___ (play).

88   Verbo + forma in -*ing* o infinito con *to* (2)

Dopo i verbi sotto elencati si può usare sia la forma in -*ing* che l'infinito con *to*, ma con diversi significati.

| *remember   forget   try   stop   go on   regret* |

1 | ***Remember/forget doing* e *remember/forget to do***

Si usa *remember/forget* + la forma in -*ing* quando ci si ricorda o dimentica di aver fatto qualcosa.

AZIONE◄────────────RICORDARSI

I **remember going** to the 1972 Olympics. (Nel 1972 sono andato alle Olimpiadi e adesso me ne ricordo.)

Have you **forgotten giving** me the money? (Ti sei dimenticato che mi hai dato i soldi?)

Si usa *remember/forget* + l'infinito con *to* quando ci si ricorda o dimentica di fare qualcosa.

RICORDARSI────────────►AZIONE

I **remembered to go** to the chemist's for you. Here's your medicine. (Me ne sono ricordato, poi ci sono andato.)

Don't **forget to give** me the money.

2 | *Try doing* e *try to do*

Si usa *try* + la forma in -*ing* per dire 'fare un esperimento' – fare qualcosa e vedere cosa succede.

*'The car won't start.'   'Why don't we **try pushing** it?*

Si usa *try* + l'infinito con *to* per dire 'fare uno sforzo' – vedere se si riesce a fare qualcosa.

*I **tried to push** the car up the hill, but I couldn't move it.*

3 | *Stop doing* y *stop to do*

Si usa *stop* + la forma in -*ing* per dire che si smette di fare qualcosa.

*I'm a vegetarian. I **stopped eating** meat 5 years ago.* (= Ho mangiato carne fino a 5 anni fa, poi ho smesso.)

Si usa *stop* + l'infinito con *to* per dire che ci si ferma per fare qualcosa (cfr. 95).

*After I'd been working for 3 hours, I **stopped to eat** lunch.* (= Mi sono fermato per poter pranzare.)

4 | *Go on doing* e *go on to do*

Si usa *go on* + la forma in -*ing* per parlare di qualcosa che continua.

*She **went on talking** about her holiday all evening.* (= Continuò a parlare . . .)

Si usa *go on* + l'infinito con *to* per dire che si passa a fare qualcosa di diverso.

*She spoke about her son, then she **went on to talk** about her daughter.*

5 | *Regret doing* e *regret to do*

Si usa *regret* + la forma in -*ing* per dire che rincresce di aver fatto qualcosa.

*I **regret saying** that he was an idiot.* (Mi rincresce di aver detto che è un idiota.)

Si usa *regret* + l'infinito con *to* per dire che rincresce di dover fare qualcosa.

*I **regret to say** that I won't be able to come to the meeting on Monday.*

Nota che *regret* + l'infinito con *to* è piuttosto formale.

ESERCIZIO 88A

Metti i verbi fra parentesi alla forma in -*ing* o all'infinito con *to*.

Esempio:

'I introduced you to Sue last month.'   'Really? I don't remember *meeting* (meet) her.'

1 'You said Ken was stupid.'   'I don't remember ＿＿ (say) that.'
2 I'll never forget ＿＿ (visit) Istanbul in 1983.
3 When I go shopping I must remember ＿＿ (buy) some bread.
4 Please remember ＿＿ (turn off) the radio before you go out.

ESERCIZIO 88B

Metti i verbi fra parentesi alla forma in *-ing* o all'infinito con *to*.

Esempio:

'I need to borrow some money.'   'Why don't you try *asking* (ask) your parents to lend you some?'

1 I'll try ____ (come) to the meeting, but I'm not sure if I'll be able to.
2 If you get hiccups, you should try ____ (drink) a glass of water. If that doesn't work, try ____ (hold) your breath.
3 You can borrow my camera, but please try ____ (be) careful with it.
4 'This soup doesn't taste very good.'   'Try ____ (put) in some more salt.'

ESERCIZIO 88C

Completa le frasi usando la forma in *-ing* o l'infinito con *to* dei verbi nel riquadro. Usa ciascun verbo una volta sola.

Esempio:

Could you stop *working* for a moment? I'd like to speak to you.

| ask   not learn   tell   ~~work~~   make |

1 He went on ____ a noise even though I'd asked him to stop.
2 She started by talking about her job. Then she went on ____ me about her family.
3 He stopped reading ____ me a question.
4 I regret ____ to play a musical instrument when I was younger.

89 *Be used to* + forma in *-ing* e *used to* + infinito

1

Confronta:

Si usa *be used to* + la forma in *-ing* per dire 'essere abituati a'.

I'm used to driving my new car now, but I found it very strange at first. (= Sono abituato a guidare la macchina ormai, non sono più impacciato.)

Si usa *used to* + l'infinito per parlare di azioni abituali nel passato, che sono cessate.

I used to drive a Mercedes, but now I drive a Citroen. (= Un tempo guidavo sempre la Mercedes, non più adesso.)

2 Si può usare *get used to* (= abituarsi) + la forma in *-ing*, p.es. *I've got used to driving my new car.*

3 Dopo *be/get used to* si può usare anche un' espressione nominale p.es. *English food, my new computer.*

He isn't used to English food.
I haven't got used to my new computer yet.

ESERCIZIO 89A

Metti i verbi alla forma corretta: *to* + la forma in *-ing* o *to* + l'infinito.

Esempio:

When I was younger, I used *to play* (play) a lot of football. Now I never play.

1 It won't take you long to get used _to working_ (work) with your new word processor.

2 My parents used _to live_ (live) in London, but now they live in Bristol.

3 Bruno is Italian, but he has lived in London for over 5 years. He has got used _to eat_ (eat) English food now, but when he first arrived in England he didn't like it very much.

4 Mike found Africa strange at first. He wasn't used _to living_ (live) in such a hot climate.

5 I normally go to bed at about 10 o'clock. I'm not used _to staying_ (stay) up late.

6 I used _to work_ (work) on a farm once and had to get up at 5 o'clock every morning. It was difficult at first because I wasn't used _to getting up_ (get up) so early.

Nota —Per *used to*, cfr. anche 51.

90 *Need* + forma in -*ing* o infinito con *to*

1 Dopo *need*, usato come verbo regolare, si può fare seguire l'infinito con *to*.

*I'm tired. I **need to get** some sleep.*
*We've got plenty of time. We **don't need to hurry**.*

2 Dopo *need*, usato come verbo regolare, si può fare seguire anche la forma in -*ing*, ma il significato diventa passivo.

*My car **needs servicing**.*
*These trousers **need cleaning**.*

Dopo *need*, si può usare anche *to be* + il participio passato con lo stesso significato passivo.

*My car **needs to be serviced**.*
*These trousers **need to be cleaned**.*

ESERCIZIO 90A

Completa ogni frase usando la forma corretta del verbo più adatto nel riquadro.
Talvolta sono possibili due forme.

Esempi:

There is a hole in my sock. It needs *repairing/to be repaired*.
Tomorrow is a holiday, so I don't need *to get up* early in the morning.

buy	adjust	~~get up~~	ask
renew	practise	feed	~~repair~~

1 Your passport is out of date. It needs _____.
2 You need _____ the piano every day if you want to improve.
3 The brakes on my car aren't working very well. I think they need _____.
4 The cat is hungry. It needs _____.
5 We've got plenty of milk. We don't need _____ any more.
6 I went to see her because I needed _____ her some questions.

91 Infinito senza *to*

1 Si usa l'infinito senza *to* dopo i verbi modali p.es. *can, must, should* (cfr. 35).

*I **can speak** Italian.*
*We **must go** now.*

Eccezione: dopo il verbo modale *ought*, si usa l'infinito con *to*, p.es. *You **ought to be** careful.*

2 Si usa l'infinito senza *to* dopo *let's* (= let us) e *why don't we/you . . .?* per fare una proposta (cfr. 30, 50.2).

*'What shall we do this afternoon?' '**Let's go** to the cinema.'*
***Why don't we have** a party next Saturday?*
***Why don't you apply** for the job?*

Si usa l'infinito senza *to* dopo *would rather* (cfr. 57.1) e *had better* (cfr. 42.2).

*'Would you like to go out this evening?' '**I'd rather stay** at home.'*
*I think it's going to rain. **You'd better take** an umbrella with you when you go out.*

3 Dopo i verbi *let* (= permettere) e *make* (= costringere o causare), si usa un complemento p.es. *their children, me, us* + l'infinito senza *to*.

> *let/make* + complemento + l'infinito senza *to*

*They **let their children stay** up late at weekends.* (= Permettono ai loro figli di stare alzati . . .)
*Will you **let me use** your camera?* (= Mi permetterai di usare . . .)
*You can't **make us go** if we don't want to.* (= . . . costringerci ad andare . . .)
*The film **made me cry**.* (= . . . mi ha fatto piangere.)

ESERCIZIO 91A

Completa ogni frase usando, una volta sola, il verbo più adatto del riquadro.

Esempio:

'Would you like a cup of tea?' 'I'd rather *have* coffee.'

> eat hurry tell type wear lend
> sit promise cry wait use ~~have~~

1 It's very cold today. You'd better ____ a coat when you go out.
2 'I haven't got any money.' 'Let me ____ you some'.
3 Chopping onions makes me ____.
4 'I'm tired of walking.' 'Let's ____ down for a while, then.'
5 I can't ____ you what Sally said. She made me ____ that I wouldn't tell anyone.
6 'Why don't we ____ dinner now?' 'I think I'd rather ____ until later.'
7 It's getting late. We'd better ____.
8 I couldn't ____ the letter because my brother wouldn't let me ____ his typewriter.

ESERCIZIO 91B

Sally sta parlando del suo ragazzo, Peter.

Completa quello che dice usando la forma
corretta di *make* o *let* e i verbi del riquadro.

| have | understand | ~~laugh~~ | feel | go |

'Peter's very funny. He *makes* me *laugh* a lot. We usually get on very well together,
but sometimes I get really angry with him because he's so jealous and won't 1___
me ___ out on my own. He 2___ me ___ jealous, too, when he talks about his ex-
girlfriends! But I always 3___ him ___ his own friends and never ask him who he is
going out with. I've talked to him about this, but I can't 4___ him ___ that his
attitude is unfair.'

Nota –Dopo verbi come *see, hear, feel* si può usare un complemento + l'infinito senza *to* o la forma
  in -*ing*. Cfr. 97.
  –Quando si collegano due verbi all'infinito con *to*, usando *or* o *and*, spesso si omette il
  secondo *to* p.es. *I'd like **to go and see** that film.*

92 Preposizione + forma in -*ing*

1 Quando il verbo segue una preposizione (p.es. *in, of, about, before, after*), assume la
forma in -*ing*.

*Are you interested **in playing** tennis tomorrow?*
*I'm thinking **of changing** my job.*
*How **about going** to the cinema this evening?*

2 **To**

Talvolta *to* è parte integrante dell'infinito del verbo.

*We've decided **to go** on holiday next month.*
*Would you like **to eat** now or later?*

Talvolta *to* è la preposizione 'a'.

*She's travelling **to** Greece tomorrow.*
*We're looking forward **to** the party.*
*Carlos isn't used **to** English food.*

Se si può mettere un sostantivo dopo *to* si tratta della preposizione. Se *to* è
preposizione, si usa la forma in -*ing* del verbo che la segue.

*I'm looking forward **to going** to the party.*
*Carlos isn't used **to eating** English food.*

ESERCIZIO 92A

Completa le frasi. Usa una preposizione del riquadro e la forma in -*ing* dei verbi tra parentesi. Usa alcune preposizioni più di una volta.

for   at   ~~about~~   in   to   of   after

Esempio:

'What shall we do this evening?'   'How *about going* (go) to the cinema?'

1 There is a good film on TV tonight. I'm really looking forward ____ (see) it.
2 Are you interested ____ (learn) to play the guitar?
3 ____ (have) breakfast, I did the washing up.

4 I'm not used ____ (eat) such spicy food.
5 Did she apologize ____ (be) late?
6 I'm tired ____ (hear) her complain.
7 We thanked her ____ (give) us a lift in her car.
8 She's very good ____ (paint) and (draw).

93 Persona + forma in -*ing*

1

Nell'inglese informale si usa regolarmente la costruzione: pronome complemento o nome proprio (p.es. *me, you, Simon*) + la forma in -*ing*.

*Do you mind **me asking** you a question?*
*They were angry about **Simon arriving** late.*

Nell'inglese formale, invece, si può usare un possessivo p.es. *my, your, Simon's* + la forma in -*ing*.

*Do you mind **my asking** you a question?*
*They were angry about **Simon's arriving** late.*

2

Dopo *see, hear, feel* e *smell*, normalmente si usa la prima costruzione (cfr. 97).

*You saw **me arriving**.* (Non: ~~*You saw **my arriving**.*~~)

ESERCIZIO 93A

Completa le frasi usando (i) complemento + forma in -*ing* e (ii) possessivo + forma in -*ing*.

Esempio:

Do you mind ____ (I | open) the window?
 (i) *Do you mind me opening the window?*   (ii) *Do you mind my opening the window?*

1 I don't mind ____ (you | borrow) my car.
2 Do you mind ____ (I | switch on) the TV?
3 They insisted on ____ (we | stay) for dinner with them.
4 How do you feel about ____ (they | get) married?
5 Annie's parents don't like ____ (she | go) to bed late.
6 I was surprised about ____ (Sue | forget) to come to the meeting.

94 Forma in *-ing* e infinito con *to* in funzione di soggetto

---

1 | Si può usare la forma in *-ing* come soggetto.

Smoking *is a terrible habit.*
Knowing *how to drive is useful.*
Playing *tennis in England isn't expensive.*

2 | Si può usare anche l'infinito con *to* come soggetto (p.es. **To know** *how to drive is useful*) ma questo è abbastanza raro. In casi simili si preferisce cominciare la frase con *it* (come 'soggetto preliminare').

It *is useful* **to know** *how to drive.*
It *isn't expensive* **to play** *tennis in England.*

ESERCIZIO 94A

Che cosa significa *it* in ciascuna di queste frasi? Usa la forma in *-ing* delle espressioni nel riquadro per rispondere.

Esempio:

It can be dangerous, especially at midday. *Sunbathing can be dangerous, especially at midday.*

live on your own   babysit   ~~sunbathe~~   smoke
read English   swim   watch late night horror films

1 It is a big responsibility, especially with very
   young children.
2 It is a very good way of keeping fit.
3 It can give you nightmares.
4 It is quite difficult if you are used to being
   with a lot of people.
5 It is much easier than speaking it.
6 It can cause lung cancer.

ESERCIZIO 94B

Collega ogni frase di **A** con la frase più adatta di **B**, usando la forma dell'infinito con *to*, come nell'esempio.

Esempio:

1 *It is very strange to see yourself on video.*

A | **B**
1 It is very strange — | eat well
2 It isn't necessary | live on a pension
3 It can be dangerous | — see yourself on video
4 It doesn't have to be expensive | have your car serviced every month
5 It is difficult for old people | leave medicine lying around

95 Infinito con *to* per indicare scopo

1 Si può usare l'infinito con *to* per esprimere lo scopo, il motivo per cui si fa una cosa.

*I'm going out **to do** some shopping.*
*She's saving up **to buy** a motorbike.*
*I went to a restaurant **to have** some lunch.*

Nello stile formale si usa *in order to* o *so as to*.

*I went to Paris **in order to learn** French.*
*We left early **so as to have** plenty of time.*

2 Nelle frasi negative normalmente si usa *in order not to* o *so as not to* (non *not to* da solo).

*We left early **so as not to be** late./We left early **in order not to be** late.* (Non: ~~We left early not to be late.~~)

Per altre espressioni indicanti scopo, cfr. 163–164.

ESERCIZIO 95A

Dove sei andato ieri, e perché ci sei andato?

1 Chemist's   **2** Post Office   **3** Cinema
4 Hairdresser's   **5** Car Rental Agency   **6** Park

Componi delle frasi usando *I went to the* (luogo) *to* + i verbi del riquadro.

Esempio:

1 *I went to the chemist's to buy some medicine.*

hire	a haircut
buy	tennis
have	a film
play	some letters
post	a car
see	some medicine

ESERCIZIO 95B

Collega ogni frase di **A** con una di **B**, usando (i) *in order (not) to* e (ii) *so as (not) to*.

Esempio:

1 (i) *He drank lots of black coffee in order to keep awake.*
(ii) *He drank lots of black coffee so as to keep awake.*

A	**B**
1 He drank lots of black coffee	disturb the neighbours
2 I often write things down	save time
3 She took an umbrella	get a better job
4 We'll use the computer	forget them
5 I want to pass the exams	keep awake
6 We turned down the music	get wet

96 Nome/pronome/aggettivo + infinito con *to*

1 | **Nome o pronome + l'infinito con *to***

Si può usare l'infinito con *to* dopo alcuni nomi e pronomi (spesso per dire quello che bisogna fare con le cose indicate da tali nomi o pronomi).

*I've got some **letters to write**.*
*We need some **scissors to cut** this paper.*
*Would you like **something to read?***

Si può usare anche la costruzione: aggettivo + nome + l'infinito con *to*.

*That's an **impossible question to answer**.*

2 | **Aggettivo + l'infinito con *to***

a | Si può usare l'infinito con *to* dopo diversi aggettivi.

*I'm very **pleased to see** you.*
*I was **disappointed to hear** that you didn't pass the exam.*
*He'll be **surprised to get** your letter.*
*It isn't **easy to learn** a foreign language.*

b | Si può usare la costruzione: *of* + pronome/nome + l'infinito con *to* dopo i seguenti aggettivi:

> nice   kind   generous   polite   good   mean
> silly   careless   clever   wrong   stupid

*It's **kind of you to help**.*
*It was **stupid of me to say** that.*

c | Si può usare la costruzione: *for* + l'infinito con *to* dopo i seguenti aggettivi:

> *easy   important   essential   (un)usual   (un)necessary*
> *common   normal   rare*

*It won't be **easy for us to get** tickets for the concert now.*
*It's **important for everyone to be** here on time.*

Si può usare questa costruzione anche dopo alcuni nomi e verbi.

*It was a **mistake for me to come** here.*
*I'm **waiting for my sister to phone** me.*

ESERCIZIO 96A

Completa le frasi usando l'infinito con *to* dei verbi nel riquadro.

Esempio:

Are you hungry? Would you like something *to eat?*

> say   unlock   catch   wear   ~~eat~~   write   tell

1 Have you got a key ____ this door?
2 Can we meet today? I've got something important ____ you.
3 I'm staying at home this evening. I've got some letters ____.
4 'Why are you so quiet?'   'I haven't got anything ____.'
5 I need some new clothes ____ to the party.
6 I really must go now. I've got a train ____.

ESERCIZIO 96B

Completa le frasi usando la forma corretta delle parole nel riquadro.

Esempio:

Goodbye. It was very *nice to meet* you.

> impossible | finish   please | hear   safe | go
> ~~nice | meet~~   easy | use   interesting | plan

1 My new video recorder looks complicated, but it's actually very ____.
2 That is a very dangerous part of the city. It isn't ____ out there at night.
3 I was ____ that you had passed your exam.
4 I don't like package holidays. I think it's much more ____ your own holiday.
5 It's ____ all that work today. There just isn't enough time.

ESERCIZIO 96C

Componi delle frasi cominciando con le parole fra parentesi, come negli esempi.

Esempi:

You lent me the money. (It was kind)
It was kind of you to lend me the money.
I forgot my keys. (It was stupid)
It was stupid of me to forget my keys.

1 She sent me a birthday card. (It was nice)
2 He opened your letter. (It was wrong)
3 You found the answer. (It was clever)
4 I left my keys at home. (It was careless)

ESERCIZIO 96D

Riscrivi le frasi. Usa le parole fra parentesi + *for* + complemento + l'infinito con *to*, come negli esempi.

Esempi:

You needn't explain. (It isn't necessary)
It isn't necessary for you to explain.
She isn't normally late for work. (It's unusual)
It's unusual for her to be late for work.

1 You needn't pay me back the money. (It's unnecessary)
2 We must leave immediately. (It's essential)
3 Everyone should try to keep calm. (It's important)
4 He doesn't normally complain. (It's unusual)

Nota   –Per l'uso dell'infinito con *to* preceduto da *too* (p.es. *It's **too** early (for me) **to go** to bed*) o da *enough* (p.es. *Is he old **enough to drive** a car?*), cfr. 138.4–5.

97 *See someone doing* e *see someone do*, ecc.

Dopo i verbi *see*, *hear*, *feel*, *watch*, *listen to* e *notice* si può usare un complemento +
...-ing o l'infinito senza *to*.

| verbo + complemento + ...-ing | verbo + complemento + l'infinito senza *to* |

We saw Peter leaving.
I heard them going out.

We saw Peter leave.
I heard them go out.

Spesso il significato è diverso. Confronta:

Si usa la forma in -*ing* quando si vede, si
sente, ecc. solo una parte dell'azione in
corso.

*As I drove past the park, I saw some
people playing football.* (= Erano nel
bel mezzo della partita.)

Si usa l'infinito senza *to* quando si vede,
si sente, ecc. l'intera azione.

*Last week I went to London and saw
England play Brazil in the big football
match.* (= Ho visto l'intera partita.)

ESERCIZIO 97A

Metti i verbi fra parentesi alla forma in -*ing* o all'infinito senza *to*.

Esempio:

I saw Sue *drop* (drop) the bag and pick it up again.

1 As I walked past the room, I heard two people
____ (argue).
2 We stopped for a moment and watched them
____ (build) the new hospital.
3 Did you see someone ____ (break) the
window?

4 We watched them ____ (climb) up to the top
of the hill and then come down again.
5 We saw the man ____ (post) a letter and walk
down the street.
6 As I looked out of the window I noticed the
woman ____ (repair) her car.

98 Riepilogo della forma in -*ing* e dell'infinito

ESERCIZIO 98A

Completa le frasi mettendo i verbi alla forma in -*ing* o all'infinito con o senza *to*.
Talvolta sono possibili due costruzioni.

Esempi:

You really should *try* (try) to stop *smoking* (smoke).

1 I hate ____ (work) at weekends.
2 Would you like ____ (come) to a disco this
evening?
3 Can I help you ____ (move) your things?

4 I had hoped ____ (see) the musical *Rainbow*,
but I couldn't ____ (get) any tickets.
5 Stop ____ (make) so much noise. People are
trying ____ (sleep).

6 Would you like something ___ (drink)?
7 You should ___ (try) to avoid ___ (drive) through the city centre at the rush hour.
8 I want a few days ___ (think) about their offer before ___ (make) a decision.
9 What time do you need ___ (leave) ___ (catch) your bus?
10 It's unusual for him ___ (be) ill.
11 It was horrible to work as an au pair. My family expected me ___ (work) seven days a week.
12 Do you prefer ___ (ski) to ___ (ice-skate)?
13 I'm very fond of ___ (walk) by the sea.
14 I rang the doorbell, but no one seemed ___ (be) at home.
15 It was good of you ___ (explain) everything to me.
16 I'd advise you ___ (not | walk) alone in that part of the city. It can be very dangerous there at night.
17 I remember ___ (meet) her once, but I can't remember her name.
18 I'd like ___ (make) a copy of a letter. Could you ___ (show) me how ___ (use) the photocopier? I've never used it before.
19 I feel like ___ (not | do) anything at all this evening.
20 We're very much looking forward to ___ (see) you next week.
21 I mustn't ___ (forget) ___ (phone) the doctor tomorrow morning.
22 The customs officer made me ___ (empty) my suitcases.
23 ___ (eat) too many sweets is bad for your teeth.
24 Sarah has decided ___ (not | go) away on holiday this summer.
25 They stopped ___ (work) at one o'clock ___ (have) something ___ (eat).

ESERCIZIO 98B

Completa ogni frase usando la forma corretta dei verbi nel riquadro. Usa ciascun verbo una volta sola.

Esempio:

I phoned my bank manager and I arranged *to meet* him next Tuesday.

```
repair   open   have   travel   sunbathe
meet   fall   go   lend   shop   switch off
```

1 It was very kind of her ___ you the money.
2 I can't stand ___ by Underground.
3 These shoes need ___. They've got holes in them.
4 I wouldn't recommend ___ in that supermarket. It's very expensive.
5 Would you mind ___ the door for me, please?
6 When you leave the room, don't forget ___ all the lights.
7 They saw Maria ___ in the garden as they drove past.
8 Autumn is coming. The leaves are starting ___ from the trees.
9 I'm tired. I regret ___ to bed so late last night.
10 I like ___ my eyes tested regularly.

99 Aggettivi participiali (in -*ed* e in -*ing*)

Confronta gli aggettivi terminanti in -*ed* con quelli terminanti in -*ing*:

-*ed*

*She's **annoyed**.*

Gli aggettivi terminanti in -*ed*
descrivono i sentimenti di una persona.

*I'm **interested** in photography.*
*Everyone was **excited**.*
*We all feel **relaxed**.*

-*ing*

*The noise is **annoying**.*

Gli aggettivi terminanti in -*ing*
descrivono la persona o la cosa che
suscita quei sentimenti.

*I think photography is **interesting**.*
*It was an **exciting** tennis match.*
*We're having a **relaxing** holiday.*

ESERCIZIO 99A

Scegli la desinenza giusta.

Esempio:

I enjoyed the book. It was very ~~interested~~/
interesting.

1 Are you *interested*/*interesting* in art?
2 They were *shocked*/*shocking* when they heard
  the news.
3 I thought the story was quite *amused*/*amusing*.
4 We were all very *worried*/*worrying* when he
  didn't come home.
5 It was *surprised*/*surprising* that she didn't
  come to the meeting.

ESERCIZIO 99B

Completa le frasi con aggettivi formati
aggiungendo -*ing* o -*ed* alle parole fra parentesi.

Esempio:

I don't get *embarrassed* very easily. (embarrass)

1 I find it quite ___ to talk in front of a group of
  people. (embarrass)
2 I think reading newspapers is ___. (depress)
3 I'm ___ in all kinds of sport. (interest)
4 I find walking in the countryside very ___.
  (relax)
5 I think learning a language is very ___.
  (interest)
6 I get ___ when people smoke in restaurants.
  (annoy)
7 I don't normally get ___ when I watch
  horror films. (frighten)

E tu, su che cosa sei d'accordo?

100 Frasi participiali (in -*ing*)

1 Si può usare il participio presente p.es. *sitting, playing* per fare una 'frase participiale'.

*Simon is the boy **sitting in the corner**.*
*I had an accident **driving to work**.*

2 Alcune di queste frasi fungono da aggettivo: dicono qualcosa di più sul nome.

*Simon is the boy **sitting in the corner**.*
*The girl **wearing the black dress** is Sarah.*

3 Altre fungono da avverbio in quanto possono esprimere, per esempio, rapporti temporali o causali tra le frasi:

a Si può usare una frase in -*ing* per indicare un'azione che avviene nel corso di un'altra, interrompendola.

*I had an accident **driving to work**.* (= Ho avuto un incidente mentre stavo andando al lavoro.)

b Si può usare una frase in -*ing* per indicare un'azione che avviene contemporaneamente a un'altra.

*I walked out of the room **smiling to myself**.* (= Sono uscito dalla stanza sorridendo tra me e me.)

c Si può usare *having* + il participio passato per indicare un'azione che avviene prima di un'altra.

***Having finished** breakfast, I went out for a walk.* (= Avendo finito la colazione, sono uscito per fare una passeggiata.)

Si può usare una frase in -*ing* per indicare un'azione che avviene immediatamente prima di un'altra.

***Taking a book out of his pocket**, he started to read.* (= Prese un libro dalla tasca e subito lo cominciò a leggere.)

d Si può usare una frase in -*ing* per spiegare la causa, il motivo di un fatto.

***Knowing you wanted to go to the concert**, I bought a ticket for you.* (= Sapendo che volevi andare al concerto . . .)
***Having failed the exam the first time**, he decided to take it again.* (= Poiché non aveva passato l'esame la prima volta . . .)

ESERCIZIO 100A

Forma una frase in -*ing* per collegare due frasi, come negli esempi.

Esempi:

Who is that man? He's playing tennis with Maria.
Who is that man playing tennis with Maria?
That woman is my boss. She's talking to Peter.
That woman talking to Peter is my boss.

1 That woman is Kate Robinson. She's wearing the green coat.
2 That boy is Sally's brother. He's sitting over there.
3 Who is that girl? She's looking at us.
4 All those people want to see you. They're waiting outside.

ESERCIZIO 100B

Ieri Peter ha avuto una giornataccia. Cosa gli è successo? Completa le frasi costruendo frasi participiali con le parole del riquadro.

Esempio:

1 *He fell off a ladder changing a light bulb.*

1 He fell off a ladder ____.
2 He burnt himself ____.
3 He ran out of petrol ____.
4 He lost his keys ____.
5 He broke a cup ____.

> drive to work
> get out of his car
> do the washing-up
> ~~change a light bulb~~
> cook his dinner

ESERCIZIO 100C

Collega le frasi costruendo una frase participiale, come nell'esempio.

Esempio:

I was sitting in the park. I was writing a letter.
I was sitting in the park writing a letter.

1 The woman was driving along. She was listening to her car radio.
2 I arrived at the examination hall. I was feeling very nervous.
3 He came into the room. He was carrying a suitcase.
4 They were walking down the street. They were holding hands.

ESERCIZIO 100D

Riscrivi le frasi usando *Having* + il participio passato, come nell'esempio.

Esempio:

I finished the washing up, then I sat down and watched TV.
Having finished the washing up, I sat down and watched TV.

1 He typed the letters, then he put them all in envelopes.
2 I did all the housework, then I went out for a walk.
3 He got out of bed, then he had a shower.
4 She locked all the doors, then she went to bed.

ESERCIZIO 100E

Riscrivi le frasi formando una frase participiale, come negli esempi.

Esempi:

Because she didn't want to miss the train, she ran all the way to the station.
Not wanting to miss the train, she ran all the way to the station.
Because I had just eaten, I wasn't hungry. *Having just eaten, I wasn't hungry.*

1 Because she is a little deaf, she wears a hearing aid.
2 Because I don't like classical music, I didn't go to the concert.
3 Because she is rich, she can afford expensive holidays.
4 Because I had finished the book, I decided to take it back to the library.
5 Because they had gone to bed so late the night before, they felt quite tired the next day.

Nota   –Il soggetto della frase participiale deve essere lo stesso della frase principale p.es. *Having just eaten, I wasn't hungry.* (= Poiché **io** avevo appena mangiato, **io** non avevo fame.) E' sbagliato comporre frasi participiali con il soggetto diverso da quello della frase principale; non si può dire *Running down the street, the envelope fell out of my hand* (altrimenti sembra che sia stata la busta a correre per strada!)

101   Nomi: singolare e plurale (1)

1 | **Plurali regolari**

		NOME SINGOLARE	NOME PLURALE
a	La maggior parte dei nomi forma il plurale aggiungendo -s alla forma singolare.	book day girl	books days girls
b	I nomi terminanti in -ch, -sh, -s, -x aggiungono -es.	church dish bus box	churches dishes buses boxes
c	Alcuni nomi terminanti in -o (*tomato, potato, echo, hero, negro* sono tra i più comuni) aggiungono -es.	tomato potato hero	tomatoes potatoes heroes
	Altri nomi terminanti in -o aggiungono solo -s.	piano radio	pianos radios
d	I nomi terminanti in -y preceduta da una consonante cambiano -y in i, poi aggiungono -es.	baby factory	babies factories

2 | **Plurali irregolari**

	NOME SINGOLARE	NOME PLURALE

a   Alcuni nomi terminanti in *-f/-fe* perdono *-f/-fe* poi aggiungono *-ves* p.es. *half, thief, leaf, loaf, self, shelf, wolf, knife, wife, life.*

half	*halves*
thief	*thieves*
leaf	*leaves*
knife	*knives*
wife	*wives*
life	*lives*

b   Alcuni nomi formano il plurale cambiando una o più vocali.

Il plurale di *mouse* è *mice.*

foot	*feet*
tooth	*teeth*
goose	*geese*
man	*men*
woman	*women* /'wɪmɪn/
mouse	*mice*

c   Alcuni nomi formano il plurale con *-en.*

child	*children* /'tʃɪldrən/
ox	*oxen*

d   Alcuni nomi rimangono invariati.

sheep	*sheep*
deer	*deer*
fish	*fish**
aircraft	*aircraft*
hovercraft	*hovercraft*
spacecraft	*spacecraft*
series	*series*
species	*species*

e   Alcuni nomi di derivazione greca o latina mantengono la forma greca o latina del plurale.

crisis	*crises*
phenomenon	*phenomena*
cactus	*cacti*

f   Il plurale di *person* è, di norma, *people* (non *persons*).

person	*people*

* *fish* rimane invariato al plurale; esiste anche la forma *fishes*, ma è poco usata.

Per la pronuncia di *-(e)s*, cfr. 187.1.

ESERCIZIO 101A

Completa le frasi facendo il plurale dei nomi fra parentesi.

Esempio:

I like *oranges, apples, peaches* and *strawberries.* (orange | apple | peach | strawberry).

  1 They've got five ＿＿, three ＿＿ and two ＿＿. (child | girl | boy)
  2 London has many different ＿＿, ＿＿, ＿＿ and ＿＿.
     (restaurant | theatre | cinema | disco)

3 When he fell over, he broke two of his ____. (tooth)
4 We've got enough ____, but we need some more ____ and ____. (plate | knife | fork)
5 On their tour of Europe, they visited seven ____ in six ____. (country | day)
6 ____ hunt ____. (cat | mouse)
7 Do you know those ____ over there? (person)
8 These ____ are too small for me. They hurt my ____. (shoe | foot)
9 We've got some ____ and ____, but we haven't got any ____.
   (egg | tomato | potato)
10 Autumn is coming. The ____ are starting to all from the ____. (leaf | tree)

102 Nomi: singolare e plurale (2)

1 Normalmente si usano nomi singolari con verbi e pronomi singolari, e nomi plurali con verbi e pronomi plurali.

'Where's the key?' *'It's on the table.'*   *'Where are the keys?'* *'They're on the table.'*

Ma cfr. 2–9 sotto.

2 Con i nomi collettivi p.es. *family, team, group, crowd, class, company, government* si possono usare verbi e pronomi sia singolari che plurali:

a Si usano verbi e pronomi plurali quando si considerano questi gruppi come un insieme di varie persone.

My family are on holiday.
The government think they can solve the problem.

b Si usano verbi e pronomi singolari quando si considera il gruppo come un'entità singola e impersonale.

The family is a very important part of society.

3 Con *people, (the) police* e *cattle*, si usa sempre il plurale.

People are strange, aren't they?
The police in Britain wear blue uniforms.

4 Si usano nomi, verbi e pronomi plurali con *a number of* e *a group of*.

A number of my friends are planning a holiday together. They hope to go to Greece and Turkey.

Per *a lot of,* cfr. 116.

5 Dopo *one of my/his/her* ecc. si usa il nome al plurale e il verbo al singolare.

One of my friends is coming to see me.

6 Quando si parla di cifre o quantitativi spesso si usano verbi e pronomi al singolare anche con nomi al plurale.

Ten thousand pounds is a lot of money.
'The nearest town is five kilometres from here.' *'That isn't very far.'*

7	Alcuni nomi hanno soltanto la forma plurale p.es. *trousers, jeans, pyjamas, shorts, tights, glasses, scissors.*
	These jeans are *very old.*
	There **are** *some* **scissors** *in the kitchen.*
	Con questi nomi si può usare anche il verbo al singolare + *a pair of.*
	There **is a pair of scissors** *in the kitchen.*
8	Alcuni nomi terminano in -s ma sono singolari p.es. *news, politics, mathematics, physics, economics, athletics, billiards, rabies.*
	The news is *depressing.*
	Mathematics is *an interesting subject.*
9	I nomi non numerabili, cioè che non possono essere accompagnati da numerali, p.es. *milk, money,* non hanno in genere forma plurale.
	There **is** *some* **milk** *in the fridge.*
	Money isn't *the most important thing in life,* **is it?**
	Per i nomi non numerabili, cfr. 107.

ESERCIZIO 102A

Scegli la forma corretta. In una frase sono possibili due costruzioni.

Esempio:

There *were*/~~was~~ a lot of people at the party.

1 Economics *is/are* an interesting subject.
2 My trousers *have/has* got a hole in *it/them*.
3 Rabies *isn't/aren't* a very common disease in Britain.
4 My family *lives/live* in the North of England.
5 The news *was/were* quite surprising.
6 '*Is this/Are these* your scissors?' 'Yes, *they are/it is*.'
7 Two weeks *isn't/aren't* a very long time, *is it/ are they?*
8 My hair *is/are* quite greasy. *It needs/They need* washing.

103 Nomi composti

1	Un nome composto è un sostantivo formato da due (o più) parole:
	a **toothbrush** *a* **tin-opener**
a	Molti nomi composti sono formati da due sostantivi, di cui il primo funge da aggettivo. Il primo sostantivo è quasi sempre al singolare (anche quando il significato è plurale).
	a **toothbrush** (uno spazzolino da denti)
	a **shoe shop** (un negozio di scarpe)
	a **taxi driver** (un conducente di tassì)

Ci sono alcune eccezioni p.es. *clothes, sports, men, women.*

a clothes shop   **a sports car**   **women doctors**

b   Alcuni nomi composti formano un'unica parola p.es. *toothbrush*, altri sono separati da un trattino p.es. *tin-opener*, altri infine sono scritti in due parole distinte p.es. *shoe shop.*

Alcuni di questi si possono scrivere in tutti e tre i modi p.es. *babysitter, baby-sitter, baby sitter* (non esistono norme precise).

c   Alcuni nomi composti sono formati dal participio presente di un verbo + un nome o da un aggettivo + un nome.

a shopping bag   **a waiting room**   **drinking water**
a greenhouse

2   Il plurale dei nomi composti si forma, di regola, aggiungendo *-(e)s* alla seconda parola.

a shoe shop | *shoe shops*
a toothbrush | *two toothbrushes*

Nota però che i nomi composti terminanti in *-in-law* aggiungono *-s* alla prima parola.

one brother-in-law | *two brothers-in-law*
my mother-in-law | *some mothers-in-law*

Qualche altro nome composto aggiunge *-s* alla prima parola p.es. *passer-by* (= passante).

a passer-by | *some passers-by*

ESERCIZIO 103A

Forma dei nomi composti plurali, usando le parole del riquadro, per descrivere gli oggetti illustrati.

Esempi:

1 *alarm clock*   2 *T-shirts*   3 *crossroads*

screw	mower
hole	suit
alarm	roads
cork	hangers
bottle	shirts
cross	driver
clothes-	punch
T-	screw
track-	opener
lawn	clock

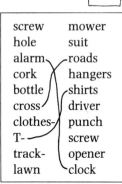
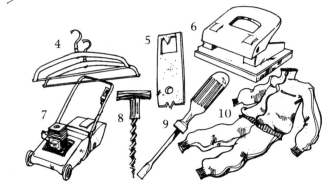

104 Possessivo con 's (genitivo sassone)

1 | **Uso**

Sally's *motorbike*   **Andrew's** *bedroom*

a Spesso si aggiunge 's (genitivo sassone) ai nomi propri di persona (p.es. *Sally*, *Andrew*) per indicare un rapporto di possesso o di specificazione.

Sally's *motorbike* (la motocicletta di Sally)
Andrew's *bedroom* (la camera di Andrew)
my sister's *school* (la scuola di mia sorella)

Si usa 's anche con i pronomi personali indefiniti p.es. *someone, nobody*.

someone's *passport*   **nobody's** *problem*

b Si può usare 's anche con nomi di animali.

a **dog's** *life*   *the* **cat's** *milk*

c Si può usare 's con nomi che indicano gruppi di persone, luoghi di lavoro, città ecc.

the **company's** *office*   *the* **club's** *rules*
the **world's** *problems*   **London's** *traffic*

d Si usa 's con alcune espressioni temporali.

yesterday's *newspaper*   **last week's** *football match*
next year's *plans*

Si usa 's con espressioni che indicano un periodo di tempo.

two days' *work*

2 | **Forma**

a Dopo un nome singolare si aggiunge 's.

> *my father's car*
> *Sally's clothes*

b Dopo un nome plurale che termina in -*s* si aggiunge solo '.

> *my parents' car*
> *ladies' clothes*

c Dopo un nome plurale che non termina in -*s* si aggiunge 's.

> *the men's car*
> *children's clothes*

d | Talvolta si aggiunge solo *'* a un nome singolare che termina in *-s*.

Sherlock Holmes' best friend   *Archimedes' Law*

Si preferisce però aggiungere *'s*.

Mrs Jones's husband   *Chris's idea*

e | Se il rapporto di possesso o specificazione riguarda più di un nome, si aggiunge *'s* all'ultimo nome.

Sue and Frank's *daughter*

Ma se il rapporto di possesso o specificazione riguarda un nome collegato a un'intera frase, si usa *. . . of . . .* p.es. *the daughter **of** the Australian couple who live next door* (cfr. 105).

f | Spesso si usa *'s* senza far seguire nessun nome (se è chiaro di che cosa si sta parlando).

*My car is next to **Ken's**.* (= *. . . next to Ken's car.*)

In questo modo si sottintendono spesso negozi, ambulatori ecc.

*She has just been to the **hairdresser's**.*
*I went to the **doctor's** yesterday.*

Per la pronuncia della *'s* del genitivo sassone, cfr. 187.1.

ESERCIZIO 104A

Osserva l'albero genealogico poi forma delle frasi usando *'s* e le parole del riquadro.

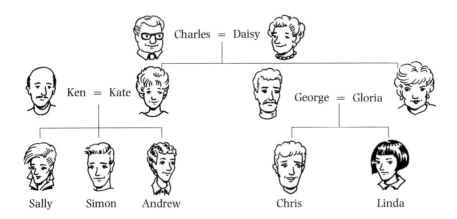

Esempi:

Kate–Ken
Kate is Ken's wife.
Simon and Andrew–Sally
Simon and Andrew are Sally's brothers.
Gloria–Ken
Gloria is Ken's sister-in-law.

1 Gloria–Chris and Linda
2 Linda–Chris
3 George–Chris and Linda
4 Chris–George and Gloria
5 Charles–Ken
6 Daisy–Linda and Chris
7 Kate–Chris and Linda
8 Sally, Simon and Andrew–Chris and Linda

~~wife~~	mother	father
sister	~~brother~~	son
aunt	grandmother	
cousin	sister-in-law	
father-in-law		

ESERCIZIO 104B

Completa le frasi usando la forma corretta del possessivo.

Esempio:

What is your friend*'s* name?

1 Sarah found somebody ____ credit cards in the street.
2 The Eiffel Tower is Paris ____ most famous landmark.
3 The boys ____ bedroom has just been painted.
4 I read about a murder in this morning ____ newspaper.
5 Can you borrow your parents ____ car at the weekend?
6 I need to get some medicine. Is there a chemist ____ near here?

105 Possessivo con 's o con . . . *of* . . .

1	Di regola si usa 's con nomi di persone o animali.	Di regola si usa . . . *of* . . . con nomi di cose.
	***Andrew's** school* ***Sarah's** book* ***my parents'** car* ***the cat's** food*	*the name **of the school*** *the middle **of the book*** *the front **of the car*** *the smell **of the food***

2 Si usa . . . *of* . . . invece di 's quando il rapporto di possesso o specificazione riguarda un nome collegato a un'intera frase.

*Yesterday I met the daughter **of the Australian couple who live next door**.* (Invece di: *Yesterday I met **the Australian couple who live next door's** daughter.*)

ESERCIZIO 105A

Completa le frasi con le parole tra parentesi dopo averle collegate tra loro con 's o con . . . *of* . . ., come negli esempi.

Esempi:

Have you seen *Steven Spielberg's new film*? (the new film | Steven Spielberg)
Have you repaired *the wheel of the bicycle*? (the wheel | the bicycle)

1 We had to leave the cinema early so we didn't see ____. (the end | the film)
2 We met Sue and Frank at ____. (the party | Sarah)
3 My flat is on ____. (the top floor | the house)
4 The bus crashed into ____. (the back | my car)
5 We heard the news from ____. (a friend | the woman who works in the post office)
6 There's a hospital at ____. (the end | this road)
7 I've spoken to ____. (the parents | the girls)
8 The police want to interview ____. (the manager | the Black Cat Club)

106 Doppio possessivo

Si può usare *...of...* e un'altra forma possessiva, costruendo un 'doppio possessivo'.

> *...of...* + forma possessiva

*Sarah is **a friend of Simon's**.* (= una delle amiche di Simon)
*A **cousin of mine** is coming to visit me.* (= un mio cugino)
*Sue is having lunch with **some colleagues of hers**.* (= alcuni suoi colleghi)

Nota che dopo *of* si usa un pronome possessivo p.es. *mine, hers* ecc. non un pronome personale p.es. *me, her* ecc.

ESERCIZIO 106A

Componi nuove frasi usando *...of...* + un'altra forma possessiva, come nell'esempio.

Esempio:

I met one of my friends in London.   *I met a friend of mine in London.*

1 Robert visited one of his relatives.
2 One of our neighbours is going to babysit for us.
3 Sally is going on holiday with some of her friends.
4 Simon has borrowed some of Sarah's records.
5 Two of my colleagues are ill at the moment.

107 Nomi numerabili e non numerabili

1

a

I nomi possono essere numerabili o non numerabili:

Sono numerabili i nomi che designano persone, oggetti concreti ecc. separati e distinti che possono essere accompagnati da numerali; questi nomi hanno forma singolare e plurale.

*one **book**   two **books***   *a **man**   some **men***

Sono non numerabili i nomi indicanti massa, materia, realtà astratte ecc. che non possono essere accompagnati da numerali; questi nomi non hanno forma plurale.

milk   rice   weather

b

I nomi numerabili possono avere il verbo sia al singolare che al plurale.

*This **book** is expensive.*   *These **books** are expensive.*
*That **man** lives next door.*   *Those **men** live next door.*

I nomi non numerabili hanno sempre il verbo al singolare.

Milk is good for you.
*The **weather** was very good yesterday.*

c Un nome numerabile può essere preceduto da *a/an*, oltre che da numerali.

a man   **one book**   **two books**

Un nome non numerabile di solito non viene preceduto da *a/an* o da numerali: non si dice *a weather, two weathers* ecc. Qualche volta, però, si usa l'articolo indeterminativo o un numerale davanti a nomi quali *coffee, tea, beer*, se si intende una tazza o un bicchiere di queste bevande, per esempio quando si ordina al ristorante.

Excuse me, waiter. Could we have **two coffees** *and* **a tea**, *please?*

Si usa *a* davanti ai nomi numerabili che cominciano per consonante, p.es. *a book, a man*, e *an* davanti a quelli che cominciano per vocale, p.es. *an apple, an egg* (cfr. 108.1).

d Si usa *some* davanti ai nomi numerabili plurali e ai nomi non numerabili (cfr. 115).

some books   **some rice**
some men   **some milk**

2 Alcuni nomi possono essere considerati numerabili o non numerabili, con diversi significati. Per esempio:

NUMERABILI   NON NUMERABILI

a glass

glass (= il vetro)

a hair

her hair (= i capelli)

a paper (= un giornale)

some paper (= carta da scrivere)

an iron (= un ferro da stiro)

iron (= il ferro)

some potatoes

some potato

3 | Alcuni nomi non sono numerabili in inglese, ma lo sono in altre lingue. I più comuni sono qui elencati assieme alle espressioni a cui si ricorre quando si ha bisogno di usare questi nomi come numerabili.

NON NUMERABILI	NUMERABILI
accommodation	*a place to live/stay*
advice	*a piece of advice*
bread	*a loaf/slice/piece (of bread) a (bread) roll*
furniture	*a piece of furniture*
information	*a piece of information*
luggage	*a piece of luggage; a suitcase/bag*
money	*a note/coin; a sum (of money)*
news	*a piece of news*
traffic	*a car/bus etc*
travel	*a journey/trip*
work	*a job; a piece of work*

Confronta:

*I've just had some **news**.*	*I've just had **a piece of news**.*
*Where is your **luggage**?*	*Where are your **suitcases**?*
*We need some **bread**.*	*We need **a loaf of bread**.*

Invece di *a piece of*, si può usare *a bit of* nello stile informale p.es. *a bit of advice*.

4 | Si possono usare nomi sia numerabili che non numerabili in espressioni di quantità con *of*.

*a box **of** matches*	*a bottle **of** water*
*two tins **of** tomatoes*	*two loaves **of** bread*

ESERCIZIO 107A

(i) Guarda gli oggetti delle illustrazioni. Qui sono nomi numerabili (Nu) o non numerabili (No)?

Esempi:

(ii) Elenca gli oggetti illustrati usando *a/an* o *some*.

Esempi:

Some cheese, a banana . . .

ESERCIZIO 107B

Scegli la forma corretta.

Esempio:

I'd like some *information*/~~informations~~ about hotels in London.

1 Sue is the woman with blonde *hair*/~~hairs~~ who lives opposite.
2 Did you have a good ~~travel~~/*journey* from Switzerland?
3 I've got a problem and I'd like some *advice*/~~advices~~.
4 Don't forget to buy ~~a bread~~/*some bread* when you go shopping.
5 I'd like to find out what's on TV this evening. Have you got *a paper*/~~some paper~~?
6 There *is*/~~are~~ usually a lot of *traffic*/~~traffics~~ in the city at this time of the day.
7 He's trying to find ~~a work~~/*job* at the moment, but there *isn't*/~~aren't~~ much *work*/~~works~~ available.
8 *Is*/~~Are~~ good *accommodation*/~~accommodations~~ difficult to find in the city centre?

108 Articoli: *a/an* e *the*

1

a

Forma e pronuncia

Si usa *a* /ə/ con le parole che cominciano per consonante.

a book /ə bʊk/
a car /ə kɑː/
a day /ə deɪ/
a friend /ə frend/
a girl /ə gɜːl/

Si usa *an* /ən/ con le parole che cominciano per vocale.

an apple /ən 'æpl/
an egg /ən eg/
an interview /ən 'ɪntəvjuː/
an old coat /ən əʊld kəʊt/
an umbrella /ən ʌm'brelə/

b

Si usa *the*, pronunciato /ðə/, con le parole che cominciano per consonante.

the book /ðə bʊk/
the car /ðə kɑː/
the day /ðə deɪ/

Si usa *the*, pronunciato /ðiː/, con le parole che cominciano per vocale.

the apple /ðiː 'æpl/
the egg /ðiː eg/
the interview /ðiː 'ɪntəvjuː/

c

Si usa *a* e *the*, pronunciato /ðə/, con le parole che cominciano per vocali consonantiche /j/.

a university /ə ˌjuːnɪ'vɜːsətɪ/
the university /ðə ˌjuːnɪ'vɜːsətɪ/

Si usa *an* e *the*, pronunciato /ðiː/, con le parole che cominciano per *h* muta.

an hour /ən 'aʊə(r)/
the hour /ðiː 'aʊə(r)/

2 | **Uso di *a/an***

Per i nomi numerabili e non numerabili, cfr. 107.

a | Si usa *a/an* davanti ai nomi numerabili singolari.

a student   *a book*   *an idea*

Non si usa *a/an* davanti ai nomi numerabili plurali: non si può dire ~~*a students*~~ o ~~*an ideas*~~. Di norma si usa *a/an* nemmeno davanti ai nomi non numerabili: non si può dire ~~*a water*~~ o ~~*a music*~~ (ma cfr. 107.1–2).

Non si usano i nomi numerabili singolari da soli, senza *a/an*, *the*, *my*, *this* ecc.

I'm a student. (Non: ~~*I'm student.*~~)

b | Si usa *a/an* quando chi ascolta o legge non sa con precisione a chi o che cosa ci si riferisce.

There is a book on the table. (Non si sa quale libro.)
He met a girl last night. She works in a bank. (Non si sa né quale ragazza né quale banca.)

Si usa *a/an* per dire che lavoro fa una persona o com'è una cosa.

I'm an architect.   *He's a vegetarian.*   *It was a good film.*

3 | **Uso di *the***

Per i nomi numerabili e non numerabili, cfr. 107.

a | Si usa *the* sia con i nomi numerabili singolari e plurali che con i nomi non numerabili.

the man   *the shoes*   *the water*

b | Si usa *the* quando chi ascolta o legge sa esattamente a chi o che cosa ci si riferisce:

■ Si usa *the* per parlare di persone o cose che sono già state introdotte nel discorso.

I met a girl and a boy. I didn't like the boy much, but the girl was very nice.
My father bought a shirt and some shoes. The shoes were quite expensive.

■ Si usa *the* quando si indica chi o che cosa si intende.

Who is the man over there talking to Sue?

■ Si usa *the* quando è chiaro dal contesto a chi o che cosa ci si riferisce.

'Where's Simon?'   'He's in the bathroom.' (= nel bagno di questa casa)
Are you hot? I'll open the window. (= la finestra di questa stanza)
I got into a taxi. The driver asked me where I wanted to go. (= l'autista del tassì che ho preso)

■ Si usa *the* con nomi che indicano cose uniche in nature p.es. *the sun*, *the sky*, *the earth*, *the world*.

I enjoy lying in the sun.
Would you like to travel round the world?

ESERCIZIO 108A

Metti le parole nella colonna giusta: A o B.

A	B
a e *the* /ðə/	*an* e *the* /ði:/
clock	orange

~~clock~~	aunt	sandwich	house	school	examination
~~orange~~	old car	dog	hospital	onion	ice-cream
envelope	university	game	hour	umbrella	

ESERCIZIO 108B

Aggiungi *a* o *an* se necessario.

Esempi:

I'd like *a* hamburger, please.
Sarah and Simon are —— students.

1 There's ____ post office in West Street.
2 I've got ____ envelope, but I haven't got ____ stamp.
3 We ate ____ cheese and drank ____ wine.
4 Can you see those two men? They're ____ policemen.
5 Would you like ____ cup of tea?
6 I saw ____ very good film on TV last night.

ESERCIZIO 108C

Completa le frasi con *a, an* o *the*.

Esempio:

The Queen of England lives in Buckingham Palace in London.

1 Who is ____ best footballer in ____ world?
2 My brother works in ____ large garage in Brighton. He's ____ engineer.
3 Did you enjoy ____ party you went to on Saturday?
4 ____ earth moves round ____ sun.
5 I had ____ cup of coffee and some toast for breakfast this morning. ____ coffee was delicious.
6 Could you switch off ____ TV? Nobody is watching it.
7 'What's ____ capital of India?' 'Delhi.'
8 'What do you think of Lynne?' 'She's ____ extremely nice person.'

109　Parlando in generale: omissione dell'articolo o *a/an*

1

Quando si parla di qualcosa in generale si usano i nomi numerabili al plurale e quelli non numerabili senza *the*.

***Shoes** are expensive.* (= le scarpe in generale)
***Milk** is good for you.* (= il latte in generale)

Quando si parla di qualcosa in particolare si usa *the*.

*These are **the shoes** which I bought last week.* (= le scarpe che ho comprato la scorsa settimana)
*Could you pass **the milk**, please?* (= il latte che è sul tavolo)

Altri esempi:

GENERALE	PARTICOLARE
*I like **horses**.*	*Look at **the horses** in that field.*
***Life** isn't easy.*	*I've got a book about **the life** of J. F. Kennedy.*
*He only cares about **money**.*	*Where is **the money** I gave you yesterday?*

Non è sempre facile sapere se qualcosa è inteso in senso generale o particolare. Per esempio:

GENERALE	PARTICOLARE
*I enjoy talking to **old people**.* (= le persone anziane in generale)	*Do you know **the old people** sitting over there?* (= quelle persone anziane sedute laggiù)

2   Si può parlare di qualcosa in generale usando *a/an* (con il significato di 'qualsiasi') con un nome numerabile al singolare.

*A **vegetarian** doesn't eat meat.*
*An **architect** designs buildings.*

ESERCIZIO 109A

Aggiungi *the* quando è necessario.

I find ⁔ history an interesting subject.
We studied *the* history of the Spanish Civil War at school.

1 Andrew hates ＿＿ examinations.
2 How did you get on in ＿＿ examination yesterday?
3 Do you take ＿＿ sugar in ＿＿ coffee?
4 'Where is ＿＿ coffee I bought?' 'It's in ＿＿ kitchen.'
5 I'm a vegetarian, I don't eat ＿＿ meat or ＿＿ fish.
6 I'll put ＿＿ shopping away. Shall I put ＿＿ meat into ＿＿ freezer?
7 Do you like ＿＿ English beer?
8 Do you think ＿＿ love is the most important thing in ＿＿ life?

ESERCIZIO 109B

Riscrivi queste frasi usando *a/an* come nell'esempio.

Esempio:

Carpenters make things from wood.
A carpenter makes things from wood.

1 Florists sell flowers.
2 Children need love.
3 Corkscrews take corks out of bottles.
4 Large cars are expensive to run.
5 Teetotallers don't drink alcohol.

110   Parlando in generale: *the*

1	***The* + nome**
a	Talvolta si usa *the* con un nome numerabile singolare per parlare di qualcosa in generale. Questo, per esempio, con i nomi di animali, fiori e piante.

The dolphin *is an intelligent animal.*
The orchid *is a beautiful flower.*

(*the dolphin* = i delfini in generale; *the orchid* = le orchidee in generale)

b	Si usa *the* in senso generale anche con i nomi di strumenti musicali e di invenzioni scientifiche.

She can play **the guitar** *and* **the saxophone.**
Marconi invented **the radio.**

c	Alcuni nomi comuni, usati con *the*, assumono un significato generale p.es. *the town, the country(side), the sea(side), the mountains, the rain, the wind, the sun(shine), the snow.*

I enjoy going for long walks in **the country.**
They often go to **the mountains** *at weekends.*
I like the sound of **the rain.**

d	Si usa anche *the cinema* e *the theatre* con significato generale.

Which do you prefer, **the cinema** *or* **the theatre?**

2	***The* + aggettivo**
a	Si può usare *the* davanti ad alcuni aggettivi p.es. *young, old, rich, poor, blind* con significato generale.

The young *should listen to* **the old.**

(*the young* = i giovani in generale; *the old* = i vecchi in generale)

b	Si usa *the* anche davanti ad alcuni aggettivi di nazionalità p.es. *English, Italian, French, Swiss, Japanese* per indicare 'le persone di quella nazione'.

The English *drink a lot of tea.*

Nota che questi aggettivi sostantivati terminano tutti in *-sh* (p.es. *the English, the Irish*), *-ch* (p.es. *the French, the Dutch*), o *-ese* (p.es. *the Japanese, the Chinese*).

Con altre nazionalità, indicate dall'aggettivo sostantivato al plurale terminante in *-s*, si può usare *the* oppure ometterlo p.es. *(the) Indians, (the) Germans.*

ESERCIZIO 110A

Completa ogni frase usando *the* e il nome più adatto del riquadro.

Esempio:

The blue whale is the largest animal in the world.

> piano   radio   tulip   sea
> ~~blue whale~~   country   swan

1 ___ is a large white bird with a long neck.
2 Do you often listen to that programme on ___?
3 My grandmother has lived in a small village in ___ all her life.
4 ___ has a bell-shaped flower.
5 Chopin wrote a lot of music for ___.
6 Do you ever go swimming in ___?

ESERCIZIO 110B

Come ci si riferisce a queste persone? Usa
the + gli aggettivi del riquadro.

Esempio:

people who are unable to hear
the deaf

> blind   sick   ~~deaf~~   unemployed   dead

1 people who are no longer alive
2 people who have no jobs
3 people who cannot see
4 people who are unwell

ESERCIZIO 110C

Come si chiamano i popoli di queste nazioni?

Esempio:

Portugal
the Portuguese

1 Britain
2 Australia
3 Spain
4 France
5 Greece

111 Nomi comuni senza articolo

1 *School, the school, church, the church* ecc.

a Spesso si usano i seguenti nomi senza articolo.

> school   university   college
> hospital   prison   church   bed

*Maria goes to **school** every morning.*
*I studied history at **university**.*
*Mr Woods has gone into **hospital**.*
*John has been in **prison** for three years.*
*I think I'll go to **bed** early tonight.*

Si usano questi nomi senza articolo quando si considera la funzione del luogo. Confronta:

*I think I'll go to **bed** early tonight.* (per dormire)	*There are some shoes under **the bed**.*
*Maria goes to **school** every morning.* (per studiare)	***The school** was painted last month.*
*Mr Woods has gone into **hospital**.* (per cure mediche)	*Sarah met Simon outside **the hospital**.*

b Normalmente *work* e *home* si usano senza articolo.

*What time do you usually go to **work**?*
*Would you like to stay at **home** this evening?*

2 **Mezzi di trasporto**

Si usa *by car/bus/train/plane* ecc. senza articolo, per indicare il mezzo di trasporto.

*I usually go to school **by car**.*
*We went to Rome **by train**.*

Si dice anche *on foot* (= a piedi) p.es. *I came home **on foot**.*

3 **Pasti**

Normalmente non si usa l'articolo con i nomi dei pasti.

*What time do you usually have **breakfast**?*
*When would you like to have **dinner**?*

Però si usa *the* quando segue una specificazione p.es. *I enjoyed **the dinner** we had last night.*

Si può anche dire *a/the meal* p.es. *We had **a meal** on the plane.* Si usa *a/an* anche quando *breakfast/lunch/dinner* ecc. sono preceduti da un aggettivo.

*They had **a large breakfast**.*

ESERCIZIO 111A

Aggiungi *the* quando è necessario.

Esempi:

Mrs Woods goes to —— church every Sunday.
There is a cemetery behind *the* church.

1 What time does Annie normally go to ____ school?
2 They are painting ____ school at the moment.
3 I went to ____ bed at 10 o'clock last night.
4 I was lying on ____ bed reading a book.
5 Kate arrives ____ home from ____ work at about 6.00 every evening.
6 Did you go to ____ work by ____ bus or on ____ foot yesterday?
7 Sue went to ____ prison to visit John last month.
8 My mother has gone into ____ hospital for an operation.
9 The ABC cinema is opposite ____ hospital.
10 I usually have coffee and toast for ____ breakfast.

Nota   –Per le espressioni temporali con e senza articolo p.es. *in the* morning, *at* night, *on* Monday, *in (the)* summer, cfr. 169.

112 Nomi geografici con e senza *the*

1

a

Nomi geografici senza *the*	
Normalmente non si usa *the* con i nomi di:	
continenti	*Africa Europe Australia*
nazioni, stati, regioni ecc.	*England Spain Brazil California Hampshire*
città, paesi e villaggi	*Sydney Tokyo Bilbao*
isole singole	*Crete Long Island*
laghi	*Lake Michigan Lake Geneva*
monti	*Mount Everest Mount Fuji*
strade	*Oxford Street North Road*

b Però si usa *the* con questi nomi quando essi comprendono un nome numerabile p.es. *union, republic, states, kingdom, isle.*

the Soviet **Union**   **the** United **States**   **the** United **Kingdom**

c Si usa *the* anche con i nomi geografici plurali p.es. **the** *Netherlands,* **the** *West Indies,* **the** *Alps.*

d | Si usa *the* anche con una serie di altri nomi geografici p.es. *the North/South Pole,*
the Arctic/Antarctic, the Middle East, the Far East, the Costa Brava, the Ruhr.

2 | **Nomi geografici con *the***

a | Normalmente si usa *the* con nomi di:

oceani e mari	*the Pacific* *the Mediterranean*
fiumi	*the Mississippi* *the Nile*
canali	*the Panama Canal* *the Suez Canal*
deserti	*the Sahara* *the Kalahari*
arcipelaghi	*the Canaries* *the West Indies*
alberghi, cinema	*the Plaza Hotel* *the Cannon Cinema*
gallerie, locali	*the Prado Museum* *the Black Cat Club*
ristoranti, pub	*the Hard Rock Café* *the Swan (pub)*

b | Però non si usa *the* con alberghi, ristoranti ecc. che prendono il nome del
proprietario + *'s.*

Macy's Hotel (Non: ~~the Macy's Hotel~~)   *Brown's* (Non: ~~the Brown's~~)

Questi nomi sono spesso scritti senza apostrofo (') p.es. *Lloyds Bank, Woolworths.*

Non si usa *the* con le chiese che portano il nome di un santo + *'s.*

St Peter's Church   *St Paul's Cathedral*   *(St = Saint)*

c | Si usa *the* con i nomi seguiti da *of.*

the Statue of Liberty   *the Bank of Scotland*
the University of London (o: *London University*)

ESERCIZIO 112A

Rispondi alle domande usando *the* se necessario. Si possono trovare le risposte tra
parentesi!

Esempi:

Which is the longest river in Europe? (GOVAL)   *the Volga*
What's the capital of India? (HELDI)   *Delhi*

1 What's the capital of Australia? (BRECARAN)
2 Which country has the largest population in the world? (NICAH)
3 Which is the largest city in the world? (EXCOMI YICT)
4 Which is the largest desert in the world? (HAAARS)
5 In which state of the USA is Los Angeles? (FLIARIACON)
6 Which is the largest lake in the world? (KEAL PERSOIRU)
7 Which is the largest ocean in the world? (AIPFCIC)
8 Which is the highest mountain in the world? (TUMON STEERVE)
9 Which are the highest mountains in Europe? (LAPS)

ESERCIZIO 112B

Aggiungi *the* se necessario.

Esempio:

The Louvre Museum is in ══ Paris.

1 Ron Lewis was born in ___ Manchester, but he lives in ___ Bristol now. He's a lecturer at ___ University of Bristol.
2 ___ Luigi's restaurant is between ___ Albany Hotel and ___ Jimmy's Wine Bar in ___ Cambridge Road.
3 When we were in ___ Rome we visited ___ St Peter's Church, ___ Castle of St Angelo and ___ National Roman Museum.

113 Riepilogo degli articoli: *a/an, the* o loro omissione

ESERCIZIO 113A

Aggiungi *a, an* o *the* se necessario.

Esempi:

We saw *an* interesting film at *the* cinema last night.
I start ══ work at 9 o'clock every morning.

1 ___ Soviet Union is ___ biggest country in ___ world.
2 Have you ever been to ___ St Peter's Square in ___ Rome?
3 ___ weather was lovely when I woke up yesterday morning; ___ sun was shining and there was ___ beautiful blue sky.
4 My sister works in ___ large hospital in ___ London. She's ___ doctor.
5 Who was ___ woman you were talking to just now?
6 'Where's Kate?' 'She's in ___ living room.'
7 What time do you usually have ___ lunch?
8 Do you prefer cooking with ___ gas or ___ electricity?
9 We visited ___ Prado Museum when we were in ___ Madrid.
10 What time does Andrew finish ___ school?
11 There are 20 classrooms in ___ school.
12 Who invented ___ telescope?
13 How long have you been looking for ___ work?
14 Did you go to ___ Scotland by ___ car or by ___ train?
15 ___ Japanese export a lot of cars.
16 Sue and Frank have got two children; ___ girl and ___ boy. ___ girl is ___ student and ___ boy is ___ engineer.
17 ___ Giovannis' restaurant is next to ___ Midland Bank in ___ Bath Road.
18 Are you interested in ___ politics?
19 ___ Atlantic Ocean is larger than ___ Indian Ocean.
20 ___ Mont Blanc is higher than ___ Mount Etna.
21 Sue's brother is ill in ___ hospital.
22 The government plan to help ___ poor and ___ unemployed.

114 Espressioni di quantità: schema generale

Per parlare di quantità si usano espressioni come:

some, any (cfr. 115)	*all, every, each* (cfr. 118)
much, many, a lot, (a) little, (a) few (cfr. 116)	*both, either, neither* (cfr. 119)
no, none (cfr. 117)	*more, most, half*

1 Queste espressioni (eccetto *none, a lot, half*) possono essere usate direttamente davanti a un nome.

There are **some eggs** in the fridge.   There are **no letters** for you today.
We haven't got **any milk**.   **Both films** were very good.

2 Queste espressioni (eccetto *no, every*) possono essere usate davanti a *of* + *the, her, your, this* ecc. + un nome.

I've finished writing **some of the letters**.
Can **either of your parents** speak French?

Queste espressioni (eccetto *no, every*) possono essere usate davanti a *of* + un pronome complemento p.es. *them, us, it*.

Not all of these books are mine. **Some of them** are Peter's.
Neither of us saw the film.

Dopo *all, half, both* si può omettere *of* se questo precede *the, her, my, your, this* ecc.

I switched off **all (of) the lights**.
Half (of) my friends are on holiday at the moment.
I enjoyed **both (of) the films**.

Ma dopo *all, half, both* non si può omettere *of* se questo precede un pronome complemento p.es. *them, us, it*.

'Have you read these books?'   'Not **all of them**.' (Non: ~~... all them~~.)
I haven't finished my homework. I've done about **half of it**. (Non: ~~... half it~~.)
She invited **both of us** to the party. (Non: ~~... both us ...~~)

Si può usare anche *every one of* davanti a *the, her, my* ecc. o davanti a un pronome complemento.

Every one of the students passed the exam.
I've read some of those books, but not **every one of them**.

3 Queste espressioni (eccetto *no, every*) possono essere usate anche da sole, senza il nome.

If you want some coffee, I'll make **some**.
'Were there a lot of people on the train?'   'No, not **many**.'

Però, invece di *all* e *each* da soli, si usa spesso *all of* + un pronome complemento p.es. *them, it*, ecc. e *each one*.

I like some Elvis Presley records, but not **all of them**.
They've got three children and **each one** goes to a different school.

Anche *every one* può essere usato da solo.

I've read some of these books, but not **every one**.

ESERCIZIO 114A

Scegli l'espressione giusta.

Esempio:

I've finished ~~most~~/most of my homework.

1 Not all/~~all of~~ birds can fly.
2 The teacher interviewed each/~~each of~~ student in turn.
3 I've heard ~~some~~/some of those records, but not ~~all~~/all of them.
4 I can't lend you any/~~any of~~ money because I haven't got any/~~any of~~.
5 Most/~~Most of~~ people like Kate.
6 ~~Neither~~/Neither of my parents will be at home this evening.
7 ~~Neither~~/Neither of these jackets fits me properly.
8 'How much/~~much of~~ coffee have we got?' 'Not a lot/~~a lot of~~.'
9 A few/A few of Simon's friends went to the concert, but not many/~~many of~~.
10 Are there many/~~many of~~ museums in Brighton?
11 We tried several chemists' and ~~every~~/every one of them was closed.
12 He spends ~~most~~/most of his time watching TV.
13 My sister has read nearly every/~~every one of~~ book in the library.
14 I answered each/~~each of~~ question carefully.
15 Do ~~either~~/either of these books belong to you?
16 We haven't painted the whole house yet, but we've done about ~~half~~/half of it.
17 They've got five children and ~~each of~~/each one is quite different.

115   *Some* e *any*

1 Si usa *some* e *any* con i nomi numerabili plurali e con i nomi non numerabili per parlare di quantità indefinite:

some letters   **any** letters
some money   **any** money

2 In generale si usa *some* nelle frasi affermative, *any* in quelle negative.

*There are **some** letters for you.*   *There aren't **any** letters for you.*
*I've got **some** money.*   *I haven't got **any** money.*

Ma cfr. 3, 4 e 6 di seguito.

3 Si usa *any* dopo espressioni di significato negativo come *without, never, seldom, rarely, hardly.*

*I found a taxi **without any** trouble.*
*You **never** do **any** homework.*
*There are **hardly any** eggs left.*

4 Si può usare sia *some* che *any* dopo *if.*

*If you need **some**/**any** money, tell me.*

5 | Di norma si usa *any* nelle domande cosiddette 'a risposta aperta', quando cioè non si prevede la risposta.

*Have you got **any** writing paper?*
*Is there **any** tea in the cupboard?*

Spesso però si usa *some* quando ci si aspetta una risposta positiva.

*Have you got **some** paper I could have, please?* (Penso che tu abbia della carta; mi aspetto quindi che tu dica di sì.)

Si usa *some* nelle domande anche quando si vuole incoraggiare una risposta positiva, per esempio in caso di richieste e offerte.

*'Can you let me have **some** paper?'   'How much do you want?'*
*'Would you like **some** more tea?'   'Oh, yes, please.'*

6 | Si usa *any* nel significato di 'non importa quale', 'qualsiasi'.

*You can get the tickets from **any** travel agency.*
*I can come and see you **any** day next week.*

7 | Si usa *some* (con pronuncia enfatizzata) per sottolineare un contrasto.

***Some** people like lying in the sun, others don't.*

ESERCIZIO 115A

Completa le frasi con *some* o *any*. Talvolta è possibile usare entrambi.

Esempio:

He hasn't got *any* brothers or sisters.

1 There are ____ people outside who want to see you.
2 I like ____ water sports, but not all of them.
3 Can you buy ____ butter when you go to the shops? There's hardly ____ left.
4 'Could I have ____ more coffee, please?' 'Yes, of course.'
5 'I haven't got ____ money.'   'Would you like me to lend you ____?'

6 If you need ____ more information, please ask me.
7 Phone me ____ time you like tomorrow. I'll be at home all day.
8 I've done ____ revision for the exams, but not much.
9 ____ museums are worth visiting, but others aren't.
10 Tell me if you want ____ help.

Nota –Per *some* e *any*, cfr. anche 114.
–*Some time* significa 'in un qualche momento' p.es. *Let's meet **some time** next week*; *sometimes* significa 'qualche volta' p.es. *We **sometimes** meet after school.*
–La differenza tra *something* e *anything*, *somebody/someone* e *anybody/anyone* è come quella tra *some* e *any*. Cfr. 125.

116 *Much, many, a lot of, (a) little, (a) few*

1 Si usa *much* e *(a) little* con i nomi non numerabili, *many* e *(a) few* con i nomi numerabili plurali.

much milk **much** rice	**many** cars **many** books
(a) little wine **(a) little** sugar	**(a) few** jobs **(a) few** eggs

Si usa *a lot of, lots of* e *plenty of* sia con i nomi non numerabili che con i nomi numerabili plurali.

a lot of milk	**a lot of** cars
lots of rice	**lots of** books
plenty of wine	**plenty of** jobs

Nota: *a lot/lots* = una grande quantità; *plenty* = più che sufficiente.

2 *Much, many, a lot (of)*

Si usa *much* e *many* per lo più nelle frasi interrogative e negative.

*How **much** milk have we got?*	*We haven't got **much** milk.*
*Is there **much** rice left?*	*There isn't **much** rice left.*
*Has he got **many** books?*	*He hasn't got **many** books.*

Nelle frasi affermative si usa, di norma, *a lot (of), lots (of)* e *plenty (of)*, non *much* o *many*.

*We've got **a lot of** milk.* (Non: *We've got **much** milk.*)
*There's **lots of** rice left.* (Non: *There is **much** rice left.*)
*He's got **plenty** of books.* (Non è consueto dire: *He's got **many** books.*)

Spesso, però, *much* e *many* vengono usati in frasi affermative, quando sono preceduti da *too, as, so* e *very*.

*We've got far **too much** milk.*
*Take **as much** rice as you want.*
*I've got **so many** jobs to do today.*
*We enjoyed the party **very much**.*

3 *(A) little, (a) few*

A little e *a few* indicano concetti positivi. Il primo significa 'poco, ma sufficiente', il secondo 'pochi, ma sufficienti'.

*There's still **a little** work to do before we go home.* (= un po' di lavoro, poco, ma abbastanza)
*The exam was extremely difficult, but **a few** students passed it.* (= pochi, ma in numero soddisfacente)

Little e *few* senza *a* esprimono concetti negativi. Il primo significa 'poco, quasi niente', il secondo 'pochi, quasi nessuno'.

*There's **little** work left to do. We've already finished most of it.* (= poco lavoro, quasi niente)
*The exam was extremely difficult and **few** students passed it.* (= quasi nessuno)

Little e *few* (senza *a*) sono piuttosto formali. Nell'inglese di tutti i giorni si preferisce usare *not much, not many, only a little, only a few* o *hardly any* (= quasi nessuno).

*There isn't **much** time left.*
***Hardly any** students passed the exam.*

Very little e *very few* sono invece abbastanza frequenti nell'inglese di tutti i giorni.

*I've got **very little** money.*
***Very few** people went to the football match.*

ESERCIZIO 116A

Completa le frasi usando *much, many, a lot (of), a little, a few*. Qualche volta è possibile usare più di una espressione.

Esempi:

There are so *many* jobs to do today and we haven't got *much/a lot of* time.
There were only *a few* people in the cinema.

1 I know ____ people in London, but not many.
2 We've got ____ coffee left, but not much.
3 He earns ____ money in his job.
4 She's got ____ classical music records.
5 We had ____ wine with our meal, but not very much.

6 Have we got ____ potatoes left?
7 How ____ money did you spend on holiday?
8 I didn't enjoy the party on Saturday very ____. There were far too ____ people there, and there wasn't ____ food or drink, so everybody was hungry and thirsty.

ESERCIZIO 116B

Scegli l'espressione giusta.

Esempio:

I've got *a little/~~little~~* money, so I could lend you some if you want.

1 I'm sorry, but I've got very *~~a little~~/little* money at the moment. I'm afraid I can't lend you any.
2 He has very *a few/few* friends and he gets rather lonely.
3 She has *a few/few* friends in London and she's very happy there.
4 It is an extremely poor country: it has *a few/few* natural resources and *a little/ little* good agricultural land.
5 Would you like *a little/little* more wine? There's still *a little/little* left in the bottle.
6 It won't take long to drive into town. There's very *a little/little* traffic on the road at this time of the day.
7 I think Peter went out *a few/few* minutes ago.
8 It's a very boring little town; there's very *a little/little* to do there.

117 *No e none*

1 | Si usa *no* (= 'not a', 'not any') come aggettivo.

*There's **no lock** on the door.*
*There are **no letters** for you today.*
*We've got **no milk**.*

Si può usare *no* davanti ai nomi numerabili singolari p.es. *lock*, o plurali
p.es. *letters*, ma non davanti ai nomi non numerabili p.es. *milk*.

No è più enfatico di *not a* e *not any* p.es. *There isn't **a** lock on the door. There aren't
any letters for you today.*

2 | *None* è un pronome, si usa pertanto senza nome.

'Are there any letters for me today?'   *'No, **none**, I'm afraid.'*
'How much milk have we got?'   *'**None**.'*

Davanti a *my, this, the* ecc. o a un pronome complemento p.es. *us, them*, si usa *none
of*.

***None of my** friends have seen the film.*
***None of the** photographs were very good.*
***None of us** have any money.*

Quando si usa *none of* con un nome plurale, il verbo può essere al singolare o al
plurale.

*None of my **friends have/has** seen the film.*

Il verbo al singolare è più formale.

ESERCIZIO 117A

Completa le frasi usando *no* o *none*.

Esempio:

We really must hurry. There's *no* time to lose.

1 —— of my family are rich.
2 Unfortunately, there were —— tickets left for the concert.
3 He's so serious. He's got —— sense of humour.
4 I've got —— idea what I'm going to do when I leave school.
5 —— of the students failed the examination.
6 I haven't got any money at the moment, —— at all.
7 My friends and I would all like to go to the concert, but —— of us has got a
   ticket.

118 *All, every, everybody, everything, whole*

1

All e *every*

Every ha un significato simile a *all*; vuol dire 'tutti senza eccezione'. Confronta:

All *the students in the class passed the exam.*
Every *student in the class passed the exam.* (= tutti gli studenti senza eccezione)

Nota che *all* si può usare con parole al plurale, ma *every* soltanto con parole al singolare.

All children like *playing.*   **Every child likes** *playing.*

Si può usare *all* ma non *every* con i nomi non numerabili.

Do you like **all** *pop music?* (Non: ~~... every pop music?~~)

2

All, everybody, everything

a

Normalmente non si usa *all* da solo, senza un nome, nel significato di *everybody* o *everyone.* Confronta:

All the people *stopped talking.*	**Everybody** *stopped talking.* (Non: ~~All stopped ...~~)
I have invited **all the students** *in my class to the party.*	*I have invited* **everyone** *in my class to the party.* (Non: ~~... all in my class ...~~)

b

All non viene usato spesso nel significato di *everything.*

Everything *is so expensive these days.* (Non: ~~All is so expensive these days.~~)
Have you got **everything**? (Non: ~~Have you got all?~~)

Ma si può usare *all* con il significato di *everything* nella costruzione: *all (that)* + frase relativa.

Have you got **all (that) you need**?
He's forgotten **all (that) I told him.**

Si usa *all* anche nell'espressione *all about.*

Tell me **all about** *yourself.*

Si può usare *all* anche per dire 'l'unica cosa che' o 'nient'altro'.

I'm not hungry. **All** *I want is a cup of tea.*

3

All e *whole*

a

Whole significa 'intero' o 'ogni parte di'. Di norma si usa con i nomi numerabili singolari.

I didn't see the **whole film**. *I missed the first part.* (= tutto il film, dall'inizio alla fine)
I've spent my **whole salary** *on clothes last month.* (= tutto lo stipendio, l'intero stipendio)

Si usa sempre *the, my, this* ecc. davanti a *whole* + un nome singolare p.es. **the** *whole film*, **my** *whole salary.*

Si può usare *the, my, this* ecc. anche con *all*, ma cambia l'ordine delle parole. Confronta:

all *the film*   *the* **whole** *film*
all *my salary*   *my* **whole** *salary*

b | Si può usare *a whole* davanti a un nome (singolare).

*Mike ate **a whole chicken** himself.*

c | Di norma non si usa *whole* con i nomi non numerabili.

*We've finished **all the coffee**.* (Non: ~~... the whole coffee.~~)

4 | ***All day, every day*, ecc.**

Si usa *all* con alcuni nomi numerabili singolari p.es. *day, morning, week, year* per dire 'tutto', 'intero'; si usa *every* con gli stessi nomi per dire 'ogni'. Confronta:

*I work hard **all day**.* (= tutto il giorno)   *I work hard **every day**.* (= ogni giorno)

Si può usare *the whole day/morning* ecc. invece di *all day/morning* ecc.

*We've been waiting **the whole morning/all morning**.*

The whole è più forte di *all* in questo caso.

ESERCIZIO 118A

Completa le frasi usando *all, every, everybody, everything*. Talvolta è possibile usare due espressioni.

Esempio:

Have you spent *all* the money I gave you?

1 I tried ____ key in the lock, but none of them fitted.
2 ____ enjoyed the film except Peter.
3 I'm really tired. ____ I want to do is go to bed.
4 Listen to me. I can explain ____.
5 Has Sarah told you ____ about her holiday in Austria?
6 It was late when Simon arrived home and ____ was asleep.
7 Did you remember to switch off ____ the lights?
8 I believe ____ word he says.
9 Have you packed ____ into this suitcase?
10 I learn't ____ I know about physics at school.

ESERCIZIO 118B

Completa le frasi usando *all (the)* o *the whole*. Talvolta è possibile usare entrambe le espressioni.

Esempi:

We've finished *all the* wine.
I didn't see *all the/the whole* film.

1 ____ family went on holiday together.
2 Have you spent ____ money I gave you?
3 The tap was dripping ____ night.
4 Did you understand ____ information I gave you?

ESERCIZIO 118C

Scegli l'espressione giusta.

Esempio:

My favourite TV programme is on at 8.30 ~~all~~/ *every* Tuesday evening.

1 What time do you normally get up *all/every* morning?
2 The weather was terrible yesterday, so we spent *all/every* day at home.
3 Peter was late for work *all/every* day last week.
4 My neighbours had a party last night and the noise kept me awake *all/every* night.

Nota   –Confronta *every* con *each*: si usa *every* quando si considerano gli individui indistintamente, come parte del gruppo nel suo insieme; si usa *each* quando si considerano gli individui separatamente.

every	***each***
*I asked **every** person in the room the same question.*	***Each** person gave a different answer.*

–Per *all*, *every* e *each*, cfr. anche 114.

119   *Both, either, neither*

1   ***Both***

Si può usare *both* (= 'entrambi', 'sia l'uno che l'altro') davanti a un nome numerabile plurale.

***Both films** were very good.*
*I spoke to **both girls**.*

Si usa *both of* davanti a *the, your, these,* ecc. + un nome numerabile plurale; in questo caso spesso si omette *of.*

***Both (of) the films** were very good.*
*Do **both (of) your parents** like dancing?*

Si usa *both of* davanti ai pronomi complemento plurali *you, us, them*; in questo caso non si può omettere *of.*

*She invited **both of us** to the party.* (Non: ~~... **both us** ...~~)

Si può usare *both* dopo un pronome complemento.

*She invited **us both** to the party.*

2   ***Either* e *neither***

Si può usare *either* (= 'o l'uno o l'altro') e *neither* (= 'né l'uno né l'altro') davanti a un nome numerabile singolare.

*We could meet on Saturday or Sunday. **Either day** is fine with me.*
***Neither road** goes to the station.*

Si usa *either of* e *neither of* davanti a *your, these, the* ecc. + un nome numerabile plurale.

*Can **either of your parents** speak French?*
***Neither of these roads** goes to the station.*

Si usa *either of* e *neither of* anche davanti ai pronomi complemento plurali *you, us, them.*

*Can **either of you** type?*
***Neither of us** went to the party.*

Dopo *neither of* il verbo può essere al singolare o al plurale.

***Neither of** these roads **goes/go** to the station.*
***Neither of** us **is/are** hungry.*

Il verbo al singolare è più frequente nello stile formale.

(N)either ha due pronunce: /ˈnaɪðə(r)/ o /ˈniːðə(r)/.

3   *Both, either* e *neither* fungono inoltre da congiunzioni correlative nelle seguenti costruzioni:

> *both . . . and . . .*
> *either . . . or . . .*
> *neither . . . nor . . .*

*I spoke to **both** Sally **and** Peter.*
*John is **both** thoughtful **and** generous.*
*She **both** speaks Japanese **and** writes it.*

*I don't like **either** football **or** rugby very much.*
*We can **either** stay in **or** go out.*

***Neither** Mrs Woods **nor** her husband were at home.*
*He **neither** apologised **nor** explained.*

ESERCIZIO 119A

Completa le frasi usando *both, both of, either, either of, neither, neither of.* In un caso sono possibili due espressioni.

Esempi:

The tennis match was very exciting. *Both* players were very good.

1 'Have your parents got a car?' 'No, ＿＿ them can drive.'
2 They don't like each other and I made the mistake of inviting them ＿＿ to my party.
3 'What does "ambidextrous" mean?' 'It means being able to use ＿＿ hand with equal skill.'
4 'Which of these shirts do you prefer?' 'I don't really like ＿＿ them very much.'
5 'What's the capital of Switzerland, Geneva or Zurich?' '＿＿. It's Berne.'
6 Simon had a very bad accident when he was younger. He fell from a tree and broke ＿＿ his legs.

ESERCIZIO 119B

Collega questi concetti completando le frasi.

Esempio:

Sue plays the piano. And she sings.
Sue both *plays the piano and sings.*

1 We could eat now. Or we could wait until
later. We could either ____ .
2 My father couldn't read Arabic. And he couldn't
write it. My father could neither ____ .
3 Ken didn't know the address. And Kate didn't
know the address. Neither Ken ____ .

4 I didn't see his sister. And I didn't see his
brother. I didn't see either ____ .
5 Simon passed the exam easily. And Sarah
passed the exam easily. Both Simon ____ .
6 The journey wasn't very comfortable. And it
wasn't very interesting. The journey was
neither ____ .
7 My new flat is larger than my old flat. And it
is closer to my office. My new flat is both ____ .

Nota –Per *both, either* e *neither* cfr. anche 114; per *Neither do I, I don't either,* ecc. cfr. 151.

120 Pronomi personali

1 I pronomi personali sono:

	PRONOMI SOGGETTO		PRONOMI COMPLEMENTO	
	SINGOLARE	PLURALE	SINGOLARE	PLURALE
1ª persona	*I*	*we*	*me*	*us*
2ª persona	*you*	*you*	*you*	*you*
3ª persona	*he* *she* *it*	*they*	*him* *her* *it*	*them*

2 Si usano i pronomi personali al posto dei nomi quando è chiaro di chi o che cosa si
sta parlando.

a Si usano i pronomi personali soggetto come soggetti dei verbi.

'Where's Simon?'   'He's in the kitchen.'
Sue didn't go out last night. **She** *stayed at home.*

Nota che in inglese, di norma, il soggetto della frase viene sempre espresso.

'Where's Simon?'   'He's in the kitchen.' (Non: ~~*Is in the kitchen.*~~)

b Si usano i pronomi complemento come complementi dei verbi e delle preposizioni.

verbo + pronome complemento	preposizione + pronome complemento

Help **me.**
I like **him.**
Can you see **it?**

I've written to **her.**
Look at **them.**
They're waiting for **us.**

Si possono usare i pronomi complemento anche come complementi indiretti.

*Can you lend **me** some money?*
*I'll send **him** a postcard.*

Si possono usare i pronomi complemento dopo *than* e *as* nei comparativi.

*I'm older than **him**.*
*She isn't as tall as **me**.*

Nello stile formale si usa però il pronome soggetto + il verbo.

*I'm older than **he is**.*

Si possono usare i pronomi complemento dopo il verbo *be*.

*'Who's there?'   'It's **me**.'*

In questo caso si possono usare anche i pronomi soggetto, p.es. *It's I*, ma si tratta di una costruzione molto formale e poco frequente.

Si usano i pronomi complemento anche nelle risposte formate semplicemente da un pronome.

*'Who has got my book?'   '**Me**.'* (Non: ~~I~~)

3   Si usa:

a   *I/me* per la persona che parla.

b   *we/us* per le persone che parlano.

c   *you* per la persona o le persone che ascoltano.

d   *he/him* per la persona e per alcuni animali di sesso maschile di cui si parla.

e   *she/her* per la persona e per alcuni animali di sesso femminile di cui si parla.

f   *it* per la cosa o l'animale di cui si parla, se il sesso non è specificato o importante.

g   *they/them* per le persone o cose di cui si parla.

Cfr. 4–9 di seguito.

4   Si può usare *you* con significato impersonale 'la gente in generale, compresi tu e io'.

***You** can easily lose your way in Rome.*
***You** can drive a car in Britain when you're 17.*

Si può anche usare *one* in questo caso, in particolare nello stile formale.

***One** can easily lose **one's** way in Rome.*

5   Si può usare *they* con significato impersonale 'la gente in generale, esclusi tu e io'.

***They** say she's a good teacher.*

Si usa *they* per riferirsi al governo o alle persone in posizioni di responsabilità.

*'What are the government's plans?'   '**They're** going to increase taxes.'*
***They** say the new motorway will be finished by next April.*

6 | Spesso si usano i pronomi personali plurali *they* e *them* con significato singolare, particolarmente nello stile informale.

*Somebody forgot to lock the door, didn't **they**?*
*If anyone phones for me while I'm out, tell **them** I'll phone **them** back later on.*

In frasi come queste si usa *they* invece di '*he*' o '*she*' e *them* invece di '*him*' o '*her*' (se non si specifica il sesso della persona).

7 | *We* può comprendere o meno chi ascolta. Confronta:

*Why don't **we** go to the cinema this evening? (we comprende chi ascolta)* | *We're going to the cinema this evening. Why don't you come with us? (we non comprende chi ascolta)*

8 | Si può usare *it* per le persone in frasi dove si chiede o dice chi è qualcuno.

*'There's someone at the door. Who is **it**?'   'It's Peter.'*

9 | Si usa *it* come soggetto 'vuoto' in varie espressioni, per esempio riferite alle ore, alle date, al clima.

It's 8 o'clock.
It's the first of June.
*How far is **it** to the next town?*
It's usually very warm here in the summer.

10 | Spesso si comincia una frase con *it* come 'soggetto preliminare' invece dell'infinito con *to* o di *that* + l'indicativo.

*It is interesting **to study** a foreign language.* (Invece di: **To study** *a foreign language is interesting.*)
*It was lucky **that** we didn't miss the bus.* (Invece di: **That** *we didn't miss the bus was lucky.*)

ESERCIZIO 120A

Scegli le risposte giuste.

Esempio:

We/~~Us~~ met Sally yesterday afternoon. She/~~Her~~ came to the cinema with ~~we~~/us.

1 I phoned Sarah last night and gave *she/her* the message.
2 My brother is older than *I/me*, but *he/him* isn't as tall as *I/me* am.
3 'Who wants a cup of coffee?'   '*I/Me*.'
4 'Have you seen Simon today?'   'Yes. *I/Me* saw *he/him* this morning. *He/Him* was going to the swimming pool.'
5 'What did those people want?'   '*They/Them* asked *I/me* to help *they/them*.'

ESERCIZIO 120B

Completa le frasi usando i pronomi del riquadro.

Esempio:

'I'm looking for Andrew. Have you seen *him*?'   'Yes, *he* was here a few minutes ago.'

I	you	he	she	it	we	they
me	you	him	her	it	us	them

1 Peter and I are going out this evening. ＿＿ 're going to the cinema. Would you like to come with ＿＿?
2 Where are my keys? I put ＿＿ on the table a moment ago, but now ＿＿ 've disappeared.
3 ＿＿ 's usually quite cold in New York in the winter.
4 'What did you think of the film, Simon?'   '＿＿ enjoyed ＿＿ very much.'
5 ＿＿ 's strange that Kate didn't come to the meeting.
6 'What do the government plan to do about education?'   '＿＿ say that ＿＿ 're going to build more schools.'
7 ＿＿ aren't allowed to drive a car in Britain until ＿＿ 're 17 years old.
8 If you have any problems, just tell someone and ＿＿ 'll help you.
9 How far is ＿＿ from Madrid to Paris?
10 My sister and I are quite different. ＿＿ 's much more serious than ＿＿ am.

121 Aggettivi e pronomi possessivi

1 Gli aggettivi e i pronomi possessivi sono:

	AGGETTIVI POSSESSIVI		PRONOMI POSSESSIVI	
	SINGOLARE	PLURALE	SINGOLARE	PLURALE
1ª persona	my	our	mine	ours
2ª persona	your	your	yours	yours
3ª persona	his / her / its	their	his / hers / —	theirs

2 Si usa l'aggettivo possessivo davanti a un nome per indicare appartenenza.

*I can't find **my** keys.*
*Sally bought **her** motorbike last year.*

3 | Si usa il pronome possessivo quando il nome è sottinteso.

'Is this Peter's book?'   *'No, it's **mine**.'* (= il mio libro)
*I've got my coat, but Maria can't find **hers**.* (= il suo cappotto)
*Their flat is smaller than **ours**.* (= il nostro appartamento)

4 | ***My own/your own/his own, ecc.***

Si usa *my own/your own/his own*, ecc. per enfatizzare che qualcosa appartiene solo a una persona, non è né condivisa né presa in prestito. Confronta:

*This is **my** office.*	*I've got **my own** office now. I don't share with anyone else.*
*This isn't **my** bicycle.*	*This isn't **my own** bicycle. I only borrowed it.*

Si usa sempre *my/your/his/her* ecc. davanti a *own*. Non si può dire
~~*an own room/book*~~ ecc.

Nota la costruzione: *of my own/of your own/of his own* ecc.

*I've got an office **of my own** now. I don't share with anyone else.*

Si usa *my own/your own*, ecc. per enfatizzare che una persona fa qualcosa da sé invece di farlo fare a qualcun altro. Confronta:

*Clean **your** room.*	*Clean **your own** room! I'm not going to do it for you.*

On my own/on your own, ecc. può voler dire 'da solo' o 'senza aiuto'.

*I don't live **on my own**, I share a flat with two friends.*
*I can't move this table **on my own**. It's too heavy.*

ESERCIZIO 121A

Scegli le espressioni giuste.

Esempio:

Have you seen *my*/~~*mine*~~ coat?

1 We know *their/theirs* telephone number, but they don't know *our/ours*.
2 *My/Mine* car wasn't as expensive as *her/hers*.
3 'How are *your/yours* children?'   'Fine, thanks. How are *your/yours*?'
4 Maria has got *her/hers* suitcase, but *her/hers* friends haven't got *their/theirs*.
5 *Our/Ours* flat isn't as big as *their/theirs*, but *our/ours* is much more comfortable.

ESERCIZIO 121B

Completa le frasi usando *my own, your own, his own, her own*, ecc.

Esempio:

I don't have *my own* telephone yet, so I have to use the public phone.

1 Sarah shares a flat with some friends. She would prefer to have a flat of ____, but she can't afford one.
2 'That isn't ____ camera, is it?'   'No, I borrowed it from my father.'
3 You can wash ____ dirty clothes! I'm not going to wash them for you.
4 We helped them move the piano; they couldn't have done it on ____.
5 Sometimes I'm allowed to use my parents' car, but I wish I had a car of ____.
6 He's always using my shampoo. Why doesn't he buy ____?

Nota –Si può usare *by myself, by yourself*, ecc. invece di *on my own, on your own*, ecc. p.es. *I don't live **by myself**.* Cfr. 122.4.

122 Pronomi riflessivi

1

I pronomi riflessivi sono:

	SINGOLARE	PLURALE
1ª persona	myself	ourselves
2ª persona	yourself	yourselves
3ª persona	himself herself itself	themselves

2

Si usano i pronomi riflessivi quando il soggetto e il complemento oggetto di una frase sono identici.

*I burnt **myself** cooking the dinner.*
***Annie** hurt **herself** when she fell over.*

Nota: *enjoy yourself* = divertiti; *help yourself* (to something) = serviti.

*Did you **enjoy yourself** at the circus?*
***Help yourself** to some more coffee.*

3

Dopo le preposizioni si usano i pronomi complemento p.es. *me*, *him*, invece dei pronomi riflessivi quando è chiaro a chi ci si riferisce. Confronta:

*I'll take some money with **me**.* (E' chiaro che li porterò con me, non con qualcun altro!) | *I'm very angry with **myself**.* (Potrei essere arrabbiato con qualcun altro!)

4

By myself/by yourself, ecc. può voler dire 'da solo' o 'senza aiuto'.

*I don't live **by myself**, I share a flat with two friends.*
*I can't move this table **by myself**. It's too heavy.*

Si usa anche *on my own/on your own*, ecc. con questo significato. (Cfr. 121.4.)

5

Normalmente non si usano i pronomi riflessivi dopo *feel*, *relax* o *concentrate*.

*I **feel** fine.* (Non: ~~.... feel myself fine~~.)
*I must try to **relax**.* (Non: ~~.... relax myself~~.)
*I can't **concentrate**.* (Non: ~~.... concentrate myself~~.)

Normalmente non si usano i pronomi riflessivi per parlare di azioni che uno fa da sé p.es. *wash, shave, dress*.

*Ken got up. Then he **washed**, **shaved** and **dressed**.* (Non: ~~.... washed himself~~, ecc.)

Però si dice *dry myself/yourself*, ecc. p.es. *I got out of the bath and **dried myself**.*

6

Si possono usare i pronomi riflessivi anche per enfatizzare 'proprio quella persona'.

*Nobody helped me build the swimming pool. I built it **myself**.*
*I'm not going to clean your room for you. You clean it **yourself**!*

Quando si usano i pronomi riflessivi a questo proposito, di solito si mettono in fondo alla frase, ma possono anche seguire il soggetto.

*The manager **himself** told me the news.*
*I **myself** prefer golf to tennis.*

7   Confronta *-selves* (p.es. *themselves, ourselves*) con *each other*:

*They're looking at **themselves**.*

*They're looking at **each other**.*

Altri esempi:

*Sue and I can take care of **ourselves**.* (= Sue può badare a se stessa e io a me stesso.)	*Sue and I can take care of **each other**.* (= Sue può avere cura di me e io di lei.)

Si può usare *one another* invece di *each other*.

*They're looking at **one another**.*

Nota però che è preferibile usare *each other* per due persone o cose, e *one another* per più di due. Confronta:

*Chris and Sue often help **each other**.*   *We should all try to help **one another**.*

ESERCIZIO 122A

Completa le frasi usando *myself, yourself, himself, herself, itself, ourselves, yourselves, themselves*.

Esempio:

I taught *myself* to play the guitar; I've never had lessons.

1 Sue's children are too young to look after ____.
2 An elephant hurt ____ when it tried to get out of the zoo yesterday.
3 I couldn't borrow my mother's car last night because she was using it ____.
4 I don't need any help. I can take care of ____.
5 Mr Woods fell over and hurt ____ when he was running for a bus.
6 Would you all like to help ____ to sandwiches and cakes?
7 Sarah and I didn't really enjoy ____ at the disco last night.

ESERCIZIO 122B

Completa ogni frase usando *by* + un pronome riflessivo.

Esempio:

The dog opened the door *by itself.*

1 'Who did you go to the cinema with?'   'Nobody, I went ____.'
2 Since the old lady's husband died, she's been living ____.
3 Did someone help you move all the furniture, or did you do it all ____?
4 They need some help; they can't manage ____.

ESERCIZIO 122C

Mercoledì scorso Sarah è rimasta alzata fino a tardi per preparare un esame.

Sarah spiega cosa le è successo mercoledì sera. Completa quello che dice aggiungendo *myself* se necessario.

'I was really annoyed with *myself* for leaving all my revision to the last moment, so I decided to stay up and work. At first, I felt __1__ fine and I even started to congratulate __2__ on all the work I was doing. But at about 3 o'clock in the morning I started to feel __3__ tired. I went to the kitchen and made __4__ a strong black coffee. Then I went back to work, but I couldn't concentrate __5__. In the end, I started to feel sorry for __6__, so I went to my bedroom, undressed __7__ and went to bed to get some sleep. Then, of course, I couldn't relax __8__ because I couldn't stop thinking about all the work I had to do!'

ESERCIZIO 122D

Completa le frasi usando un pronome riflessivo.

Esempio:

Sally didn't buy that sweater, she made it *herself.*

1 I didn't buy the cake from the shop. I made it ____.
2 'Who built your swimming pool for you?' 'Nobody. We built it ____.'
3 Did someone phone the doctor for you? Or did you phone him ____?
4 'Who told you they were moving?' 'They told me ____.'
5 Mr Mason ____ offered me the job.

ESERCIZIO 122E

Completa le frasi usando *each other* o *-selves.*

Esempio:

My penfriend and I write to *each other* every month.

1 They're good friends. They like ____ very much.
2 Mike and Sue phone ____ every evening.
3 We all enjoyed ____ at the party.
4 A lot of people can take care of ____.

123 Riepilogo dei pronomi personali, dei pronomi e degli aggettivi possessivi e dei pronomi riflessivi

ESERCIZIO 123A

Completa la tabella.

PRONOME PERSONALE		AGGETTIVO	PRONOME	PRONOME
SOGGETTO	COMPLEMENTO	POSSESSIVO	POSSESSIVO	RIFLESSIVO
I	*me*	*my*	____	____
____	____	____	____	*yourself*
he	____	____	____	____
____	*her*	____	____	____
it	____	____	____	____
____	____	____	*ours*	____
____	*you*	____	____	____
they	____	____	____	____

ESERCIZIO 123B

Completa le frasi usando il pronome o l'aggettivo giusto.

Esempi:

Could *you* lend *me* some money? (you | I)
Why didn't *she* ask *us* to help *her*? (she | we | she)
Do *you* ever talk to *yourself* when *you*'re on *your* own? (you | you | you | you)

1 ____ house is much bigger than ____. (they | we)
2 Is this book ____ or ____? (you | I)
3 'Is Lynne going on holiday with ____ friend?' 'No, ____'s going by ____.' (she | she | she)
4 How long have ____ been waiting for ____? (they | we)
5 Don't blame ____; ____ wasn't ____ mistake. (you | it | you)
6 ____ was very angry with ____ for being so stupid. (I | I)
7 ____ was very angry with ____ when ____ broke ____ camera. (he | I | I | he)
8 Someone came to see ____ while ____ were out. ____ told ____ that ____ would be back at 2 o'clock. (you | you | I | they | you)
9 'Who painted ____ flat?' 'Nobody. ____ painted it ____. (you | we | we)
10 ____'s a coincidence that ____ birthday is on the same day as ____. (it | he | her)

124 One(s)

1 Spesso si usa *one* invece di ripetere il nome:

My new flat is much bigger than my old one. (= quello vecchio)
'Which of those girls is your sister?' *'She's the one with the blonde hair.'* (= quella bionda)

Si usa *ones* al posto di un nome numerabile plurale.

I like these shoes more than the other ones. (= le altre)

2 *A/an* viene usato con *one* solo quando precede un aggettivo p.es. *a blue one*, non *a one*. Confronta:

I'm looking for a tie.	*I'm looking for a tie.*
I want a blue one.	*I want one with stripes.*

3 Si può usare *one* dopo gli aggettivi dimostrativi *this*, *that*.

Which picture do you prefer, this one or that one?

Normalmente, però, si usa il plurale *ones* dopo *these* o *those* solo in presenza di un aggettivo p.es. *those black ones*. Confronta:

I like these shoes more than those.	*I like these brown shoes more than those black ones.*

4 Si usa *which one(s)* nelle domande.

I like the green shirt best. Which one do you prefer?

5 Si può usare *one* dopo *each*.

I've got three children, and each one goes to a different school.

6 *One(s)* può sostituire solo i nomi numerabili; con i nomi non numerabili p.es. *milk*, *sugar*, si ripete il nome o, come spesso avviene, lo si omette.

There's some brown sugar in the cupboard, but there isn't any white (sugar).

ESERCIZIO 124A

Completa ogni frase usando *one* o *ones*. Che cosa significa *one(s)* in ciascun caso?

Esempio:

The best road to the centre of town is the *one* on the left.   one = road

1 'Would you like a drink?' 'Oh yes, please, I'd love _____.'
2 My new glasses are much stronger than my old _____.
3 'Which of the women in this photo is your aunt?' 'She's the _____ with the dark hair.'
4 There are two films on TV this evening. Which _____ would you prefer to see?

Nota –Nello stile formale si può usare *one* anche per parlare di persone in generale. Cfr. 120.4

125 *Something, anything, somebody, anybody, ecc.*

1   Si possono formare pronomi indefiniti composti unendo *some, any, no* e *every* con *-thing, -body, -one* e *-where*.

	some	any	no	every
-thing	*something* (qualcosa)	*anything*	*nothing*	*everything*
-body	*somebody* (qualcuno)	*anybody*	*nobody*	*everybody*
-one	*someone* (qualcuno)	*anyone*	*no-one*	*everyone*
-where	*somewhere* (da qualche parte)	*anywhere*	*nowhere*	*everywhere*

2   La differenza tra *something/somebody*, ecc. e *anything/anybody*, ecc. è simile a quella tra *some* e *any*:

a   In generale, si usa *something, somebody*, ecc. nelle frasi affermative, *anything, anybody*, ecc. nelle frasi negative e interrogative.

*I've got **something** to ask you.*
*There's **somebody** at the front door.*

*I **don't** want to do **anything** this evening.*
*I **can't** see **anybody** outside.*

*Have you got **anything** to say?*
*Did **anybody** phone for me?*

b   Si usa però *something, somebody* ecc. nelle frasi interrogative, se ci si aspetta o si sollecita una risposta affermativa, p.es. in caso di richieste o proposte.

*Could I have **something** to eat?*
*Would you like **someone** to help you?*

Per ulteriori dettagli sulla differenza tra *some* e *any*, cfr. 115.

3   Tutti questi pronomi indefiniti composti sono singolari.

***Something** is wrong. What **is** it?*
*There **was nobody** at home when I phoned.*
***Everything** is so expensive these days.*

Talvolta, però, soprattutto nello stile informale, si usano forme plurali come *they, them, their*, per riferirsi ai pronomi indefiniti composti terminanti in *-body* o *-one*, p.es. *somebody/someone, anybody/anyone*.

***Somebody** forgot to lock the door, didn't **they**?*
*If **anybody** phones for me while I'm out, tell **them** I'll phone **them** back later on.*
*Look. **Someone** has left **their** bag on this seat.*

In frasi del genere si usa *they* invece di 'he' o 'she', *them* invece di 'him' o 'her' (se il genere, maschile o femminile, non è specificato).

ESERCIZIO 125A

Completa le frasi usando i pronomi indefiniti composti del riquadro.

something	anything	nothing	everything
somebody	anybody	nobody	everybody
somewhere	anywhere	nowhere	everywhere

Esempio:

Somebody has written in my book.

1 There's ____ in this envelope. It's empty!
2 Why don't we go out ____ for dinner this evening?
3 There's ____ waiting outside to see you. She didn't tell me her name.
4 They've got ____ to live; they're homeless.
5 There isn't ____ watching the TV at the moment.
6 He lost ____ in the fire: his house and all his possessions.

7 Lynne is the only one in the office at the moment. ____ else has gone home.
8 'Shall I make you ____ to eat?'   'Oh, yes, please. I'm really hungry. I've had hardly ____ all day.'
9 It's a secret. ____ knows about it.
10 Have you seen my glasses? I've looked ____ for them, but I can't find them ____.

126   Forma, posizione e ordine degli aggettivi

1   **Forma**

In inglese gli aggettivi hanno una sola forma, che si usa con i nomi sia singolari che plurali.

an *old* man	*old* men
an *old* woman	*old* women
an *old* car	*old* cars

Se un nome viene usato come aggettivo, non cambia al plurale. Confronta:

two hours	a *two-hour* film
three weeks	a *three-week* holiday

2   **Posizione**

a   Gli aggettivi si possono collocare in due posizioni diverse:

■ davanti al nome

a *young* man	*new* shoes
an *empty* house	a *nice* girl

■ dopo i verbi *be, look, appear, seem, feel, taste, smell, sound* (e qualche altro) quando si descrive il soggetto.

He is *young*.	These shoes are *new*.
The house looks *empty*.	She seems *confident*.
That soup smells *good*.	

b | Qualche aggettivo p.es. *asleep, alone, alive, awake, afraid, ill, well* può seguire il verbo, ma non precedere il nome. Per esempio, si può dire *he is **asleep**,* non *an **asleep** man*. Davanti ai nomi si usano altri aggettivi p.es. *sleeping* invece di *asleep, living* invece di *alive, frightened* invece di *afraid, sick* invece di *ill, healthy* invece di *well*.

*a **sleeping** man*   *a **frightened** animal*
***sick** children*   ***healthy** people*

c | In espressioni di misura, normalmente l'aggettivo segue il nome dell'unità di misura.

*He's eighteen years **old**.*   *I'm 1.80 metres **tall**.*

3 | **Ordine**

a | Quando si usano due o più aggettivi, gli aggettivi che descrivono 'opinioni' (p.es. *interesting, beautiful*) normalmente precedono quelli che descrivono 'fatti' (p.es. *new, blue*).

*an **interesting new** film*   *a **beautiful blue** dress*

b | Quando due o più aggettivi relativi a 'fatti' precedono il nome, normalmente vanno messi nell'ordine seguente:

dimensione + età + forma + colore + provenienza + materiale + scopo + NOME

*a **small rubber** ball* (dimensione + materiale)
*a **young Spanish** woman* (età + provenienza)
*a **large round** hat* (dimensione + forma)
***white leather running** shoes* (colore + materiale + scopo)

ESERCIZIO 126A

Come si possono descrivere queste persone e cose?

Esempi:

a child who is four years old   *a four-year-old child*

a journey which takes six hours   *a six-hour journey*

1 a concert which lasts for two hours
2 a man who is fifty years old
3 a delay which lasts for twenty minutes
4 a letter which has ten pages
5 a meeting which lasts for two hours

ESERCIZIO 126B

Quali parole sono aggettivi?

Esempio:

'You look tired.' 'Yes, I don't feel very well.'
Aggettivi: *tired, well*

1 It's a very long book, but it's not at all boring.
2 Were you late for work today?
3 You seem sad. Is something wrong?
4 The boss sounded angry when I spoke to him on the phone.
5 He's quite a shy person. He often feels embarrassed when he meets people.

ESERCIZIO 126C

Metti le parole nell'ordine giusto.

Esempi:

is | a | generous | Kate | woman | very | .   *Kate is a very generous woman.*
look | very | Simon | angry | did | ?   *Did Simon look very angry?*

1 children | asleep | the | are | ?
2 very | city | is | a | Sydney | modern | .
3 building | over | old | that | 500 years | is | .
4 don't | happy | very | you | sound | .
5 a | he | very | man | healthy | looks | .
6 bridge | long | is | 1.55 kilometres | the | .
7 blue | seen | have | my | you | T-shirt | ?

ESERCIZIO 126D

Metti gli aggettivi del riquadro nella categoria giusta.

Opinione	Dimensione	Età	Forma	Colore	Provenienza	Materiale	Scopo
horrible	*short*	*old*	*round*	*grey*	*English*	*glass*	*shopping*
___	___	___	___	___	___	___	___
___	___	___	___	___	___	___	___

English   old   horrible   grey   glass   round   shopping
short   middle-aged   plastic   Italian   beautiful   sports
ugly   square   leather   red   German   small   young   white
writing   curly   large

ESERCIZIO 126E

Metti gli aggettivi fra parentesi nell'ordine giusto.

Esempio:

an (German | interesting | young) woman   *an interesting young German woman*

1 a (fat | short) man
2 a (middle-aged | tall) woman
3 two (white | small | paper) cups
4 some (Japanese | tiny) TV sets
5 a (young | handsome) doctor
6 a (red | plastic | cheap) raincoat
7 an (blue | long | attractive) coat
8 a pair of (leather | expensive | black) shoes

Nota   –Un aggettivo, in genere, ha la stessa forma sia al singolare che al plurale (cfr. 126.1). Nota però che gli aggettivi dimostrativi *this* e *that* cambiano in *these* e *those* con i nomi plurali p.es. *this man, these men.*

127 Aggettivi: comparativo e superlativo

1 **Forma**

a Aggettivi monosillabi

Gli aggettivi monosillabi
formano il comparativo
aggiungendo -er e il
superlativo aggiungendo
-est.

AGGETTIVO	COMPARATIVO	SUPERLATIVO
small	*smaller*	*smallest*
high	*higher*	*highest*
young	*younger*	*youngest*
cold	*colder*	*coldest*

Quando si aggiunge -er o -est ci possono essere variazioni di ortografia p.es. *big* →
bigger. Cfr. 188.3,4,6.

b Aggettivi polisillabi

Gli aggettivi di tre o più
sillabe formano il com-
parativo premettendo
more e il superlativo
premettendo *most*.

Gli aggettivi bisillabi
terminanti in -y preceduta
da una consonante,
cambiano -y in -i, poi
aggiungono -er o -est.

Alcuni aggettivi bisillabi
formano il comparativo
con -er e il superlativo
con -est p.es. *quiet, clever,
simple, narrow, gentle.*

La maggior parte degli
altri aggettivi bisillabi
forma il comparativo con
more e il superlativo con
most.

Alcuni aggettivi bisillabi
possono avere entrambe
le forme -er/-est o *more/
most* p.es. *polite, common,
pleasant, stupid.*

AGGETTIVO	COMPARATIVO	SUPERLATIVO
exciting (ex-cit-ing)	**more** *exciting*	**most** *exciting*
interesting (in-ter-est-ing)	**more** *interesting*	**most** *interesting*
happy (hap-py)	*happier*	*happiest*
sunny (sun-ny)	*sunnier*	*sunniest*
quiet (qui-et)	*quieter*	*quietest*
clever (clev-er)	*cleverer*	*cleverest*
honest (hon-est)	**more** *honest*	**most** *honest*
careful (care-ful)	**more** *careful*	**most** *careful*
polite (po-lite)	*politer*/**more** *polite*	*politest*/**most** *polite*
common (com-mon)	*commoner*/**more** *common*	*commonest*/**most** *common*

c Comparativi e superlativi irregolari

Gli aggettivi *good, bad, far* e *old* hanno comparativi e superlativi irregolari.

AGGETTIVO	COMPARATIVO	SUPERLATIVO
good	*better*	*best*
bad	*worse*	*worst*
far	*farther/ further*	*farthest/ furthest*
old	*older/ elder*	*oldest/ eldest*

Anche *little* e *much/many* hanno comparativi e superlativi irregolari.

little	*less*	*least*
much/many	*more*	*most*

2 Uso del comparativo

a Si usa il comparativo quando si confronta una persona, una cosa, ecc. con un'altra.

*Martin is **taller** than Annie.*

Altri esempi:

*The Amazon is **longer** than the Mississipi.*
*Good health is **more important** than money.*

Dopo il comparativo spesso si usa *than* p.es. taller **than**, longer **than**, more important **than**.

b Si può usare la costruzione: comparativo + *and* + comparativo p.es. *colder and colder, more and more expensive* per esprimere il concetto 'sempre più ...'.

*The weather is getting **colder and colder**.*
*Things are becoming **more and more expensive** all the time.*

c Si puo usare la costruzione: *the* + comparativo ..., *the* + comparativo per dire che due cose cambiano contemporaneamente o che una dipende dall'altra.

***The smaller** a car is, **the easier** it is to park.*
***The colder** the weather, **the higher** my heating bills are.*

d Davanti al comparativo si può usare *(very) much, a lot, a little, a (little) bit, rather* o *far* (= molto).

***very much** taller   **a lot** more important   **a little** cheaper*
***a bit** more expensive   **rather** colder   **far more** interesting*

3   **Uso del superlativo**

a   Si usa il superlativo quando si confronta una persona o una cosa di un gruppo con due o più persone o cose dello stesso gruppo.

Martin

Martin is the **tallest** of the three children.

Altri esempi:

*I'm the **youngest** in my family.*
*Which is the **most beautiful** place you've ever been to?*

Normalmente si usa *the* con il superlativo p.es. ***the** tallest, **the** youngest, **the** most beautiful*.

b   Davanti al superlativo si usa spesso *by far* o *easily* p.es. ***by far** the tallest, **easily** the most interesting*.

ESERCIZIO 127A

Completa le frasi usando il comparativo degli aggettivi fra parentesi + *than*.

Esempio:

My brother is *younger than* my sister. (young)

1 Today is a lot ____ yesterday. (cold)
2 My new car is much ____ my old one. (comfortable)
3 This restaurant is ____ the one we went to yesterday. (good)
4 I'm a little ____ my father. (tall)
5 The film was much ____ I'd expected. (interesting)

ESERCIZIO 127B

Maria è una studentessa straniera a Londra. Parla dei problemi che ha per imparare l'inglese.

Completa quello che dice usando il comparativo degli aggettivi fra parentesi, aggiungendo *than* se necessario.

'Oh, why is English such a difficult language! I think it's *much more difficult than* (much | difficult) French. Sometimes I feel that my English is getting ____(1)____ (bad), not ____(2)____ (good)! When you first start learning English, it seems ____(3)____ (a lot | easy) other languages and the grammar looks ____(4)____ (much | simple). However, when you become ____(5)____ (a little | advanced), it gets ____(6)____ (a lot | complicated). There are also so many words in English! The dictionary I bought when I first came to Britain is far too small. I'm already looking for something ____(7)____ (rather | big) and ____(8)____ (comprehensive).'

ESERCIZIO 127C

Completa queste frasi relative al mondo d'oggi usando la costruzione: comparativo + *and* + comparativo.

Esempio:

Computers are becoming *more and more important* in our lives. (important)

1 The world's population is getting ____. (big)
2 The problem of feeding all the people in the world is getting ____. (bad)
3 Many of the world's seas, rivers and lakes are becoming ____. (polluted)
4 Life is becoming ____. (automated)

ESERCIZIO 127D

Forma delle frasi usando la costruzione: *the* + comparativo . . ., *the* + comparativo.

Esempio:

(small) a house is | (easy) it is to look after
The smaller a house is, the easier it is to look after.

1 (big) a car is | (expensive) it is to run
2 (bad) the weather | (dangerous) it is to drive on the roads
3 (old) he gets | (thoughtful) he becomes
4 (complicated) the problem | (hard) it is to find a solution

ESERCIZIO 127E

Completa le frasi usando *the* e il superlativo degli aggettivi fra parentesi.

Esempio:

What's *the most precious* (precious) metal in the world?

1 Who's ____ (good) footballer in Europe?
2 This was ____ (cheap) watch that they had in the shop.
3 I bought ____ (reliable) washing machine I could find.
4 This is one of ____ (expensive) restaurants in Milan.
5 The blue whale is ____ (large) of all the animals.
6 He's one of ____ (stupid) people I know.
7 ____ (old) university in the world is in Morocco.
8 I think that was one of ____ (bad) days of my life.
9 Sydney Opera House is one of ____ (famous) modern buildings in the world.

Nota   –*Further* (ma non *farther*) può voler dire 'più' o 'ulteriore' p.es. *Tell me if you have any* **further** *problems* (= ulteriori problemi).
–Si usa *older/oldest* (ma non *elder/eldest*) nei comparativi p.es. *My sister is* **older** *than me.* (Non: ~~. . . elder than me.~~) Si usa *elder/eldest* (spesso davanti a un nome p.es. *sister, son, brother*) soprattutto per parlare dei familiari p.es. *my* **elder** *sister.*
–Dopo il superlativo si usa *in* se seguono nomi di luoghi p.es. *Mount Everest is the highest mountain* **in the world**.
–Nello stile informale si usano i pronomi complemento p.es. *me, him* dopo *than* p.es. *She's older than* **me**. Nello stile formale si usa il pronome soggetto p.es. *I, he* + il verbo p.es. *She's older than* **I am**. Alcuni grammatici considerano questa forma più corretta.
–Talvolta si usa *most* + aggettivo nel significato di 'very' p.es. *It was* **most kind** *of you to lend me the money* (= molto gentile).

128 *As ... as*

1

Si usa *as ... as* per dire che due persone, cose, ecc. sono in qualche modo uguali.

*Judy is **as tall as** Martin.*

> *as* + aggettivo + *as*

*Judy is **as tall as** Martin*
*I'm **as old as** you are.*
*Was the exam **as difficult as** you'd expected?*

2

Dopo *not* si può usare sia *as ... as* che *so ... as*.

> *not as/so* + aggettivo + *as*

*Judy isn't **as/so tall as** Carla.*
*Today isn't **as/so cold as** yesterday.*

ESERCIZIO 128A

Completa le frasi usando *as ... as* e gli aggettivi del riquadro.

Esempio:

'Are you *as old as* Mike?'   'No, I'm younger than he is.'

> interesting   cheap   ~~old~~   clever   tall

1 Jill is almost ＿＿ her father. She's 164 cm and he's 166 cm.
2 I'm not ＿＿ my brother. He's very intelligent.
3 The film wasn't ＿＿ I'd thought it would be. In fact, it was quite boring.
4 Going by train is almost ＿＿ taking the coach. They both cost around £5.

ESERCIZIO 128B

Forma il comparativo usando *isn't as . . . as* e gli aggettivi fra parentesi.

Esempio:

Japan | India   (large | industrialised)
Japan isn't as large as India.
India isn't as industrialised as Japan.

1 a giraffe | an elephant   (tall | strong | fast)
2 iron | gold   (strong/valuable)
3 a gorilla | a human   (intelligent | strong)
4 a car | a bicycle   (expensive | fast | easy to park)

Nota   –Nello stile informale si usano i pronomi complemento, p.es. *me, him*, dopo *as*: *You aren't as tired as **me***. Nello stile formale si usa il pronome soggetto p.es. *I, he* + il verbo: *You aren't as tired as **I am***. Alcuni grammatici considerano questa costruzione più corretta.

129 Riepilogo dei comparativi, dei superlativi e di *as . . . as*

ESERCIZIO 129A

Completa le frasi usando la forma corretta degli aggettivi fra parentesi. Aggiungi *than, the* o *as*, se necessario.

Esempi:

A mile is *longer than* a kilometre (long)
Today isn't as *sunny as* yesterday. (sunny)
What's *the best* holiday you've ever had? (good)

1 Baseball is ＿＿ sport in the USA. (popular)
2 She's much ＿＿ her brother. (serious)
3 He wasn't as ＿＿ he usually is. (friendly)
4 That was ＿＿ film I've ever seen. (good)
5 He's much ＿＿ any of his brothers. (generous)
6 You aren't as ＿＿ you think you are. (clever)
7 Where's ＿＿ place in the world? (hot)
8 Debbie is far ＿＿ she used to be. (self-confident)
9 My brother is one of ＿＿ people I know. (strange)
10 Which is ＿＿ building in the world? (tall)
11 Our holiday was much ＿＿ we'd expected. (cheap)
12 That was one of ＿＿ times of my life. (enjoyable)

130 Aggettivi e avverbi di modo

1 Gli avverbi di modo precisano **come** avviene qualcosa.

*She sings **beautifully**.*
*I passed the exam **easily**.*

Confronta gli aggettivi con gli avverbi di modo:

Un aggettivo di modo ci dice qualcosa del nome p.es. *singer, worker, exam*.	Un avverbio di modo ci dice qualcosa del verbo p.es. *sings, works, passed*.
*She's a **beautiful** singer.* *He's a **slow** worker.* *The **exam** was **easy**.*	*She **sings beautifully**.* *He **works slowly**.* *I **passed** the exam **easily**.*

2 La gran parte degli avverbi di modo si forma aggiungendo *-ly* all'aggettivo.

AGGETTIVO	AVVERBIO
beautiful	*beautifully*
slow	*slowly*
clever	*cleverly*

Nota però che l'avverbio di *good* e *well*.
*You're a **good** swimmer.   You swim very **well**.*

Fast, hard, early e *late* si usano sia come aggettivi che come avverbi.

*It's a **fast** car.*	*The car goes very **fast**.*
*It was **hard** work.*	*We worked **hard**.*
*I was **early**.*	*I arrived **early**.*

3 Non tutte le parole che terminano in *-ly* sono avverbi. Alcuni aggettivi terminano in *-ly* p.es. *friendly, lovely, lonely, silly, ugly*. Questi aggettivi non hanno una forma per l'avverbio; si usano invece costruzioni diverse p.es. *in a . . . way*.

*She smiled **in a friendly way**.* (Non: ~~She smiled friendly/friendily~~.)

4 Quando si aggiunge *-ly* agli aggettivi ci possono essere variazioni di ortografia p.es. *easy → easily*. Cfr. 188.3,4.

ESERCIZIO 130A

Scegli la parola giusta.

Esempio:

Simon is a *good*/~~well~~ guitarist and he sings quite ~~good~~/*well*, too.

1 She learnt to swim very *easy/easily*.
2 How *fast/fastly* were you driving when the accident happened?
3 He speaks extremely *slow/slowly*, doesn't he?
4 I can't sing very *good/well*.
5 I'm taking some exams next month, so I'm studying very *hard/hardly* at the moment.
6 England played very *bad/badly* in the football match last night.
7 This spaghetti tastes *delicious/deliciously*. You're a very *good/well* cook.
8 This is a very *serious/seriously* problem and it needs thinking about *careful/carefully*.

131 Avverbi di modo, luogo e tempo

1 Un avverbio può essere costituito da una parola singola p.es. *quickly* o da una serie di parole (cioè da una 'locuzione avverbiale').

Un avverbio che indica **come** avviene qualcosa p.es. *carefully, well* è un avverbio di modo.

Un avverbio che indica **dove** avviene qualcosa p.es. *here, in the park* è un avverbio di luogo.

Un avverbio che indica **quando** avviene qualcosa p.es. *now, yesterday* è un avverbio di tempo (in questo caso determinato).

2 **Posizione**

a Gli avverbi di modo, di luogo e di tempo (determinato) di regola seguono il complemento oggetto.

> complemento oggetto + avverbio

*I read **the letter carefully**.*
*We saw **Maria in the park**.*
*He bought **a camera yesterday**.*

b Se non c'è nessun complemento oggetto, di regola l'avverbio segue il verbo.

> verbo + avverbio

*She **drove carefully**.*
*He **lives here**.*

c Se ci sono più avverbi, l'ordine usuale è:

> modo + luogo + tempo

*I slept **very well last night**.* (modo + tempo)
*He lives **here now**.* (luogo + tempo)
*We worked **hard at school yesterday**.* (modo + luogo + tempo)

d Nota che l'avverbio di regola non va tra il verbo e il complemento oggetto.

> verbo + complemento oggetto + avverbio

I like Maria very much. (Non: ~~I like very much Maria.~~)
He drank his coffee quickly. (Non: ~~He drank quickly his coffee.~~)
We played tennis yesterday. (Non: ~~We played yesterday tennis.~~)

e | Alcuni avverbi di modo, di luogo e di tempo possono essere collocati anche all'inizio della frase (se si vuole dar loro enfasi).

***Slowly**, he started to walk away.*
***In London**, we went to the zoo.*
***Tomorrow** I have to go to the doctor's.*

ESERCIZIO 131A

Completa le frasi mettendo le parole tra parentesi nell'ordine: complemento oggetto + modo + luogo + tempo.

Esempio:

Annie did ____ (last night | her homework | very quickly)
Annie did her homework very quickly last night.

1 Sue can play ____ (now | very well | tennis)
2 I posted ____ (early this morning | in the town centre | your letters)
3 The children have been playing ____ (this afternoon | in the park | football)
4 It snowed ____ (yesterday evening | heavily | in the north of Scotland)
5 They studied ____ (carefully | later on in the day | the map)
6 He walked ____ (out of the room | at the end of the meeting | angrily)
7 She played ____ (at the concert | last night | beautifully | the guitar)

Nota | –Alcuni avverbi di modo possono precedere il verbo p.es. *He **angrily** walked* out of the room. Lo stesso vale per certi avverbi di tempo indeterminato (p.es. *still, already, just*) e di frequenza (p.es. *always, never*): *I **still** love you. He **always** starts* work at 8.00. Per altri dettagli sulla posizione degli avverbi rispetto ai verbi, cfr. 132.

132 Posizione degli avverbi rispetto ai verbi

Certi avverbi p.es. *usually, never, always, probably, certainly, still, already, just, almost, only* possono essere usati con i verbi:

1 | L'avverbio normalmente precede il verbo.

avverbio + verbo

*They **usually watch** TV in the evenings.*
*I **never eat** sweets.*
*He **probably knows** what to do.*
*We **still live** here.*

2 Però l'avverbio normalmente segue il verbo *be* o un altro verbo ausiliare p.es. *have, will, can.*

> *be* + avverbio

*They're **usually** in bed by 11.30.*
*He's **probably** at home now.*
*We're **still** here.*

> verbo ausiliare + avverbio

*I've **never** eaten Chinese food.*
*We'll **probably** be late this evening.*
*I **can never** remember your phone number.*

3 Quando ci sono più verbi ausiliari p.es. *have been*, l'avverbio normalmente va dopo il primo.

*These curtains **have never** been cleaned.*
*Ken **has probably** been working all day.*

4 Nelle frasi negative gli avverbi di valutazione p.es. *probably, certainly*, normalmente precedono l'espressione negativa *won't, not*, ecc.

*We **probably won't** be here tomorrow./We'll **probably not** be here tomorrow.*

ESERCIZIO 132A

Metti l'avverbio fra parentesi al posto giusto.

Esempio:

He'll be in Paris until next Friday. (probably)
He'll probably be in Paris until next Friday.

1 They've been trying to contact us. (probably)
2 She went to the meeting last week. (probably)
3 They take their summer holidays in May. (normally)
4 Have you lived in a foreign country? (ever)
5 I've eaten Indian food. (never)
6 Do you live in the same flat? (still)
7 He wants to borrow the money. (only)
8 I won't see Martin again until next weekend. (probably)
9 We've finished painting the outside of the house. (almost)
10 I try to go jogging at least three times a week. (always)
11 We haven't got any time to lose. (certainly)
12 I can lend you some money until next week. (certainly)
13 He's complaining about something. (always)
14 I don't watch this TV programme. (usually)

133 Tempo: *still, yet* e *already*

1 Si usa *still* (= ancora) davanti al verbo, ma dopo *be* o un altro verbo ausiliare (cfr. 132).

*My brother is 18, but he **still behaves** like a child.*
*'Has Andrew woken up?'   'No, he's **still** asleep.'*
*I **can still** remember the first time we met.*

Si usa *still* dopo il soggetto nelle frasi negative; in questo caso *still* può esprimere impazienza o sorpresa.

*They received the bill a month ago and **they still** haven't paid it.*
*I've known Mike for years, but **I still** don't understand him.*

2 Si usa *yet* (= neancora) solo nelle frasi interrogative e negative; *yet* viene in genere collocato in fondo alla frase.

*Have you had your exam results **yet**?*
*I wrote to her a week ago, but she hasn't answered my letter **yet**.*

Spesso si usa *yet* dopo *not* nelle risposte brevi negative.

*'Have you passed your driving test yet?'   'No, **not yet**.'*

3 Di regola si usa *already* (= già) davanti al verbo, ma dopo *be* o un altro verbo ausiliare (cfr. 132).

*You don't need to tell Ken the news; he **already knows**.*
*'What time is Sue going to be here?'   'She's **already** here.'*
*'Could you do the washing up?'   'I've **already** done it.'*

Si può collocare *already* anche in fondo alla frase per dare enfasi.

*I've seen the film **already**.*
*Have you finished **already**?*

ESERCIZIO 133A

Completa le frasi usando *still, yet* o *already*.

Esempio:

Is Lynne *still* here, or has she gone home?

1 When we arrived at the cinema, the film had ____ started.
2 Paul has been looking for a job for ages, but he ____ hasn't found one ____.
3 Do you ____ drive the same car or have you sold it?
4 Have you had your exam results, or are you ____ waiting for them?
5 She only started the book yesterday, but she's finished it ____.
6 'They started the job ages ago. Haven't they finished it ____?'   'No, not ____.'

ESERCIZIO 133B

Metti gli avverbi fra parentesi al posto giusto. Talvolta sono possibili due
costruzioni.

Esempio:

The meeting started three hours ago and it *still* hasn't finished. (still)

1 You needn't clean the kitchen; I've done it. (already)
2 You don't need to tell me; I know what to do. (already)
3 Haven't you received your invitation to the party? (yet)
4 I can't decide what to do this evening. (still)
5 I can remember the first time I flew in a plane. (still)
6 Robert works for the same company in London. (still)

134   Tempo: *any more, any longer e no longer*

Si può usare *not . . . any more, not . . . any longer* e *no longer* per dire che una
situazione non è più come prima.

1 *Any more* e *any longer* vanno in fondo alla frase.

*Annie doesn't live here **any more**. She moved last year.*
*My father is not a young man **any longer**.*

2 Normalmente *no longer* precede il verbo, ma segue *be* o un altro verbo ausiliare.

*Annie **no longer lives** here. She moved last year.* | *My father **is no longer** a young man.*

In genere, in questi casi, non si usa *no more*.

ESERCIZIO 134A

Metti l'espressione giusta fra parentesi al posto giusto.

Esempio:

I don't want to stay here. (any more/no longer)
I don't want to stay here any more.

1 Sue works for the same company in London. (any longer/no longer)
2 My brother isn't a young child. (any more/no longer)
3 Her father is unemployed. (any longer/no longer)
4 There is a large ship-building industry in Britain. (any more/no longer)

135 Avverbi di frequenza

Gli avverbi di frequenza precisano **quanto spesso** accade qualcosa.

Esempi:

always   normally   usually   frequently   often   sometimes
occasionally   rarely   seldom   hardly ever   never   ever

1 Questi avverbi normalmente precedono il verbo, ma seguono *be* o un altro verbo ausiliare.

They **usually watch** TV.	They're **usually** in bed by 11.30.
She **never eats** sweets.	She's **never** eaten Chinese food.
I **always go** to work by bus.	I'll **always** remember you.

Quando ci sono più verbi ausiliari p.es. *have been*, l'avverbio normalmente va dopo il primo.

These curtains **have never** been cleaned.
Have you **ever** been invited to one of his parties?

2 *Sometimes, usually, normally, frequently, often* e *occasionally* possono andare anche all'inizio o in fondo alla frase.

Sometimes I walk to work.
Do you see your parents **often**?

3 Le locuzioni avverbiali di frequenza p.es. *every evening, once a week*, normalmente vanno in fondo o all'inizio della frase.

They watch TV **every evening**.
I go swimming **once a week**.

4 Gli avverbi di frequenza determinati p.es. *daily, weekly, monthly, yearly* normalmente vanno in fondo alla frase.

The post is delivered here twice **daily**.

ESERCIZIO 135A

Metti gli avverbi in ordine di frequenza.

seldom   never   ~~usually~~   often   sometimes not ever   frequently   ~~normally~~   ~~always~~ hardly ever   rarely

all the time	(1)	*always*	
	(2)	*normally*	*usually*
	(3)	____	____
	(4)	____	
	(5)	____	____
	(6)	____	
at no time	(7)	____	____

ESERCIZIO 135B

Metti gli avverbi al posto giusto. Talvolta sono possibili più soluzioni.

Esempio:

She *always* tries to visit her parents at the weekends.   (always)

1 I've seen that programme on TV.   (never)
2 He's late for appointments.   (hardly ever)
3 They go to the cinema nowadays.   (rarely)
4 Is he bad-tempered?   (often)
5 They listen to the radio.   (every morning)
6 I'm at home before 8 o'clock.   (seldom)
7 Have you had a really serious illness? (ever)
8 I'll forget our holiday together.   (never)
9 She's been interested in music.   (always)
10 I brush my teeth.   (always/three times a day)

136   Avverbi di valutazione

Gli avverbi di valutazione precisano **quanto sicuri** si è di qualcosa.

Esempi:

certainly   definitely   obviously   probably

1   Questi avverbi normalmente precedono il verbo, ma seguono *be* o un altro verbo ausiliare (cfr. 132).

He **probably knows** your address.
They **definitely saw** me.
She **obviously likes** you.

He's **probably** at home now.
They've **definitely** gone out.
She **can obviously** do the job.

2   Nelle frasi negative gli avverbi di valutazione normalmente precedono l'espressione negativa *won't, isn't, not,* ecc.

She **probably won't** be late.
He **certainly isn't** at home now.
They're **obviously not** very happy.

3   *Perhaps* e *maybe* normalmente vanno all'inizio della frase.

Perhaps *I'll see you later.*
Maybe *you're right.*

Maybe è abbastanza informale.

ESERCIZIO 136A

Metti gli avverbi i posto giusto.

Esempio:

In the future, machines will *probably* do many of the jobs that people do today.
(probably)

1 Simon is at Sarah's house at the moment.
   (probably)
2 There will be an election early next year.
   (probably)
3 We'll play tennis later this afternoon.
   (perhaps)
4 They enjoyed the film very much. (obviously)

5 You should go and see the doctor. (definitely)
6 I don't want to be home late tonight.
   (definitely)
7 Computers are becoming more and more
   important in our lives. (certainly)
8 The bridge has been repaired by now.
   (probably)

137   *Fairly, quite, rather* e *pretty*

1 Gli avverbi *fairly, quite, rather* e *pretty* modificano gli aggettivi o altri avverbi.
Normalmente precedono l'aggettivo o l'avverbio che modificano.

*The film was **quite good**.* (avverbio + aggettivo)
*I know her **fairly well**.* (avverbio + avverbio)

2 Confronta:

fairly	*quite*	*rather/pretty*	*very*
good	*good*	*good*	*good*

a *Quite* è più forte di *fairly*.

*I'm **fairly** tired, but I don't think I'll go to bed yet.*
*I'm **quite** tired. I think I'll go to bed now.*

b *Rather* è più forte di *quite*; lo si può usare per dire 'più del normale', 'più del voluto'
o 'più di quanto ci si aspettasse'.

*The TV is **rather** loud. Shall I turn it down?*
*We're **rather** late. We'd better hurry.*
*The concert was **rather** good. I was surprised.*

c Si può usare *pretty* con un significato simile a *rather*, nello stile informale.

*We're **pretty** hungry. We haven't eaten all day.*

d Nota però che il significato di *fairly, quite, rather* e *pretty* può anche dipendere
dall'intonazione della voce e dall'enfasi.

*He's **quite** 'nice.* (più forte)
*He's '**quite** nice.* (meno forte)

3 | *Quite* va prima di *a/an*, *fairly* e *pretty* lo seguono. Confronta:

*He's **quite a** young man.*	*He's **a fairly** young man.*
*It was **quite an** interesting film.*	*It was **a pretty** interesting film.*

Rather può precedere o seguire *a/an*.

*It was **rather an** interesting film./It was **a rather** interesting film.*

4 | *Quite* e *rather* possono modificare anche il verbo: lo precedono, se è un verbo principale, lo seguono se è un verbo ausiliare (cfr. 132).

*She **quite enjoyed** the film.*
*I **rather like** driving at night.*
*He's **quite** enjoying himself.*

5 | *Rather*, ma non *fairly*, *quite* o *pretty*, può precedere un comparativo.

rather colder   **rather more** expensive

6 | *Quite* può essere usato anche come rafforzativo di alcuni aggettivi, nel significato di 'assolutamente', 'completamente' ecc.

*The animal was **quite dead**.* (= morto e stramorto)

Quite è usato al riguardo solo con aggettivi 'non graduabili' come *dead* (non si può essere più o meno morti: si è morti o no).

Altri esempi:

*The meal was **quite perfect**.* (= assolutamente squisito)
*The story is **quite untrue**.* (= completamente falsa)

Quite, con questa funzione, può accompagnare anche certi avverbi e verbi.

*She sang **quite perfectly**.* (= in modo assolutamente perfetto)
*I **quite understand**.* (= capisco perfettamente)

ESERCIZIO 137A

Completa le frasi usando uno dei due avverbi fra parentesi. Talvolta sono possibili entrambi.

Esempi:

She's *quite* a generous woman. (quite/fairly)
It's *rather/fairly* cold in this room. (rather/fairly)

1 I've made ____ a stupid mistake. (pretty/rather)
2 She ____ enjoys working at night. (fairly/quite)
3 It was a ____ boring football match. (pretty/rather)
4 I'm ____ looking forward to the party on Saturday. (pretty/quite)
5 The weather was ____ worse than we'd expected. (quite/rather)
6 My grandfather was ____ an amazing man. (quite/fairly)
7 Maria speaks English ____ well, doesn't she? (quite/pretty)
8 I'm feeling ____ better today. (fairly/rather)

ESERCIZIO 137B

Completa le frasi usando, una volta sola, l'espressione più adatta del riquadro.

Esempio:

There was nothing in the envelope.
It was *quite empty*.

quite useless   quite sure   quite impossible
quite original   ~~quite empty~~   quite different

1 He's not at all like his sister; they're ___.
2 This clock keeps on breaking down. It's ___ really.
3 I like your idea. It's really ___; I've never heard anything like it before.
4 'What are you going to do this evening?'   'I'm not ___.'
5 We can't finish the job by tomorrow. It's ___.

138   *Too e enough*

1 | *Too* precede gli aggettivi e gli avverbi; *enough* li segue.

*I don't think I'll go out tonight. I'm **too tired**.*
*Slow down! You're driving **too fast**.*

*Are you **warm enough**, or do you want me to switch on the heating?*
*We aren't working **quickly enough**. We'd better hurry.*

2 | Si usa *too many, too much* e *enough* davanti ai nomi:

a | Si usa *too many* davanti ai nomi numerabili plurali (p.es. *eggs*), e *too much* davanti ai nomi non numerabili (p.es. *salt*).

*I bought **too many eggs**.*
*There's **too much salt** in this soup.*

b | Si usa *enough* davanti ai nomi sia numerabili che non numerabili.

*We can't make an omelette. We haven't got **enough eggs**.*
*There's **enough salt** in the soup. It doesn't need any more.*

Si può usare *too many, too much* e *enough* anche senza il nome.

*'Is there enough salt in the soup?'   'There's **too much**. I can't eat it.'*
*We need more eggs. We haven't got **enough**.*

3 | Dopo *too* e *enough* si può usare *for* + complemento.

*This jacket is **too small for me**.*
*The flat isn't really **big enough for all of us**.*

4 | Dopo *too* e *enough* si può usare l'infinito con *to*.

*It's **too early to have** dinner.*
*He isn't **old enough to drive** a car.*

5 | Si può usare la costruzione: *too/enough* + *for* + complemento + l'infinito con *to*.

It's too early for us to have dinner.
This jacket isn't large enough for me to wear.

6 | *Too* (ma non *enough*) può essere rafforzato con *much, a lot, far* o indebolito con *a little, a bit, rather*.

much too *heavy*   **far too** *cold*   **a bit too** *fast*

7 | Confronta *very* con *too*:

Too (ma non *very*) ha il significato negativo di 'più del necessario' o 'più di quello che va bene'.

*She's a good worker. She works **very** quickly.*	*He works **too** quickly and makes a lot of mistakes.*
*They arrived at the airport **very** late, but they just caught their plane.*	*They arrived at the airport **too** late and missed their plane.*

ESERCIZIO 138A

Completa ogni frase usando *too* o *enough* e un aggettivo o avverbio del riquadro.

Esempio:

Annie can't go to school today. She has got a temperature and isn't *well enough* to get up.

warm   dark   ~~well~~   early   quietly   loud

1 We couldn't see what was in the room because it was ____.
2 I couldn't hear everything she said because she spoke ____.
3 They missed their plane because they didn't leave home ____.
4 He told them the music was ____ so they turned it down.
5 We didn't go to the beach yesterday because the weather wasn't ____.

ESERCIZIO 138B

Completa le frasi usando *too much, too many* o *enough*.

Esempio:

We've been so busy today we didn't even have *enough* time for lunch.

1 I'd like to go to the cinema, but I haven't got ____ money.
2 I can't drink this soup. It's got ____ salt in it.
3 Doctors say that ____ sugar is bad for you.
4 We didn't really enjoy the party; there were far ____ people there.
5 We couldn't make an omelette because we didn't have ____ eggs.

ESERCIZIO 138C

Collega queste frasi usando *too/enough* + l'infinito con *to* o *too/enough* + *for* + complemento + l'infinito con *to*.

Esempi:

Annie isn't old enough. She can't leave school.
Annie isn't old enough to leave school.
The weather was too bad. We couldn't go out.
The weather was too bad for us to go out.

1 I'm too tired. I can't go to the cinema this evening.
2 The table was too heavy. I couldn't move it.

3 The children aren't tall enough. They can't reach that shelf.
4 They arrived too late. They didn't see the beginning of the film.
5 Our old flat was much too small. We couldn't live in it.
6 He spoke too quietly. The people at the back of the room couldn't hear.

139 *So e such*

---

1 Si usa *such* davanti a un nome, con o senza aggettivo.

*She's **such a nice woman**.*
*Don't be **such a fool**!*

Si usa *so* davanti a un aggettivo non accompagnato dal nome.

*She's **so nice**.*
*Don't be **so foolish**!*

Si può usare *so* anche con un avverbio.

*He works **so slowly**.*

2 Si può usare *so*, ma non *such*, con *many* e *much*.

*There were **so many** people on the train, we couldn't find a seat.*
*I've got **so much** to do today. I'm really busy.*

Si può usare *such*, ma non *so*, davanti a *a lot* (*of*).

*There were **such a lot of** people on the train, we couldn't find a seat.*
*I've got **such a lot** to do today. I'm really busy.*

3 Dopo *so* e *such* si può usare *that* + l'indicativo per esprimere una conseguenza (cfr. 162.2).

*The table was **so heavy that** I couldn't move it.*
*It was **such** a beautiful afternoon **that** we went to the beach.*

ESERCIZIO 139A

Completa le frasi usando *so* o *such*.

Esempio:

It was *such* a good film. I really enjoyed it.

1 She's ___ shy. She always gets very nervous when she meets people.

2 You shouldn't eat ___ quickly; you'll give yourself indigestion.

3 It's ___ an interesting town; there really is ___ much to do there.

4 I was ___ disappointed when I failed my driving test.

5 He felt ___ tired that he decided not to go out.

6 It was ___ a hot day that they had to open all the windows.

7 I've made ___ many mistakes in this letter, I think I'll type it again.

8 He had ___ a lot of luggage that we couldn't get it all into the car.

Nota   –Si usa *so* per introdurre una frase che esprima una conseguenza p.es. *I was hungry so I made something to eat.* Cfr. 162.2.

–Si usa *so that* e *so as to* per introdurre una frase che esprima uno scopo p.es. *I gave her my address so that she could write to me.* Cfr. 163.3.

140 Avverbi: comparativo e superlativo

1 **Forma**

La maggior parte degli avverbi forma il comparativo premettendo *more* e il superlativo premettendo *most*.

beautifully	more beautifully	most beautifully
carefully	more carefully	most carefully

Gli avverbi monosillabi p.es. *fast, hard, late, long, soon* aggiungono *-er* per il comparativo e *-est* per il superlativo.

fast	faster	fastest
hard	harder	hardest

Nota: anche *early (ear-ly)* aggiunge *-er/-est: earlier* → *earliest*.

Quando si aggiunge *-er/-est* ci possono essere variazioni di ortografia p.es. *early* → *earlier*. Cfr. 188.3,4,6.

Gli avverbi *well, badly* e *far* hanno il comparativo e il superlativo irregolare.

well	better	best
badly	worse	worst
far	farther/further	farthest/furthest

2 | **Costruzioni comparative con gli avverbi**

Si usano le stesse costruzioni comparative degli aggettivi anche con gli avverbi.

a | comparativo (cfr. 127.2)

*You should drive **more carefully**.*
*They arrived **later** than I'd expected.*

b | comparativo + *and* + comparativo (cfr. 127.2)

*It snowed **more and more heavily** as the day went on.*

c | *the* + comparativo . . ., *the* + comparativo (cfr. 127.2)

***The sooner** we leave, **the earlier** we'll arrive.*

d | superlativo (cfr. 127.3)

*She runs **the fastest** of all the girls.*

e | *as . . . as* (cfr. 128)

as + avverbio + *as*

*I'm working **as fast as** I can.*
*Mike can't play the guitar **as/so well as** Sarah.*

ESERCIZIO 140A

Completa le frasi usando la forma corretta delle parole fra parentesi. Aggiungi *than,*
the o *as* dov'è necessario.

Esempi:

Of all those cars, the Alfa Romeo goes *the fastest*. (fast)
I don't work as *hard as* Sally does. (hard)
We finished the job a lot *more quickly than* we'd expected. (quickly)

1 She always arrives at work much ____ anyone else. (early)

2 The children are behaving far ____ they normally do. (badly)

3 Of all the animals in the world, which one lives ____? (long)

4 Our new central heating system works a lot ____ our old one did. (efficiently)

5 He doesn't speak French as ____ his sister. (fluently)

6 The car went ____ and ____ down the hill. (fast)

7 They normally play much ____ they did last night. (well)

8 Andrew is studying a lot ____ usual now that his exams are getting closer. (hard)

Nota | –Nello stile informale spesso si usano i pronomi complemento p.es. *me, him* dopo *than* e *as* p.es. *You run faster than **me**. I can't swim as well as **him**.* Nello stile formale si usa il pronome soggetto p.es. *I, he* + il verbo p.es. *You run faster than **I** do. I can't swim as well as **he can**.* Alcuni grammatici considerano più corretta quest'ultima forma.

141 Frasi negative

Si rende negativa un'affermazione mettendo *not* (contrazione *n't*) dopo un verbo ausiliare (p.es. *be, have, can*).

We're leaving. ⟶ *We **aren't** leaving.*
They've finished. ⟶ *They **haven't** finished.*
He can swim. ⟶ *He **can't** swim.*
I may go to the party. ⟶ *I **may not** go to the party.*

Not/n't viene posto dopo *be* anche quando *be* funge da verbo principale, e dopo *have* in *have got*.

I'm hungry. ⟶ *I'**m not** hungry.*
She's got a car. ⟶ *She **hasn't** got a car.*

Per il presente e per il passato remoto, tempi formati senza ausiliare, si usa *do/does* e *did*, rispettivamente, seguito da *not/n't*.

I smoke. ⟶ *I **don't** smoke.*
She lives in London. ⟶ *She **doesn't** live in London.*
We went out last night. ⟶ *We **didn't** go out last night.*

Nota che, dopo *do, does* e *did*, il verbo è sempre all'infinito senza *to* p.es. *smoke, live, go*.

In presenza di due o più ausiliari, *not/n't* segue il primo.

He's been working. ⟶ *He **hasn't** been working.*

Per le contrazioni negative p.es. *aren't* (= *are not*), *don't* (= *do not*), cfr. 189.

ESERCIZIO 141A

Rendi negative queste frasi.

Esempi:

I'm going to apply for the job.
I'm not going to apply for the job.
She got up very early this morning.
She didn't get up very early this morning.

1 I like travelling by train.
2 He was late for the appointment.
3 We've got a lot of time.
4 I'm enjoying myself very much.
5 Robert works for a company in Manchester.
6 The weather is very nice today.
7 She can come to the party on Saturday.
8 I've been working too hard recently.
9 She's got a very interesting job.
10 They may have gone home.
11 We saw you at school yesterday.
12 The bank opens on Saturday afternoons.
13 My sister is going to work tomorrow.
14 The telephone has been repaired.
15 We play tennis every weekend.
16 I'll be seeing Martin tomorrow.

Nota –Si forma l'imperativo negativo facendolo precedere da *do* + *not/n't* p.es. ***Don't** shout.* Cfr. 30.1.
–Si possono usare altre espressioni negative p.es. *never*, per rendere negativa una frase p.es. *I **never** smoke.*

142 Domande 'a risposta chiusa'

1 | Se una domanda può avere come risposta semplicemente *sì* o *no*, viene chiamata, in inglese, domanda 'a risposta chiusa'.

'Is Sue coming?' *'Yes.'/'No.'*
'Have they finished?' *'Yes.'/'No.'*

2 | Si passa dalla forma affermativa a quella interrogativa scambiando la posizione del soggetto (p.es. *Sue, they, he*) con quella del verbo ausiliare (p.es. *be, have, can*).

Sue is coming. ⟶ ***Is Sue** coming?*
They have finished. ⟶ ***Have they** finished?*
You can cook. ⟶ ***Can you** cook?*

Lo stesso vale per *be*, quando funge da verbo principale.

They are English. ⟶ ***Are they** English?*

Se il verbo principale è *have got*, si inverte la posizione tra soggetto e *have*.

He has got a car. ⟶ ***Has he** got a car?*

Se la frase contiene due o più verbi ausiliari, si inverte la posizione tra il soggetto e il primo ausiliare.

He has been waiting. ⟶ ***Has he** been waiting?*

Per formulare una domanda al presente o al passato remoto, tempi formati senza ausiliare, si usa *do/does* e *did*, rispettivamente.

They live here. ⟶ ***Do they** live here?*
She likes tennis. ⟶ ***Does she** like tennis?*
He enjoyed the film. ⟶ ***Did he** enjoy the film?*

Nota che, dopo *do, does* e *did*, il verbo è sempre all'infinito senza *to* p.es. *live, like, enjoy*.

ESERCIZIO 142A

Formula delle domande 'a risposta chiusa' con queste frasi.

Esempi:

She lives in London.   *Does she live in London?*
You'd like a cup of coffee.   *Would you like a cup of coffee?*

1 They played tennis yesterday.
2 He's doing his homework.
3 She's got a lot to do today.
4 They've bought a new car.
5 You know Simon Robinson.
6 He can play the piano and the guitar.
7 The shop closes at 6 o'clock.
8 You'd like to go swimming.
9 The job will be finished soon.

ESERCIZIO 142B

Completa le domande 'a risposta chiusa' come negli esempi.

Esempi:

'I'll be at home this evening.'   '*Will you be* there at 7 o'clock?'
'He likes most sports.'   '*Does he like* tennis?'

1 'They visited Milan.'   '____ Rome?'
2 'She bought some coffee.'   '____ any milk?'
3 'She's got two sisters.'   '____ any brothers?'
4 'I speak Italian.'   '____ Spanish?'
5 'They've gone out.'   '____ into town?'
6 'I can play the guitar.'   '____ the piano?'
7 'He works eight hours a day.'   '____ on Saturdays?'
8 'I'm going to the cinema.'   '____ on your own?'

Nota   –Talvolta si formulano domande 'a risposta chiusa' con la stessa costruzione di una frase affermativa, ma facendo salire l'intonazione della voce p.es. *You're ~~English~~?* Questo succede spesso nei casi in cui si pensa di sapere qualcosa e se ne chiede semplicemente conferma, oppure se si vuole esprimere sorpresa p.es. *You're ~~only 14~~? I thought you were at least 18!*

143 Domande con *Wh-*

1 Molte domande sono introdotte da espressioni che, in inglese, cominciano quasi tutte con *wh-*: *what, where, who, whose, when, why, which, how* (cfr. 145).
   What is she reading?
   Where do they live?

2 Si formula la domanda cambiando la posizione del soggetto (p.es. *she, they, we*) con quella del verbo ausiliare (p.es. *be, have, can*).

   She is reading. ——————————→   What **is she** reading?
   They have gone. ——————————→   Where **have they** gone?
   We can start. ——————————→   When **can we** start?

   Lo stesso dicasi per *be* come verbo principale.

   He is here. ——————————→   Why **is he** here?

   Se il verbo principale è *have got*, si inverte la posizione tra soggetto e *have*.

   He has got your key. ——————————→   Why **has he** got your key?

   Se la frase contiene due o più ausiliari, si inverte la posizione tra il soggetto e il primo ausiliare.

   He has been reading. ——————————→   What **has he** been reading?

   Per formulare la domanda al presente o al passato remoto, tempi formati senza ausiliare, si usa *do/does* e *did*, rispettivamente (ma cfr. 144).

They start work. —————————→	*When **do they** start work?*
She goes to school. —————————→	*Where **does she** go to school?*
He arrived. —————————→	*When **did he** arrive?*

Nota che, dopo *do/does* e *did*, il verbo è sempre all'infinito senza *to* p.es. *start, go, arrive.*

ESERCIZIO 143A

Completa le domande, come negli esempi.

Esempi:

'They went to the station.'   'What time *did they go* there?'

'I've got some money.'   'How much *have you got?*'

1 'We're going.'   'Where ____?'
2 'I'm worried.'   'Why ____ worried?'
3 'I was reading.'   'What ____?'
4 'He visits his grandparents.'   'How often ____ them?'
5 'They'll do it.'   'When ____ it?'
6 'She's been waiting outside.'   'How long ____ there?'

7 'I come from Australia.'   'Which part of Australia ____ from?'
8 'I've got a car.'   'What kind of car ____?'
9 'We bought some wine.'   'How much wine ____?'
10 'She likes pop music.'   'What kind of pop music ____?'
11 'We saw a film.'   'Which film ____?'
12 'She was talking to someone.'   'Who ____ to?'

144   Domande sul soggetto e sul complemento

1   *Who*, nelle domande, può riferirsi sia al soggetto che al complemento. Confronta:

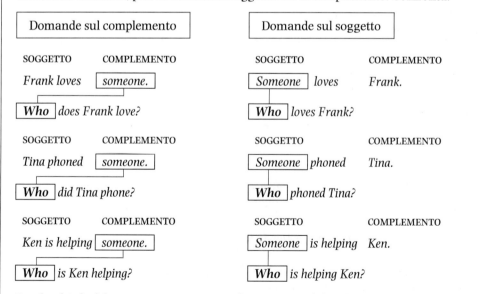

Se *who* chiede del soggetto, viene seguito direttamente dal verbo p.es. *loves, phoned, is helping*, senza l'ausiliare *do/does* nel presente e *did* nel passato remoto. La struttura è quindi come in una frase affermativa.

2 | Si può usare anche *what, which* e *how many* per fare domande sul soggetto.

'**What made** that noise?'   'It was the cat.'
'**Which car goes** the fastest?'   'The Mercedes.'
'**How many people went** to the party?'   'About fifty.'

ESERCIZIO 144A

Formula delle domande che comincino con *who* o *what*.

Esempi:

She wants to see someone.   *Who does she want to see?*
Someone wants to see her.   *Who wants to see her?*
Someone told me.   *Who told you?*

1 I told someone.
2 Someone wrote to me.
3 I wrote to someone.
4 Something is making that noise.
5 He's making something.
6 Someone makes the decisions.

7 They helped someone.
8 Someone helped them.
9 She was looking for someone.
10 Someone was looking for her.
11 Something moved.
12 Someone gave me the book.

145 Espressioni interrogative

1 | ***What, who* e *which***

a | Si usa *what* ('quale', 'che', 'che cosa') come aggettivo o pronome (p.es. *what colour, what nationality*) per fare domande soprattutto sulle cose.

__What__ colour is your car?
__What__ nationality is Maria?
__What__ is Ken doing?
__What__ would you like to drink?

Tavolta si usa però anche riferendosi alle persone.

__What__ actors do you like?

b | Si usa *who* ('chi') solo come pronome per fare domande sulle persone.

__Who__ is your favourite actor?
__Who__ told you the news?

c | Si usa *which* ('quale', 'che', 'che cosa') come aggettivo o pronome per fare domande sia sulle persone che sulle cose, se la scelta è limitata.

__Which__ colour do you like best – red, blue or yellow?
__Which__ actor do you prefer – Robert de Niro or Dustin Hoffman?
__Which__ would you like – wine or beer?

Spesso, però, anche se la scelta è limitata, si usa *who*.

Who *do you prefer – Robert de Niro or Dustin Hoffman?*

Inoltre, sempre in questi casi di scelta limitata, si usa spesso *which one* invece di *who* o *what*.

Which one *do you prefer – Robert de Niro or Dustin Hoffman?*
Which one *do you want – the red one or the blue one?*

Si può usare anche *which of . . . .*

Which of *these colours do you like best?*

2 | **Whose**

Si usa *whose*, seguito o meno da un nome, per chiedere 'di chi?'

*'***Whose*** book is this?'   'It's Maria's.'*
*'***Whose*** are these?'   'They're mine.'*

3 | **Where, when, why e how**

a | Si usa *where* per chiedere 'dov'è?'

*'***Where*** are you going on holiday?'   'To Greece.'*
*'***Where*** does Sue live?'   'In London.'*

b | Si usa *when* per chiedere 'quando?'

*'***When*** were you born?'   'In 1970.'*
*'***When*** is she leaving?'   'At 2 o'clock.'*

c | Si usa *why* per chiedere 'perché?'

*'***Why*** are you late?'   'Because my car broke down.'*
*'***Why*** did you go out?'   'To do some shopping.'*

d | Si usa *how* per chiedere 'come?'

*'***How*** did you get here?'   'I came by bus.'*
*'***How*** do you spell your name?'   'D-A-V-I-S.'*

Si usa *how* nei saluti e nelle presentazioni, e per chiedere lo stato di salute.

*'***How*** are you?'   'I'm fine, thanks. And you?'*
*'***How*** do you do?'   '***How*** do you do? I'm pleased to meet you.'*
How *is your mother now? Is she feeling any better?*

Si usa *how* con aggettivi (p.es. *old, tall*), avverbi (p.es. *often, well*) e con *much* e *many*.

*'***How old*** are you?'   'I'm 18.'*
*'***How often*** do you go to the cinema?'   'About once a week.'*
How much *money have you got with you?*
How many *brothers and sisters have you got?*

ESERCIZIO 145A

Osserva le risposte, poi completa le domande usando le parole del riquadro.

Esempio:

'*How old* are you?'   'I'm 20.'

> what   who   which   whose   where   when   why   how
> how often   how much   how many   ~~how old~~   how long

1 '____ do you do?'   'I'm a student.'
2 '____ do you live?'   'In London.'
3 '____ have you lived there?'   'For two years.'
4 '____ brothers and sisters have you got?'   'Two brothers and two sisters.'
5 '____ is your favourite pop singer?'   'Michael Jackson.'
6 '____ is your birthday?'   'November the 3rd.'
7 '____ do you play tennis?'   'About once a week.'
8 '____ does it cost to play tennis in Britain?'   'It's not very expensive.'
9 '____ bag is this?'   'I think it's Simon's.'
10 '____ do you usually get to work?'   'By car.'
11 '____ of those girls is your sister?'   'She's the one in the black skirt.'
12 '____ are you smiling?'   'Oh, I've just thought of something funny.'

146   Domande negative

1

Si formula una domanda negativa collocando di solito la contrazione *n't* dopo un verbo ausiliare (p.es. *be, have, can*).

Aren't you watching TV?
Haven't they finished yet?
Can't he swim?

Not/n't viene posto dopo *be* anche quando *be* funge da verbo principale, e dopo *have* in *have got*.

Aren't you Simon Robinson?
Haven't they got any money?

In presenza di due o più ausiliari, *n't* segue il primo.

Haven't you been listening?

Per formulare la domanda negativa al presente o al passato remoto, tempi senza ausiliare, si usa *do/does* e *did* rispettivamente, davanti a *n't*.

Don't you smoke?
Doesn't she live here any more?
Didn't they go to the cinema?

2 | L'ordine delle parole cambia usando la forma piena *not*. Confronta:

***Are you not** watching the TV?*	***Aren't** you watching the TV?*
***Does she not** live here any more?*	***Doesn't** she live here any more?*

Le forme con *not* sono più formali e meno frequenti.

3 | Spesso si formulano domande negative per esprimere sorpresa, delusione o fastidio.

***Don't** you smoke? I thought you did.*
***Hasn't** she finished the letter yet? She's been typing it all morning!*

La costruzione propria di una domanda negativa è frequente in quella che è invece una frase esclamativa.

***Isn't** it a terrible day!*

Si usa questa costruzione anche per chiedere conferma di qualcosa che si pensa di sapere.

*'**Aren't** you Simon Robinson?'   'Yes, that's right.'   'I thought you were.'*

4 | Nota il significato di *yes* e *no* in risposta a una domanda negativa.

*'**Didn't** they see the film?'   'Yes.'* (= Sì, l'hanno visto.)/*'**No.**'* (= No, non l'hanno visto.)

ESERCIZIO 146A

Formula delle domande negative usando *n't* e le parole fra parentesi.

Esempio:

I posted the letter to you over a week ago! *Haven't you received it yet?* (you | have | received it yet?)

1 Why aren't you eating your dinner? (you | do | like it?)
2 'Look! ____ (that | is | your brother over there?)' 'Oh, yes.'
3 'I really must go now.' 'But it's only half past nine. ____ (you | can | stay a little longer?)'
4 '____ (she | is | a pretty child!)' 'Yes, lovely.'
5 ____ (I | have | met you somewhere before?) I'm sure I know your face.
6 'Sally is still in bed.' '____ (she | is | going to work today?)'
7 ____ (you | do | want to come to the concert tonight?) I thought you said you did.

147 Domande 'coda'

1 | Osserva queste frasi.

*It's cold today, **isn't it**?*
*You haven't seen my keys, **have you**?*

Domande 'coda' vengono dette, in inglese, espressioni come *isn't it?*, *have you?*, equivalenti a 'vero?', 'non è vero?', collocate in fondo alla frase.

2 Le domande 'coda' sono formate da un verbo ausiliare (p.es. *be, have, can*) + un pronome personale (p.es. *it, you*).

*You aren't listening to me, **are you?***
*You haven't seen my keys, **have you?***
*He can swim, **can't he?***

Queste domande hanno lo stesso verbo ausiliare della frase principale.

Se la frase principale ha *be* come verbo principale, si usa *be* nella domanda 'coda'.

*It's cold today, **isn't it?***

Se la frase principale ha *have got*, si usa *have* nella domanda 'coda'.

*You **haven't got** a stamp, **have you?***

In presenza di due o più verbi ausiliari, nella domanda 'coda' si ripete il primo.

*He **hasn't been** waiting long, **has he?***

Per formulare la domanda 'coda' al presente o al passato remoto, si usa *do/does* e *did*, rispettivamente.

*You don't like football, **do you?***
*Simon lives in London, **doesn't he?***
*You saw the film, **didn't you?***

3 Di solito una domanda 'coda' negativa segue una frase affermativa e viceversa. Confronta:

−	+		+	−

*It **isn't** cold today, **is it?*** | *It's cold today, **isn't it?***
*You **don't** like football, **do you?*** | *You **like** football, **don't you?***
*He **can't** swim, **can he?*** | *He can swim, **can't he?***

4 Il significato di una domanda 'coda' dipende dall'intonazione della voce.

a Se si intende fare una domanda vera e propria, l'intonazione sale.

*You haven't seen my keys, **have you**?*  (= Hai visto le mie chiavi?)

b Ma se si è sicuri della risposta e si vuole avere solo una conferma, l'intonazione cala.

*It's cold today, **isn't it**?*  (= Fa freddo, oggi, vero?)

c Spesso si usa una frase negativa + una domanda 'coda' affermativa per chiedere un favore, un aiuto, un'informazione.

−	+

*You **couldn't** lend me some money, **could you?***
*You **don't** know where Peter lives, **do you?***

5

a Nota:

La domanda 'coda' di *I am* è *aren't I?*

*I'm right, **aren't I?***

b Dopo l'imperativo si può usare, come domanda 'coda', sia *will/would you?* che *can/can't/could you?* quando si vuole che qualcuno faccia qualcosa.

Switch** on the light, **will you?
Help** me with these bags, **could you?

Dopo l'imperativo negativo si usa *will you?*

Don't forget** to post my letter, **will you?

c Dopo *let's* si usa *shall we?* per proporre qualcosa.

Let's** listen to some music, **shall we?

d Si usa *they* nelle domande 'coda' dopo *somebody/someone, everybody/everyone* e *nobody/no one.*

Somebody** told you, **didn't they?
No one** phoned for me, **did they?

e Si usa *it* nelle domande 'coda' dopo *nothing.*

Nothing** is wrong, **is it?

f Si può usare *there* come soggetto di una domanda 'coda'.

There** won't be any problems, will **there?

ESERCIZIO 147A

Formula una domanda 'coda' dopo ogni frase. Talvolta è possibile più di una costruzione.

Esempio:

It's a good restaurant.
It's a good restaurant, isn't it?

1 You don't like this music.
2 Robert isn't at work today.
3 I'm too late.
4 You haven't seen the newspaper.
5 Lynne speaks French and German.
6 They didn't go to the concert.
7 You'd like to have something to eat.
8 We're leaving tomorrow.
9 You couldn't do me a favour.
10 You don't know where Sarah is.
11 Switch on the light for me.
12 Don't forget to lock the door.
13 Nobody was watching the TV.
14 Everyone will be here soon.
15 Nothing terrible has happened.
16 There's plenty of time.
17 Pass me that magazine.
18 Let's have a cup of tea.

148 Domande di commento

1 Osserva queste frasi.

'I'm going to bed now.' *'**Are you?** Oh, good night, then.'*
'He can't swim.' *'**Can't he?** I thought he could.'*

Spesso si commenta quello che una persona dice con una domanda breve formata da un verbo ausiliare e da un pronome personale p.es. *Are you?* o *Can't he?*

Non si tratta di una domanda vera e propria, bensì di un modo per dimostrare che si sta ascoltando. Inoltre, con queste 'domande' si fa spesso un 'commento', esprimendo tutta una serie di sentimenti come interesse, sorpresa o rabbia, secondo l'intonazione della voce.

2 In queste domande di commento si usa lo stesso verbo ausiliare della frase in questione.

*'**I'm** going to bed now.'* *'**Are you?** Oh, good night, then.'*
*'**We've** finished.'* *'**Have you?**'*

Se la frase in questione ha *be* come verbo principale, si usa *be* nella domanda di commento.

*'**I'm** hungry.'* *'**Are you?** I'll make you something to eat.'*

Se la frase in questione ha *have got*, si usa *have* nella domanda di commento.

*'**I've got** a headache.'* *'Oh, **have you?** Do you want some aspirin?'*

Se la frase ha due o più ausiliari, nella domanda di commento si ripete il primo.

*'**I've been** waiting for an hour.'* *'**Have you?**'*

Per formulare la domanda di commento nel presente e nel passato remoto si usa *do/does* e *did*, rispettivamente.

*'I **like** football.'* *'**Do you?**'*
*'She **lives** in Brighton.'* *'**Does she?**'*
*'We **saw** the film.'* *'**Did you?**'*

3 Si formulano domande affermative come commento a frasi affermative e domande negative come commento a frasi negative. Confronta:

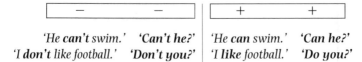

− −	+ +
*'He **can't** swim.'* *'**Can't he?**'*	*'He **can** swim.'* *'**Can he?**'*
*'I **don't** like football.'* *'**Don't you?**'*	*'I **like** football.'* *'**Do you?**'*

Si può commentare una frase affermativa anche con una domanda negativa, calando l'intonazione della voce. Questo significa che si vuole enfatizzare che si è d'accordo.

'It was a fantastic film.' *'Yes, **wasn't it?** I really enjoyed it.'*

ESERCIZIO 148A

Immagina di essere seduto su una panchina, quando ti si avvicina un mendicante
e comincia a parlare.

Commenta con delle domande quello che dice.

Tramp: It's a lovely day.
You: Yes, *isn't it?*
Tramp: This is my bench, you know.
You: Oh, *is it?* I'm sorry, I didn't know.
Tramp: It's all right. You can sit here. You may
not believe this, but I was very rich once. I
was almost a millionaire.
You: __1__? That's amazing.
Tramp: Yes, but I gave all my money away.
You: __2__? What, all of it?
Tramp: Yes, every penny. I gave it away to my
friends, to my relatives. But they didn't thank
me.
You: __3__?
Tramp: No. Still, I'm much happier now.
You: __4__?
Tramp: Yes, I like the simple life. I like sleeping
in the park under the stars.
You: __5__? Don't you get cold?
Tramp: No, I don't feel the cold. I'm used to it.
You: __6__? Really? Even in winter?
Tramp: Yes, I've been sleeping on this bench for
over twenty years.
You: __7__? Really? That's a long time.
Tramp: Yes, the only problem is my health. I've
got a bad heart condition.
You: Oh, __8__?
Tramp: Yes, I haven't got long to live.
You: __9__?
Tramp: No, but I'm going to enjoy my last few
weeks. I'm going to eat and drink well ... But
food and drink are so expensive nowadays.
You: Yes, they are, aren't they?
Tramp: Yes, if I had some money, I'd go and
have a good meal.
You: __10__?
Tramp: Yes ... You couldn't let me have a few
pounds, could you?

149 Domande introdotte da un'altra frase

1 Quando si chiedono informazioni, a volte si introduce la domanda con frasi quali
Could you tell me . . .? Do you know . . .? o *Can you remember . . .?* Confronta:

DOMANDA DIRETTA	DOMANDA INTRODOTTA DA UN'ALTRA FRASE
Where is the station?	*Could you tell me **where** the station **is**?*
When will they finish the job?	*Do you know **when** they **will** finish the job?*

Nelle domande così introdotte l'ordine delle parole è come nelle frasi affermative
p.es. *the station is, they will finish.*

2 Nota i mutamenti che avvengono quando si formula una domanda in questo modo
al presente o al passato remoto.

*What time **does** the shop **close**?*	*Can you tell me **what time** the shop **closes**?*
*What **did** she **say**?*	*Can you remember **what** she **said**?*

In queste domande non si usa il verbo ausiliare *do* (*do, does, did*).

3 Se manca un pronome o avverbio interrogativo p.es. *what, who, where,* si può usare
if o *whether* per introdurre la domanda.

Is she at home now?	*Do you know **if** she is at home now?*
Can he speak Italian?	*I wonder **whether** he can speak Italian?*

ESERCIZIO 149A

Usa le frasi tra parentesi per introdurre queste domande.

Esempio:

Where is the Tourist Information office? (Could you tell me)
Could you tell me where the Tourist Information office is?

 1 When does the last bus leave? (Can you tell me)
 2 Is he over 18? (Do you know)
 3 Can she speak French? (Do you know)
 4 How does this machine work? (Can you explain)
 5 Where are you going on holiday? (Have you decided)
 6 What did he tell you? (Do you remember exactly)
 7 Will you be here tomorrow? (Do you know)
 8 Does she like horse riding? (Have you got any idea)
 9 Did you switch off all the lights? (Can you remember)
10 Has everyone gone home? (Do you know)

Nota –I mutamenti visti sopra avvengono anche passando da una domanda diretta a una
indiretta p.es. *'Where do you live?'* —→ *He asked me **where** I **lived**.* Cfr. 78.

150 Risposte brevi

1

Spesso si risponde a una domanda 'a risposta chiusa' con una risposta breve, formata dal soggetto + un verbo ausiliare (p.es. *be*, *have*, *can*).

'*Are you going out?*'   '*Yes, **I am.**'* (= Sì, esco)
'*Has he seen the film?*'   '*No, **he hasn't.**'* (= No, non l'ha visto)
'*Can she speak French?*'   '*Yes, **she can.**'* (= Sì, lo sa parlare)

Se la domanda ha *be* come verbo principale, si usa *be* nella risposta breve.

'***Are** you angry?*'   '*No, **I'm not.**'*

Se la domanda ha *have got*, si usa *have* nella risposta breve.

'***Have** you **got** a car?*'   '*No, **I haven't.**'*

Se nella domanda ci sono due o più verbi ausiliari, nella risposta breve si usa il primo.

'***Have** you **been** working?*'   '*Yes, **I have.**'*

Per formulare la risposta breve al presente o al passato remoto, si usa *do/does* e *did*, rispettivamente.

'*Do you know Kate?*'   '*Yes, **I do.**'*
'*Does Simon smoke?*'   '*No, **he doesn't.**'*
'*Did they see the film?*'   '*Yes, **they did.**'*

2

Si possono formulare risposte brevi anche per controbattere o per rafforzare un'affermazione.

'*I'm not angry.*'   '*Yes, **you are.**'*
'*Sue lives in Western Road.*'   '*No, **she doesn't.**'*
'*Simon is very helpful.*'   '*Yes, **he is.**'*

ESERCIZIO 150A

Completa le risposte brevi a queste domande, come nell'esempio.

Esempi:

'Have you ever been to the USA?'   'No, *I haven't.*'
'Is she coming to the party?'   'Yes, *she is.*'

1 'Can you play the guitar?'   'No, ____.'
2 'Are you over 21?'   'Yes, ____.'
3 'Did Andrew go to school yesterday?'   'Yes, ____.'
4 'Do you smoke?'   'No, ____.'
5 'Does Sarah like tennis?'   'Yes, ____.'
6 'Have you got time for a coffee?'   'No, ____.'
7 'Is Ken working today?'   'No, ____.'
8 'Were you at home last night?'   'Yes, ____.'
9 'Will you be seeing Martin tonight?'   'Yes, ____.'
10 'Have they been living here very long?'   'No, ____.'
11 'Has Lynne got any brothers or sisters?'   'No, ____.'
12 'Does Simon want to go to university?'   'Yes, ____.'

ESERCIZIO 150B

Tutte queste affermazioni sono false. Controbattile formulando delle risposte brevi.
Esempi:

'Rio de Janeiro is the capital of Brazil.'   *'No, it isn't.'*
'Marconi didn't invent the radio.'   *'Yes, he did.'*

1 'Penguins can fly.'
2 'The earth doesn't move around the sun.'
3 'Shakespeare was born in London.'
4 'The population of the world isn't increasing.'
5 'The Second World War ended in 1940.'
6 'Spaghetti grows on trees.'

151   *So/neither am I, so/neither do I, so/neither can I, ecc.*

1   Osserva queste frasi.

'I'm going out later.'   **'So am I.'** (= Anch'io.)
He can play the guitar, and **so can I.'** (= ... e so suonarla anch'io.)
'I'm not feeling very well.'   **'Neither am I.'** (= Neanch'io.)
She can't drive, and **neither can I.'** (= ... e nemmeno io so guidare.)

Si può usare *so* (= 'anche') e *neither* (= 'neanche', 'nemmeno') davanti a un verbo ausiliare (p.es. *be, can*) + soggetto (p.es. *I, he*).

In questa costruzione si usa *be* se c'è *be* come verbo principale nella frase precedente; si usa *have*, se c'è *have got* come verbo principale.

'I'm thirsty.'   **'So am I.'**
You haven't got any money and **neither have I.**

Se ci sono due o più verbi ausiliari, si usa il primo dopo *so* e *neither*.

'I've been studying.'   **'So have I.'**

Nel presente e nel passato remoto si usa *do/does* e *did*, rispettivamente, dopo *so* e *neither*.

'I like tennis.'   **'So do I.'**
I don't want anything to eat, and **neither does Sue.**
'I went to the concert last week.'   **'So did I.'**

2   Si può usare *nor* invece di *neither*.

'I haven't got a car.'   *'**Nor**/**Neither** have I.'*

3   Si può usare *not ... either* invece di *neither* e *nor*.

'I'm not cold.'   *'**Neither** am I./**Nor** am I./I'm **not either**.'*
I can't swim, and **neither** *can you./and* **nor** *can you./and you can't* **either**.

4   *(N)either* ha due pronunce: /'(n)aɪðə(r)/ o /'(n)iːðə(r)/.

ESERCIZIO 151A

Concorda o meno con queste affermazioni usando '*So . . . I'* o *'Neither . . . I'*.

Esempi:

'I don't like noisy people.'   *'Neither do I.'*
'I'm a very tidy person.'   *'So am I.'*

  1 'I'm not very interested in football.'
  2 'I enjoy travelling.'
  3 'I've never been to Australia.'
  4 'I'd like to go there one day.'
  5 'I haven't got a very good memory.'
  6 'I haven't been working very hard recently.'
  7 'I often forget things.'
  8 'I went to bed quite late last night.'
  9 'I should go to bed earlier.'
10 'I always tell the truth.'
11 'I'd rather die than tell a lie.'
12 'I didn't tell lies even when I was a child.'

Nota –Per *either* e *neither* cfr. anche 119.2.

152 *I think so, I hope so, I expect so,* ecc.

1 Osserva queste frasi.

'Is she ill?'   *'I think so.'* (= Penso di sì.)
'Do you think the weather will be nice tomorrow?'   *'I hope so.'* (= Lo spero.)
'Do you think you'll come to the party?'   *'I expect so.'* (= Penso di sì.)

Si usa *so* dopo verbi come *think, hope, expect, imagine* e *suppose* per evitare di ripetere quanto è stato già detto.

Si usa *so* anche con l'espressione *be afraid.*

'Is she seriously ill?'   *'I'm afraid so.'*

2 Con i verbi *suppose, imagine* e *expect* si può fare la forma negativa in due modi:

soggetto + verbo + *not*	soggetto + *do not* + verbo + *so*

I suppose not. | *I don't suppose so.*
I imagine not. | *I don't imagine so.*
I expect not. | *I don't expect so.*

Si usa sempre soggetto + verbo + *not* con *hope* e *be afraid.*

'Do you think you will be late tonight?'   *'I hope not.'* (= Spero di non fare tardi.)
'Did he pass the exam?'   *'I'm afraid not.'* (= Temo di no.)

Di regolo con *think* si usa soggetto + *do not* + *so.*

'Is she ill?'   *'I don't think so.'* (= Penso di no.)

ESERCIZIO 152A

Da' risposte brevi usando le parole fra parentesi. Talvolta sono possibili due risposte.

Esempi:

'Do you think it will be a good concert?'   'Yes, I hope so.' (Yes | hope)
'Do you think we'll be late?'   'No, I hope not.' (No | hope)

1 'Are you going to sell your car?' (Yes | think)
2 'Will you give him the money?' (Yes | suppose)
3 'Have your parents heard the news?' (No | think)
4 'Will you be able to help us?' (No | afraid)
5 'Is she going to apply for the job?' (Yes | imagine)
6 'Do you think they will come with us?' (No | expect)
7 'Will he have to go into hospital?' (Yes | afraid)
8 'Will you have time to go shopping this afternoon?' (No | suppose)
9 'Do you think everything will be all right?' (Yes | expect)
10 'Does he know about the accident yet?' (Yes | imagine)

153   Frasi relative determinative con *who, that* e *which*

<table>
<tr><td>1</td><td>

Osserva queste frasi:

*I spoke to the woman **who owns the hotel**.*
*Did you see the letter **that came this morning**?*

Who owns the hotel e *that came this morning* sono 'frasi relative determinative.' Esse indicano a chi o a cosa si riferisce la persona che parla (p.es. *who owns the hotel* ci dice quale donna; e *that came this morning* ci dice quale lettera).

</td></tr>
<tr><td>2</td><td>

Si usa *who* per le persone. Confronta:

*I spoke to the woman. **She** owns the hotel.* *The man was very nice. **He** interviewed me.*	*I spoke to the woman **who** owns the hotel.* *The man **who** interviewed me was very nice.*

Si usa *that* per le cose. Confronta:

*Did you see the letter? **It** came this morning.* *The keys have disappeared. **They** were on this table.*	*Did you see the letter **that** came this morning?* *The keys **that** were on this table have disappeared.*

Nota che *who* e *that* sostituiscono il pronome personale.

*I spoke to the woman **who** owns the hotel.* (Non: ~~I spoke to the woman **who she** owns the hotel.~~)

</td></tr>
</table>

3 | Si può usare *which* invece di *that* (per parlare di cose) in una frase relativa determinativa.

*Did you see the letter **which** came this morning?*
*The keys **which** were on this table have disappeared.*

Nello stile informale, è anche possibile usare *that* invece di *who* (per parlare di persone).

*I spoke to the woman **that** owns the hotel.*

4 | Nota che *who, that* e *which* si possono omettere quando sono complementi di frasi relative determinative p.es. *He's the man **(who) we met last night**.* Cfr. 154.

ESERCIZIO 153A

Collega ogni coppia di frasi usando *who* per le persone e *that* per le cose.

Esempi:

That's the woman. She works in the post office.
That's the woman who works in the post office.
The man wasn't English. He spoke to us.
The man who spoke to us wasn't English.

1 He's the man. He painted my house.
2 What is the name of the boy? He telephoned you.
3 What's happened to the money? It was on my desk.

4 They're the people. They offered Sue a job.
5 The car has now been found. It was stolen.
6 She's the person. She gives me a lift to work every day.
7 The lock has now been repaired. It was broken.
8 Most of the people are very nice. They work in Peter's office.

154 Omissione di *who, that* e *which* nelle frasi relative determinative

1 | *Who, that* e *which* possono essere sia soggetto che complemento oggetto di una frase relativa determinativa.

Marianne is the girl | who | *invited us to the party.*

who è soggetto: | she | invited us to the party

Marianne is the girl | who | *we met last night.*

who è complemento oggetto: we met | her | last night

2 | Spesso, nelle frasi relative determinative, *who, that* e *which* vengono omessi quando sono complemento oggetto.

*Marianne is the girl **we met last night**.* (La ragazza *che* abbiamo incontrato ieri sera)
*Have you seen the book **I put on this table**?* (Il libro *che* ho messo su questo tavolo)

3 | *Who, that* e *which* non possono però essere omessi quando sono soggetto della frase relativa determinativa.

*Marianne is the girl **who invited us to the party**. (Non: ~~Marianne is the girl **invited us…**~~)*

*Have you seen the book **that was on this table?** (Non: ~~Have you seen the book **was on this table?**~~)*

4 | Nelle frasi relative determinative si può usare *whom* invece di *who* (per le persone) quando questo è complemento oggetto del verbo.

*I met a woman **whom I know**.* (*che* io conosco)

Ma *whom* è alquanto formale e poco usato nel linguaggio di tutti i giorni. Si usa invece *who* o *that* (o si omette).

*I met a woman **(who) I know**.*

ESERCIZIO 154A

Completa le frasi usando *who* per le persone e *that* per le cose; se è possibile omettere *who* o *that*, scrivili comunque tra parentesi.

Esempi:

I can't find the envelopes *(that)* I bought this morning.
Have you seen the film *that* is on TV tonight?

1 John Murray is the man _who_ owns the Grand Hotel.
2 The man _x_ we spoke to wasn't very nice.
3 This is the sweater _x_ I bought on Saturday.
4 What is the name of the company _x_ you work for?

5 A bi-lingual person is someone _who_ can speak two languages equally well.
6 Who's that boy _x_ Sally is dancing with?
7 Are these all the letters _that_ came in this morning's post?
8 Have you found the money _x_ you lost?
9 The people _who_ used to live in that house have moved.
10 I don't like films _that_ are very violent.

155 Frasi relative determinative con *whose, where, when* e *why/that*

1 | *Whose*

Si usa *whose* nelle frasi relative (al posto di *his, her, their* ecc.) per esprimere possesso o specificazione. Confronta:

*I've got a friend. **His** brother is an actor.*	*I've got a friend **whose** brother is an actor.*
*They're the people. **Their** house caught fire.*	*They're the people **whose** house caught fire.*

Non confondere *whose* e *who's*; *who's* = *who is* o *who has*.

*I've got a friend **who's** at university.* (= *che è all'università*)

2 | ***Where, when* e *why/that***

a | Si può usare *where* ('dove', 'in cui') e *when* ('quando', 'in cui') nelle frasi relative.

*The factory **where I work** is going to close down.*
*Is there a time **when we can meet?***

b | Dopo la parola *reason*, si può usare *why* o *that* nelle frasi relative.

*Is there a **reason why/that you want to leave now?***

c | *When, why* e *that* possono essere omessi.

*Is there a time **we can meet?***
*Is there a reason **you want to leave now?***

Si può omettere anche *where* se si usa una preposizione.

*The factory **I work in** is going to close down.*

ESERCIZIO 155A

Collega ogni coppia di frasi usando *whose*.

Esempio:

I know someone. His mother is an opera singer.
I know someone whose mother is an opera singer.

1 She's the woman. Her husband teaches at Annie's school.
2 He's the man. His flat was broken into.
3 They're the couple. Their children were injured in the accident.
4 That's the girl. Her friend lent me the money.
5 I'm the person. My credit cards were stolen.
6 Are you the one? Your mother phoned the police.

ESERCIZIO 155B

Completa le frasi usando *where, when* o *why/that*.

Esempio:

That is the church *where* Ken and Kate were married.

1 Did they tell you the reason _____ they wanted you to do that?
2 What's the name of the restaurant _____ you had lunch?
3 I can remember a time _____ there was no television.
4 It that the hospital _____ you had your operation?
5 I don't understand the reason _____ he was late.
6 Do you remember the time _____ your car broke down on the motorway?

---

156 Frasi relative determinative e frasi relative accessorie

1 | Le frasi relative 'determinative' identificano dei nomi: esse precisano a chi o a che cosa si riferisce la persona che parla. Cfr. 153 e 154.

*I spoke to the woman **who owns the hotel**.* (*who owns the hotel* precisa quale donna)
*The house **which Sue has bought** is over 100 years old.* (*which Sue has bought* precisa quale casa)

2 Le frasi relative 'accessorie' non identificano a chi o a che cosa si riferisce la persona che parla; esse comunicano un'informazione semplicemente aggiuntiva su una persona o una cosa già identificata.

*Ken's mother, **who is 69**, has just passed her driving test.* (*who is 69* non precisa quale donna; si sa già che è *Ken's mother*)
*Sue's house, **which is in the centre of town**, is over 100 years old.* (*which is in the centre of town* non precisa quale casa; si sa già che è *Sue's house*)

Le frasi relative accessorie sono più comuni nello stile formale, soprattutto nella lingua scritta e, in genere, sono chiuse tra virgole.

*Last weekend I met Sue, **who told me she was going on holiday soon**.*
*Frank Morris, **who is one of my best friends**, has decided to go and live in France.*

3 In una frase relativa accessoria si usa sempre *who* per le persone e *which* per le cose; non si può usare *that*.

*She gave me the key, **which** I put in my pocket.* (Non: ~~She gave me the key, that I put in my pocket.~~)

In una frase relativa accessoria non si può omettere *who* o *which*.

*My uncle John, **who lives in Manchester**, is coming to visit me next week.* (Non: ~~My uncle John, lives in Manchester, is coming …~~)
*She gave me the key, **which I put in my pocket**.* (Non: ~~She gave me the key, I put in my pocket.~~)

ESERCIZIO 156A

Aggiungi la virgola dove è necessaria.

Esempi:

Robert's parents __,__ who are both retired __,__ now live in Spain.

1 The people ____ who live next door ____ helped us to move the furniture.
2 Have you still got the money ____ that I gave you?
3 Sydney ____ which has a population of more than three million ____ is Australia's largest city.
4 Peter's sister ____ who I've known for years ____ is a very nice person.
5 We saw Sue last night with that man ____ who works in the library.
6 The chair ____ that was broken ____ has now been repaired.

ESERCIZIO 156B

Completa le frasi usando *who*, *that* o *which*, ma soltanto dove è necessario – lascia uno spazio vuoto, se è possibile ometterli. In una frase sono possibili due costruzioni.

Esempio:

Is that the same song ____ we heard yesterday?

1 Maria, ____ has only been in Britain for a few weeks, speaks excellent English.
2 Who was the girl ____ you were speaking to just now?
3 My sister, ____ wasn't feeling very hungry, didn't want to go to the restaurant.
4 I've lost all the money ____ you gave me.
5 This is the letter ____ came in today's post.
6 Mr and Mrs Woods, ____ live next door to us, have gone on holiday.
7 Brighton, ____ is a tourist centre on the south coast of England, is about 85 kilometres from London.

157 Frasi relative accessorie con *whose, where, when* e *whom*

Si può usare *whose, where* e *when* (cfr. 155) nelle frasi relative accessorie.

*Tina Harris, **whose brother is the actor Paul Harris**, is a good friend of mine.*
*We visited a town called Christchurch, **where we had lunch in an Italian restaurant.***
*We're going on holiday in September, **when the weather isn't so hot.***

Nelle frasi relative accessorie si può usare *whom* invece di *who*, quando questo è complemento oggetto del verbo (cfr. 154.4).

*Sarah Ross, **who/whom you met in Madrid last summer**, will be at the party tonight.*

ESERCIZIO 157A

Peter andrà negli Stati Uniti il prossimo anno. Completa quello che dice al riguardo usando *whose, who/whom, where* e *when*.

'I'm going to the States at the beginning of January *when*, hopefully, it won't be too cold. I'm flying to New York, ___(1)___ my friend Brian has been living for the past two years. I'm really looking forward to meeting his American girlfriend Cyndy, ___(2)___ I met when they both came over to London last year. Cyndy, ___(3)___ brother is quite a famous jazz musician, has promised to take me to Greenwich Village, ___(4)___ there are a lot of jazz clubs. After two weeks in New York, I'll take the Greyhound bus to Cleveland, Ohio. I'm going to stay there with my Aunt Jackie, ___(5)___ son – my cousin Abe – I met last summer in England. Then, if I have enough money, I'll travel south to New Orleans. I hope to get there by the first two weeks of February, ___(6)___ the Mardi Gras Festival takes place.'

158 Frasi relative con preposizione + *which* e *whom*

1 | Frasi determinative

Si può usare una preposizione davanti a *which* e *whom*, p.es. *in which, with whom* in una frase relativa determinativa.

*That's the town **in which he was born**.*
*The people **with whom I stayed** were very kind.*

Ma nel linguaggio di tutti i giorni si preferisce mettere la preposizione in fondo alla frase e omettere il pronome *which, whom*, ecc.

*That's the town **he was born in**.*
*The people **I stayed with** were very kind.*

2 | **Frasi accessorie**

a Nello stile formale si può usare una preposizione davanti a *which* e *whom* anche in una frase accessoria relativa.

*She's studying chemistry, **about which I know very little**.*
*Mr and Mrs Morris, **with whom we went on holiday**, live in Bristol.*

Ma nel linguaggio di tutti i giorni si preferisce mettere la preposizione in fondo alla frase e usare *who* invece di *whom*.

*She's studying chemistry, **which I know very little about**.*
*Mr and Mrs Morris, **who we went on holiday with**, live in Bristol.*

Nota che non si può omettere il pronome *which, who*, ecc. in una frase relativa accessoria.

b Nota la costruzione *some of/any of/many of/much of/none of/all of/* ecc. + *which/whom*.

*A number of my friends, **some of whom** you've met before, will be at the party.*
*He gave me a lot of advice, **much of which** was very useful.*

ESERCIZIO 158A

Collega ogni coppia di frasi senza usare *who, whom* o *which*.

Esempi:

The restaurant was in West Street. We went to it.
The restaurant we went to was in West Street.
The woman is a good friend of mine. I borrowed the money from her.
The woman I borrowed the money from is a good friend of mine.

1 The man is Sue's cousin. I introduced you to him.
2 The hotel overlooked the sea. We stayed at it.
3 The shop is closed. I bought the shoes from it.
4 The people like him very much. He works with them.

ESERCIZIO 158B

Collega ogni coppia di frasi usando (i) *who* o *which*, e (ii) una preposizione + *whom* o *which*, come nell'esempio.

Esempio:

Mr Jones is a teacher at Annie's school. I was talking to him a moment ago.
 (i) *Mr Jones, who I was talking to a moment ago, is a teacher at Annie's school.*
 (ii) *Mr Jones, to whom I was talking a moment ago, is a teacher at Annie's school.*

1 Peter's party is next Saturday evening. We are all invited to it.
2 Mr Mason apologized for the mistake. We complained to him.
3 The film *Family Life* is showing next week. I've heard good reports about it.

ESERCIZIO 158C

Una donna si sta lamentando di un uomo che non le piace affatto. Completa quello che dice usando le parole fra parentesi e *of which* o *of whom*.

'He's always giving people lots of advice, *much of which* (much) is complete nonsense. He also talks about all the famous people he says he knows, ___(1)___ (most) I'm sure he's never even met. He boasts about the hundreds of books he says he's read, ___(2)___ (many) I'm sure he's never opened in his life. He talks about his 'three lovely children', ___(3)___ (all) are, in fact, as horrible as their father. He talks constantly about what a good son he is, and how often he visits his parents, ___(4)___ (neither) ever actually see him. And what else? Well, he spends lots of money, ___(5)___ (none) is his, and drives two big cars, ___(6)___ (both) belong to his wife!'

159 *Which* riferito a un'intera frase

Si può usare *which*, nel significato di 'il che', 'la qual cosa', per fare riferimento a un'intera frase precedente. Confronta:

| *He offered to help me.* | **This** | *was very kind of him.* |

| *He offered to help me,* | **which** | *was very kind of him.* |

which = il fatto che si sia offerto di aiutarmi

ESERCIZIO 159A

Collega ogni frase di **A** con la frase più adatta di **B** usando *which*.

Esempio:

1 *She lent me the money, which was very generous of her.*

A	**B**
1 She lent me the money.	This made driving dangerous.
2 They had to wait for over an hour.	It made us all feel very hungry.
3 There was a lot of snow on the roads.	That is why I didn't buy you a ticket.
4 I knew you didn't want to go to the concert.	It meant I had to take a taxi.
5 There was a bus strike.	This annoyed them very much.
6 There was a delicious smell coming from the kitchen.	This was very generous of her.

160 Tempo: *when, as, while, as soon as, before, after, until*

1   Quando si vuole dire che certe cose avvengono nello stesso momento, si può usare *when, as, while.*

When I was watching TV, the telephone rang.
As they were walking down the street, they saw Sue.
I often listen to the radio **while** I'm having breakfast.

Nota che normalmente si usa *when, as* o *while* + la forma progressiva (p.es. *when I was watching, as they were walking, while I'm having*) per l'azione più duratura.

Spesso si usa *(just) as* per due azioni brevi che avvengono nello stesso momento p.es. *The baby started crying* (**just**) **as** *I got into bed.*

2   Quando si vuole dire che certe cose avvengono una dopo l'altra, si può usare *when, as soon as, before, after.*

When I had finished breakfast, I went out.
I'll phone you **as soon as** I get home.
The train had left **before** they arrived at the station.
After he left school, he started working in a bank.

Nota che, quando si parla del futuro, normalmente si usa il presente dopo *when, as soon as, before,* ecc. p.es. *I'll phone you* **as soon as** *I get home.* Cfr. 22.

3   *When* può avere lo stesso significato di *while/as, before* o *after.*

When/While/As I was watching TV, the telephone rang.
The train had left **when/before** they arrived at the station.
When/After he left school, he started working in a bank.

4   Si usa *until* (o *till*) per dire 'fino al momento in cui'.

We waited **until** she arrived.
I knew nothing about it **until** you told me.

ESERCIZIO 160A

Scegli l'espressione giusta.

Esempio:

I'm not going out now. I'll wait *until*/~~when~~ it stops raining.

1   ~~While~~/When I had locked all the doors, I went to bed.
2   I fell off the chair *while*/~~until~~ I was changing the light bulb.
3   They waited ~~when~~/until everybody was there *before*/~~until~~ they started the meeting.
4   My grandfather worked hard all his life *until*/~~when~~ he retired.
5   I usually get up ~~before~~/as soon as I wake up.
6   It started to rain ~~until~~/just as we got to the park.
7   I broke my leg ~~as soon as~~/when I was skiing.
8   The film had already started ~~when~~/just as we sat down in the cinema.

161 Contrasto: *although, even though, though, in spite of, despite, while, whereas, however*

1 Si può usare *although* e *even though* per sottolineare un contrasto. Dopo *although* e *even though* occorre una frase intera, con soggetto e verbo.

Although she doesn't enjoy her job, she works hard.
She passed the exam, although she hadn't studied for it.
Even though they were late, they didn't hurry.

Even though è più enfatico di *although*.

Si può usare *though* invece di *although* specialmente nello stile informale.

Though they were late, they didn't hurry.

Se *though* viene collocato in fondo alla frase, assume il significato di 'tuttavia' (cfr. 5 di seguito).

The room is very small. It's quite comfortable though.

2 Si può anche usare *in spite of* o *despite* per indicare contrasti. Dopo *in spite of/despite* si può usare un nome o la forma in *-ing*.

In spite of the bad weather, we went out for a walk.
Despite being late, they didn't hurry.

Si dice anche *in spite of/despite the fact (that)* ....

In spite of the fact that the weather was bad, we went out for a walk.
They didn't hurry despite the fact that they were late.

3 Confronta *in spite of/despite* e *although*:

In spite of the rain/Despite the rain, we started to play tennis.	*Although it was raining, we started to play tennis.*

4 Si può sottolineare un contrasto tra due fatti usando *while* e *whereas*.
He is quiet and shy, while/whereas his sister is lively and talkative.

5 Si può esprimere un contrasto anche usando l'avverbio *however* tra due frasi.
She said she didn't want to change her job. However, she may change her mind.

ESERCIZIO 161A

Riscrivi le frasi cominciando con le parole fra parentesi.

Esempio:

She has plenty of money, but she is very mean. (although)
Although she has plenty of money, she is very mean.

1 They have a car, but they rarely use it. (though)
2 He was innocent, but he was sent to prison. (although)
3 He has a number of relatives living nearby, but he never visits them. (even though)
4 She never takes any kind of exercise, but she is quite fit and healthy. (even though)

ESERCIZIO 161B

Riscrivi le frasi usando le parole fra parentesi seguite da un nome, come negli esempi.

Esempi:

They went out for a walk, even though the weather was bad. (despite)
They went out for a walk despite the bad weather.
She managed to write, even though her hand was injured. (in spite of)
She managed to write in spite of her injured hand.

1 All the trains were on time, even though the snow was heavy. (despite)
2 Our coach didn't arrive late, even though the traffic was terrible. (in spite of)
3 A lot of people buy those houses, even though the prices are high. (despite)

ESERCIZIO 161C

Riscrivi le frasi usando le parole fra parentesi e (i) la forma in -*ing*, (ii) *the fact (that) . . . .*

Esempio:

He stayed up late, even though he was very tired. (despite)
 (i) *He stayed up late despite being very tired.*
(ii) *He stayed up late despite the fact (that) he was very tired.*

1 I didn't buy the car, even though I had enough money. (despite)
2 He stayed outside in the cold weather, even though he felt ill. (despite)
3 People continue to smoke, even though they know the dangers. (in spite of)

ESERCIZIO 161D

Sally e Peter sono buoni amici, ma sono molto diversi.

Confrontali. Collega una frase di **A** (descrizione di Sally) con una di **B** (descrizione di Peter), usando *while/whereas* per sottolinearne le differenze.

Esempio:

1 *She likes hard work, while/whereas he's quite lazy.*

A	**B**
1 She likes hard work.	He prefers classical music.
2 She likes jazz and pop music.	He prefers staying at home.
3 She likes going out a lot.	He can be rather mean.
4 She's very practical.	He's quite lazy.
5 She's very generous.	He's quite idealistic.

162 Causa e conseguenza: *because, because of, as, since, so, as a result, therefore, so/such ... (that)*

1	**Causa:** *because, because of, as, since*
a	Si usa *because* davanti a un'intera frase.

*He ran to the station **because** he was late.*
*We didn't go out **because** it was raining.*

Si usa *because of* davanti a un nome.

*We didn't go out **because of** the rain.*
*We arrived late **because of** the traffic.*

b	Si può usare anche *as* o *since* per introdurre una frase causale; questa, allora, si colloca spesso prima della principale.

***As** it was raining, we didn't go out.*
***Since** you haven't got any money, I'll lend you some.*

2	**Conseguenza:** *so, as a result, therefore, so/such ... (that)*
a	Si può usare *so, as a result* e *therefore* per indicare la conseguenza o l'effetto di qualcosa.

Si usa *so* (con o senza *and*) davanti a un'intera frase.

*He was late **(and) so** he ran to the station.*

Si usa anche *and as a result* e *and therefore* davanti a un'intera frase.

*It was raining hard **and as a result** we didn't go out.*
*I failed my driving test the first time **and therefore** I took it again.*

Therefore può stare anche tra il soggetto e il verbo p.es. *... and I **therefore took** it again.*

Si usa *as a result* e *therefore* anche dopo il punto fermo.

*It was raining hard. **As a result**, we didn't go out.*
*I failed my driving test the first time. **Therefore**, I took it again.*

Therefore è piuttosto formale.

b	Si può usare anche *so/such ... (that)* quando si parla delle conseguenze o dell'effetto di qualcosa.

*The film was **so** good **(that)** I went to see it again.*
*It was **such** a beautiful afternoon **(that)** we decided to go out for a walk.*

So può precedere anche un aggettivo o un avverbio p.es. *so good, so well*, mentre *such* può precedere solo un nome (con o senza aggettivo) p.es. *such a beautiful afternoon, such an idiot*. Cfr. 139.1.

ESERCIZIO 162A

Completa le frasi di **A** usando *because* o *because of* e un concetto di **B**. Usa ciascun concetto di **B** una volta sola.

Esempio:

1 *He phoned the police because he'd lost his wallet.*

A	**B**
1 He phoned the police ＿＿	his bad leg
2 I didn't have any lunch ＿＿	I thought it might rain
3 Our plane was delayed ＿＿	I wasn't hungry
4 He went to Paris ＿＿	~~he'd lost his wallet~~
5 I took an umbrella ＿＿	the fog
6 He couldn't run very fast ＿＿	he wanted to learn French

ESERCIZIO 162B

Scegli le espressioni giuste.

Esempio:

I haven't got much money ~~as~~/*so* I can't afford a new car.

1 *As/As a result* it was such a beautiful day, we decided to have a picnic.
2 It was his birthday *because/so* we decided to buy him a present.
3 *As a result/Since* all the seats on the train were taken, we had to stand.
4 The banks were closed and *as a result/because* we couldn't get any money.
5 I didn't find the book very interesting and *so/as* I didn't finish it.
6 We couldn't drive across the bridge *as a result/because* it was closed.
7 She had the best qualifications and she *so/therefore* got the job.

ESERCIZIO 162C

Collega ogni coppia di frasi usando *so/such . . . (that)*.

Esempio:

He's got a very good memory. He never needs to write anything down.
He's got such a good memory (that) he never needs to write anything down.

1 It was a very warm evening. We had dinner outside in the garden.
2 He was very nervous. He couldn't eat anything.
3 Our neighbours' party was very noisy. We couldn't sleep.
4 The restaurant was very crowded. They couldn't find anywhere to sit down.
5 We were all having a good time. We didn't want to stop.

163   Scopo: *to, in order to, so as to, for, so that*

1   Si può usare l'infinito con *to* per parlare dello scopo per cui si fa qualcosa.

*I went to Paris **to learn** French.*

*I'm going out **to do** some shopping.*

Nello stile formale si usa *in order to* o *so as to*.

*I went to Paris **in order to learn** French.*
*We got up early **so as to have** plenty of time.*

Nelle frasi negative di solito si usa *in order not to* o *so as not to* (non *not to* da solo).

*We got up early **so as not to be** late./We got up early **in order not to be** late. (Non: ~~We got up early **not to be** late.~~)*

2 | Si può usare *for* per introdurre lo scopo di una persona ma solo se è seguito da un nome (non da un verbo).

*We went to a restaurant **for lunch**.*
*I'm going out **for a walk**.*

Si usa *for* + la forma in *-ing* per parlare dello scopo o della funzione di qualcosa.

*A thermometer is used **for measuring** temperature.*
*We use this knife **for cutting** bread.*

3 | Si usa anche *so (that)* per comporre una frase finale. In questo caso tale frase contiene spesso *can, can't, will* o *won't*.

*I'll give you a key **so (that)** you **can** unlock the door.*
*We'll leave early **so (that)** we **won't** arrive late.*

Spesso si usa *so (that)* con *could(n't)* e *would(n't)* riferendosi al passato.

*I gave you a key **so (that)** you **could** unlock the door.*
*We left early **so (that)** we **wouldn't** arrive late.*

ESERCIZIO 163A

Rispondi a ogni domanda di **A** formando una frase finale con *to* o *for* e il concetto più adatto di **B**.

Esempi:

1 *I'm going to the library to return a book.*
2 *She's gone to the greengrocer's for some potatoes.*

A	B
1 Why are you going to the library?	go jogging
2 Why has she gone to the greengrocer's?	a drink
3 Why is he taking the car to the garage?	invite me to his party
4 Why did he phone you?	~~some potatoes~~
5 Why do you get up early every day?	~~return a book~~
6 Why have they gone to the pub?	have it serviced

ESERCIZIO 163B

A che cosa servono queste cose? Componi delle frasi usando le parole del riquadro.

Esempio:

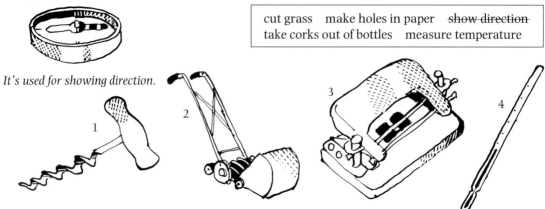

> cut grass   make holes in paper   ~~show direction~~
> take corks out of bottles   measure temperature

It's used for showing direction.

ESERCIZIO 163C

Collega queste frasi usando le espressioni fra parentesi.

Esempio:

I wrote down the number. I didn't want to forget it. (so as not to)
I wrote down the number so as not to forget it.

1 He's started walking to work. He wants to get more exercise. (so as to)
2 The government are going to increase taxes. They want to raise more money. (in order to)
3 We took a map with us on the journey. We didn't want to get lost. (so as not to)
4 They stopped work at 1 o'clock. They wanted to have lunch. (in order to)

ESERCIZIO 163D

Collega le frasi usando *so that* e le espressioni fra parentesi.

Esempio:

She got up early. She didn't want to be late for work. (wouldn't)
She got up early so that she wouldn't be late for work.

1 He switched on the light. He wanted to see what he was doing. (could)
2 I turned down the music. I didn't want to disturb the neighbours. (wouldn't)
3 She repeated everything. She wanted us to remember it. (would)
4 She's saving money. She wants to buy a new car. (can)

164   Scopo: *in case*

1   Si usa *in case* per indicare qualcosa che si fa allo scopo di premunirsi di fronte a determinate evenienze.

*Take an umbrella with you **in case** it rains.* (. . . in caso dovesse piovere.)
*I'll take some food with me **in case** I'm hungry on the journey.* (. . . in caso mi venisse fame durante il viaggio.)
*I'll write down the telephone number **in case** I forget it.* (. . . in caso dovessi dimenticarlo.)

Dopo *in case* si usa il presente per riferirsi al futuro p.es. . . . *in case I forget it*.
Cfr. 22.

2 Confronta *if* (cfr. 66) con *in case*:

*We'll buy another concert ticket **if** Simon wants to come with us.* (Aspettiamo a comprare un altro biglietto: prima vediamo se Simon vuole venire.)	*We'll buy another concert ticket **in case** Simon wants to come with us.* (Compriamo un altro biglietto adesso, così ne abbiamo già uno in più se Simon vuole venire.)

3 Si può usare *in case* anche con il passato.

*I wrote down the phone number **in case** I **forgot** it.*
*We bought another concert ticket **in case** Simon **wanted** to come with us.*

4 Dopo *in case* si può usare *should* se si pensa che l'evenienza contro cui ci si vuole premunire sia meno probabile. Confronta:

*Take an umbrella with you **in case** it **rains**.* (Penso che forse pioverà.)	*Take an umbrella with you **in case** it **should rain**.* (Forse pioverà, ma ne sono meno sicuro.)

ESERCIZIO 164A

Collega una frase di **A** con una di **B** tramite *in case*.

Esempio:

1 *You'd better hurry up in case you miss your train.*

A	**B**
1 You'd better hurry up ____	you (get) sunburnt.
2 Take a book on the journey ____	you (catch) a cold.
3 Put on some sun cream ____	~~you (miss) your train.~~
4 Wear a coat when you go out ____	someone (try) to steal it.
5 You should lock the car ____	you (get) bored.

ESERCIZIO 164B

Completa le frasi usando *if* o *in case*.

Esempio:

I'll write down the address *in case* I forget it.

1 We'll walk home ____ we miss the last bus.
2 Go and see the doctor ____ you don't feel well.
3 You should carry some kind of identification with you ____ you have an accident.
4 I'll come and see you later today ____ I have enough time.
5 We'll close all the windows ____ it rains while we're out.

Nota –*In case of* è diverso da *in case*. *In case of*, di frequente usato negli avvisi scritti, significa 'in caso di', 'nell'evenienza di un . . .' p.es. **In case of** *fire, press the alarm*. (= In caso di incendio . . . .)

165 Stato in luogo: *in, at, on*

1 | Si usa *in* quando si considera un luogo come tri-dimensionale.

*Simon is **in** his room.*
*Do you like swimming **in** the sea?*

Si usa *in* anche quando si considera un luogo come area geografica.

*We went for a walk **in** the park.*
*He's got a flat **in** Milan.*

2 | Si usa *at* quando si considera un luogo come punto specifico.

*I waited **at** the bus stop for twenty minutes.*
*I'll meet you **at** the station.* (luogo d'incontro)

3 | Si usa *on* quando si considera un luogo come superficie.

*What's that **on** the floor?*
*I'll put this picture **on** the wall.*

Si usa *on* anche quando si considera un luogo come linea.

*Memphis is **on** the Mississippi River.*
*Brighton is **on** the south coast of England.*

4 | Con le città e i paesi si usa *at* quando li si considera come punto p.es. sosta di un viaggio.

*Our train stops **at** Brighton.*

Ma si usa *in* quando si pensa al luogo in sé e per sé p.es. *He's got a flat **in** Milan.*

5 | Con gli edifici si può usare *at* o *in*.

*We had lunch **at/in** Luigi's restaurant.*
*She works **at/in** the post office.*

Normalmente si preferisce *at* quando si pensa all'edificio come funzione che esplica.

*'Where were you last night?' 'I was **at** the cinema.'*
*My brother is **at** university.*

Però si usa *in* quando si pensa all'edificio in sé. Confronta:

*We stayed **at** the Queens Hotel.*   *There are fifty bedrooms **in** the Queens Hotel.*

6 | Con gli indirizzi si usa *at* quando si dà il numero civico; nell'inglese britannico si usa *in* se si dà soltanto il nome della strada.

*I live **at** 42 East Street.*   *I live **in** East Street.*

Si usa *on* quando si indica il numero del piano di un edificio p.es. *I live in a flat **on** the first floor/second floor* ecc.

ESERCIZIO 165A

Completa le frasi usando le preposizioni *at, in* o *on*. Talvolta è possibile usarne più di una.

Esempio:

What have you got *in* your pocket?

1 There's some tea ____ the shelf ____ the cupboard.
2 Does your train stop ____ Lyon?
3 My friend works ____ a chemist's ____ the town centre.
4 Turin is ____ the north of Italy, ____ the River Po.
5 Shall we meet ____ the coach station?
6 'Is Ken ____ the living room?' 'No, he's ____ the garden.'
7 They're staying ____ the Metropole Hotel while they are ____ Brighton.
8 Rio de Janeiro is ____ the south-east coast of Brazil.
9 There's a chemist's ____ the corner ____ the end of the street.
10 We had lunch ____ Mario's cafe ____ Main Road ____ our way home.

166 Stato in luogo e moto: *in, into, out of, on, onto, off, inside, outside*

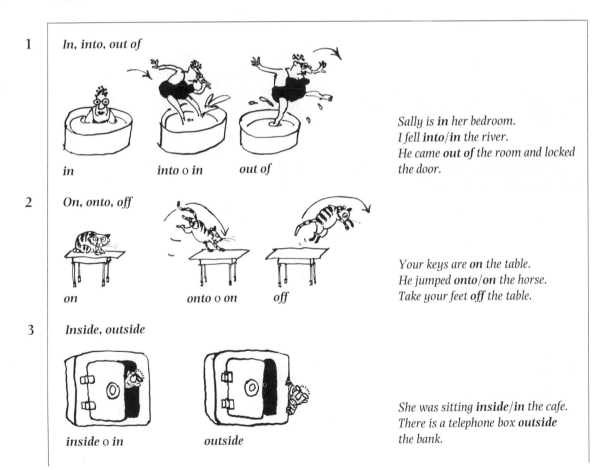

1 *In, into, out of*

in   *into* o *in*   *out of*

Sally is **in** her bedroom.
I fell **into/in** the river.
He came **out of** the room and locked the door.

2 *On, onto, off*

on   *onto* o *on*   *off*

Your keys are **on** the table.
He jumped **onto/on** the horse.
Take your feet **off** the table.

3 *Inside, outside*

inside o *in*   *outside*

She was sitting **inside/in** the cafe.
There is a telephone box **outside** the bank.

4

Nota che si usa *in* con le automobili, ma *on* con i trasporti pubblici p.es. gli autobus e i treni.

*I usually go to work **in** my car.*
*Did you come to school **on** the bus?*

Si dice *get in(to)/out of* un'automobile, ma *get on(to)/off* un autobus, un treno ecc.

*She **got into** her car and started the engine.*
*Two policemen **got on** the train at Oxford.*

Per *by car/train* ecc. cfr. 175.

ESERCIZIO 166A

Completa ogni frase usando la preposizione più adatta del riquadro. Talvolta è possibile usarne più di una.

Esempio:

There was an envelope lying *on* the floor.

in   into   out of   on   onto   off   inside   outside

1 Ken fell ____ the ladder when he was changing the light bulb.
2 Andrew normally goes to school ____ the bus.
3 When I was ____ my hotel room, I started to take my clothes ____ my suitcase.
4 There's a bus stop right ____ our house.
5 Sally came ____ the house, got ____ her motorbike and rode away.
6 My car broke down this morning so I went to work ____ a taxi.
7 The cat jumped ____ the roof of the car and looked down at the dog.
8 Annie jumped ____ the diving board ____ the swimming pool.
9 Robert came ____ the telephone box and got ____ his car.

167   Stato in luogo e moto: *above, below, over, under, underneath, on top of*

1

Sia *above* che *over* vogliono dire 'più in alto di'; sia *below* che *under* vogliono dire 'più in basso di'.

a

Over e *under* descrivono un rapporto diretto verticale.

Ⓐ
|
Ⓑ

*A is **over** B.*
*B is **under** A.*

*The nurse leaned **over** the sick child.*
*I pushed the letter **under** the door.*

b | Si usa *above* e *below* quando una cosa non è direttamente sopra o sotto un'altra.

*A is **above** B.*
*B is **below** A.*

*We stayed at a hotel **above** the lake.*
*From the top of the hill we could see a house **below** us in the valley.*

c | Si usa *over* per dire 'sopra, in tutta la sua estensione' e *under* per dire sotto, in tutta la sua estensione'.

*He put his hand **over** his face.*
*What are you wearing **under** your coat?*

d | Si usa *over* per dire 'attraverso' (cfr. anche 168.5).

*We walked **over** the fields to the village.*

2 | Si può usare *underneath* invece di *under*.

*What are you wearing **underneath** your coat?*

3 | Si usa *on top of* per dire che una cosa è 'sopra e a contatto' di un'altra.

*The magazine is **on top of** the fridge.*

ESERCIZIO 167A

Scegli la preposizione giusta.

Esempio:

I found some money on the floor *under/~~below~~* the sofa.

1 The house was on a hill *above/over* the village.
2 The cat was sitting *below/under* the kitchen table.
3 On our way to the village we drove *above/over* a small bridge.
4 There are some old shoes *above/on top of* the wardrobe.
5 He sat down *below/under* an apple tree.
6 She was wearing a long dress *below/underneath* her raincoat.

168 Altre preposizioni di stato in luogo e moto

1   *In front of, behind*

     in front of   **behind**

*I'll meet you **in front of** the post office.*
*There is someone hiding **behind** that tree.*

2   *Opposite, between*

      opposite   **between**

*The bank is **opposite** the cinema.*
*There is a coach service **between** Sydney and Melbourne.*

3   *Near, next to, by, beside*

      near   **next to**

*They live **near** the sea.*
*The police station is **next to** the cinema.*

By e *beside* hanno lo stesso significato 'a lato di'.
*Come and sit **by**/**beside** me.*

4   *Along, across, through*

     along   **across**   **through**

*They walked **along** the street looking in all the shop windows.*
*A small bridge goes **across** the river.*
*We drove **through** the city.*

5 | ***Across, over***

Si usa sia *across* che *over* per dire 'dall'altra parte di', o 'sull'altra parte di'.

*The cafe is just **across**/**over** the road.*   *A small bridge goes **across**/**over** the river.*

Si preferisce *over* per indicare scavalcamento di un alto ostacolo.
*He climbed **over** the wall. (Non: . . . ~~across the wall.~~)*

6 | ***Up, down***

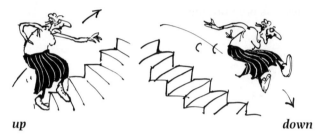

up   down

*She went **up** the stairs. Then she came **down** again.*

7 | ***Past, (a)round***

past

*The policeman just walked **past** the man.*

Si usa *round* per indicare stato in luogo attorno a qualcosa di rotondo, e moto circolare o curvilineo.

round   round

*They were all sitting **round** the table.*
*I live just **round** the corner.*

Si usa *round* anche nel significato di 'in tutte le parti di' o 'dappertutto'.
*We walked **round** the town centre.*

Si può usare *around* invece di *round* p.es. *We walked **around** the town centre.*

8 | *From, to, towards*

*We flew **from** Paris **to** Madrid.*
*Who is that woman walking **towards** us?*

9 | *Get to, arrive at/in*

Si dice *arrive in/at* (un luogo), ma *get to* (un luogo).

*She **arrived in/got to** Paris last night.*

Si dice *arrive in* con nomi di stati o città, ma *arrive at* con nomi di altri luoghi.

*She **arrived in** France/Paris last night.*
*She **arrived at** the hotel just after 10 o'clock.*

10 | Con *home*, dopo verbi di moto non si usa nessuna preposizione.

*I went **home** after school.*

Dopo verbi di stato in luogo si dice invece *at home*.

*I was **at home** last night.*

ESERCIZIO 168A

Completa le frasi usando la preposizione giusta tra quelle del riquadro. Talvolta è possibile usarne più di una.

| through   across   up   down   in   ~~round~~   between   along   to   opposite |
| in front of   next to   from   at   towards   behind   over   past |

Esempio:

What's that you've tied *round* your waist?

1 I was sitting ____ the driver in the back seat of the car.
2 A tall man was sitting ____ me at the cinema and I couldn't see much of the film.
3 There is a shoe shop ____ the chemist's and the library.
4 We walked ____ the stairs to the top floor, then we walked ____ to the bottom again.
5 What time did you arrive ____ work yesterday?
6 Who was the first person to swim ____ the Atlantic?
7 There was a woman sitting ____ the driver ____ the front passenger seat of the car.
8 We're flying ____ Paris ____ Amsterdam tomorrow. We arrive ____ Amsterdam at 6.00.
9 I got ____ the cinema late and missed the beginning of the film.
10 There's a post office right ____ my office. You can see it from my window.
11 The burglars got into the building by climbing ____ a window.
12 We were driving ____ the road looking for a petrol station for about half an hour.
13 We walked ____ the bridge to the other side of the river.
14 The dog jumped ____ the wall into someone's garden.
15 When the bus came I put out my hand, but it just went ____ me without stopping.
16 We couldn't see the man's face because he was standing with his back ____ us.

169 Tempo: *at, in, on*

1 | Si usa *at, in* e *on* come segue:

a + l'ora	***at** 2 o'clock* ***at** 6.30* ***at** midnight* ***at** noon* (= a mezzogiorno) ***at** lunchtime*
in + il momento della giornata Si dice però *at night*.	***in** the morning* ***in** the afternoon* ***in** the evening*
on + il giorno della settimana	***on** Monday* ***on** Wednesday* ***on** Saturday* ***on** Christmas day*
on + il giorno + il momento della giornata	***on** Monday morning* ***on** Wednesday evening* ***on** Saturday night*
on + la data	***on** 4th July* ***on** 1st January*
at + la parola *weekend*	***at** the weekend* ***at** weekends*
at + le festività	***at** Christmas* ***at** Easter*
in + periodi di tempo più lunghi p.es. mesi, stagioni, anni, ecc.	***in** July* ***in** the summer* ***in** 1983* ***in** the 19th century*

2 | Non si usa *at, on* e *in* davanti a *next, last, this, every, all, each, some, any* e *one*.

*We're leaving **next Monday**.*
*I'll see you **this evening**.*
*They play tennis **every weekend**.*

Non si usa *at, on* o *in* davanti a *tomorrow* e *yesterday*.

*What are you doing **tomorrow evening**?*

3 | Normalmente si omette *at* quando si chiede *(At) what time . . .?*

***What time** are you leaving?*

4 | Si usa *in* anche per riferirsi a un periodo di tempo futuro.

*I'll be finished **in** half an hour.* (= fra mezz'ora)
*We're meeting **in** two weeks.* (= fra due settimane)

Nota l'espressione *in . . . 's/' time*.

*We're meeting **in** a week's time*.

Si usa *in* anche per dire quanto si impiega per fare qualcosa.

*I can walk from my house to the town centre **in** twenty minutes.* (= impiego 20 minuti)

ESERCIZIO 169A

Aggiungi *at, on* o *in* se necessario.

Esempio:

Can you meet me *at* 2 o'clock ⸺ next Saturday afternoon?

1 Kate doesn't normally work ⎯ weekends, but she had to work ⎯ last Saturday.
2 We're leaving ⎯ tomorrow morning, but we'll be back ⎯ three weeks' time.
3 Did she send you a card ⎯ your birthday?
4 ⎯ what time does the meeting start ⎯ Monday?
5 I can normally get home from work ⎯ about half an hour ⎯ Friday evenings.
6 They went on holiday to Spain ⎯ Easter and then again ⎯ the summer.
7 The bridge was built ⎯ the 16th century.
8 Do you enjoy driving ⎯ night?
9 I'm taking my driving test ⎯ 4.30 ⎯ July 3rd.
10 He was born ⎯ 1900 and died ⎯ 1972.
11 I'm going to a conference in Egypt ⎯ a week.

170   *On time* e *in time*

1   *On time* significa 'in perfetto orario'.

The buses are very unreliable. They never arrive **on time**. (= in perfetto orario, puntuali)

In my school, the classes always start **on time**. (= in perfetto orario, puntuali)

2   *In time* significa 'in tempo per'.

He discovered the fire **in time** *to stop it spreading*. (= giusto in tempo per impedire che si propagasse)

I hope my leg gets better **in time** *for the football match on Saturday*. (= giusto in tempo per la partita)

ESERCIZIO 170A

Completa le frasi usando *on time* o *in time*.

Esempio:

I didn't arrive *in time* to see her before she left.

1 The bus service is terrible; the buses are never ⎯.
2 I hope your cold gets better ⎯ for the party.
3 She's very punctual. She always arrives ⎯.
4 She didn't arrive ⎯ to say goodbye to him.
5 The fire brigade arrived at the factory ⎯ to put out the fire.

171 *At the end* e *in the end*

1	*At the end* significa 'alla fine di'.
	*We're going on holiday **at the end** of this week.*
	***At the end** of the film I felt very sad.*
2	*In the end* significa 'alla fine', 'dopo un po' di tempo', 'infine'.
	*We couldn't decide what to do yesterday evening. **In the end** we decided to stay at home.*
	*At first, I didn't like him, but **in the end** we became good friends.*

ESERCIZIO 171A

Completa le frasi usando *at the end* o *in the end*.

Esempio:

We were going to walk home, but *in the end* we decided to take a taxi.

1 I hated school at first, but ＿＿ I quite enjoyed it.
2 They're going to Italy ＿＿ of next week.
3 At first, he didn't want to come with us on holiday, but ＿＿ he changed his mind.
4 I looked everywhere for my wallet and ＿＿ I found it in my jacket.
5 She's starting work ＿＿ of May.
6 We were all exhausted ＿＿ of the journey.

172 Tempo: *in, during, for, while*

1		*In* e *during*
	a	Si può usare sia *during* che *in* per dire 'durante' un periodo di tempo; spesso il significato è identico.
		*We were in Rome **during**/**in** the summer.*
		*It snowed **during**/**in** the night.*
	b	Si preferisce *during* per sottolineare che qualcosa continua per tutto un periodo di tempo.
		*We were in Rome **during** the whole of the summer.* (Non: ~~... in the whole of the summer.~~)
	c	Si usa *during*, non *in*, se ci si riferisce a un'attività p.es. una visita o un pasto (invece che a un periodo di tempo).
		*We visited the Colosseum **during** our visit to Rome.* (Non: ~~... in our visit to Rome.~~)
		***During** lunch I explained my plans.* (Non: ~~In lunch ...~~)
2		*During, for* e *while*
	a	*During* indica quando accade qualcosa, *for* da quanto tempo dura. Confronta:
		*It snowed **during** the morning.* | *It snowed **for** four hours.*
		*We were in Rome **during** the summer.* | *We were in Rome **for** ten days.*

b | *While* è simile a *during*, ma con una differenza, la stessa che c'è in italiano tra 'mentre' e 'durante': *while* viene usato solo davanti a una frase, *during* solo davanti a un nome. Confronta:

during + nome		*while* + frase

He broke his arm **during the fight**. | | He broke his arm **while they were fighting**.
It started to rain **during the picnic**. | | It started to rain **while they were having a picnic**.

ESERCIZIO 172A

Completa le frasi usando *during, in, for* o *while*. Talvolta è possibile più di una soluzione.

Esempio:

Someone broke into their flat *while* they were away on holiday.

1 Some people were talking in the cinema ___ the film.
2 We've been waiting ___ almost an hour.
3 Something woke me up ___ the night.

4 I was on holiday ___ two weeks ___ the spring.
5 I saw Sue ___ my visit to London.
6 They stopped work ___ half an hour ___ the afternoon.
7 We visited some interesting places ___ we were in London.
8 I'll be in France ___ the whole of September.

Nota | –Per *for, since, ago* e *before* cfr. 174.

173   Tempo: *by, until, from, to/until, before, after*

1 | **By e until**

Si usa *until* (o *till*) per dire 'fino al momento in cui'; si usa *by* per dire 'non più tardi di'. Confronta:

I'll stay **until** Sunday lunchtime. (= fino a domenica mezzogiorno) | I'll have to leave **by** Sunday lunchtime. (= non più tardi di domenica mezzogiorno)
He'll be out **till** 10 o'clock. (= fino alle 10) | He'll be home **by** 10 o'clock. (= non più tardi delle 10)

2 | **From ... to/until**

The shop opens **from** 8.30 **to** 5.30 every day.
I'll be on holiday **from** Monday **until/till** Friday next week.

3 | **Before e after**

I'll be home **before** 6 o'clock.
After dinner we went for a walk.

ESERCIZIO 173A

Completa le frasi usando *by, until, from* o *to*. Talvolta è possibile più di una soluzione.

Esempio:

The film starts at 8.10, so we must be at the cinema *by* 8.00 at the latest.

1 I waited ＿＿ half past eight ＿＿ nine o'clock, but she didn't come.
2 They hope to finish the job ＿＿ Thursday next week.
3 He normally works ＿＿ Monday ＿＿ Friday.
4 How many more weeks are there ＿＿ your holiday?
5 If you want a ticket for the concert, let me know ＿＿ next Wednesday at the latest.
6 We won't start the meeting ＿＿ everyone is here.

174 Tempo: *for, since, ago, before*

1 Si usa *for* con un periodo di tempo per riferirsi alla durata di qualcosa nel passato, nel presente o nel futuro.

*We were in Rome **for ten days** last August.*
*They usually go on holiday **for two weeks** every summer.*
*I'll be in Manchester **for the next three days**.*

2 Spesso si usa il passato prossimo con *for* e *since* per sottolineare la continuità di qualcosa. Confronta:

*I've been watching TV **for two hours**.*	*I've been watching TV **since 7 o'clock**.*
*I've known her **for three months**.*	*I've known her **since November**.*
Si usa *for* quando si indica la durata del periodo p.es. **two hours, three months**.	Si usa *since* quando si indica il momento di inizio del periodo p.es. **7 o'clock, November**.

3 *Ago* è un avverbio che significa 'fa'.

*It's 10 o'clock now. Sue left two hours **ago**.* (= Sue è partita due ore fa.)

Ago segue espressioni di tempo.

*She left **a few minutes ago**.*
***Six months ago** they moved to Manchester.*

Nota la domanda *How long ago . . .?* p.es. **How long ago** *did she leave?*

Si usa *ago* con il verbo al passato remoto, non al passato prossimo: non si può dire ~~She has left a few minutes ago~~.

4 Confronta *ago* con *for*:

*I went to New York two weeks **ago**.* (= due settimane fa)	*I went to New York **for** two weeks.* (= ci sono stato due settimane)

5 | Confronta *ago* con *before*:

ago = 'prima di adesso'; *before* = 'prima di allora'

*John left school three years **ago**; Jane had already left school three years **before**.*

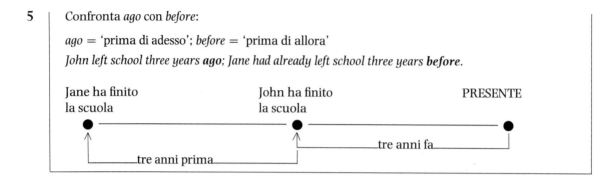

Jane ha finito la scuola   John ha finito la scuola   PRESENTE

tre anni prima

tre anni fa

ESERCIZIO 174A

Completa le frasi usando *for, since, ago* e *before*.

Esempio:

Tina moved away from Newcastle five years *ago* and she hasn't been back there *since* then.

1 My grandparents visited Edinburgh ___ two weeks in 1980. They had been there five years ___, so it wasn't completely new to them.
2 My brother has been interested in music ___ quite a long time. He was given his first guitar 20 years ___.
3 John worked in a travel agency ___ six months in 1985. He already had some experience of the tourist industry because he had worked in a Tourist Information office in London two years ___.
4 Patricia started working as a journalist with a newspaper in Madrid ten years ___. She's been working for the same newspaper ever ___ then.

Nota | –Per *for* e *since* cfr. anche 11.

175   Mezzi di trasporto: *by, on, in*

1 | Si usa *by* + il nome del mezzo di trasporto per dire come si viaggia.

> *by car   by bus   by coach   by bicycle   by motorbike*
> *by train   by Underground/Tube   by tram   by plane*
> *by boat/ship   by road   by rail   by air   by sea*

*I always come to school **by bus**.*
*They travelled to Paris **by rail**.*

Si dice però *on foot* (= a piedi).

*Does he usually go to school **on foot**?*

2 | Con *my/a/the* ecc. davanti a *car/bus/train* ecc., non si può usare *by*. Si usa *in* con le automobili e *on* con le biciclette, le moto e i mezzi pubblici p.es. gli autobus e i treni.

*I usually go to work **in my car**.* (Non: ~~... **by my car.**~~)
*They went for a ride **on a motorbike**.* (Non: ~~... **by a motorbike.**~~)
*Did you go to London **on the train**?* (Non: ~~... **by the train?**~~)

ESERCIZIO 175A

Completa le frasi usando *by, on* o *in*.

Esempio:

I'm not going to Rome *on* my motorbike. I've decided to go *by* train instead.

1 Annie usually goes to school ＿＿ her bicycle, but sometimes she goes ＿＿ bus.
2 The journey takes 10 minutes ＿＿ bus and about 25 minutes ＿＿ foot.
3 Robert didn't come to work ＿＿ his car yesterday morning. His car had broken down and he had to come ＿＿ taxi.
4 Did you travel right across London ＿＿ the Underground?
5 We've decided to travel to New York ＿＿ sea rather than go ＿＿ air.

176 *Like, as* e *as if*

1 | *Like* e *as*

a | Si può usare *like* o *as* nel significato di 'come'.

Like

*My sister is quite **like** me.*
*He eats **like** a pig!*
*This steak is very tough. It's **like** eating leather.*

In questi casi *like* funge da preposizione; la si usa davanti a un nome p.es. *like a pig*, a un pronome p.es. *like me*, o alla forma in *-ing* p.es. *like eating*.

As

*Your hair looks nice **as** it is now.*
*Nobody else can sing **as** she can.*

In questi casi *as* funge da congiunzione; la si usa davanti a una frase intera con soggetto e verbo p.es. *as it is, as she can*.

Nello stile informale spesso si usa *like* come congiunzione, invece di *as*.

*Nobody can sing **like** she can.*

Alcuni grammatici pensano che non sia corretto usare *like* in questo modo.

b Si usa *as* come preposizione per parlare del lavoro di una persona o della funzione di una cosa.

*I once worked **as** a postman.*
*Please don't use my shoe **as** a hammer.*

Confronta *as* con *like*:

*He works **as** a cleaner.* (E' addetto alle pulizie, è il suo lavoro.)
*She uses the living room **as** her office.* (E' il suo ufficio.)

*He looks **like** a pop singer.* (In realtà non è veramente un cantante pop.)
*My children treat our house **like** a hotel.* (Ma non è un albergo.)

c Si può usare *like* per introdurre un esempio.

*She enjoys some water sports, **like** sailing and windsurfing.*

2 *As if*

a Si usa *as if* + soggetto e verbo per dire che sembra che qualcuno o qualcosa . . .

*You look **as if** you're cold.*
*It looks **as if** it's going to stop raining.*

Qualche volta si usa *as if* + il passato remoto per parlare del presente.

*My brother sometimes behaves **as if** he **was** my father.*

La frase non si riferisce al passato; si usa il passato (*he **was** my father*) perché l'ipotesi è irreale (infatti lui **non è** mio padre).

Spesso si usa *were* invece di *was* dopo *as if* per esprimere ipotesi irreali, specie nello stile formale.

*My brother sometimes behaves **as if** he **were** my father.*

b Si può usare as *though* invece di *as if*.

*You look **as though** you're tired.*
*My brother sometimes behaves **as though** he were my father.*

c Nello stile informale, invece di *as if/though*, si usa qualche volta *like*.

*It looks **like** it's going to stop raining.*

ESERCIZIO 176A

Completa le frasi usando *like* o *as*. Talvolta entrambi sono possibili.

Esempio:

Sarah looks a lot *like* her brother.

1 I joined the company ____ a secretary.
2 Their garden is in a terrible mess. It looks ____ a jungle.
3 I prefer bright colours, ____ yellow and red.
4 When you've finished, put everything back ____ it was before.
5 The building looks more ____ a church than a bank.
6 Stop behaving ____ a fool.
7 Nobody else can make me laugh quite ____ she can.

ESERCIZIO 176B

Componi delle frasi sulle persone raffigurate nelle illustrazioni, usando le parole dei riquadri.

He/She/It looks	as if ___
They look	

> they're in love   they've been running
> ~~she's just woken up~~   he's going to fall
> they're having fun   she's just had some good news

Esempio:

She looks as if she's just woken up.

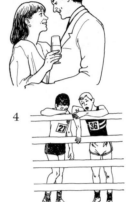

ESERCIZIO 176C

Completa ogni frase di **A** usando *as if* e il concetto più adatto di **B**. Usa i verbi fra parentesi al passato remoto.

Esempio:

1 *She's 50 years old, but she looks as if she was/were 30.*

A

1 She's 50 years old, but she looks ___
2 He's only a receptionist, but he acts ___
3 They're quite rich, but they behave ___
4 He's only got a cold, but he acts ___
5 It's my car, but he treats it ___

B

(own) the hotel
(belong) to him
(be) dying
(be) poor
~~(be) 30~~

177   *With* (= che ha) e *in* (= che indossa)

1   Si può usare *with* per dire quello che ha qualcuno o qualcosa.

*He is a tall man **with** brown hair.* (= ha i capelli castani)
*London is a large city **with** a population of over 9 million.* (= ha una popolazione di oltre 9 milioni)

2   Si può usare *in* per dire quello che indossa qualcuno.

*He often goes to work **in** his jeans.* (= con i jeans)
*Who's that woman **in** the black dress?* (= in nero)

ESERCIZIO 177A

Completa le frasi usando *with* o *in*.

Esempio:

My suitcase is the brown one *with* the blue stripe down the side.

1 We're looking for a flat ____ three bedrooms.
2 Who's that man over there ____ the green sweater?
3 The police are looking for a short man ____ black curly hair and brown eyes.
4 She's a lively woman ____ a great sense of humour.
5 A fat man ____ a dark blue suit came out of the bank ____ a black briefcase.

178 Aggettivo + preposizione

Dopo certi aggettivi si usano determinate preposizioni. Per esempio, si dice *afraid of*, *interested in* e *bored with*.
Ecco alcuni esempi di queste combinazioni aggettivo + preposizione:

■ *excited about   worried about   nervous about*
  angry about   annoyed about   furious about

I'm **excited about** having my birthday party tomorrow.
Are you **worried about** your exam?
I'm **angry about** all the mess you've made.

■ *good at   bad at   clever at   hopeless at*

I'm not very **good at** mathematics.
You're not **bad at** chess.

■ *surprised at/by   shocked at/by   astonished at/by   amazed at/by*

We were **surprised at/by** the size of the house.

■ *famous for   well known for   responsible for*

Brazil is **famous for** its coffee.
Who is **responsible for** breaking this window?

■ *different from/to*

He's very **different from/to** his sister.

■ *interested in*

I'm quite **interested in** photography.

■ *afraid of   frightened of   scared of   proud of   full of*
  ashamed of   jealous of   envious of   suspicious of   short of
  aware of   conscious of   capable of   fond of   tired of

*Are you **afraid of** spiders?*
*I'm very **proud of** you.*
*Are you **jealous of** his success?*
*He's very **fond of** her.*
*My homework was **full of** mistakes.*
*We're a bit **short of** milk. Can you buy some more?*
*I'm **tired of** doing the same things every day.*

■ *nice/kind/good/friendly/polite/rude/stupid of someone*

*It was **nice of** Simon to lend you the money.*

■ *keen on*

*She's not very **keen on** tennis.*

■ *engaged to   married to   similar to*

*Marianne is **engaged to** Alan.*
*Your camera is **similar to** mine.*

■ *nice/kind/good/friendly/polite/rude to someone*

*A shop assistant should be **polite to** customers.*

■ *pleased with   bored with   disappointed with   happy with*

*You look very **pleased with** yourself.*
*I became **bored with** the book and stopped reading it.*
*We were **disappointed with** the football match.*

■ *angry/annoyed/furious with someone for (doing) something*

*Are you **angry with** me **for** being late?*

ESERCIZIO 178A

Completa le frasi con le preposizioni del riquadro. Talvolta è possibile usarne due.

Esempio:

I'm getting bored *with* my present job.

of	by	with	on	about	in	from	for	at	to

1 They're very proud ____ their children.
2 My sister has just got engaged ____ her boyfriend.
3 Are you worried ____ your driving test?
4 You're very good ____ explaining things.

5 Sydney in Australia is famous ____ its Opera House.
6 She's quite capable ____ doing the job.
7 We're getting really excited ____ our holiday.

8 Are you interested ____ playing tennis tomorrow?

9 He's not very keen ____ football.

10 It was very kind ____ them to give us a lift to the station.

11 We were very disappointed ____ the film.

12 Are you afraid ____ flying?

13 I was shocked ____ the news of the accident.

14 The garden is full ____ roses.

15 We're a bit short ____ petrol. We'd better stop at the next petrol station.

16 I'm not very good ____ drawing.

17 My grandparents are very fond ____ their old cat.

18 Cricket is quite different ____ baseball.

19 You're hairstyle is quite similar ____ mine.

20 She was very angry ____ me ____ losing her key.

Nota –Dopo alcuni degli aggettivi sopra elencati, è possibile usare altre preposizioni p.es. *frightened by*, *annoyed at*, *disappointed in*. Per altri dettagli, consulta un buon dizionario.

179 Nome + preposizione

Dopo certi nomi si usano determinate preposizioni. Per esempio, si dice *(a) reason for*, *(an) example of*, *(an) increase in*.
Ecco alcuni esempi di queste combinazioni nome + preposizione:

■ *difference between*

There are a lot of **differences between** living in the country and living in a city.

■ *reason for   demand for   need for*

What was the **reason for** the accident?
There is a **need for** more houses in this area.

■ *increase/decrease in   rise/fall in*

There has been an **increase in** the price of petrol.

■ *difficulty in* doing something

Does he have much **difficulty in** doing his schoolwork?
Ma nota *difficulty with* something
Does he have much **difficulty with** his schoolwork?

■ *example of   cause of   picture/photograph of*

This building is an **example of** good modern architecture.
What was the **cause of** the accident?
Have you got a **photograph of** your family?

■ *answer to   solution to   reply to   invitation to   reaction to*

Have you had an **answer to** your letter?
Where are the **answers to** the exercise?
I got an **invitation to** dinner yesterday.

> ■ *attitude to/towards*
>
> *What's your* **attitude to/towards** *this idea?*
>
> ■ *relationship with*
>
> *Our company has a good* **relationship with** *the bank.*
> Ma nota: *relationship between*
> *The* **relationship between** *our company and the bank is very good.*

ESERCIZIO 179A

Completa le frasi usando le parole del riquadro. In una frase, ne sono possibili due.

Esempio:

I've had an invitation *to* a wedding next month.

towards   of   between   for   in   with   to

1 I have a good relationship ＿＿ my boss.
2 He refused to give me an answer ＿＿ my question.
3 What are the main differences ＿＿ the two countries?
4 We need a solution ＿＿ the world's population problem.
5 Smoking is one of the causes ＿＿ heart disease.
6 Has there been an increase ＿＿ unemployment recently?
7 The government want to improve the relationship ＿＿ the police and the general public.
8 He is very shy and has great difficulty ＿＿ making friends.
9 I thought her attitude ＿＿ you was rather unpleasant.
10 There is no need ＿＿ you to shout. I can hear you.
11 Nobody knows the reason ＿＿ his decision.
12 The artist drew a picture ＿＿ my mother.

Nota –Dopo alcuni dei nomi sopra elencati è possibile usare diverse preposizioni. Per altri dettagli, consulta un buon dizionario.

180 Preposizione + nome

Si usano determinate preposizioni davanti a certi nomi. Per esempio, si dice *on television* e *by mistake*.
Ecco alcuni esempi di queste combinazioni preposizione + nome:

Section C

- *by mistake*   *by accident*   *by chance*

*I put salt in my coffee **by mistake**.*

- Si dice: (to pay) *by cheque/by credit card*, ma (to pay) *in cash* o (to pay) *cash*.

*I'd like to pay **by credit card**.*

- (a book/film/painting, ecc.) *by someone*

*I'm reading a book **by** James Joyce.* (= scritto da James Joyce)

- (to go/come) *for a drink/a meal/a walk/a swim*

*Would you like to go **for a drink**?*

- (to have something) *for breakfast/lunch/dinner*

*We had spaghetti **for lunch**.*

- Si dice *for example*.

*I'd like to go somewhere warm on holiday, **for example** Greece or Turkey.*

- (to be/fall) *in love with* someone/something

*Jimmy is **in love with** Angela.*

- *in* someone's *opinion*

***In my opinion** you should phone the police.*

- (to be/go/come) *on holiday/a journey/a trip/business*

*I'm going **on holiday** in April.*
Ma nota: (go/come) *for a holiday*
*I'd like to go to Jamaica **for a holiday**.*

- *on television/the radio*

*What's **on television** this evening?*

ESERCIZIO 180A

Completa le frasi usando le preposizioni del riquadro.

Esempio:

In my opinion you're wrong.

```
by   with   in   on   for
```

1 We're going to Italy ____ a short holiday in May.
2 Robert has gone away ____ holiday for two weeks.
3 The book, *Gone With the Wind*, was written ____ Margaret Mitchell.
4 I didn't mean to do that; I did it ____ mistake.
5 I could pay you ____ cheque or ____ cash. Which would you prefer?
6 I heard an interesting programme ____ the radio last night.
7 ____ chance, I happened to have his address with me.
8 Lynne and Bruno are very much ____ love ____ each other.

Nota   –Per altri dettagli sulle combinazioni preposizione + nome, consulta un buon dizionario.

181   Verbo + preposizione

Dopo certi verbi si usano determinate preposizioni. Per esempio, si dice *believe in* e *concentrate on.*
Ecco alcuni esempi di queste combinazioni verbo + preposizione:

■ *apologize to* someone *for* (doing) something

*I **apologized to** her **for** being late.*

■ *apply for*

*Are you going to **apply for** the job?*

■ *believe in*

*Do you **believe in** life after death?*

■ *belong to*

*Does this book **belong to** you?*

■ *care about* (= pensare che qualcuno o qualcosa sia importante)

*I don't **care about** money. Money can't buy happiness.*

Ma: *care for* (= curare, avere cura di)

*She's very good at **caring for** sick animals.*

■ *take care of* (= badare a)

*Could you **take care of** the baby while I go out shopping?*

■ *complain to* (someone) *about* (something)

*The workers **complained to** the manager **about** the working conditions.*

■ *concentrate on*

***Concentrate on** the road when you're driving.*

■ *crash into*   *run into*   *drive into*   *bump into*

*When I was driving home I almost **crashed into** a bus.*

■ *depend on*

*'Are you going to the beach tomorrow?'   'It **depends on** the weather.'*

■ *die of*

*A lot of people are **dying of** AIDS.*

■ *dream about* (sognare, mentre si è addormentati)

*I was **dreaming about** Sue when I suddenly woke up.*

Ma: *dream of* (= immaginare)

*When I was younger I **dreamt of** being a famous pop-singer.*

Anche: *dream of* (= prendere in considerazione)

*I wouldn't **dream of** changing my job.*

■ *hear about* (= sentire di)

*Have you **heard about** Jimmy? He broke his leg in a skiing accident.*

Ma: *hear from* (= ricevere notizie da)

*We haven't **heard from** Mike since he wrote to us last May.*

Anche: *hear of* (= sapere dell'esistenza di qualcuno o qualcosa)

*Have you **heard of** a disco called The Dance Factory?*

■ *laugh at*   *smile at*

*Who's that girl **smiling at** you?*

- *listen to*

Would you like to **listen to** *some music?*

- *look at* (= guardare)

Look at *this photograph.*

Ma: *look for* (= cercare qualcosa)
Can you help me, please? I'm **looking for** *West Street.*

Anche: *look after* (= avere cura di)
Could you **look after** *the baby while I go out shopping?*

- *rely on*

You can't **rely on** *the post. It's always late.*

- *search for*

I've been **searching for** *the missing letters.*

- *shout at* (p.es. quando si è arrabbiati)

Don't **shout at** *me! I can hear you!*

- *speak to   talk to*

I **spoke to** *Sue this morning.*

- *suffer from*

He **suffers from** *asthma.*

- *think about* (= pensare a)

You look sad. What are you **thinking about**?

Ma: *think of/about* (= prendere in considerazione di)
I'm **thinking of/about** *changing my job.*

Anche: *think of* (= avere un'opinione)
'What do you **think of** *Sue?'   'She's very nice.'*

Anche: *think of* (= venire in mente)
I can't **think of** *any reason why the accident happened.*

- *wait for*

How long have you been **waiting for** *the bus?*

- *write to*

I'll **write to** *you soon.*

ESERCIZIO 181A

Completa le frasi usando le espressioni del riquadro. In una frase, sono possibili due soluzioni.

Esempio:

I was worried and found it difficult to concentrate *on* my work.

for	from	after	to	of	on	at	about	in	into

1 When he gets angry he always starts shouting ____ everyone.
2 This car isn't mine. It belongs ____ Mike.
3 Selfish people only care ____ themselves.
4 He complained ____ the children ____ the mess they'd made.
5 I won't tell anyone what happened. You can rely ____ me.
6 She apologized ____ me ____ losing her temper.
7 I've written ____ the company and applied ____ the job.
8 Mrs Woods suffers ____ bronchitis.
9 My grandfather died ____ old age.
10 We're thinking ____ going to the cinema.
11 Have you ever thought ____ moving to another country?
12 I remember his face, but I can't think ____ his name.
13 'We went to the concert.'   'What did you think ____ it?'
14 'Do you know a disco called The Zap Club?'   'No, I've never heard ____ it.'
15 Excuse me. We're looking ____ the sports centre. Could you tell us how to get there?
16 Thank you for looking ____ my mother while she was ill.
17 I don't believe ____ horoscopes.
18 She dreams ____ being an actress one day.
19 I dreamt ____ my grandmother last night.
20 She searched through her bag ____ a pen.
21 We're depending ____ you to help us.
22 The car went out of control and crashed ____ the back of a bus.

Nota   –Per altri dettagli sulle combinazioni verbo + preposizione, consulta un buon dizionario.

182 Verbo + complemento + preposizione

Dopo certi verbi si usa il complemento oggetto seguito da determinate preposizioni.
Per esempio, si dice *borrow* something *from* someone.
Ecco alcuni esempi di queste combinazioni verbo + complemento + preposizione.

■ *accuse* someone *of* (doing) something

*The police **accused** the man **of** murder.*

■ *blame* someone/something *for* something

*Don't **blame** me **for** what happened. It wasn't my fault.*

Ma: *blame* something *on* someone/something

*Don't **blame** what happened **on** me. It wasn't my fault.*

■ *borrow* something *from* someone

I **borrowed** *some money from my mother.*

■ *congratulate* someone *on* (doing) something

We **congratulated** *them on getting married.*

■ *explain* something *to* someone

I **explained** *the problem to the police.*

■ *invite* someone *to* something

Mike has **invited** *me to the cinema this evening.*

■ *remind* someone *about* something (= dire a qualcuno di non dimenticare qualcosa)

Simon **reminded** *me about Sarah's birthday, so I bought her a card.*
Ma: *remind* someone *of* something/someone (= far venire in mente a qualcuno qualcosa)
This song **reminds** *me of the first time we met.*

■ *tell* someone *about* something

Did they **tell** *you about their holiday?*

■ *warn* someone *about* something/someone

His boss has **warned** *him about being late for work.*

ESERCIZIO 182A

Completa le frasi usando le espressioni del riquadro.

Esempio:

They blamed the accident *on* the driver of the lorry.

| from   on   to   about   of   for |

1 Don't blame other people ____ your own mistakes.
2 This town reminds me ____ the place where I was born.
3 Will you remind Peter ____ the party next Saturday?
4 Congratulations ____ getting the new job!
5 I borrowed the umbrella ____ a friend of mine.
6 The woman accused me ____ trying to steal her bag.
7 They've invited us ____ their house for dinner.
8 We've warned him ____ swimming in that part of the river.

Nota –Per altri dettagli sulle combinazioni verbo + complemento + preposizione, consulta un buon dizionario.

183 Riepilogo delle preposizioni

ESERCIZIO 183A

Completa la descrizione della scenetta illustrata usando, una sola volta, ciascuna parola del riquadro.

behind	in front of	outside	inside	up	down	
on	onto	off	into	out of	along	across	at
round	towards	~~between~~	near	past	next to	opposite

There is a cafe *between* a supermarket and a post office. A woman is coming __1__ the supermarket. Some people are sitting __2__ the cafe. __3__ the post office is a bank. A man is getting __4__ a bus __5__ the bank. __6__ the bus there is a girl getting __7__ a motorbike. An old man is going __8__ some steps __9__ the post office; a young woman is coming __10__ the steps. Another woman is walking __11__ the road __12__ the bank. Some children and a dog are running __13__ the street __14__ the cafe. A car is waiting __15__ some traffic lights __16__ the supermarket. Some people are crossing the road __17__ the car. There is a telephone box __18__ the corner of the street __19__ the supermarket. A young man is walking __20__ the corner.

ESERCIZIO 183B

Completa le frasi usando le espressioni del riquadro. Talvolta è possibile usarne più
di una.

Esempio:

We're going away *on* holiday *for* two weeks *in* July.

```
at  in  on  since  for  from  of  to
during  between  about  with  under
```

1 We're meeting ____ the clock tower ____
   North Street ____ 8 o'clock this evening.
2 I went shopping ____ town ____ Friday
   afternoon.
3 We're thinking ____ going ____ the concert
   ____ Saturday. Are you interested ____
   coming?
4 She's been studying ____ the University ____
   Manchester ____ the past three years.
5 He had great difficulty ____ finding a job
   when he was living ____ the north of
   England.
6 They live ____ 148 Dyke Road. Their flat is
   ____ the second floor.
7 We took a lot of photographs ____ our visit
   ____ Rome last summer.
8 ____ my opinion they show too many old
   films ____ TV.
9 They went away ____ holiday ____ the end
   of last week.
10 They've been staying ____ the International
   Hotel ____ Oxford Street ____ they arrived
   ____ England.
11 He's suffered ____ bad headaches ____ he
   had the accident.
12 At first I didn't want to go swimming in the
   river, but ____ the end I changed my mind.
13 My brother worked ____ a tourist guide ____
   London ____ three months ____ the summer.
14 I found an old photograph ____ the floor
   ____ the bed ____ my room.
15 When she was a child, she dreamt ____
   being a famous dancer.
16 I'm not very good ____ making decisions.
17 You can depend ____ him to arrive ____
   time; he's never late.

18 We've arranged to meet ____ a cafe ____ a
   drink ____ 9 o'clock this evening.
19 I have a very good relationship ____ my
   sister.
20 There is no need ____ you to worry ____ me.
   I'll be all right.
21 You're very different ____ your mother, but
   quite similar ____ your father.
22 They're looking ____ a house ____ four
   bedrooms and a garden.
23 The police accused the woman ____ stealing
   the money.
24 'Do you know a pop band called Running
   Heads?' 'No, I've never heard ____ them.'
25 Newcastle is a large, commercial and
   industrial city ____ a population of about
   300,000. It is ____ the north-east of
   England, ____ the River Tyne.
26 Is there very much difference ____ the two
   word processors?
27 I've always wanted my parents to be proud
   ____ me.
28 People are angry ____ the increase ____ food
   prices.
29 I complained ____ the shop assistant ____
   the hole ____ the sweater.
30 My parents first went ____ Greece ____ a
   short holiday ____ 1980.

184 Complementi indiretti con o senza *to* e *for*

1 Alcuni verbi p.es. *give, buy* possono avere due complementi: uno diretto e l'altro indiretto. Di norma il complemento indiretto si riferisce a una persona e precede l'altro.

> verbo + complemento indiretto + complemento diretto

*I'll give **Sally the money**.*
*Richard bought **me some flowers**.*

2 Si può anche usare la costruzione:

> verbo + complemento diretto + *to/for* + complemento indiretto

*I'll give **the money to Sally**.*
*Richard bought **some flowers for me**.*

Si usa questa costruzione per esempio quando si vuole dare particolare enfasi al complemento indiretto.

*I'll give the money to **Sally**, not Peter.*

a Alcuni verbi di uso frequente che hanno la costruzione con *to* sono:

> *bring   give   lend   offer   owe   pass   pay   post*
> *promise   read   recommend   sell   send   show   take*
> *teach   tell   throw   write*

*They're going to offer **the job to Sue**.*
*He showed **the letter to a friend**.*

b Alcuni verbi di uso frequente che hanno la costruzione con *for* sono:

> *bring   build   buy   change   choose   cook   do   fetch*
> *find   fix   get   keep   make   order   prepare   save*

*She bought **some books for her brother**.*
*I'll cook **a meal for you**.*

3 Quando il complemento diretto è un pronome p.es. *them, it*, di regola questo precede l'altro p.es. *She gave **them** to her brother*. (Invece di: *She gave her brother **them**.*)

ESERCIZIO 184A

Riscrivi le frasi con o senza *to* o *for*.

Esempi:

Give this message to Martin.
Give Martin this message.
I'll make some coffee for you.
I'll make you some coffee.

1 Have you sent the letter to your brother?
2 I'll get a present for Sally.
3 Have you told the news to your parents?
4 I bought some stamps for you.
5 She lent her car to Peter.
6 I kept a seat for you.
7 He's prepared a meal for us.
8 Will you give this message to Mrs Woods?

ESERCIZIO 184B

Metti nell'ordine giusto le varie parti della frase.

Esempi:

Sarah | I | my new camera | lent | .
I lent Sarah my new camera.
to your mother | have | the money | given | you | ?
Have you given the money to your mother?

1 they | the job | me | didn't offer | .
2 for her son | she | a book | bought | .
3 the salt | pass | can | me | you | ?
4 you | this package | will | to your
   parents | take | ?
5 a taxi | ordered | they | us | have | .
6 he | to all | showed | the photographs |
   his friends | .

185 Verbi fraseologici: introduzione

1 Sono così chiamati i verbi che cambiano il significato originario quando si aggiungono particelle avverbiali diverse p.es. *down, away, on, in, up, after, off, across.*

Please **sit down**.
I'll **throw away** the rubbish.
Could you **turn on** the TV?

2 In alcuni casi il significato di questi verbi è una combinazione dei significati delle parti componenti.

Come in.

Sit down.

3 In altri casi il significato è diverso da quello delle parti componenti.

*He's **given up** eating meat.* (= Ha smesso di mangiar carne.)
*Sue **takes after** her mother.* (= Sue assomiglia alla madre.)
***Looking after** a baby is hard work.* (= Avere cura di un neonato è faticoso.)

4 Per i diversi tipi di verbi fraseologici, cfr. 186.

ESERCIZIO 185A

Completa le frasi usando la forma corretta dei verbi fraseologici del riquadro. Usa ciascun verbo una volta sola.

Esempio:

It was lucky that nobody was killed when the bomb *went off*.

speak up (= parlare più forte)   *fill in* (= compilare)
come across (= trovare per caso)   *keep on* (= continuare)
turn down (= rifiutare)   *go up* (= aumentare)
~~*go off*~~ (= esplodere)   *hold up* (= ritardare)

1 Could you ____ this application form, please?
2 They just ____ making a noise even though I'd asked them to stop.
3 The price of coffee has ____ again.
4 We can't hear you very well. Could you ____ a bit, please?
5 The coach was ____ by the heavy traffic and didn't arrive in London until 8.00.
6 Unfortunately, your request for a pay rise has been ____.
7 He ____ some old photographs when he was cleaning the attic.

186 Verbi fraseologici: quattro gruppi

I verbi fraseologici sono formati da un verbo e da particelle avverbiali p.es. *away, up, down, out, of, after, in, on.*

I'll **throw away** the rubbish.   He's **given up** smoking.

Questi verbi si dividono in quattro gruppi fondamentali:

1° gruppo

Il verbo non ha complemento oggetto.

verbo + particella

Sit down.
Look out! (= fa' attenzione)
We **set off** on our journey. (= siamo partiti)

2° gruppo

Il verbo ha il complemento oggetto. Questo, se è un nome, può essere collocato davanti o dopo la particella avverbiale.

verbo + particella + complemento		verbo + complemento + particella

I'll **throw away** the rubbish.   I'll **throw** the rubbish **away**.
Take off your shoes.   **Take** your shoes **off**.

Quando però il complemento oggetto è un pronome, p.es. *it, them*, questo deve sempre precedere la particella avverbiale.

I'll **throw** it **away**. (Non: ~~I'll throw away it.~~)
Take them **off**. (Non: ~~Take off them.~~)

3° gruppo

Il verbo ha il complemento oggetto, ma questo non può separare il verbo dalla particella avverbiale.

> verbo + particella + complemento

Sue **takes after** her mother. (Non: ~~Sue takes her mother after.~~)
Looking after a baby is hard work. (Non: ~~Looking a baby after is hard work.~~)

4° gruppo

Il verbo consiste di tre parti: verbo + particella + preposizione p.es. *look forward to*. Il verbo, che prende il complemento, non può essere separato dalle altre parti.

> verbo + particella + preposizione + complemento

I'm **looking forward to** the weekend.
You go now and I'll **catch up with** you later.
You shouldn't **go back on** your promises.

ESERCIZIO 186A

Completa le frasi usando il tempo giusto dei verbi fraseologici (1° gruppo) del riquadro. Usa ciascun verbo una sola volta.

Esempio:

The lift *has broken down* and isn't working at the moment.

> break out   take off   ~~break down~~   grow up
> get up

1 Our plane ____ from New York at 6 o'clock yesterday evening.
2 My younger sister wants to be a doctor when she ____.
3 A fire ____ in the offices of the ABC cinema last night.
4 Do you like ____ early in the mornings?

ESERCIZIO 186B

Completa le frasi usando i verbi fraseologici (2° gruppo) tra parentesi. Talvolta sono possibili due costruzioni.

Esempio:

Could you | the light? (switch on)
Could you switch on the light?/Could you switch the light on?

1 Would you like to | this jacket? (try on)
2 I don't enjoy playing football any more. I think I'll | it. (give up)
3 My wife wants me to | my moustache. (shave off)
4 I have to speak to Mr Mason. I'd better | him. (ring up)
5 That music is rather loud. Would you | it? (turn down)

ESERCIZIO 186C

Sostituisci i verbi in corsivo con i verbi fraseologici (3° gruppo) del riquadro.

Esempio:

We've *examined* the problem very carefully.
We've *gone into* the problem very carefully.

get over   ~~go into~~   run into
come into   look after

1 Who is going to *take care of* the children while you go to the pub?
2 Although she had very good medical care, it took her a long time to *recover from* her illness.
3 Jane *inherited* a great deal of money when her grandmother died.
4 I *met* an old friend *by chance* in town yesterday afternoon.

ESERCIZIO 186D

Sostituisci i verbi in corsivo con i verbi fraseologici (4° gruppo) del riquadro.

get rid of   put up with   come up with
~~go back on~~   look back on

Esempio:

You shouldn't *break* a promise.
You shouldn't *go back on* a promise.

1 Have you *thrown away* your old typewriter?
2 We must try to *find* a solution to the problem.
3 When you *remember* the past, it's easy to see the mistakes you've made.
4 I don't think I can *tolerate* this awful weather much longer.

ESERCIZIO 186E

Sostituisci il nome in corsivo con un pronome. (Nota che, qualche volta, dovrai cambiare l'ordine delle parole.)

Esempi:

Could you look after *the children*?
Could you look after them?
I'll turn off *the TV*.
I'll turn it off.

1 He's going to give up *his job*.
2 I've thrown away *the ticket*.
3 He's looking after *his sick mother*.
4 Are you looking forward to *the party*?
5 Can you fill in *the form*?
6 She takes after *her father*.
7 He can't do without *his car*.

187 Pronuncia delle desinenze -*(e)s* e -*ed*

Confronta i suoni 'sonori' con quelli 'sordi':

SONORO

Con un suono sonoro si può sentire una vibrazione.

SORDO

Con un suono sordo non si può sentire nessuna vibrazione.

1 | **Pronuncia della desinenza -(e)s**

Le regole per la pronuncia della desinenza -(e)s sono uguali a quelle per i nomi plurali (p.es. *books*, *churches*), per il possessivo con 's/s' (p.es. *Ken's*, *my parents'*) e per la terza persona singolare del verbo al presente (p.es. *he plays*, *she watches*).

La desinenza -(e)s ha tre pronunce.

a | -(e)s viene pronunciata /ɪz/ dopo i suoni /tʃ/, /ʃ/, /s/, /z/, /dʒ/, /ʒ/.

/tʃ/	/ʃ/	/s/
watches /wɒtʃɪz/	*washes* /wɒʃɪz/	*kisses* /kɪsɪz/
churches /tʃɜːtʃɪz/	*wishes* /wɪʃɪz/	*Chris's* /krɪsɪz/

/z/	/dʒ/	/ʒ/
loses /luːzɪz/	*bridges* /brɪdʒɪz/	*garages* /gærɑːʒɪz/
realizes /rɪəlaɪzɪz/	*George's* /dʒɔːdʒɪz/	

b | -(e)s viene pronunciata /s/ dopo i suoni sordi (eccetto quelli in **a**).

stops /stɒps/	*my parents'* /peərənts/	*books* /bʊks/
hopes /həʊps/	*waits* /weɪts/	*Mick's* /mɪks/
laughs /lɑːfs/	*months* /mʌnθs/	
wife's /waɪfs/	*maths* /mæθs/	

c | -(e)s viene pronunciata /z/ dopo i suoni sonori (eccetto quelli in **a**).

plays /pleɪz/	*cars* /kɑː(r)z/	*Ken's* /kenz/	*dogs* /dɒgz/
wives /waɪvz/	*ends* /endz/	*clothes* /kləʊðz/	*trees* /triːz/

2 | **Pronuncia della desinenza -ed**

La desinenza -ed viene usata per formare il passato remoto e il participio passato dei verbi regolari (p.es. *played*, *watched*).

La desinenza -ed ha tre pronunce.

a | -ed viene pronunciata /ɪd/ dopo i suoni /t/ e /d/.

/t/	/d/
waited /weɪtɪd/	*ended* /endɪd/
started /stɑːtɪd/	*needed* /niːdɪd/

b | -ed viene pronunciata /t/ dopo i suoni sordi (eccetto /t/).

stopped /stɒpt/	*looked* /lʊkt/	*watched* /wɒtʃt/
hoped /həʊpt/	*worked* /wɜːkt/	*touched* /tʌtʃt/
washed /wɒʃt/	*kissed* /kɪst/	*laughed* /lɑːft/
wished /wɪʃt/	*danced* /dɑːnst/	*coughed* /kɒft/

c | -ed viene pronunciata /d/ dopo i suoni sonori (eccetto /d/).

played /pleɪd/	*opened* /əʊpənd/	*lived* /lɪvd/	*filled* /fɪld/
showed /ʃəʊd/	*raised* /reɪzd/	*agreed* /əˈgriːd/	*used* /juːzd/

ESERCIZIO 187A

Dividi queste parole in tre gruppi secondo la pronuncia della desinenza -(e)s.

~~opens~~	~~waits~~	~~washes~~	Mick's	cars	
stops	teaches	Sally's	misses	drives	
dishes	Alice's	watches	admits	shows	
books	Bert's	studies	brings	hopes	

1	**2**	**3**
/ɪz/	/s/	/z/
washes	*waits*	*opens*

ESERCIZIO 187B

Dividi questi verbi in tre gruppi secondo la pronuncia della desinenza -ed.

~~passed~~	~~failed~~	~~painted~~	loved	finished
ended	hoped	opened	planned	invented
danced	studied	worked	waited	
lived	watched	remembered	admitted	

1	**2**	**3**
/ɪd/	/t/	/d/
painted	*passed*	*failed*

188 Ortografia delle desinenze -(e)s, -ing, -ed, -er, -est, -ly

I nomi, i verbi, gli aggettivi e gli avverbi possono prendere le seguenti desinenze:

Nome + -(e)s (plurale)	*chairs*
Verbo + -(e)s (terza persona singolare del presente	*waits* *watches*
Verbo + -ing (participio presente o gerundio)	*waiting* *watching*
Verbo + -ed (passato remoto o participio passato)	*waited* *watched*
Aggettivo + -er (comparativo) Aggettivo + -est (superlativo)	*slower* *slowest*
Aggettivo + -ly (avverbio)	*slowly*

Quando si aggiungono queste desinenze ci possono essere variazioni di ortografia:

1   **Aggiunta di -e davanti a -s**

a   Se una parola termina in -ch, -sh, -s, -x, o -z, si aggiunge -e davanti a -s.

watch	watches
dish	dishes
bus	buses
mix	mixes
fizz	fizzes

b   Anche i nomi *tomato, potato, echo, hero, negro* e i verbi *do* e *go* aggiungono -e davanti a -s.

tomato	tomatoes
potato	potatoes
do	does
go	goes

2	**Nomi che terminano in *-f(e)***	
	Alcuni nomi che terminano in *-f* o *-fe* perdono *-f*/*-fe* e aggiungono *-ves* nel plurale p.es. *half, thief, leaf, loaf, self, shelf, wolf, knife, wife, life*.	*half* — *halves* *thief* — *thieves* *knife* — *knives* *wife* — *wives* *life* — *lives*
3	**Caduta della *-e***	
a	Se una parola termina in *-e*, di norma perde *-e* davanti a *-ing, -ed, -er, -est*. Eccezione: *be/being*.	*live* — *living* *move* — *moved* *white* — *whiter* *large* — *largest*
b	I verbi terminanti in *-ee* non perdono *-e* davanti a *-ing*.	*see* — *seeing* *agree* — *agreeing*
c	Gli aggettivi terminanti in *-e* non perdono *-e* davanti alla desinenza *-ly*, per formare l'avverbio.	*nice* — *nicely* *complete* — *completely*
d	Ma gli aggettivi terminanti in *-le* cambiano *-le* in *-ly* per formare l'avverbio. Eccezioni: *true/truly, whole/wholly*.	*simple* — *simply* *possible* — *possibly*
4	**Da *-y* a *-i***	
a	Se una parola termina in *-y* preceduta da una consonante, cambia *-y* in *-ie* davanti a *-s*.	*city* — *cities* *carry* — *carries*
b	Se una parola termina in *-y* preceduta da una consonante, cambia *-y* in *-i* davanti a *-ed, -er, -est, -ly*.	*carry* — *carried* *happy* — *happier* *friendly* — *friendliest* *easy* — *easily*
c	*-y* rimane invariata davanti a *-ing*.	*carry* — *carrying* *fly* — *flying*
d	*-y* rimane invariata dopo una vocale. Eccezioni: *day/daily, pay/paid, say/said, lay/laid*.	*boy* — *boys* *pray* — *prayed* *grey* — *greyer*
5	**Da *-ie* a *-y***	
	Se una parola termina in *-ie*, cambia *-ie* in *-y* davanti a *-ing*.	*tie* — *tying* *lie* — *lying*

6 | **Raddoppio della consonante finale**

a | Se una parola monosillaba termina con una consonante preceduta da una vocale, raddoppia la consonante finale davanti a -ing, -ed, -er, -est.

sit	*sitting*
drop	*dropped*
big	*bigger*
fat	*fattest*

b | Ma non si raddoppia -y, -w, -x in fine di parola.

play	*playing*
slow	*slower*
mix	*mixed*

c | Se una parola di due o più sillabe termina con una consonante preceduta da una vocale, raddoppia la consonante finale solo se la sillaba finale è accentuata.

forget	*forgetting*
(for'get)	
prefer	*preferred*
(pre'fer)	
admit	*admitted*
(ad'mit)	

Se la sillaba finale non è accentuata, la consonante finale non viene raddoppiata.

open	*opening*
('open)	
visit	*visited*
('visit)	

Eccezione: Nell'inglese britannico si raddoppia -l in fine di parola anche se la sillaba finale non è accentuata.

travel	*travelling*
('travel)	
cancel	*cancelled*
('cancel)	

ESERCIZIO 188A

Aggiungi la desinenza -s/-es a queste parole, mettendole nel gruppo giusto: 1, 2, 3 o 4.

~~wait~~	~~shelf~~	~~copy~~	~~catch~~	buzz	plate
worry	miss	run	pay	admit	wife
finish	fly	knife	spy	disco	tomato
teach	marry				

1 + -s	**2** + -es	**3** -y + -ies	**4** -f/-fe + -ves
waits	catches	copies	shelves

ESERCIZIO 188B

Aggiungi la desinenza -ing a queste parole, mettendole nel gruppo giusto: 1, 2, 3 o 4.

~~stop~~	~~die~~	~~dry~~	~~come~~	play	knit	show
fix	make	tie	offer	visit	travel	write
plan	marry	shop	behave	stay	admit	
leave						

1 + -ing	**2** -e + -ing	**3** -ie + -ying	**4** × 2 + -ing
drying	coming	dying	stopping

ESERCIZIO 188C

Aggiungi la desinenza -ed a queste parole, mettendole nel gruppo giusto: 1, 2, 3 o 4.

~~apply~~ ~~rob~~ ~~wash~~ ~~arrive~~ trap pull
move empty drop carry discover
phone pray hope travel study
show admit save

1
+ -ed
washed

2
~~e~~ + -ed
arrived

3
~~y~~ + -ied
applied

4
× 2 + -ed
robbed

ESERCIZIO 188D

Aggiungi le desinenze -er e -est a queste parole, mettendole nel gruppo giusto: 1, 2, 3 o 4.

~~happy~~ ~~big~~ ~~high~~ ~~nice~~ wet late
busy slow simple short wide fat
easy thin cheap white red black
funny

1
+ -er/-est
higher – highest

2
~~e~~ + -er/-est
nicer – nicest

3
~~y~~ + -ier/-iest
happier – happiest

4
× 2 + -er/-est
bigger – biggest

ESERCIZIO 188E

Aggiungi la desinenza -ly a queste parole, mettendole nel gruppo giusto: 1, 2 o 3.

~~late~~ ~~happy~~ ~~gentle~~ hopeful real horrible idle
quick beautiful lucky dry sudden definite
polite heavy probable temporary

1
+ -ly
lately

2
~~le~~ + -ly
gently

3
~~y~~ + -ily
happily

189 Contrazioni

1 Le 'contrazioni' sono forme abbreviate di soggetto e verbo come *I'm* (= I am), *you've* (= you have), o di verbo e *not* come *isn't* (= is not) e *don't* (= do not).

Spesso si usano le contrazioni nell'inglese parlato e nell'inglese scritto informale p.es. in lettere agli amici.

Quando si usano le contrazioni, si mette un apostrofo (') per sostituire la lettera o le lettere che si omettono.

I'm (= I am; ' = a)   **you've** (= you have; ' = ha)
isn't (= is not; ' = o)   **don't** (= do not; ' = o)

2 Le contrazioni più comuni sono:

I'm /aɪm/ (= I am)
I've /aɪv/ (= I have)
I'll /aɪl/ (= I will o I shall)
I'd /aɪd/ (= I had o I would)

you're /jʊə(r)/ (= you are)
you've /juːv/ (= you have)
you'll /juːl/ (= you will)
you'd /juːd/ (= you had o you would)

he's /hiːz/ (= he is o he has)
he'll /hiːl/ (= he will)
he'd /hiːd/ (= he had o he would)

she's /ʃiːz/ (= she is o she has)
she'll /ʃiːl/ (= she will)
she'd /ʃiːd/ (= she had o she would)

it's /ɪts/ (= it is o it has)
it'll /'ɪtl/ (= it will)
it'd /ɪtəd/ (= it had o it would)

we're /wɪə(r)/ (= we are)
we've /wiːv/ (= we have)
we'll /wiːl/ (= we will)
we'd /wiːd/ (= we had o we would)

they're /ðeə(r)/ (= they are)
they've /ðeɪv/ (= they have)
they'll /ðeɪl/ (= they will)
they'd /ðeɪd/ (= they had o they would)

let's /lets/ (= let us)

isn't /'ɪznt/ (= is not)
aren't /ɑːnt/ (= are not)
wasn't /'wɒznt/ (= was not)
weren't /wɜːnt/ (= were not)
don't /dəʊnt/ (= do not)
doesn't /'dʌznt/ (= does not)
didn't /dɪdnt/ (= did not)
haven't /'hævnt/ (= have not)
hasn't /'hæznt/ (= has not)
hadn't /'hædnt/ (= had not)
can't /kɑːnt/ (= cannot)
couldn't /'kʊdnt/ (= could not)
won't /wəʊnt/ (= will not)
wouldn't /'wʊdnt/ (= would not)
shan't /ʃɑːnt/ (= shall not)
shouldn't /'ʃʊdnt/ (= should not)
oughtn't /'ɔːtnt/ (= ought not)
mustn't /'mʌsnt/ (= must not)
needn't /niːdnt/ (= need not)
mightn't /maɪtnt/ (= might not)
daren't /deənt/ (= dare not)

Nota
's può essere *is* o *has*

She's a student. (= She is a student.)
She's got two brothers. (= She has got two brothers.)

'd può essere *had* o *would*

I'd seen the film before. (= I had seen the film before.)
I'd like a coffee. (= I would like a coffee.)

am not diventa *aren't* /ɑːnt/ nelle domande p.es. **Aren't I right?**

Talvolta sono possibili due diverse contrazioni negative. Per esempio, si può dire *she **isn't*** o *she's **not***, *you **aren't*** o *you're **not***, *he **won't*** o *he'll **not***.

3 | Si usano le forme contratte per lo più dopo un pronome personale p.es. *I'm, you've* o nella forma negativa p.es. *isn't, don't*. Ma qualche volta si può usare la forma contratta (specialmente *'s*) dopo un nome.

Maria's *a student.* (= *Maria is a student.*)
*My **father's*** *got a new car.* (= *My father has got a new car.*)

Si può usare la forma contratta anche dopo un pronome o avverbio interrogativo p.es. *what, where, who* e dopo *there, here, that* e *now.*

What's *the time?* (= *What is the time?*)   ***There'll*** *be trouble.* (= *There will be trouble.*)
Where's *Peter gone?* (= *Where has Peter gone?*)   ***That's*** *right.* (= *That is right.*)

4 | Non si può usare la contrazione affermativa *'s, 've*, ecc. in fondo alla frase (perché il verbo in tale posizione ha l'accento tonico).

*Do you know who she **is**?* (Non: ~~Do you know who she's?~~)
*'Have you finished?'   'Yes, I **have**.'* (Non: ~~'Yes, I've.'~~)

Ma si può usare la forma negativa *isn't, haven't*, ecc. in fondo alla frase.

*'Is she English?'   'No, she **isn't**.'*
*You've finished, but I **haven't**.*

Nota

–Nell'inglese 'non-standard' (l'inglese che non è considerato 'corretto') *ain't* /eɪnt/ viene spesso usato come contrazione di *am not, are not, is not* e *have not, has not* p.es. *I **ain't** hungry.* (= *I am not hungry.*)
–Non confondere *it's* (= *it is* o *it has*) con *its* (forma possessiva di *it*) p.es. *The cat ate **its** food.*

190 Verbi irregolari

I verbi possono essere regolari o irregolari:

1 Verbi regolari

I verbi regolari (p.es. *work, play, move*) aggiungono *-ed* all'infinito per formare il passato remoto e il participio passato.

INFINITO	PASSATO REMOTO	PARTICIPIO PASSATO
work	worked	worked
play	played	played
move	moved	moved

2 Verbi irregolari

I verbi irregolari non aggiungono *-ed* all'infinito per formare il passato remoto e il participio passato:

a Alcuni verbi irregolari hanno la stessa forma nell'infinito, nel passato remoto e nel participio passato.

INFINITO	PASSATO REMOTO	PARTICIPIO PASSATO	INFINITO	PASSATO REMOTO	PARTICIPIO PASSATO
bet	bet	bet	put	put	put
burst	burst	burst	read /ri:d/	read /red/	read /red/
cost	cost	cost	set	set	set
cut	cut	cut	shut	shut	shut
hit	hit	hit	split	split	split
hurt	hurt	hurt	spread	spread	spread
let	let	let			

b Altri verbi irregolari hanno due forme uguali.

INFINITO	PASSATO REMOTO	PARTICIPIO PASSATO	INFINITO	PASSATO REMOTO	PARTICIPIO PASSATO
beat	beat	beaten	fight	fought	fought
become	became	become	find	found	found
bend	bent	bent	get	got	got
bleed	bled	bled	hang	hung	hung
breed	bred	bred	have	had	had
bring	brought	brought	hear	heard	heard
build	built	built	hold	held	held
burn	burnt*	burnt*	keep	kept	kept
buy	bought	bought	lay	laid	laid
catch	caught	caught	lead	led	led
come	came	come	lean	lent*	lent*
creep	crept	crept	learn	learnt*	learnt*
deal	dealt	dealt	leap	leapt*	leapt*
dig	dug	dug	leave	left	left
dream	dreamt*	dreamt*	lend	lent	lent
feed	fed	fed	light	lit	lit
feel	felt	felt	lose	lost	lost

INFINITO	PASSATO REMOTO	PARTICIPIO PASSATO	INFINITO	PASSATO REMOTO	PARTICIPIO PASSATO
make	made	made	stand	stood	stood
mean	meant	meant	stick	stuck	stuck
meet	met	met	sting	stung	stung
pay	paid	paid	strike	struck	struck
run	ran	run	sweep	swept	swept
say	said	said	swing	swung	swung
sell	sold	sold	teach	taught	taught
send	sent	sent	tell	told	told
shine	shone	shone	think	thought	thought
shoot	shot	shot	understand	understood	understood
sit	sat	sat	win	won	won
sleep	slept	slept	wind	wound	wound
smell	smelt*	smelt*			
speed	sped	sped			
spell	spelt*	spelt*			
spend	spent	spent			
spill	spilt*	spilt*			
spit	spat	spat			
spoil	spoilt*	spoilt*			

* Esiste anche la forma regolare: *burned, dreamed, leaned, leaped, learned, smelled, spelled, spilled, spoiled.*

c Altri verbi irregolari hanno tutte e tre le forme diverse.

INFINITO	PASSATO REMOTO	PARTICIPIO PASSATO	INFINITO	PASSATO REMOTO	PARTICIPIO PASSATO
be	was/were	been	ring	rang	rung
begin	began	begun	rise	rose	risen
bite	bit	bitten	see	saw	seen
blow	blew	blown	sew	sewed	sewn*
break	broke	broken	shake	shook	shaken
choose	chose	chosen	show	showed	shown
do	did	done	shrink	shrank	shrunk
draw	drew	drawn	sing	sang	sung
drink	drank	drunk	sink	sank	sunk
drive	drove	driven	speak	spoke	spoken
eat	ate	eaten	spring	sprang	sprung
fall	fell	fallen	steal	stole	stolen
fly	flew	flown	stink	stank	stunk
forbid	forbade	forbidden	swear	swore	sworn
forget	forgot	forgotten	swim	swam	swum
forgive	forgave	forgiven	take	took	taken
freeze	froze	frozen	tear	tore	torn
give	gave	given	throw	threw	thrown
go	went	gone	wake	woke	woken
grow	grew	grown	wear	wore	worn
hide	hid	hidden	write	wrote	written
know	knew	known			
lie	lay	lain			
mistake	mistook	mistaken			
ride	rode	ridden	* Esiste anche la forma regolare: *sewed.*		

Appendice: l'inglese americano

Le differenze grammaticali tra l'inglese britannico e l'inglese americano non sono notevoli. Le principali sono le seguenti:

a Gli americani, per dare una notizia, usano molto spesso il passato remoto in casi in cui gli inglesi usano invece il passato prossimo (cfr. 6.c).

INGLESE AMERICANO
*Did you **hear** the news?*
*My sister **had** a baby!*

INGLESE BRITANNICO
*Have you **heard** the news?*
*My sister **has had** a baby!*

Gli americani usano spesso il passato remoto con *just, already* e *yet* in casi in cui gli inglesi usano il passato prossimo (cfr. 8).

INGLESE AMERICANO
*He **just went** out.*
*I **already had** breakfast.*
*Did you **write** the letter **yet**?*

INGLESE BRITANNICO
*He's **just gone** out.*
*I've **already had** breakfast.*
*Have you **written** the letter **yet**?*

b Gli americani usano spesso *have* con *do/does* nelle frasi negative e interrogative in casi in cui gli inglesi usano *have got* (cfr. 33).

INGLESE AMERICANO
*I **have** a brother.*
*He **doesn't have** a job.*
*Do you **have** a pen?*

INGLESE BRITANNICO
*I've **got** a brother.*
*He **hasn't got** a job.*
*Have you **got** a pen?*

c Nell'inglese americano *get* ha due participi: *gotten* e *got*; nell'inglese britannico ne ha solo uno: (cfr. 190.2).

INGLESE AMERICANO
*I've **gotten/got** a ticket.*

INGLESE BRITANNICO
*I've **got** a ticket.*

d Gli americani usano spesso l'infinito senza *to* dopo verbi quali *suggest, insist, recommend*, ecc. (cfr. 55.1).

*I **suggested** (that) he **see** the doctor.*
*They **insisted** (that) she **take** the money.*

Questa costruzione è usata anche nell'inglese britannico, specialmente nello stile formale.

e Ci sono differenze nell'uso di alcune preposizioni. Per esempio:

INGLESE AMERICANO
on the weekend/weekends
*Monday **through**/to Friday*
*different **from**/than*
*stay home/stay **at** home*
*write somebody/write **to** somebody*

INGLESE BRITANNICO
at the weekend/weekends (cfr. 169.1)
Monday to Friday (cfr. 173.2)
*different **from**/to* (cfr. 178)
*stay **at** home* (cfr. 168.10)
*write **to** somebody* (cfr. 181)

f Nell'inglese americano di norma non si raddoppia *-l* in fine di parola se la sillaba non è accentuata (cfr. 188.6c).

INGLESE AMERICANO
'traveled ('travel)

INGLESE BRITANNICO
'travelled

g I verbi *burn, dream, lean, leap, learn, smell, spell, spill* e *spoil* sono di norma regolari nell'inglese americano p.es. *burned, dreamed, leaned, leaped, learned* ecc. (cfr. 190.2b).

Dizionario grammaticale

Questo dizionario elenca i termini grammaticali usati nel testo.

accento la maggiore intensità di voce con cui si pronuncia la sillaba di una parola; nel verbo *forget*, l'accento è sulla seconda sillaba *for'get*.

affermazione frase che dà un'informazione, esprime un'idea o descrive un fatto in forma positiva (affermativa) p.es. *I'm a student; They went to the cinema.*

agente nelle frasi passive l'agente è la persona o cosa dalla quale viene compiuta l'azione p.es. *The radio was invented by Marconi.*

aggettivo parte del discorso che si aggiunge al nome o al pronome per descriverlo p.es. *a red car, an old man; it's red; he's old.*

aggettivo graduabile *good, large* ecc. sono aggettivi graduabili, in quanto le persone o le cose lo possono essere più o meno. *Dead* non è graduabile in quanto non si può essere più o meno morti.

aggettivo possessivo aggettivo che esprime idea di possesso o relazione: *my, your, his, her its, our, their.*

apostrofo il segno ortografico (') p.es. *my friend's car*

articolo parte del discorso usata per indicare il nome cui si premette; si distingue in **articolo determinativo**, *the*, e **articolo indeterminativo**, *a/an*.

avverbio parte del discorso che modifica verbi, aggettivi, altri avverbi o un'intera frase. Risponde a domande quali 'come?', 'quando?', 'dove?' p.es. *She works **slowly**. He's **very** old. I'll see you **tomorrow**. Come **here**.*

avverbio interrogativo avverbio come *when, how* che si usa per introdurre una domanda.

comparativo forma che esprime una gradazione di qualità in relazione a un paragone p.es. *older, slower, more intelligent* sono comparativi di *old, slow, intelligent.*

complemento (oggetto) ogni parola che completa il senso della frase; può essere accompagnato o meno da una preposizione: nel primo caso si dice **indiretto**, nel secondo **diretto**. A volte la preposizione *to* è sottintesa p.es. nella frase *I give it to you, it* è complemento diretto, *to you* complemento indiretto; si può omettere *to*, invertendo l'ordine dei complementi: *I gave you the book.*

condizionale modo che esprime ipotesi, supposizioni; la frase condizionale è introdotta da *if* o altre congiunzioni p.es. *If I see Martin, I'll give him your message. If I knew the answer, I'd tell you.* Si usa il **condizionale** anche in altre costruzioni p.es. con *would* (o *should* con *I* e *we*) p.es. *He would come; I would/should like some coffee.*

congiunzione parte del discorso che collega due o più parole o frasi p.es. *and, but, when, if.*

consonante ogni lettera dell'alfabeto escluse le vocali; è così chiamata perché non può 'suonare' se non è accompagnata da una vocale. Cfr. anche **vocale**.

contrazione forma abbreviata di soggetto + verbo o verbo + *not* p.es. *I'm* (= I am); *they've* (= they have); *don't* (= do not).

dimostrativo aggettivo o pronome che indica qualcosa in relazione alla vicinanza o lontananza di chi parla o scrive: *this, that, these, those.*

discorso diretto discorso in cui si riportano esattamente parole altrui, chiuse tra virgolette p.es. in *He said: 'I'm cold.'*, la frase *'I'm cold.'* è formulata con il discorso diretto.

discorso indiretto discorso in cui si riferiscono parole altrui p.es. in *He said he was cold.*, la frase *he was cold* è formulata con il discorso indiretto.

domanda a risposta chiusa domanda la cui risposta può essere solo sì o no, p.es. *Are you working? Did she go out? Can we start now?*

domanda 'coda' domanda come *isn't it?* o *have you?* collocata in fine di frase p.es. *It's cold, **isn't it**?*

domanda con wh- domanda che viene introdotta da avverbi o pronomi che, in inglese, iniziano tutti con *wh-* p.es. ***What** are you doing? **Where** did she go? **When** can we start?*

domanda di commento si tratta di una domanda apparente, che di fatto esprime un commento di chi ascolta a quanto è stato detto; può anche comunicare diversi sentimenti, come sorpresa, interesse ecc. p.es. *'I'm leaving now.' 'Are you?'*

domanda introdotta da un'altra frase spesso, per rendere più cortese e meno diretta una domanda, la si introduce con un'altra frase in forma interrogativa come *Do you know . . .? Could you tell me . . .?* p.es. *Do you know where Ken is?*

enfasi maggiore importanza data a certe parole nella frase.

esclamazione espressione o frase che esprime un sentimento improvviso p.es. *Stop! How incredible!* Viene seguita dal punto esclamativo.

forma affermativa l'opposto di **forma negativa** p.es. *I know* è in **forma affermativa**, mentre *I don't know* è in **forma negativa**.

forma attiva il verbo è nella forma attiva quando il suo soggetto compie l'azione. Nella frase *I told Peter*, il verbo *told* è **attivo**. Cfr. anche **forma passiva**.

forma in -ing forma del verbo terminante in *-ing* p.es. *working, running*, che equivale al participio presente e al gerundio italiano. Cfr. anche **gerundio** e **participio presente**.

forma passiva il verbo è nella forma passiva quando il soggetto subisce l'azione. Nella frase *Peter was told*, il verbo *was told* è **passivo**. Cfr. anche **forma attiva**.

forma progressiva il verbo è nella forma progressiva quando si vuole sottolineare che qualcosa è in corso in un preciso momento; viene costruita con *be* + *-ing* p.es. *I'm working* (presente progressivo); *I was working* (passato progressivo), *I've been working* (passato prossimo progressivo).

forma regolare forma che segue le stesse regole della maggior parte delle altre espressioni, l'opposto di **irregolare**, p.es. *cars, books, rooms* sono forme regolari del plurale dei nomi (terminanti in -*s*), mentre *men, children* sono forme plurali irregolari.

frase l'unione di più parole, di regola con un soggetto e un verbo, che abbiano un senso compiuto p.es. *I went out* e *it stopped raining*; una frase può esprimere una domanda, un ordine, un'esclamazione. Più frasi formano un **periodo**, p.es. *I went out when it stopped raining*. Cfr. anche **frase principale**.

frase principale nel periodo: *I phoned Maria when I got home*, la frase principale è *I phoned Maria*; *when I got home* è la frase secondaria. Una frase principale può stare da sola, non invece una frase secondaria.

frase relativa accessoria frase relativa che non identifica la persona o cosa a cui si riferisce chi parla, bensì comunica solo un'informazione aggiuntiva sulla persona o cosa già identificata p.es. *Mrs Higgins, **who is 48**, has just had a baby.* (*Who is 48* non ci dice chi, si sa già che si tratta di **Mrs Higgins**.) Cfr. anche **frase relativa determinativa**.

frase relativa determinativa frase che identifica a chi o a che cosa si riferisce chi parla p.es. *I spoke to the man **who works in the post office**.* (*Who works in the post office* identifica quale uomo.) Cfr. anche **frase relativa accessoria**.

genitivo sassone in inglese si intende con questo il rapporto di possesso o specificazione, il più delle volte riferito a persone o animali, che viene indicato con *'s* o *'* p.es. *John's room, my parents' house*.

gerundio la forma in -*ing*, altrimenti detta participio, quando viene usata come nome p.es. *Walking is good for you.*

imperativo modo che esprime un ordine, un'offerta ecc. p.es. *Wait here. Be quiet. Have some more tea.* si forma con l'infinito senza *to*.

infinito uno dei modi indefiniti del verbo; esprime genericamente l'idea del verbo senza specificare la persona e il tempo; nelle frasi *I can drive, you must come*, *drive* e *come* sono **infinito senza *to***; nelle frasi *I'd like to drive, you have to come*, *to drive* e *to come* sono **infinito con *to***.

intonazione tono della voce che sale o scende.

linguaggio formale linguaggio che si usa con le persone che non si conoscono, nelle forme di cortesia e in situazioni in cui si vuole mostrare rispetto p.es. sul lavoro e quando si scrivono lettere commerciali. Si usa invece il **linguaggio informale** con gli amici, in situazioni appunto informali e nelle forme colloquiali.

locuzione espressione formata da due o più parole p.es. *as a matter of fact*.

nome parte del discorso che designa esseri animati, cose, concetti, fatti, sentimenti p.es. *student, girl, car, bedroom*.

nome composto nome formato da due parole p.es. *toothbrush* (*tooth* + *brush*), *something* (*some* + *thing*).

nome non numerabile nome che non può essere preceduto né da un numerale né dall'articolo indeterminativo *a/an* e che ha solo forma singolare p.es. *money, music*. Cfr. anche **nome numerabile**.

nome numerabile nome di cose, persone ecc. p.es. *book, egg, girl* che può essere preceduto da un numerale e dall'articolo *a/an*; ha forma sia singolare che plurale: *a book, two books; an egg, six eggs; one girl, three girls*.

ortografia parola di origine greca che significa corretto modo di scrivere; l'insieme delle regole usate allo scopo.

participio passato forma verbale usata per fare i tempi composti, come il passato prossimo p.es. *I've cleaned my room*, e il passivo p.es. *The room has been cleaned*. Il participio passato dei verbi regolari termina in -*ed*, p.es. *cleaned, worked*. Il participio passato dei verbi irregolari ha forme diverse p.es. *break* ⟶ *broken*, *see* ⟶ *seen* (cfr. 190).

participio presente forma verbale in -*ing* usata per fare la forma progressiva o una frase participiale p.es. *I hurt my leg playing tennis*; può fungere anche da aggettivo p.es. *a worrying problem*.

periodo unione di due o più frasi con un senso compiuto.

plurale forma usata per indicare più di uno. *Car* e *he/she* sono al **singolare**, mentre *cars* e *they* sono al **plurale**.

preposizione parte del discorso p.es. *in, on, of, at, for* che si premette a un elemento della frase (nome, pronome ecc.) per formare i complementi, cioè per stabilire un rapporto tra le parole.

prima persona colui o coloro che parlano = *I, we*; segue poi la **seconda persona**, cioè colui o coloro che ascoltano = *you*; e la **terza persona**, cioè colui, coloro o ciò di cui si parla = *he, she it, they*.

pronome parte del discorso che si usa al posto di un nome p.es. *she, they, them, mine*.

pronome indefinito pronome come *something, anyone* che indica qualcuno o qualcosa in modo indefinito.

pronome interrogativo pronome come *what, who, which* che si usa per introdurre una domanda.

pronome possessivo l'aggettivo possessivo usato senza il nome, in inglese ha però una forma diversa da quella dell'aggettivo: *mine, yours, his, hers, its, ours, theirs*.

pronome relativo pronome che, riferito a un nome o pronome della frase precedente, mette in relazione le due frasi; nel periodo: *I spoke to the man who works in the post office*, la parola *who* è un pronome relativo; sono pronomi relativi *who, that, which, whose, whom, what*.

pronome riflessivo pronome usato quando l'azione compiuta dal soggetto 'si riflette', cioè ricade sul soggetto stesso; sono pronomi riflessivi *myself, yourself, himself, herself, itself, ourselves, yourselves, themselves*.

risposta breve risposta formata dal soggetto e da un verbo ausiliare p.es. *Yes, **I am**. No, **she hasn't**.*

sillaba gruppo di lettere che si pronunciano con una

sola emissione di voce p.es. *remember* ha tre sillabe: re-mem-ber.

soggetto ciò di cui si parla o scrive, l'elemento fondamentale della frase, assieme al verbo; nella forma affermativa precede il verbo p.es. **John** *went to London.*

suono sonoro suono in cui si può sentire una vibrazione p.es. /d/, /b/, /n/.

suono sordo suono in cui non si può sentire nessuna vibrazione p.es. /p/, /k/, /t/.

superlativo forma che esprime il massimo grado di una qualità p.es. *old*est, *slow*est, *most* intelligent sono le forme superlative di *old, slow, intelligent.*

tempo (del verbo) forma verbale che indica quando avviene un'azione o esiste una condizione p.es. *is working* (presente), *worked* (passato).

verbo parte del discorso che indica cosa fa o in che stato si trova il soggetto; assieme a quest'ultimo è l'elemento più importante della frase. Cfr. anche **verbo principale, ausiliare, modale.**

verbo ausiliare è così chiamato un verbo come *be, have* o *do* che 'aiuta' a formare i tempi composti degli altri verbi, la forma passiva, negativa e interrogativa p.es. *We* **are** *waiting. I* **have** *finished. You* **don't** *know. It* **was** *stolen.*

verbo fraseologico verbo + particella (avverbio o preposizione) p.es. *get up, switch on, throw away,* o verbo + particella + preposizione p.es. *look forward to, go back on.*

verbo modale (ausiliare) è così chiamato un verbo che indica un modo dell'azione principale; in italiano è anche detto **servile** perché 'serve' all'infinito del verbo che contiene l'idea principale. Sono verbi modali *can, could, may, might, will, would, shall, should, ought (to), must, need* e *dare.*

verbo principale il verbo che indica l'azione, non il verbo ausiliare (*be, have, do*), né quello modale (*can, must, may* ecc.). Però anche un verbo ausiliare può essere usato come verbo principale, quando non svolge funzione di ausiliare.

virgolette il segno ortografico ('...') o ("...") usato per racchiudere il discorso diretto.

vocale lettera che corrisponde ai suoni formati con la più semplice emissione della voce (*a, e, i, o, u*).

Indice analitico

I numeri si riferiscono alle unità, non alle pagine.

Progress Tests

Gli 88 tests che seguono sono mirati alla verifica graduale e progressiva dell'apprendimento dei principali argomenti trattati in *The Heinemann English Grammar*.

Contents

Answers on pages 348–352 of the 'with answer key' edition.

1 Present simple and present continuous (Units 1–3)

(i) Put the verbs in brackets into the correct form: the present simple or the present continuous.

1 Britain ____ (have) an election at least once every four years.
2 I ____ (negotiate) a new pay deal with my boss at the moment.
3 It ____ (rain) every time I ____ (leave) my umbrella at home.
4 Please sit down! I ____ (try) to watch this TV programme.
5 American Football ____ (become) very popular in England.
6 Robert never ____ (go) abroad for his holidays. It's too expensive.
7 Many of the world's natural resources ____ (disappear).
8 Rain ____ (fall) very heavily in Bombay during June and July.
9 My parents are in America on holiday. They ____ (stay) near San Francisco.
10 The traffic ____ (move) very slowly on the motorway today. Workmen ____ (repair) the road.

(ii) Choose the correct answer—A or B.

1 ____ skiing in the French Alps every year.
  A *We go*   B *We're going*
2 ____ one of Agatha Christie's books at the moment.
  A *I read*   B *I'm reading*
3 Some modern cars ____ on unleaded petrol.
  A *run*   B *are running*
4 The St Lawrence River ____ into the North Atlantic.
  A *flows*   B *is flowing*
5 'Where's the cat?' '____ on the sofa.'
  A *It lies*   B *It's lying*
6 Drive carefully. ____ heavily this morning.
  A *It snows*   B *It's snowing*
7 Be careful! The ladder ____ down.
  A *falls*   B *is falling*

8 The planet Mercury ____ round the sun every eighty-eight days.
  A *travels*   B *is travelling*

2 Past simple and past continuous (Units 4–5)

(i) There are mistakes in some of these sentences. Find the mistakes and correct them.

1 The Titanic travelled to New York when it hit an iceberg and sank in the Atlantic.
2 The jumper was shrinking when I washed it.
3 Christopher Columbus was sailing in the Santa Maria when he discovered America.
4 I was breaking my toe when I tripped over the dog.
5 The mouse was having a heart attack when the cat jumped down from the chair.
6 The footballer ran towards the goal when he fell over.
7 James Dean drove a sports car when he was dying.

(ii) Make sentences. Put the verbs into the correct form: the past simple or the past continuous.

1 while I | write | a letter the phone | ring | .
2 you | read | the newspaper as soon as it | arrive | ?
3 she | not | lock | the door when she | leave | the office | .
4 the train | go | through the tunnel when it | suddenly | stop | .
5 Sally | wash | her hair when the doorbell | ring | .
6 John Logie Baird | invent | the television or the telephone | ?
7 they | cry | when they | hear | the bad news | .
8 the cat | lie | on the sofa when the mouse | come | into the room | .

3 *Been* and *gone* (Units 6–7)

Choose the correct answer.

1 The children are back at school now. They've *been/gone* on holiday for the summer.
2 'Have you ever *been/gone* to Niagara Falls?' 'No, but I've *been/gone* to the Great lakes.'
3 Bill worked very hard today. He's *been/gone* to bed early.
4 I've got a lot of money. I've *been/gone* to the bank today.
5 'His car isn't in the garage. I think he's *been/gone* away for the day.'

4 Present perfect with *just, yet* and *already* (Units 6, 8)

Put the words in the correct order. (Sometimes two answers are possible.)

Example:

started | have | they | to have | just | dinner | .
They have just started to have dinner.

1 just | to rain | has | it | started | .
2 you | that book | have | yet | finished | ?
3 yet | that film | seen | haven't | I | .
4 the bus | just | left | has | .
5 you | already | done | your shopping | have | ?
6 has | for several jobs | Bob | applied | already | .

5 Present perfect simple and present perfect continuous (Units 6, 9, 10)

(i) Complete the sentences using the present perfect simple or present perfect continuous of the words in the box.

| break | grow | make |
| play | put up | lose |

1 My young brother ____ three centimetres this month.
2 The young children ____ a snowman all morning.
3 I ____ my arm twice in two years.
4 I'm tired. I ____ tennis all afternoon.
5 Have you got any money? I ____ my wallet.
6 They ____ their tent for over an hour now and they still haven't finished.

(ii) Complete the questions. Use the present perfect simple or present perfect continuous.

Example:

I've saved some money.
How much *have you saved?*
How long *have you been saving?*

1 Mike is losing his hair.
   How long ____ his hair?
   How much hair ____?
2 I'm looking for a flat.
   How many flats ____ at?
   How long ____?
3 Annie is doing her homework.
   How long ____ it?
   How much homework ____?
4 They're playing tennis.
   How long ____?
   How many games ____?

6 Present perfect with *for* and *since* (Units 6, 11)

Re-write the sentences beginning with the words given. Use *for* or *since*.

Example:

Great Britain introduced decimal currency in 1971.
Great Britain has had *decimal currency since 1971.*

1 I last read *War and Peace* in 1980.
   I haven't ____.
2 Sarah started studying Spanish two years ago.
   Sarah has been ____.
3 Steven Spielberg started directing films in the 1960s.
   Steven Spielberg has been ____.
4 It started raining on Monday.
   It hasn't stopped ____.
5 My mother stopped working ten years ago.
   My mother hasn't ____.
6 My sister stopped skiing in 1989.
   My sister hasn't ____.
7 Robert de Niro began acting in the 1970s.
   Robert de Niro has been ____.

7 Present perfect and past simple (Units 6, 12)

(i) There are mistakes in some of these sentences. Find the mistakes and correct them.

1 I live in Brighton. I lived here for ten years.
2 Tolstoy has written *War and Peace*.
3 I started studying Spanish two years ago.
4 Oh, no! Look! Someone stole my car radio!
5 Who has discovered America?
6 We've played tennis yesterday afternoon.
7 When have you passed your driving test?
8 When did Neil Armstrong walk on the moon?
9 I never ate Chinese food in my life.
10 Look at Mike! He grew a beard!

(ii) Choose the correct answer—A or B?

1 I ____ to Los Angeles in 1980.
   A *have been*   B *went*
2 You ____ a lot of interesting things in your life.
   A *have done*   B *did*
3 James Dean ____ in the film *Rebel without a Cause*.
   A *has starred*   B *starred*
4 Who ____ the wheel?
   A *has invented*   B *invented*
5 I ____ coffee since 1980.
   A *haven't drunk*   B *didn't drink*
6 How many people ____ in the Second World War?
   A *have died*   B *died*
7 I work in a bank now. I ____ there for a year.
   A *have worked*   B *worked*
8 We ____ the new Steven Spielberg film last week.
   A *have seen*   B *saw*
9 ____ the news last night?
   A *Have you heard*   B *Did you hear*
10 When ____ your new car?
   A *have you bought*   B *did you buy*

8 Present perfect and present tense (Units 6, 9, 13)

There are mistakes in some of these sentences. Find the mistakes and correct them.

1 Carlo lives in Rome since three years.
2 Bob is working hard at the moment.
3 How long are you studying English?
4 My parents are married for thirty years.
5 I'm using a computer these days.
6 Sarah knows Simon for a long time.
7 Those men are waiting outside since 2.00.
8 Have you been sitting there for long?
9 My sister lives in Brighton since 1980.
10 The Rolling Stones rock group are playing together for over twenty years.

9 Past perfect simple and past simple (Unit 14)

(i) Choose the correct answer—A or B.

1 I arrived at the bus station late yesterday. When I got there, my bus ____.
   A *left* B *had left*
2 I arrived at the bus station at 10 o'clock last night. My bus ____ at 10.15.
   A *left* B *had left*
3 I was asleep when my friend phoned me last night. I ____ in bed for two hours.
   A *was* B *had been*
4 When I arrived home my father wasn't there. He ____ out.
   A *went* B *had gone*
5 I had breakfast when I ____ a shower.
   A *had* B *had had*

(ii) Make sentences. Put the verbs into the past simple or past perfect simple.

1 when I | visit | the town last month | they | build | a new hospital
2 when we | have | dinner | we | go | out for a walk
3 when Sue | look | in the fridge | all the food | go
4 I | not know | the way to John's house because I | not be | there before
5 Mike | get | really exhausted in his first marathon because he | not run | in such a long race before

10 Past perfect continuous, past simple and past continuous (Units 4, 5, 15)

There are mistakes in some of these sentences. Find the mistakes and correct them. *had been*
1 We were waiting for an hour when our train finally arrived yesterday.
2 I'd been playing football for over twenty years when I gave it up in 1980.
3 We lived in Paris for ten years when we moved to Madrid last year. *had been living*

4 After we'd been walking round the town for a few hours, we decided to have lunch. *had been working*
5 It was late and I was working since early in the morning, so I was very tired.

11 *Will* and *going to* (Units 16–18)

Complete the sentences. Use *will* or *going to* and the verbs in the box.

teach	lend	live	bite	take	look
have	buy	meet	rain		

1 'Would you like to come to the cinema with us?' 'All right. I'll *MEET* you at 7.00.'
2 Look at those black clouds. It's *GOING TO RAIN*
3 'I can't find my umbrella.' 'Don't worry. I'll *(LEND)* you mine.'
4 'Have you seen my tennis racket?' 'No. I haven't. Just a minute. I'll *LOOK* in the cupboard.'
5 'I can't play chess.' 'I'll *TEACH* you if you like.'
6 'Why are you putting on your coat?' 'I'll *GOING TO TAKE* the dog for a walk.'
7 'Why are you selling your house?' 'We *ARE GOING TO LIVE* in the country.'
8 Don't go near that dog! It'll *BITE* you!
9 'I'm going to buy Sally a Walkman for her birthday.' 'She's already got one.' 'Has she? Well, I'll *BUY* her a new sweater.'
10 Have you heard the news? Mrs Green's pregnant again. She *IS GOING TO HAVE* another baby.

12 Present continuous and *going to* (Units 19–20)

There are mistakes in some of these sentences. Which sentences have mistakes in them?

1 We're going to see a film this evening.
2 The weather forecast says it's snowing tomorrow. *GOING TO SNOW*

3 What are you doing next weekend?
4 I think England are ~~winning~~ the soccer match tonight.
   GOING TO WIN
5 I'm staying at home this evening.
6 Do you think Sarah is ~~passing~~ her exams this summer?
   GOING TO PASS

---

13 Present simple and *will* (Units 21–22)

Choose the correct answer—A or B.

1 We'll go for a picnic tomorrow if the weather ____ nice.
   A *will be*   B *is*
2 Simon will get a ticket for the U2 concert, providing he ____ all night.
   A *will queue*   B *queues*
3 If you go to Moscow, you ____ Red Square.
   A *will see*   B *see*
4 Sue will give me some money when she ____ paid.
   A *will get*   B *gets*
5 I'll phone Mike as soon as I ____ any news.
   A *will hear*   B *hear*
6 Unless you work hard, you ____ your exams.
   A *will fail*   B *fail*

---

14 Future continuous and future perfect (Units 23–24)

Ken and Kate are going to Paris tomorrow. Here is their timetable for tomorrow morning:

7.30-8.30	Drive to the airport
8.30	Check-in at the airport
10.00-11.00	Flight to Paris
11.15-11.45	Taxi to the hotel
1.00	Lunch at the hotel

Complete the sentences about Ken and Kate. Put the verbs into the future continuous or future perfect.

1 At 8.00 they ____ (leave) home and they ____ (drive) to the airport.
2 At 8.30 they ____ (arrive) at the airport and they ____ (check-in).
3 At 10.15 they ____ (fly) to Paris.
4 At 11.30 they ____ (arrive) in Paris and they ____ (drive) to their hotel.
5 At 1.10 they ____ (have) lunch at the hotel.

---

15 Future in the past: *was/were going to* (Unit 25)

Make sentences with *was/were going to . . .*, but . . . .

Example:

I | take | the dog for a walk | it | start | to rain
I was going to take the dog for a walk, but it started to rain.

1 Robert | watch | the film on TV | he | fall asleep
2 I | visit | you | I | not have | enough time
3 Sarah | change | some traveller's cheques | the bank | be | closed
4 we | go | to the concert | it | be | cancelled
5 I | finish | work early | my boss | ask | me to work late
6 my parents | fly to Scotland | they | decide | to go by train

---

16 Continuous forms with *always* (Unit 26)

Put the verbs in brackets into the most suitable form: the present simple or the present continuous.

1 You're never satisfied! You ____ (always | complain)!
2 Maria is never late for work. She ____ (always | arrive) on time.

3 Stephanie is very conceited. She ____
(always | look) at herself in the mirror.
4 Joe is very kind. He ____ (always | help)
people.
5 I never feel hungry in the mornings. I
____ (always | have) a small breakfast.

---

17 Verbs not used in the continuous (Unit 27)

Choose the correct answer—A or B.

1 Some people ____ there is life on other
planets.
   A *are believing* B *believe*
2 You look worried. What ____ about?
   A *are you thinking* B *do you think*
3 'Where's Ken?' 'I think ____ a bath.'
   A *he's having* B *he has*
4 I think Ken ____ a moustache.
   A *is having* B *has*
5 Which sports ____?
   A *are you liking* B *do you like*
6 You can switch off the radio. ____ to it.
   A *I'm not listening* B *I don't listen*
7 ____ the Russian alphabet?
   A *Are you understanding*
   B *Do you understand*
8 What's wrong? You look like ____ a
ghost!
   A *you've just been seeing*
   B *you've just seen*
9 Can you repeat that, please? ____ you.
   A *I wasn't hearing* B *I didn't hear*
10 How long ____ your best friend?
   A *have you been knowing*
   B *have you known*

---

18 Review of the present and the past (Unit 28)

(i) **Correct the mistakes in this letter using suitable present or past forms.**

```
Dear Mrs Black,

I write to you in reply to your
advertisement in last Monday's
Evening Argus.

At the moment, I working for
Sun Travel, a company in
London. I work there for two
years. Before I was joining Sun
Travel, I have worked for a
student travel company in
Spain. I work there for a year.
Before that, I have worked for
Worldwide Travel in Brighton
for a year. Now I would like to
move back to Brighton and I
look for a job with a travel
company in the town.
```

(ii) **Use these words to make the sentences in a story. Put the verbs into a suitable present or past form.**

1 What | be | the most embarrassing thing
that | ever | happen | to you in your life?
2 I | have | a terrible experience last
Saturday.
3 This | be | what | happen.
4 I | leave | my flat at 2 o'clock and | go |
into town to do some shopping.
5 I | go | shopping most Saturday
afternoons.
6 By 4 o'clock I | finish | shopping and
I | go | into a cafe for a cup of coffee.
7 While I | sit | in the cafe, I | see | a friend
called Julie Jones and she | join | me.
8 At around 4.30 Julie and I | pay | the bill
and | leave | the cafe.
9 As we | leave, | I | offer | to give Julie a lift
home in my car.

10 She | say | she would like a lift so
    we | walk | to the car park together.
11 I always | put | my car in the same car
    park near the town centre, but when
    we | get | to the car park, I | have | a big
    surprise.
12 My car | be | not | there!
13 Of course, I immediately | think | that
    someone | steal | it.
14 I | phone | the police, but luckily I | do
    not.
15 I suddenly | realise | the truth!
16 I | not | drive | into town that day!
17 I | come | on the bus instead.
18 Imagine how stupid I | feel.
19 My face | go | so red.
20 Julie just | smile | and | say | 'Don't
    worry. We can take the bus home
    together!'

(iii) Complete the sentences in this story.
Put the verbs in brackets into a suitable past
form.

One night in January 1938 Samuel Beckett
__1__ (walk) home in Paris. He __2__
(be) to the cinema and then to a cafe, where
he __3__ (spend) some time with friends.
As Beckett and his friends __4__ (walk)
along the Avenue d'Orleans, a man __5__
(stop) them and __6__ (ask) them for
money. The man __7__ (drink) heavily all
evening and he __8__ (be) very drunk.
Beckett __9__ (refuse) to give him any
money. When he __10__ (start) to walk
away the man __11__ (take) out a knife
and __12__ (stab) Beckett in the chest. A
young woman called Suzanne __13__
(pass) by at the time. She __14__ (stop)
and __15__ (help) Beckett. Later she
__16__ (visit) him in hospital. Twenty-
three years later Beckett and Suzanne
__17__ (get) married.

19 Review of the future (Unit 29)

**Choose the correct or most suitable
answer—A or B.**

1 Who do you think ___ the next
   election?
   A *is winning*   B *will win*
2 ___ my flat by next weekend.
   A *I paint*   B *I'll have painted*
3 Don't go out without a coat on. ___ a
   cold.
   A *You'll catch*   B *You're going to catch*
4 I can't come out with you on Saturday.
   ___ a friend.
   A *I meet*   B *I'm meeting*
5 At 2.00 tomorrow ___ in my office.
   A *I'll work*   B *I'll be working*
6 The concert ___ at 8.00 on Saturday.
   A *starts*   B *is going to start*
7 'Would you like a drink?' 'Oh, yes, ___
   a Coke. Thank you.'
   A *I'll have*   B *I'm going to have*
8 'Where are you going with that ladder?'
   '___ the roof.'
   A *I'll repair*   B *I'm going to repair*
9 If ___ Martha, I'll tell her the news.
   A *I see*   B *I'll see*
10 Look out! That glass ___ off the table.
    A *falls*   B *is going to fall*

20 Imperative and *let's* (Unit 30)

(i) How can you make your own yoghurt?
Complete the instructions with the verbs in
the box.

add   leave   boil   leave   stir

__1__ some milk for one minute. Then
__2__ the milk to cool for five minutes.
Next, __3__ a little natural yoghurt to the
milk and __4__. Then __5__ the mixture
in a warm place for about eight hours.

(ii) Make suggestions. Use *Let's* or *Let's not* and the words in the box.

tell   stay   hurry   make

1 We don't want to be late. ____.
2 We want to keep this a secret. ____ anyone.
3 We want to be careful. ____ any mistakes.
4 We don't want to go out now. ____ at home.

21   *Be* (Unit 31)

(i) Complete the sentences using the present or past forms of *be*.

Hello. My name __1__ John Jackson and my sister's name __2__ Anna. We __3__ from Newcastle. That __4__ in the north-east of England. I __5__ 25 years old and Anna __6__ 16. Anna __7__ born in Newcastle, but I __8__n't. I __9__ born in Liverpool. What about you? What __10__ your name? You __11__n't English. Where __12__ you from? __13__ that where you __14__ born?

(ii) Complete the sentences using the words in the box.

is('s)   isn't   are('re)   aren't
was   wasn't   were   weren't

1 '____ Steven Spielberg a film maker?' 'Yes, he ____.'
2 '____ Dallas in Arizona?' 'No, it ____. It ____ in Texas.'
3 '____ Madonna English?' 'No, she ____ American.'
4 The Rocky Mountains ____ in Mexico. They ____ in the United States and Canada.
5 '____ Pablo Picasso French?' 'No, he ____. He ____ Spanish.'

6 'Where ____ the first Olympic Games?' 'They ____ in Greece.'
7 '____ Marie and Pierre Curie American?' 'No, they ____.'

22   *There is, there are* (Unit 32)

Complete the sentences. Use *there*, *it* or *they* with a suitable form of *be*.

Example:
There's an old castle on the hill. *It's* over 500 years old.

1 ____ a film on TV tonight. ____ called *The Deer Hunter*.
2 ____ five senses. ____ sight, hearing, taste, smell and touch.
3 '____ a computer shop in the town centre?' 'Yes, ____. ____ in West Street.'
4 '____ any books about Alfred Hitchcock in the library?' 'Yes ____. ____ in the film section.'
5 ____ a closing-down sale at the ABC Carpet Store last month. ____ from the 26th to the 31st of July.
6 ____ another Olympic Games in the year 2020. ____ probably ____ held in Greece.

23   *Have* and *have got* (Units 33–34)

There are mistakes in some of these sentences. Find the mistakes and correct them.

1 I'm having a rest at the moment.
2 I'm having got a pain in my neck at the moment.
3 Had you got a good journey yesterday?
4 Have you got a new computer?
5 We're having dinner late tonight.
6 We usually have got dinner at 7 o'clock.
7 'Have you got a car?' 'Yes, I've got.'
8 I've got an appointment with the doctor.
9 Did Madonna have got blonde hair in 1991?
10 Do you have got a driving licence?

24 Ability: *can, could, be able to* (Unit 36)

Choose the correct answer—A, B or C.

1 How many languages ____?
   A *do you can speak*   B *can you speak*
   C *can you to speak*
2 Mike ____ chess very well.
   A *to can't play*   B *doesn't can play*
   C *can't play*
3 Maria ____ very fast when she was younger.
   A *can run*   B *could run*
   C *was able run*
4 The traffic was very heavy, but Peter ____ to work on time.
   A *managed to get*   B *could get*
   C *couldn't get*
5 They were whispering so I ____ what they were saying very clearly.
   A *could hear*   B *couldn't to hear*
   C *couldn't hear*
6 My grandfather was a very good footballer. He ____ a professional if he had wanted to.
   A *could be*   B *was able to be*
   C *could have been*
7 When Martha asked me for money, I ____ her some, so I did.
   A *could lend*   B *was able to lend*
   C *could have lent*
8 Sue would like ____ to buy a new car.
   A *to be able to afford*   B *to can afford*
   C *be able to afford*
9 Do you think that doctors ____ cancer in the future?
   A *will can cure*   B *will able to cure*
   C *will be able to cure*
10 I ____ the company's offer of a job in Edinburgh, but I didn't want to live in Scotland.
   A *could accept*   B *could have accepted*
   C *could to have accepted*

25 Permission: *can, could, may, might, be allowed to* (Unit 37)

There are mistakes in some of these sentences. Find the mistakes and correct them.

1 'Can I use your car this evening?' 'Yes, of course you could.'
2 The law says that you might not drive a car in Britain without a seat belt.
3 'May I ask you for a favour?' 'Of course you can.'
4 'Could I borrow your dictionary?' 'Yes, of course you might.'
5 My brother may borrow my sister's computer any time he wants to.
6 You can have a look at my newspaper if you like.
7 My sister's daughter could stay up late and watch the World Cup on TV last night.

26 Obligation and necessity (Units 38–39)

(i) Re-write the sentences using the words in brackets.

Example:

It is against the law to drive without a licence. (*mustn't*)
You mustn't drive without a licence.

1 It isn't necessary to be over 16 to get married. (*don't have to*)
2 It is important for me to pass the exam. (*must*)
3 It is necessary to have an appointment to see the manager. (*have to*)
4 It isn't necessary for you to apologise. (*don't have to*)
5 It is against the law to drive without a seat belt. (*mustn't*)

(ii) Complete each sentence using the most suitable word in the box.

> must   have to   have to   had to
> having to   have to

1 I'm sorry, but I can't see you this evening. My boss has told me I ____ work late.
2 You're always working late! You ____ work late yesterday, too!
3 I've got a terrible toothache. I really ____ go to the dentist.
4 I've got an appointment with the dentist today. I ____ be there at 2.00.
5 I hate ____ go to the dentist.
6 The law says that you ____ report a motor accident to the police.

27 Review of permission and obligation (Unit 40)

Choose the most suitable answer—A, B or C.

1 It isn't cold outside. You ____ wear a coat.
   A *mustn't* B *can* C *needn't*
2 You ____ keep out of that room. It's private.
   A *don't have to* B *mustn't* C *must*
3 You ____ fall asleep when you drive a car.
   A *mustn't* B *needn't* C *must*
4 I'm going to retire soon. Then I won't ____ work any more.
   A *must* B *have to* C *can*
5 You ____ vote in Britain until you are 18.
   A *have to* B *can* C *aren't allowed to*
6 You ____ wear a uniform in the army.
   A *can* B *have to* C *mustn't*
7 Tomorrow is a holiday. We ____ go to work.
   A *don't have to* B *aren't allowed to* C *have to*
8 You ____ ride a bicycle on a motorway in Britain.
   A *must* B *don't have to* C *can't*

28 *Needn't have* and *didn't need to* (Unit 41)

There are mistakes in some of these sentences. Find the mistakes and correct them.

1 We needn't have bought so much wine for the party because nobody drank much.
2 Mike needn't have gone to work yesterday, so he stayed at home.
3 It was nice of you to phone and thank me, but you really didn't need to.
4 Sue needn't have hurried home, so she took her time.
5 Kate needn't have made lunch when she arrived home from work because her husband had already done it.

29 Obligation and advice (Unit 42)

Choose the most suitable answer—A, B or C.

1 Language students ____ a little every day.
   A *is supposed to study* B *should study*
   C *had better study*
2 I think my car has been stolen. I ____ the police.
   A *had better phone*
   B *should have phoned*
   C *am supposed to phone*
3 I ____ tennis tomorrow, but I can't.
   A *had better play* B *am supposed to play*
   C *am not supposed to play*
4 I ____ this bill last month, but I forgot.
   A *should pay* B *had better pay*
   C *ought to have paid*
5 We have to get up early tomorrow, so we ____ to bed too late tonight.
   A *had better not go* B *ought to go*
   C *are supposed to go*
6 Everyone ____ a holiday sometimes.
   A *had better take* B *ought take*
   C *should take*

7 I've forgotten to send my friend a
  birthday card. What _____?
  A *am I supposed to do*   B *shall I do*
  C *shall I to do*
8 You _____ my new camera or I'll kill you!
  A *had better not break*
  B *shouldn't break*
  C *aren't supposed to break*
9 I've got a terrible headache. I think I
  _____ take an aspirin.
  A *am supposed to*   B *should take*
  C *had better to take*
10 You _____ with us to the beach
  yesterday. We had a very nice time.
  A *had better come*   B *should come*
  C *should have come*

---

30 Possibility: *may, might, could* (Unit 43)

**Re-write each sentence making it unsure.
Use the words in brackets.**

Example:

Sarah lent Simon some money. (*might*)
Sarah might have lent Simon some money.

1 It will rain tonight. (*may*)
2 Peter is in the Sports centre. (*could*)
3 Sally wrote to the bank. (*might*)
4 Ken didn't see me. (*may*)
5 I won't be here tomorrow. (*might*)
6 The robbers had a key to the office.
  (*may*)
7 The children aren't asleep. (*might*)
8 People will be living on the moon in the
  year 2050. (*could*)
9 Mike didn't receive my letter. (*may*)
10 Those people are waving at us. (*might*)

---

31 Possibility: *can* (Unit 44)

**Complete the second sentence so that it has
a similar meaning to the first sentence. Use
can or *may*.**

Example:

It is sometimes very hot here in the
summer.
It *can be very hot here in the summer.*

1 Perhaps it will be very hot here
  tomorrow.
  It _____.
2 Perhaps I am wrong.
  I _____.
3 It is possible for anyone to be wrong.
  Anyone _____.
4 Cats sometimes live for 20 years.
  Cats _____.
5 Perhaps your cat will live for 20 years.
  Your cat _____.

---

32 Probability: *should, ought to* (Unit 45)

**Re-write each sentence making it probable.
Use the word in brackets.**

Example:

Kate is very happy. (*should*)
Kate should be very happy.

1 Simon is in his room. (*should*)
2 I'll finish the book soon. (*ought to*)
3 Maria received the letter yesterday.
  (*should*)
4 We won't be late home tonight.
  (*shouldn't*)
5 My parents arrived at their hotel a few
  hours ago. (*ought to*)

---

33 Deduction: *must, can't* (Unit 46)

**Complete the sentences. Use *must* or *can't*
and the correct form of the verb in brackets.**

1 You haven't eaten all day. You _____
  hungry. (*be*)
2 You _____ cold. It's 30 degrees in the
  shade! (*be*)
3 There are no lights on in the office.
  Everyone _____ home. (*go*)
4 Peter _____ ill. I've just seen him playing
  tennis. (*be*)

5 I ___ my bag on the train. I can remember having it with me when I got off the train. (*leave*)

6 You drove home at night without any lights on? You ___ crazy! (*be*)

7 'I've just finished reading *War and Peace* in Russian.' 'That ___ a long time!' (*take*)

---

34 Review of possibility, probability and deduction (Unit 47)

Choose the correct answer—A, B or C.

1 It ___ a lovely day tomorrow.
   A *can be*   B *could be*   C *must be*

2 I'm getting fat. I think I ___ eating the wrong kind of food.
   A *must be*   B *can't be*   C *can be*

3 I'm not sure, but I ___ Sue in town last night.
   A *can see*   B *must have seen*
   C *may have seen*

4 Mike ___ driving to London tomorrow. He can't drive!
   A *might be*   B *can't be*   C *must be*

5 My letter ___ yesterday, but it didn't.
   A *must have arrived*   B *may arrive*
   C *should have arrived*

6 I can hear footsteps in the flat upstairs, so there ___ someone there.
   A *must be*   B *might be*   C *can't be*

7 We're very busy tomorrow so we ___ time to visit you. We aren't sure.
   A *could not have*   B *might not have*
   C *ought to have*

8 That girl ___ 20 years old. She looks about 12!
   A *may be*   B *must be*   C *can't be*

---

35 Requests, offers and suggestions (Units 48–50)

Write what you could say in these situations using the words in brackets.

Example:
You offer to make someone a cup of coffee. (*Shall?*)
Shall I make you a cup of coffee?

1 You ask to use the phone in a friend's house. (*Can?*)

2 You ask the waiter for the menu in a restaurant. (*Could?*)

3 You ask your teacher to explain something to you. (*Could?*)

4 You ask a friend to lend you some money. (*Would?*)

5 You are carrying a lot of bags. You ask a stranger to open a door for you. (*Would/mind?*)

6 You offer to give a friend a lift home in your car. (*I'll*)

7 You offer to show a friend how to use a photocopier. (*Shall?*)

8 You suggest to a friend that you have a walk in the park. (*How about?*)

9 You invite someone to the cinema this evening. (*you like?*)

10 You ask a friend to suggest where you can meet tomorrow. (*shall we?*)

11 You suggest to a friend that you go swimming this weekend. (*Let's*)

12 You suggest to a friend that you watch a video this evening. (*Why don't?*)

---

36 Habits: *used to, will, would* (Unit 51)

There are mistakes in some of these sentences. Find the mistakes and correct them.

1 I use to go swimming a lot nowadays.

2 When I was a child I used to suck my thumb.

3 I don't use to get up early these days.

4 My uncle would live in San Francisco when he was younger.

5 Mike used to live in Paris for a year.
6 Sarah uses to like Madonna, but she doesn't any more.
7 When I was younger I would go running two or three times a week.
8 When I was a student I would have a beard.
9 Where did you used to live?
10 Our neighbours will keep playing loud music. It's really annoying.

37 Refusals: *won't, wouldn't*; promises and threats: *will* (Units 52–53)

(i) **Complete each sentence using *will*, *won't* or *wouldn't* and a word in the box.**

> eat   say   go   call   be

1 My girlfriend ___ to the concert with me, so I went on my own.
2 Thank you for letting me use your new computer. I ___ very careful with it.
3 I've asked George three times now, but he still ___ why he's angry with me.
4 Leave me alone or I ___ the police.
5 Our cat ___ his food at the moment. I think he must be ill.

(ii) **Now say if each sentence is a refusal, a promise or a threat.**

38 *May/might as well* (Unit 54)

Complete the sentences using *may as well*... and the words in the box.

> sell   give up   apply   clean

1 I don't think I'll get the job. But I ___ for it. I've got nothing to lose.
2 We ___ the flat now. We've got to clean it some time and we've got nothing to do at the moment.

3 You never use your computer. You ___ it.
4 I ___ playing the piano. I'll never learn to play very well.

39 Other uses of *should* (Unit 55)

(i) **Re-write each sentence using the verb in brackets and *that...should*...**

Example:

I told my friend to sell his car. (*suggest*)
I suggested that my friend should sell his car.

1 My doctor told me to see a specialist. (*recommend*)
2 I told the shop assistant to give me my money back. (*insist*)
3 My teacher told me to buy a larger dictionary. (*suggest*)
4 The traffic warden told us to move our car. (*insist*)

(ii) **Put the two ideas together. Make sentences with *that...should*.**

Example:

Mike acted so strangely. I was surprised.
I was surprised that Mike should act so strangely.

1 You remembered my birthday. I'm pleased.
2 Sue offered me a job. I was surprised.
3 You lost your wallet. I'm very sorry.
4 John agreed with me. It was interesting.

40 *Wish* and *if only* (Unit 56)

Complete the second sentence so that it has a similar meaning to the first sentence.

1 I'd love to have more money.
  I wish ___.
2 I'm very sorry I was rude to Jim's wife.
  I wish ___.
3 Why doesn't Peter listen to me!
  If only ___.

4 Annie is sorry she ate so much chocolate.
  Annie wishes ____.
5 I'd really like to live in the country.
  I wish ____.
6 Why can't we find a cure for cancer!
  If only ____.
7 Why doesn't it stop raining!
  I wish ____.

41 *Would rather* (Unit 57)

Complete the sentences using *would rather* and the verbs in the box.

```
do   go   not play   not tell   have
```

1 I'm hungry. I ____ lunch now than later.
2 This is a secret. I ____ you ____ anyone what I said.
3 We don't want to go to Scotland by car. We ____ by train.
4 I ____ tennis now. I'm too hot.
5 'Are you going to do the shopping today?' 'I ____ you ____ it. I'm very busy.'

42 *It's time* (Unit 58)

Complete the sentences using the correct form of the verbs in the box.

```
ask   buy   clean   go
```

1 It's very late. It's time I ____ to bed.
2 My car is rather dirty. I think it's about time I ____ it.
3 I've been earning the same salary for 15 years. It's time I ____ my boss for a pay rise.
4 You're always borrowing my tennis racket! Don't you think it's about time you ____ your own?

43 The passive (Units 59–60)

(i) Re-write the sentences in the active, beginning with the words given.

Example:

The phone is being repaired now.
They *are repairing the phone now.*

1 A new motorway has been built.
  They ____.
2 The information is kept on our computer.
  We ____.
3 A man was arrested late last night.
  The police ____.
4 The medicine should be taken after meals.
  You ____.
5 The hotel will have to be sold.
  We ____.
6 Mike doesn't like being criticized.
  Mike doesn't like people ____.
7 When I returned to the town, my old school had been pulled down.
  When I returned to the town, they ____.
8 As I was walking home, I thought I was being followed.
  As I was walking home, I thought someone ____.

(ii) Re-write these sentences in the passive, leaving out *they* or *someone*.

Example:

They have sold the company.
The company has been sold.

1 They are interviewing the president on TV at the moment.
2 They deliver the post twice a day.
3 They took the old man to hospital.
4 They were repairing the traffic lights yesterday.
5 Someone has opened this letter.
6 I remember someone telling me the news.
7 They should reduce taxes.
8 Someone must have told Ann about the accident.

9 They had cancelled the 9.15 train, so I took a later train.
10 They are going to change the law soon.

(iii) Choose the correct answers.

The National Security Bank in downtown San Antonio __1__ (*robbed/was robbed*) last night. A safe __2__ (*blew open/was blown open*) and around $800,000 __3__ (*stole/was stolen*). The robbery __4__ (*took/was taken*) place between midnight and 1.00 am. The police __5__ (*are looking/are being looked*) for two men who __6__ (*saw/were seen*) getting into a black car near the bank at about 1 o'clock last night. They __7__ (*also want/are also wanted*) to hear from Mr Joe Newman, 52, who __8__ (*worked/was worked*) as a security guard at the bank. Mr Newman __9__ (*disappeared/was disappeared*) just before the robbery and he __10__ (*has not seen/has not been seen*) since then.

44 The passive with *by* and *with* (Unit 63)

There are mistakes in some of these sentences. Find the mistakes and correct them.

1 This letter was written by a typewriter.
2 The film *ET* was made by Steven Spielberg.
3 The omelette was made by three eggs.
4 *The Mona Lisa* (*La Gioconda*) was painted with Leonardo da Vinci.

45 The passive (Units 61, 62, 64)

Re-write these sentences beginning with the words given.

1 Someone will give you the information later.
   You ___.
2 Someone sent me a letter.
   A letter ___.

3 Someone knocked me over in the street.
   I ___.
4 The president is expected to visit Moscow.
   It ___.
5 It is said that golf was invented in China.
   Golf ___.
6 The Queen of England is thought to be one of the richest women in the world.
   It ___.
7 It is claimed that beings from outer space have visited the earth.
   Beings from outer space ___.
8 People say that sunbathing causes skin cancer.
   Sunbathing is supposed ___.

46 *Have something done* (Unit 65)

Re-write the sentences beginning with the words given.

Example:
They serviced Ken's car yesterday.
Ken *had his car serviced yesterday.*

1 They're repairing our roof at the moment.
   We ___.
2 They're going to fit a stereo in my car.
   I ___.
3 Someone cleans Sue's flat once a week.
   Sue ___.
4 Has anyone tested your eyes recently?
   Have you ___?
5 Someone stole John's briefcase last week.
   John ___.

47 *If* sentences, conditionals (Units 66, 68–70, 72)

(i) Choose the correct answer—A, B or C.

1 I may go to the USA next year. ___, I'll visit a friend in New York.
   A *When I go* B *If I go* C *If I'll go*
2 I'll see you ___ back from my holiday.
   A *when I'll come* B *when I come*
   C *if I come*

3 ＿ too busy tomorrow. I'll visit you.
  A *When I'm not* B *If I'm not*
  C *If I won't be*
4 ＿ more money, I'd buy a new car.
  A *When I have* B *If I have* C *If I had*
5 If I knew Alan's address, ＿ to him.
  A *I'd write* B *I'll write* C *I wrote*
6 Where would you live ＿ anywhere?
  A *if you lived* B *if you can live*
  C *if you could live*

(ii) Put the verbs in brackets into the correct form.

1 We'll go out later if it ＿ (stop) raining.
2 If I ＿ (be) you, I'd go to the doctor.
3 Do you want to watch TV? I ＿ (switch) it on if you do.
4 Simon doesn't want to come to the concert. I ＿ (buy) him a ticket if he did.
5 If we leave now, we ＿ (not | be) late.
6 If I were you, I ＿ (not | buy) that car.
7 If I ＿ (lie) in the sun, I always get sunburnt.
8 If John ＿ (not | apologize) to me, I won't speak to him any more!
9 ＿ (you | stop) working if you were a millionaire?
10 ＿ (you | phone) me tomorrow if you have time?

48 Unreal past conditionals (Unit 71)

Complete the sentences about these situations.

1 You went out for a walk without an umbrella. It rained, you got very wet and then you caught a cold.
  a) If I ＿ (take) an umbrella with me, I ＿ (not | get) wet.
  b) If I ＿ (know) it was going to rain, I ＿ (not | go) out.
  c) If I ＿ (not | go) out, I ＿ (not | catch) a cold.

2 You went to bed late last night. This morning you woke up late. Then you missed your bus and you were late for work.
  a) I ＿ (not | wake up) late this morning if I ＿ (not | go) to bed late last night.
  b) If ＿ (not | wake up) late, I ＿ (not | miss) my bus.
  c) If I ＿ (not | miss) my bus, I ＿ (not | be) late for work.

49 Conditional clauses without *if* (Unit 73)

Re-write the sentences without *if*, using the words in brackets.

Example:

If we don't take a taxi, we'll be late. (*unless*)
Unless we take a taxi, we'll be late.

1 If you don't go now, I'll be very angry. (*or*)
2 If you help me now, I'll help you later. (*provided*)
3 If you give me your address, I'll write to you. (*and*)
4 If they don't offer me a better job, I'll leave the company. (*unless*)
5 I'll stay up and watch the film if it isn't on too late. (*as long as*)
6 If you were in my place, what would you do? (*supposing*)
7 If I win the lottery, I'll give you half the money. (*should*)

50 Review of conditionals (Unit 74)

(i) There are mistakes in some of these sentences. Find the mistakes and correct them.

1 Janet will be disappointed if she'll fail the exam.
2 If Peter had been more careful, he wouldn't break the camera.
3 You can use my car tomorrow if I don't need it.

4 If I won't have much time, I usually have a sandwich for lunch.
5 If I were you, I won't lend John any money.
6 If the bus doesn't come soon, I'll walk home.
7 I'd be happier if I don't have to work so hard.

(ii) Make *if* sentences about these situations.

Examples:

Mike never takes any exercise. He's so unfit.
If Mike took some exercise, he wouldn't be so unfit.

I didn't know your address. I didn't write to you.
If I'd known your address, I would have written to you.

1 We didn't know the film was on TV. We didn't record it on our video.
2 I go to bed late every night. I'm always tired.
3 Janet wasn't in a hurry. She walked home.
4 I haven't got enough money. I can't go skiing next week.
5 We didn't have an umbrella. We got wet.

---

51 **Reported speech: statements (Units 76–78)**

(i) Peter met an American woman called Kirsty Lane last month. Look at some of the things that Kirsty told Peter. What were her actual words?

Example:

She told Peter that she lived in New York.
'I live in New York.'

1 She said that she was 25 years old.
2 She said she worked in a bank.
3 She said she had been working there for a year.

4 She told Peter that she didn't like her job very much.
5 She said she was in Europe on holiday.
6 She said she was having a great holiday.
7 She said she had arrived in London the previous week.
8 She told Peter that she had been to Britain twice before.
9 She told him that she was going to Italy the following week.
10 She said that she couldn't speak Italian very well.
11 She said she would be in Italy for a week.

(ii) Here are some things that Peter told Kirsty last month. How can you report these things now?

Example:

'I work for an export company.'
He told *her (that) he worked for an export company.*

1 'I've been working there for a year.'
He said ____.
2 'I'm looking for a better job.'
He told ____.
3 'I like travelling.'
He said ____.
4 'I've been to the United States.'
He said ____.
5 'I went to New York last summer.'
He told ____.
6 'I'd like to go to Australia one day.'
He said ____.
7 'I've got one sister.'
He told ____.
8 'Her name is Judy.'
He said ____.
9 'My sister doesn't live in England.'
He told ____.
10 'She lives in Spain.'
He said ____.

52 Reported speech: questions (Unit 78)

(i) Frank Allen had an interview for a job in a garage last week. The manager of the garage, Mr Jones, interviewed him. He asked Frank a lot of questions.

Frank is telling a friend about the interview. Read what Frank says. What were the actual questions that Mr Jones asked.

Example:

(1) *How old are you?*

First, Mr Jones asked me ___1___ how old I was. Then he asked ___2___ where I worked now, and ___3___ how long I had worked there. After that, he asked me ___4___ where I had been to school, and ___5___ what exams I had taken at school. Then he asked ___6___ if I could drive a car, ___7___ how long I had been driving, and ___8___ if I had a car of my own. After that, he asked ___9___ what my hobbies were, and ___10___ what I liked doing in my free time. Then, finally, he asked me ___11___ if I wanted the job. When I said I did, he asked me ___12___ if I could start next month.

(ii) You went to England last month. When you were there, you met an English couple who asked you a lot of questions. Report the questions beginning *They asked me . . . .*

Example:

'Where are you from?'
They asked me where I was from.

1 'Where do you work?'
2 'How long have you been working there?'
3 'Are you on holiday in England?'
4 'When did you arrive here?'
5 'Have you been to Britain before?'
6 'How long are you going to stay here?'
7 'Do you like English food?'
8 'Have you got any brothers or sisters?'
9 'How long have you been studying English?'
10 'Can you speak any other languages?'

53 Using the *to* infinitive in reported speech (Unit 79)

Report the sentences using the words in the box and the *to* infinitive form.

Example:

'Can I get you a drink?' he said to us.
He offered to get us a drink.

promised   invited   offered   advised

1 'Would you like to go to the cinema?' she asked her friend.
2 'I could post the letter for you,' he said to her.
3 'You should take more exercise,' the doctor said to me.
4 'I won't drive too fast,' I said.

54 Review of reported speech (Unit 80)

Frank was driving home last night when a police car stopped him. Read what Frank says happened. What do you think were the actual words that the policeman and Frank said?

First of all, the policeman told me ___1___ to switch off my engine. Then he asked me ___2___ where I was going. When I told him ___3___ I was going home, he asked me ___4___ where I lived. So I gave him my address. Then he asked me ___5___ where I had just come from. I said ___6___ I had been at a friend's house all evening. Then he asked ___7___ to see my driving licence. When I gave him my licence, he told me ___8___ to get out of the car. Then he wanted to know ___9___ if it was my car. I told him ___10___ I had bought it last year. After that he went back to his car and spoke on the radio for a short time. Then he told me ___11___ I could go home.

55 *-ing* form or infinitive (Units 82−98)

(i) Choose the correct answer—A, B or C.

1 Do you dislike ____ money?
   A *borrow*   B *to borrow*   C *borrowing*
2 My girlfriend persuaded me ____ my hair cut.
   A *have*   B *to have*   C *having*
3 I used ____ running every morning, but I never go now.
   A *go*   B *to go*   C *going*
4 I've decided ____ for a new job.
   A *look*   B *to look*   C *looking*
5 You needn't ____ me back that magazine. I've finished with it.
   A *give*   B *to give*   C *giving*
6 You must always remember ____ your car locked.
   A *keep*   B *to keep*   C *keeping*
7 It's very late. We really must ____ going.
   A *be*   B *to be*   C *being*
8 How about ____ tennis at the weekend?
   A *play*   B *to play*   C *playing*
9 You shouldn't encourage anyone ____.
   A *smoke*   B *to smoke*   C *smoking*
10 I'm not very good at ____ speeches.
   A *make*   B *to make*   C *making*
11 Going to the dentist always makes me ____ nervous.
   A *feel*   B *to feel*   C *feeling*
12 I stopped writing ____ the telephone.
   A *answer*   B *to answer*   C *answering*
13 I don't particularly enjoy ____.
   A *cook*   B *to cook*   C *cooking*
14 Janet promised ____ anyone what I'd said.
   A *not tell*   B *not to tell*   C *to not tell*
15 It's a lovely morning. Why don't we ____ for a walk?
   A *go*   B *to go*   C *going*
16 We haven't decided what ____ this evening.
   A *do*   B *to do*   C *doing*
17 We didn't expect England ____ the football match.
   A *win*   B *to win*   C *winning*
18 The police warned the man ____.
   A *to not move*   B *not to move*   C *not move*
19 ____ a lot of sugar is supposed to be bad for you.
   A *Eat*   B *To eat*   C *Eating*
20 I can't afford ____ a new stereo.
   A *buy*   B *to buy*   C *buying*
21 Ken switched on the radio ____ the news.
   A *hear*   B *to hear*   C *hearing*
22 All the hotels are full and we've got nowhere ____.
   A *stay*   B *to stay*   C *staying*

(ii) There are mistakes in some of these sentences. Find the mistakes and correct them.

1 I stopped to play football 20 years ago.
2 When will the car need servicing again?
3 Thanks for letting me to borrow your car.
4 Would you like to having a coffee now?
5 To walk can be very relaxing.
6 It isn't easy learn to play the piano.
7 I went to the station for get my train.
8 They wanted that I go out with them.
9 Everyone refused helping the old man.
10 I usually avoid driving at night if I can.
11 How about to play tennis at the weekend?
12 As I walked past the house I saw some men build a swimming pool.
13 Have you finished to eat your breakfast?
14 I'm used to work at night now, but I found it difficult at first.
15 Do you like to take regular exercise?
16 We're thinking of to go to a disco tonight.
17 Can you to come to my party on Saturday?
18 I'm looking forward to see you tonight.
19 We hope to have a holiday soon.
20 Do you feel like to listen to some music?
21 Annie's mother made her to eat her lunch.
22 Do you want that someone helps you for move the table?

56 Participle (-*ing* and *ed*) adjectives (Unit 99)

Re-write the sentences beginning with the words given.

1 I'm surprised by the news.
   I find ＿＿.
2 The man's behaviour was shocking.
   We were all ＿＿.
3 Kate is interested in travel.
   Kate finds ＿＿.
4 The tennis match was boring.
   We were ＿＿.
5 I felt very relaxed in the sauna.
   I found ＿＿.

57 Participle (-*ing*) clauses (Unit 100)

Join these ideas. Make sentences using -*ing* clauses, as in the examples.

Examples:

I arrived at the interview. I was feeling confident.
I arrived at the interview feeling confident.

I had a shower. I made breakfast.
Having had a shower, I made breakfast.

1 I dropped my bag. I was running for a bus.
2 We got lost. We were driving through Paris.
3 I locked all the doors. I went to bed.
4 I'd just had a drink. I wasn't thirsty.

58 Singular and plural (Units 101–103)

There are mistakes in some of these sentences. Find the mistakes and correct them.

1 Do you like my new jacket and trouser?
2 Where is your family from?
3 The news aren't very good.
4 How many persons live in Britain?
5 Where is the scissors?
6 I've bought a new teethbrush.
7 Do you eat a lot of fish?
8 How much is this blue Levi's jean?
9 Are the childrens asleep yet?
10 People are interesting.
11 Your hairs look very nice today. Have you just washed them?
12 Ten kilometre are a long way to walk.
13 One of my brother work in a shoes shop.
14 Physics were my favourite subject at school.
15 I don't like wearing pyjamas in bed.
16 What are the government going to do about the problem of homelessness?
17 There were £30 in my wallet, but now they've gone!
18 Some passer-bys stopped and helped the old man when he fell over.

59 Possessive forms (Units 104–106)

(i) Join the nouns using 's or *the . . . of . . . .*

Examples:

job | Sally
Sally's job

door | the car
the door of the car

1 news | this week
2 stolen car | the thieves
3 roof | the hotel
4 price | your meal
5 vacation | two weeks
6 end | the film
7 middle | our English lesson
8 name | the girl who came to dinner
9 girlfriend | Jim's brother
10 rising cost | petrol

(ii) Re-write the sentences beginning with the words given.

1 One of my friends is having a party.
   A friend ＿＿.
2 The only theatre in the town is closed.
   The town ＿＿.
3 Some of our neighbours have offered to help us.
   Some neighbours ＿＿.

4 Rainfall in Britain has been light this year. Britain ____.

5 We've been visiting some of our relatives. We've been visiting some relatives ____.

60 Countable and uncountable nouns (Unit 107)

Correct the mistakes.

1 The tourist office has informations about hotel accommodations.
2 You look different. Have you had your hairs cut?
3 There are traffics news on the radio every morning.
4 'Travelling light' means travelling without a lot of luggages.
5 We need a bread, some tomatoes and some spaghettis.
6 Where are the money I gave you? Have you spent them already?
7 We're having a beautiful weather at the moment.
8 Some of our furnitures were damaged when we moved.

61 Articles (Unit 108)

Complete the story. Put in a, an or the.

Last Sunday I decided to have __1__ quiet evening at home. At around 8 o'clock I was in __2__ kitchen cooking __3__ omelette for my dinner. __4__ omelette was almost ready when __5__ telephone rang. I went into __6__ hall to answer it. It was __7__ friend of mine, __8__ girl called Lisa. Lisa is __9__ student at __10__ London School of Music and Art. She told me she was taking __11__ important exam __12__ following day. She said she was sure she would fail __13__ exam. She sounded very worried. We talked for about __14__ quarter of __15__ hour. Then I suddenly remembered __16__ omelette on __17__

cooker! I put down __18__ phone and rushed into __19__ kitchen. It was terrible! __20__ room was full of smoke and __21__ omelette was completely black. It took me more than __22__ hour to clean up all __23__ mess.

62 Articles (Unit 109)

Choose the correct answer.

1 *Noise/The noise* is a form of pollution.
2 I'm worried about *noise/the noise* coming from my car.
3 Don't go swimming in this river. *Water/The water* here is polluted.
4 *Water/The water* turns to ice when it freezes.
5 The man gave *money/the money* to charity throughout his life.
6 Have you already spent *money/the money* I gave you yesterday?

63 Articles (Units 108–113)

(i) Put in a, an or the where necessary.

1 Have you ever been in ____ hospital for ____ serious operation?
2 Phil Collins can play ____ drums, ____ piano and ____ harmonica.
3 ____ giraffe is ____ tallest animal in ____ world.
4 My grandmother often listens to ____ radio in ____ bed at night.
5 I won't be at ____ home at 6 o'clock this evening. I'll still be at ____ work.
6 We'd like to live in ____ small cottage in ____ country.
7 There's ____ good film on at ____ cinema this evening.
8 Which is your favourite meal, ____ breakfast, ____ lunch or ____ dinner?
9 What is ____ government going to do for ____ unemployed of ____ Great Britain?
10 Don't you think ____ English are strange people?

(ii) Correct the mistakes.

1 The Canberra is capital of the Australia.
2 The San Diego is in the Southern California.
3 Is Amazon a longest river in the Latin America?
4 The Jamaica is island in Caribbean Sea.
5 The Snowdon is highest mountain in the England and Wales.
6 The Lake Michigan is in United States.
7 The Gobi desert is in the Asia.
8 Uffizi is one of a most famous museums in world.
9 Statue of Liberty was made in the France.
10 The Macy's is famous department store on the 34th Street in the New York.

64 Quantity (Units 114–119)

(i) Choose the correct answer: A, B, C or D.

1 There are ___ envelopes on my desk.
  A *much* B *some* C *any* D *a little*
2 There isn't ___ money in my pocket.
  A *no* B *some* C *any of* D *any*
3 Have you got ___ good computer games?
  A *any* B *any of* C *a lot* D *many of*
4 Do you like Madonna? Have you got ___ her records?
  A *some* B *every of* C *any* D *all*
5 There isn't ___ time before our flight leaves.
  A *much* B *many* C *some* D *no*
6 I've got ___ idea where Mike is.
  A *none* B *none of* C *no* D *any*
7 Do you know ___ people living in England?
  A *much* B *many* C *much of*
  D *many of*
8 You've had ___ interesting experiences.
  A *any* B *a lot* C *much* D *a lot of*
9 Would you like ___ more milk?
  A *little* B *a little* C *few* D *a few*
10 ___ my friends want to see the concert.
  A *No* B *Any of* C *None* D *None of*

(ii) Re-write the sentences beginning with the words given.

Example:

He isn't reliable and he isn't hard-working.
He is neither *reliable nor hard-working*.

1 She is intelligent and she is charming.
  She is both ___.
2 My brother can't sing and he can't play the guitar.
  My brother can neither ___.
3 My girlfriend didn't enjoy the party and I didn't enjoy the party.
  Neither ___.
4 Almost nobody likes Monday mornings.
  Few ___.
5 I've seen all Steven Spielberg's films.
  I've seen every ___.
6 She said that she only wanted a cup of coffee for breakfast.
  She said that all ___.
7 He can only speak a little French.
  He can't speak ___.
8 Almost no houses have video phones.
  Few ___.
9 All my sisters are single.
  None ___.
10 All my friends have passed their driving test.
  None ___.

65 Pronouns, etc (Units 120–125)

(i) Correct the mistakes.

1 Look! There's Sally and his boyfriend! Can you see them?
2 My brother he looks very young, but is older than I.
3 'Who's that outside?' 'It's I.'
4 My girlfriend and me phone us every day.
5 Ours flat was cheaper than their, but their is much smaller than our.
6 Did the old man hurt him when fell out of his bed?
7 I woke up, got dressed myself and made me some breakfast.

8 Is easy to cut you when you're shaving.
9 When we warned herself not to walk home by her own, she just laughed at us.
10 We were very annoyed with us for forgetting about yours party.

(ii) Put in a suitable pronoun or adjective eg *they, you, me, our* etc.

1 ____ can get married in England at the age of 16.
2 Stephanie is very conceited. She's always looking at ____ in the mirror.
3 Someone called to see you. ____ didn't tell me ____ name.
4 How far is ____ from Barcelona to Madrid?
5 Living by ____ can be lonely.
6 ____ isn't expensive to play tennis in England.
7 The police say that ____ want to interview Joe Newman.
8 If you don't want to come to the theatre with ____, I'll go on ____ own.

---

66 *One(s)* (Unit 124)

Choose the correct answer—A, B or C.

1 I'm looking for a new shirt. I'd like to buy ____ with a button-down collar.
   A *a one*   B *one*   C *ones*
2 My sister has already got a good job, but she wants ____.
   A *a better ones*   B *better one*
   C *a better one*
3 We've got some red wine, but we haven't got any ____.
   A *white*   B *white one*   C *a white one*
4 Do you like these chairs more than ____?
   A *those one*   B *those ones*   C *those*

---

67 *Something, anything,* etc (Unit 125)

(i) Re-write the sentences beginning with the words given.

Example:

There wasn't anybody in the restaurant.
There was *nobody in the restaurant.*

1 I've eaten nothing all day.
   I haven't eaten ____.
2 There's nobody living in that house.
   There isn't ____.
3 I haven't got anything to do today.
   I've got ____.
4 We haven't been anywhere this week.
   We've been ____.

(ii) There are mistakes in some of these sentences. Find the mistakes and correct them.

1 You look worried. Is something wrong?
2 I've spent all my money. I've got anything left.
3 There isn't nothing good on TV tonight.
4 That house is empty now. There's somebody living there.
5 We've looked anywhere for the letter, but we can't find it everywhere.
6 Tina is very nice. Everybody likes her.
7 We'd like to go somewhere warm on holiday this summer.
8 There wasn't nowhere to sit down in the room, so we had to stand.

---

68 Form, position and order of adjectives (Unit 126)

Complete the sentences. Put the words in brackets in the correct order.

Example:

We ____ (antique | a | bought | vase | large).
We *bought a large antique vase.*

1 My girlfriend ____ (motorbike | has got | a | Japanese | powerful).

2 The garden ___ (beautiful | this summer | looks).

3 Your grandmother ___ (woman | very | a | seems | cheerful).

4 The man ___ (a | leather | was wearing | black | coat | long).

5 We ___ (an | restaurant | French | had lunch at | expensive).

6 The Pyramids of Egypt ___ (old | are | around 5,000 years).

---

69 Comparatives, superlatives and *as . . . as* (Units 127–129)

(i) Correct the mistakes.

1 Today is more sunny as yesterday.

2 My boyfriend isn't as clever than he thinks.

3 Ken is a very more careful driver than Simon.

4 You aren't taller as I.

5 What was the happier day of your life?

6 The more older my grandmother gets, the more forgetful she becomes.

7 Camping isn't as comfortable than staying in a hotel, but it's much healthy.

8 The problem of world pollution is getting more and more bad.

(ii) Re-write the sentences beginning with the words given, as in the examples.

Examples:

A Rolls Royce is more expensive that a Fiat.
A Fiat isn't *as expensive as a Rolls Royce.*

I've never seen a taller man than Tom.
Tom is the *tallest man I've ever seen.*

1 Playing golf isn't as cheap as playing football.
Playing football is ___.

2 None of the animals in the world is faster than a cheetah.
A cheetah is the ___.

3 There is nothing better than a cold shower to wake you up in the mornings.
A cold shower is the ___.

4 Tokyo is bigger than Paris.
Paris isn't ___.

5 There is no footballer in the world more talented than Roberto.
Roberto is the ___.

6 Listening to records isn't as exciting as hearing live music.
Hearing live music is ___.

---

70 Adjectives and adverbs (Unit 130)

Complete the second sentence beginning with the words given, as in the examples.

Examples:

She's a very quick typist.
She types *very quickly.*

He looked at me suspiciously.
He gave me a *suspicious look.*

1 You're a very slow eater.
You eat ___.

2 He drives rather recklessly.
He's a ___.

3 She's a very hard worker.
She works ___.

4 Harrison Ford acts very well.
Harrison Ford is a ___.

5 She gave me an angry stare.
She stared at me ___.

---

71 Adverb position (Units 131–136)

Put the words into the most usual order.

Example:

The car slowly out of the garage I drove.
I drove the car slowly out of the garage.

1 My parents will be next week on holiday.

2 Confidently into the exam room I walked.

3 We saw on Saturday morning them in town.

4 Last week worked hard all the students.

5 The English like very much tea.
6 Last week my grandmother into hospital went.
7 My brother helps never with the housework.
8 We start always school at 9.00.
9 My teacher never is late for class.
10 Robert plays no longer football.
11 I'll forget never the first time we met.
12 I every night sleep always 8 hours.
13 Carla hasn't finished probably yet working.
14 We for an hour already have been waiting and the bus hasn't still come.

72 Adverbs (Units 133–139)

Choose the correct answer. (Sometimes two answers are possible.)

1 They started building the road two years ago and they ____ haven't finished it.
   A *still*   B *yet*   C *already*
2 You don't need to vacuum the carpet. I've ____ done it.
   A *still*   B *yet*   C *already*
3 I sent the letter two weeks ago and they haven't received it ____.
   A *still*   B *yet*   C *already*
4 Many rivers are ____ safe to swim in nowadays.
   A *any more*   B *any longer*   C *no longer*
5 I used to smoke, but I don't ____.
   A *any more*   B *any longer*   C *no longer*
6 It was really a ____ boring journey.
   A *quite*   B *fairly*   C *rather*
7 We ____ liked the hotel we stayed at.
   A *quite*   B *fairly*   C *pretty*
8 This summer is ____ hotter than last summer.
   A *rather*   B *quite*   C *fairly*
9 I can't lift this box. It's ____.
   A *too much heavy*   B *much too heavy*
   C *heavy enough*
10 We can't all fit into my car. It isn't ____.
   A *too much big*   B *enough big*
   C *big enough*

11 ____ is supposed to be bad for you.
   A *Too much salt*   B *Too many salt*
   C *Enough salt*
12 Annie feels ill. She's eaten ____.
   A *too much chocolates*
   B *too many chocolate*
   C *too many chocolates*
13 Mike is a wonderful dancer. He dances ____.
   A *too well*   B *very well*   C *well enough*
14 Everyone likes Tina. She's ____.
   A *such a nice*   B *so nice woman*
   C *so nice*
15 It was ____ that we had breakfast outside in the garden.
   A *such a warm morning*   B *such a warm*
   C *so warm*

73 Comparison: adverbs (Unit 140)

Re-write the sentences beginning with the words given.

Example:

Peter is a better cook than Sally is.
Peter cooks *better than Sally does.*

1 I'm not as good at tennis as you are.
   I don't play tennis ____.
2 Your writing is clearer than mine is.
   You write ____.
3 My brother is a more careless driver than I am.
   My brother drives ____.
4 Annie is the best swimmer of all the students in her school.
   Annie swims the ____.

74 Negatives (Unit 141)

Correct the mistakes.

1 I no think politics is interesting.
2 It not is raining at the moment.
3 You no have got any brothers or sisters.
4 My sister works not in London.
5 Liz no would like to live in the country.

6 I did not worked yesterday.
7 Sue not will be here next weekend.
8 They not have been waiting for us.

75 Questions (Units 142–147)

Ask questions using the words in brackets, as in the examples.

Examples:

I'm cooking. (*What?*)
What are you cooking?

Judy likes pop music. (*Madonna?*)
Does she like Madonna?

I've got a brother. (*not/any sisters?*)
Haven't you got any sisters?

1 Sarah is going to Paris. (*by car?*)
2 I go swimming. (*How often?*)
3 We stayed at a hotel. (*Which hotel?*)
4 I'm thirsty. (*not/hungry?*)
5 We can stay until 8.00.
   (*not/any longer?*)
6 I've eaten Chinese food. (*Indian food?*)
7 Sue has been having piano lessons.
   (*How long?*)
8 Mike wants to stay at home.
   (*not/to come out with us?*)
9 I asked someone. (*Who?*)
10 Someone asked me. (*Who?*)

76 Question tags (Unit 147)

Add question tags to these sentences.

Example:

You haven't got a car, *have you?*

1 Sally went to the concert, ____
2 You aren't angry, ____
3 Our train leaves at 7.30, ____
4 Ken will be here tomorrow, ____
5 Let's play tennis, ____
6 You don't know my father, ____
7 Close the door, ____
8 You'd like a coffee, ____

77 Reply questions (Unit 148)

Answer these sentences using 'reply questions' eg *Is he?*, *Did you?* etc.

Example:

I can dance the tango.
Can you?

1 I haven't read that book.
2 My sister lives in New York.
3 We went skiing last winter.
4 I've found a new job.
5 Derek isn't feeling very well.

78 Indirect questions (Unit 149)

There are mistakes in some of these sentences. Find the mistakes and correct them.

1 Can you tell me where is the nearest bank?
2 What time you usually finish work?
3 Do you know whether Derek has got a car?
4 Can you remember where did you put my pen?
5 Have you decided what colour are you going to paint the flat?
6 Do you know if has the bridge been repaired yet?
7 When you started to study English?

79 Short answers (Units 150, 152)

Give short answers to the questions using the words in brackets.

Examples:

Do you like dancing? (*Yes*)
Yes, I do.

Will you be here tomorrow? (*No/think*)
No, I don't think so.

1 Did Peter have a holiday last summer? (*No*)
2 Is the car badly damaged? (*Yes/afraid*)

3 Have you been waiting long? (*Yes*)
4 Does Simon work at night? (*No/think*)
5 Will they finish the job today? (*Yes/hope*)
6 Are you going shopping today? (*Yes*)

---

80 *So/neither am I* etc (Unit 151)

Re-write the sentences using *so/neither . . . .*

Example:

I like tennis and you like tennis.
I like tennis and so do you.

1 You aren't hungry and Jim isn't hungry.
2 Peter can drive and Sally can drive.
3 I'm in a hurry and you're in a hurry.
4 I haven't seen the film and you haven't seen the film.
5 You saw what happened and we saw what happened.

---

81 Relative clauses (Units 153–159)

(i) There are mistakes in some of these sentences. Find the mistakes and correct them.

1 I've lost the key you gave me.
2 Have you seen the book which it was on my desk?
3 They are the couple my parents went on holiday with.
4 The girl which she answered the phone said you weren't at home.
5 Where's the newspaper who I bought it this morning?
6 Is that the man sold you the car?
7 She's the woman whose the briefcase was stolen.
8 Steven Spielberg's new film, who it cost more than $100 million to make, will be showing in British cinemas soon.
9 Albert Davis, which is only 25 years old, is the new manager of Acme Export Ltd.
10 The people I work with are very funny.
11 John's father gave me the taxi fare, what was very nice of him.

(ii) Add the words in the box but only where necessary. (Sometimes two answers are possible.)

> who   that   which   whose   where   why
> when   whom

1 What was the name of the man ___ phoned yesterday?
2 Is that the suit ___ you bought last week?
3 Who were those people ___ were waiting outside just now?
4 Have you finished reading the book ___ I gave you?
5 Kathy Cobuild is the woman ___ husband was kidnapped.
6 The building ___ I work isn't properly air-conditioned.
7 The office ___ you work in is very modern.
8 Can you give me one good reason ___ I should lend you the money?
9 Is there a good time ___ I can phone you?
10 Mr Ross, ___ I have known for a long time, has just become the president of a very large international company.
11 My wife, ___ mother is Italian, knows Italy very well.
12 The restaurant was full, ___ is why we had to go somewhere else for dinner.

---

82 Linking words (Units 160–164)

Choose the correct answer—A, B or C.

1 I'm not going to stop work now. I'll keep going ___ I finish.
A *when* B *until* C *while*
2 ___ we've finished lunch, we'll do the washing up.
A *When* B *Until* C *While*
3 ___ I was walking around the supermarket, I saw a friend.
A *As soon as* B *As* C *Until*
4 ___ I put my hat on, it blew off.
A *As soon as* B *While* C *Until*

5 I enjoy watching tennis on TV, ____ I prefer playing it.
   A *despite* B *because* C *although*
6 ____ having a well-paid job, she never has any money.
   A *Despite* B *Because* C *Even though*
7 Sarah is very slim ____ she eats so much.
   A *despite* B *in spite of*
   C *despite the fact that*
8 I was able to walk slowly ____ the pain in my leg.
   A *whereas* B *in spite of* C *despite of*
9 My girlfriend likes the town ____ I like the country.
   A *whereas* B *in spite of* C *because of*
10 We drove very slowly ____ the icy roads.
   A *because* B *because of* C *therefore*
11 Mike borrowed the money and ____ he was able to go on holiday with his friends.
   A *because* B *because of* C *as a result*
12 The sea was dangerous ____ we didn't go in for a swim.
   A *as* B *so* C *since*
13 We were ____ tired that we fell asleep in front of the TV.
   A *so* B *such* C *therefore*
14 Robert had ____ an awful holiday that he wanted to come home early.
   A *so* B *such* C *however*
15 We went to a restaurant ____ celebrate my birthday.
   A *for* B *to* C *for to*
16 Peter has been to the supermarket ____ some shopping.
   A *for* B *for do* C *for doing*
17 A telephone answering machine is used ____ recording telephone messages on.
   A *for to* B *for* C *so as to*
18 These tests are given in the book ____ you can check your progress.
   A *in case* B *if* C *so that*
19 We hurried ____ be late for our appointment.
   A *not to* B *in case* C *so as not to*
20 I'll take my credit card with me ____ I decide to buy something when I'm out.
   A *so that* B *in case* C *if*

83 Prepositions of place and movement (Units 165–168)

Complete the sentences by putting the words in brackets in the correct places.

1 I got ____ the crowded train and sat down ____ a young man.
   (*next to/onto*)
2 The boys got ____ the garden by climbing ____ the fence.
   (*over/into*)
3 I've got a poster of Madonna ____ my room, ____ the wall ____ my bed.
   (*above/in/on*)
4 Maria drove ____ Madrid ____ Barcelona ____ her friend's car yesterday. She arrived ____ Barcelona at 8 o'clock.
   (*to/in/from*)
5 My grandparents live ____ 42 London Road, ____ a flat ____ the top floor. A very nice Italian couple live ____ the floor ____ them.
   (*in/on/below/at*)
6 We'd been driving ____ Harbour Street for a few minutes when the car ____ us stopped suddenly and we crashed ____ it.
   (*in front of/into/along*)
7 The robbers ran ____ the bank and jumped ____ the motor bike waiting ____. Then they drove off ____ the corner.
   (*onto/outside/out of/round*)
8 When I got back ____ my hotel bedroom, I locked the door ____ me, took ____ my dressing-gown and got ____ bed.
   (*behind/off/into/inside*)
9 Don't walk ____ that ladder. Something may fall ____ ____ you.
   (*down/under/on top of*)
10 The coach drove ____ the factory, then it went ____ the tunnel and started to climb ____ the hill.
   (*past/up/through*)

11 Sally got ____ the taxi and sat down
   ____ the driver ____ the back seat.
   (*behind/in/into*)

12 London is ____ the River Thames, which
   flows ____ the city ____ west to east.
   (*from/on/through*)

13 Mrs Woods got ____ the bus and walked
   ____ the street ____ the post office.
   (*towards/off/across*)

14 My girlfriend and I often meet ____ the
   Espresso Cafe ____ East Street. Do you
   know the Espresso? It's ____ the bank
   and the school, ____ the Grand Hotel.
   (*opposite/between/at/in*)

84 Prepositions of time (Units 169–174)

Correct the mistakes.

1 My interview is on 2 o'clock in Monday.
2 We've been waiting here from ten
   minutes.
3 Are you leaving at Saturday morning?
4 I worked in a bank during five years.
5 Ken and Kate are on holiday on August.
6 I always visit my parents in Christmas.
7 Mike usually plays football the
   weekend.
8 You've known me since ten years.
9 I was born in January 3rd at 1968.
10 Sarah was listening to the radio during
   she was taking a bath.
11 The doctors operated on the man just
   on time to save his life.
12 Are you doing anything in the end of
   next week?
13 I fell asleep in front of the TV in the
   football match.
14 The builders say they'll have finished
   the job until next weekend at the latest.
15 I found my new contact lenses strange
   at first, but I got used to them at the
   end.

85 Other prepositions (Units 175–177)

**Complete the sentences using the words in
the box. (Sometimes two answers are
possible.)**

in	as	with	on	like	by	as if

1 She's a middle-aged woman ____ blue
   eyes and short blonde hair.
2 We went to Athens ____ my car.
3 Would you rather go home ____ taxi or
   ____ the bus?
4 Who's that man ____ the white hat?
5 Sue's brother is very handsome. He looks
   ____ Tom Cruise!
6 I've got a summer job in the Espresso Cafe
   working ____ a waiter.
7 Are you all right? You look ____ you
   haven't slept all night.
8 I don't want to change my flat. I like it
   just ____ it is.

86 Word and preposition combinations
(Units 178–182)

Choose the correct preposition—A, B or C.

1 I'm feeling rather nervous ____ my
   interview tomorrow.
   A *of* B *to* C *about*
2 I used to be quite good ____ dancing.
   A *in* B *at* C *on*
3 Are you afraid ____ snakes?
   A *by* B *to* C *of*
4 Pisa in Italy is famous ____ its 'Leaning
   Tower'.
   A *about* B *from* C *for*
5 I'm not really interested ____ stamp
   collecting.
   A *in* B *on* C *by*
6 There's no need ____ you to worry.
   A *to* B *for* C *of*
7 Who's responsible ____ these children?
   A *of* B *for* C *in*

8 There has been a rise ____ the number of homeless people.
   A *in* B *of* C *with*
9 I've had some difficulty ____ my new computer.
   A *with* B *of* C *in*
10 Sally met an old friend in town quite ____ chance yesterday.
   A *on* B *by* C *with*
11 Ken and Kate will be ____ holiday soon.
   A *on* B *in* C *at*
12 The film *The Birds* was made ____ Alfred Hitchcock.
   A *with* B *of* C *by*
13 My brother is thinking ____ selling his car.
   A *to* B *of* C *on*
14 I can't concentrate ____ anything at the moment.
   A *on* B *to* C *about*
15 They apologized ____ losing my letter.
   A *to* B *in* C *for*
16 When Robert was younger, he dreamt ____ being a famous footballer one day.
   A *to* B *of* C *in*
17 They're taking very good care ____ your son in hospital.
   A *about* B *for* C *of*
18 I congratulated them ____ getting engaged.
   A *on* B *of* C *in*
19 I've warned you ____ taking my things without asking me.
   A *for* B *of* C *about*
20 That smell always reminds me ____ hospitals.
   A *on* B *of* C *about*

87 Indirect objects with or without *to* and *for* (Unit 184)

Re-write the sentences without *to* or *for*.

Example:

You've lent your camera to Frank.
You've lent Frank your camera.

1 The company has given the job to Kathy Cobuild.
2 My sister made a cake for me on my last birthday.
3 The receptionist will order a taxi for us.
4 I've promised these concert tickets to someone.

88 Phrasal verbs (Units 185–186)

Replace the words in *italics* with one of the phrasal verbs in Units 185 and 186.

1 I *refused* their offer of a job.
2 We *continued* working through our lunch break.
3 Robert *stopped* playing football years ago.
4 People say that I *am like* my father.
5 What time did you *start* on your journey?
6 Unemployment has *increased* by 10% since last year.
7 Our flight was *delayed* by bad weather.
8 My grandfather never *broke* a promise.
9 Mr and Mrs James may never *recover from* the tragic death of their son.
10 The bank's computer has *stopped working* six times this week already!

Risposte agli esercizi

Per chiarimenti sull'uso delle contrazioni
p.es. I'm, she's, they've, cfr. 189.

1A *(Risposte possibili)*

1 He's reading a newspaper.
2 She's taking a photograph.
3 They're watching TV.
4 They're playing cards.
5 He's doing the washing up.

1B

1 Is Sally having, 's (is) washing
2 aren't watching
3 Are you enjoying, 'm (am) having
4 is Maria doing, 's (is) studying
5 're (are) staying
6 are rising, is getting

2A

1 make
2 don't live, live
3 covers
4 gives
5 don't come, come
6 works, doesn't work

2B

1 Do you listen
2 Does he live
3 does she finish
4 do you go
5 Do they watch
6 Does she play

3A

1 It snows
2 I'm going
3 I go
4 He's cooking
5 she's going
6 flows

4A

(i)

1 painted
2 made
3 ended
4 invented
5 discovered
6 died
7 won

(ii)

1 ended
2 won
3 invented
4 died
5 painted
6 discovered

4B

1 did you do
2 did she get up
3 Did you go
4 Did he enjoy
5 did they go
6 Did you watch

4C

1 didn't feel, stayed
2 didn't go, went
3 didn't write, didn't have
4 ordered, didn't come

5A

1 I dropped my bag when I was running for a bus.
2 I cut myself when I was shaving.
3 My car broke down when I was driving to work.
4 I saw a shark when I was swimming in the sea.
5 My clothes got dirty when I was cleaning the attic.
6 I broke a tooth when I was eating a sandwich.

5B

1 were going, stopped
2 Were they having, called
3 rang, got up, answered
4 opened, was standing
5 arrived, did you do, reported

5C

1

(i)

1 was getting
2 was turning
3 rushed
4 turned
5 asked

(ii)

1 was beginning
2 was standing
3 opened
4 turned
5 asked

(iii)

1 was sitting
2 was cutting
3 went
4 went
5 put

2

(i) a horror story
(ii) a love story
(iii) a western

6A

1 've (have) had
2 've (have) lived
3 've (have) known
4 's (has) lived
5 's (has) had

6B

1 's (has) never slept
2 've (have) ever stayed
3 Have you been
4 haven't been
5 has been
6 has changed
7 've (have) never seen
8 've (have) heard
9 Have you ever eaten
10 haven't tried

6C

1 They've done the washing up.
2 Sally hasn't cleaned the cooker yet.
3 Simon hasn't emptied the rubbish bin yet.
4 They've cleaned the windows.
5 Sally has defrosted the fridge.
6 Simon hasn't cleaned the floor yet.

7A

1 been
2 gone
3 been
4 gone
5 been, been

8A

1 Have you done your homework yet?
2 I haven't worn my new coat yet.
3 'Is Sally here?' 'No, she's just gone out.'
4 Have you just spoken to your parents?
5 It's quite early. Has Jack already gone to bed?/ Has Jack gone to bed already?
6 I've already cleaned the windows./I've cleaned the windows already.

9A

1 hasn't been living
2 have you been studying
3 have been standing
4 've (have) been working, haven't been getting
5 has she been doing, 's (has) been playing

9B

1 She's been repairing the car.
2 They've been playing in the garden.
3 He's been putting up some shelves.
4 They've been painting the kitchen.
5 He's been lying on the beach.
6 She's been chopping onions.

10A

1 They've been repairing
2 I've broken
3 has saved
4 Have you lost
5 I've always worked
6 has been eating

11A

1 for
2 since
3 for
4 since
5 for
6 since

12A

1 I've worked
2 I worked
3 were you
4 I moved
5 I've had
6 I had
7 I sold
8 I came

12B

1 have you known, did you first meet
2 Has your husband ever had, 's (has) had, had, was
3 Have you seen, saw, arrived, went
4 didn't have, haven't had

13A

1 I've been cleaning
2 He's sitting
3 have you been
4 Have you known
5 I've been learning
6 They live, They've been

14A

1 'd (had) changed, 'd (had) moved
2 hadn't driven
3 'd (had) spoken, 'd (had) already met, hadn't liked

14B

1 went
2 had disappeared
3 had started
4 started

14C

1 had done, found
2 didn't laugh, 'd (had) heard
3 left, 'd (had) had
4 discovered, had taken

15A

1 had been studying
2 hadn't been waiting
3 'd (had) just been talking
4 had he been living

15B

1 I felt very cold because I had been standing outside for over two hours.
2 I had been playing tennis so I was feeling hot and sticky.
3 The children's hair was wet because they had been swimming in the sea.
4 I hadn't been feeling well for weeks before I finally went to see the doctor.
5 They had been travelling all day so they were very tired.
6 They had been driving for about half an hour when they realized they were lost.

16A

1 The population of the world will be much bigger.
2 Scientists will control the weather.
3 People will take holidays in space.
4 Many people won't work at all during their lives.
5 People will live longer.
6 Life won't be better than it is now.

16B

1 I'll lend
2 I'll answer
3 I'll put on
4 I won't have
5 I won't go, I'll wait

16C

1 'll (will) remember
2 will the meeting last, won't finish
3 Will you be, won't get, 'll (will) phone

17A *(Risposte possibili)*

1 He's going to do the washing up.
2 They're going to get on the bus.
3 She's going to watch TV.

4 It's going to land.
5 They're going to clean the car.
6 He's going to fall off the bicycle.

17B

1 are you going to wear, Are you going to wear
2 are you going to do, 'm (am) going to decorate
3 isn't going to leave, 's (is) going to stay
4 'm (am) going to buy, are you going to pay, 'm (am) going to ask

18A

1 'm (am) going to live
2 'll (will) come
3 'm (am) going to faint
4 'll (will) get
5 're (are) going to crash
6 I'll (I will) pay

19A

1 'm (am) working
2 'm (am) not doing
3 'm (am) meeting
4 'm (am) seeing
5 'm (am) going
6 're (are) meeting
7 are you doing
8 Are you doing

20A

1 It's going to snow later tonight.
2 She's going to meet them tomorrow morning./She's meeting them tomorrow morning.
3 What are you going to do this afternoon?/What are you doing this afternoon?
4 Be careful! You're going to break that glass.
5 He isn't going to come next Saturday./He isn't coming on Saturday.
6 Look out! You're going to hurt yourself with that knife.
7 Are they going to drive to Scotland next weekend?/Are they driving to Scotland next weekend?

21A

1 starts, finishes
2 doesn't take off
3 begins, doesn't end
4 does the next train leave

22A

1 see, 'll (will) give
2 'll (will) buy, have
3 's (is), 'll (will) go
4 'll (will) look after, 're (are)
5 won't do, hears
6 won't open, push
7 'll (will) play, doesn't rain
8 'll (will) lend, pay

23A

1 At 11.00 tomorrow she'll be visiting the ABC travel company.
2 At 13.30 tomorrow she'll be having lunch with Mary and Ron King.
3 At 15.30 tomorrow she'll be visiting Derek Hall.
4 At 16.30 tomorrow she'll be taking a taxi to the airport.
5 At 17.30 tomorrow she'll be flying back to London.

23B

1 Will you be speaking
2 won't be using
3 'll (will) be getting
4 will you be visiting

24A

1 will have left
2 Will you have finished
3 'll (will) have gone
4 won't have eaten

25A

1 I was going to take a taxi home last night, but I didn't have enough money, so I had to walk.
2 We were going to write to them when we were on holiday, but we changed our minds and phoned them instead.

3 She was going to drive to Scotland last weekend, but her car broke down, so she went by train.
4 We were going to play tennis yesterday afternoon, but it rained all afternoon, so we stayed at home.
5 She was going to watch the film on TV last night, but she had seen it before, so she went to bed early.
6 I was going to change my job last year, but my boss offered me more money, so I decided to stay.

26A

1 's (is) always leaving
2 was always hitting
3 's (is) always borrowing
4 'm (am) always forgetting
5 was always breaking down
6 're (are) always winning

27A

1 are you thinking
2 do you think
3 has Simon known
4 does this word mean
5 Did you hear
6 You aren't watching
7 I didn't remember
8 Do you like
9 She has always wanted
10 I had never seen

28A

(i)
1 works
2 has been
3 is studying
4 has been
5 arrived
6 has been

(ii)
1 heard
2 got
3 was still sleeping
4 went
5 were trying
6 switched on
7 ran
8 escaped
9 had
10 heard
11 had seen
12 had phoned

28B

(i)
1 are you cooking
2 I'm making
3 I've just had
4 did you have
5 I met
6 we went
7 It looks
8 I've ever tasted

(ii)
1 Do you like
2 have you had
3 I've only had
4 I bought
5 did it cost
6 I'd been saving

(iii)
1 It's been hurting
2 I fell
3 I was cleaning
4 Do you think
5 I've broken
6 haven't broken

29A

1 It's going to rain
2 Are you doing
3 I arrive
4 I'm going to be
5 I'll have
6 is
7 I'm going to repair
8 I'll bring
9 we'll be lying
10 They'll have visited

30A

1 Don't touch that! It's hot.
2 Please take a seat, Mr Woods.
3 Put this in the fridge, could you?
4 Pass me the spanner.
5 Do turn that music down, Andrew!

30B

1 Let's go to the cinema.
2 Let's take a taxi.
3 Let's light a fire.
4 Let's buy her a present.
5 Let's stay in this evening.

31A

(i)	(ii)	(iii)
1 'm (am)	1 Am	1 are
2 are	2 are	2 're (are)
3 'm (am) not	3 's (is)	3 Are
4 's (is)	4 's (is)	4 are
5 's (is)	5 am	5 Is
6 's (is)	6 Are	6 's (is)
7 Is	7 'm (am) not	7 Are
8 isn't	8 'm (am)	8 are
		9 Is
		10 isn't

31B

1 was
2 were
3 was
4 Were
5 were
6 were
7 were
8 were
9 Were
10 was
11 was
12 was
13 was

32A

1 There's (There is)
2 were there
3 there'll be (there will be)
4 Is there
5 There were, there are
6 There's been (There has been)

32B

1 There's (There is), It's (It is)
2 There are, They're (They are)
3 Is there, it's (it is)
4 There's (There is), is it, It's (It is)
5 There's (There is), There's (There is)

33A

1 Have we got, haven't, 've (have) got
2 has got, had
3 Have you got
4 Have we got, Have you got, has got
5 Has your sister got, has
6 didn't have

34A

1 haven't had a cigarette
2 have a look
3 had a game of tennis
4 has a swim
5 Did you have a good time?
6 has just had a baby
7 have a rest
8 have a shave

36A

1 could
2 can
3 could
4 been able to
5 can
6 be able to

36B

1 were able to
2 could/was able to
3 was able to
4 Could/Were you able to, couldn't/wasn't able to
5 could/was able to

36C

1 Robert could have gone
2 He could have passed

3 he could have been
4 He could have started
5 He could have emigrated

37A

1 May I sit here?
2 Can I borrow your bike for half an hour?
3 Can I try this on?
4 Do you think I could close the window?
5 May I come in?

37B

1 You can't feed the animals./You aren't allowed to feed the animals.
2 You can't smoke in this room./You aren't allowed to smoke in this room.
3 You can park in this street./You're allowed to park in this street.
4 You can't walk on the grass./You aren't allowed to walk on the grass.
5 You can't turn left./You aren't allowed to turn left.

37C

1 was allowed to
2 could/were allowed to
3 were allowed to
4 could/was allowed to

38A

(i)	(ii)
1 must stay	1 have to take
2 must drink	2 have to continue
3 must take	3 have to stay
4 must continue	4 have to drink

38B

1 must/have to   4 had to
2 have to   5 has had to
3 must/have to   6 having to

39A

1 mustn't   4 needn't
2 don't have to   5 don't need to
3 mustn't   6 haven't got to

40A

1 must   3 can   5 must
2 can't/mustn't   4 needn't   6 needn't

40B

1 You have to be quiet.
2 You aren't allowed to overtake.
3 You don't have to be a member to get in.
4 You are allowed to park here.
5 You aren't allowed to swim here.
6 You aren't allowed to walk here.

41A

1 didn't need to get up   4 needn't have paid
2 didn't need to wear   5 didn't need to pay
3 needn't have worried   6 needn't have bought

42A

1 You should/ought to report it to the credit card company immediately.
2 Perhaps you should/ought to buy a new alarm clock!
3 Perhaps you should/ought to look for another job.
4 Perhaps you should/ought to take some aspirin.
5 Don't you think you should/ought to apologize to them?
6 I think you should/ought to sell it.

42B

1 You shouldn't/oughtn't to work so hard. You should/ought to relax more.
2 You should/ought to buy an alarm clock!
3 She shouldn't/oughtn't to have gone to work yesterday. She should/ought to have stayed in bed.
4 He shouldn't/oughtn't to have walked into the road without looking. He should/ought to have looked first.

42C

1 'd (had) better be
2 'd (had) better park
3 'd (had) better stay
4 'd (had) better hurry
5 'd (had) better not leave
6 'd (had) better put out

42D

1 aren't/'re not (are not) supposed to open
2 was supposed to go
3 aren't/'re not (are not) supposed to park
4 were supposed to arrive
5 is supposed to have

42E

1 shall I invite   3 Shall I tell
2 shall I put   4 shall I paint

43A

1 You could be right.
2 She might win the race.
3 She may have forgotten about the meeting.
4 They might have been asleep.
5 He may not know the address.
6 They could have left early.
7 He might not be coming.
8 I may see you tomorrow.
9 They could be going on holiday.
10 She may not have caught the bus.

44A

1 can live   3 could cross   5 could grow
2 can reach   4 can survive   6 can make

45A

1 should receive/ought to receive
2 should have won/ought to have won
3 should sell/ought to sell
4 should have passed/ought to have passed
5 shouldn't take/oughtn't to take
6 should have arrived/ought to have arrived

46A

1 They can't be Greek. They're speaking Italian.
2 He must be ill. He's got a high temperature.
3 The heating can't be on. It's very cold in here.
4 They must be asleep. Their bedroom lights are off.
5 She must be happy. She's just passed her driving test.
6 He can't be a doctor. He's too young.

46C

1 Palmer can't/couldn't have stayed in bed all morning yesterday. Someone saw him in town at 10.00 yesterday morning.
2 He can't/couldn't have had lunch at Luigi's restaurant. Luigi's restaurant was closed all day yesterday.
3 He can't/couldn't have gone for a drive in his car yesterday afternoon. His car was outside his flat all yesterday afternoon.
4 He can't/couldn't have stayed at home last night. Someone phoned his flat at 9.00 last night and there was no reply.

5 He must have been inside the Central Art Gallery. His fingerprints were found in the gallery.

47A

SI'	definitely	must
↓	probably	should; ought to
	possibly	may; might; could
NO	definitely not	can't

47B

1 She might phone later.
2 I should be at home by 6 o'clock.
3 They could have gone home.
4 He can't be telling the truth.
5 You must have heard the news.
6 I may not go out this evening.
7 She can't have seen us.
8 The bus must have left.
9 He might not have applied for the job.
10 She ought to be here soon.

48A

1 Could you tell me where the hospital is, please?
2 May I have the menu, please?
3 Will you switch on the TV for me, please?
4 Would you answer the phone, please?
5 Would you mind changing places with me?
6 Can you pass me the cloth, please.

49A

1 I'll help you do the washing up.
2 Could I carry some bags for you?
3 Shall I switch off the light?
4 I can lend you an umbrella if you like.
5 Can I take your coat?
6 Would you like me to phone for the doctor?

50A

1 How about   3 shall we   5 could
2 Let's   4 Why don't we   6 Let's

51A

1 used to be, isn't
2 never goes, used to go
3 used to be, is
4 used to have, doesn't have
5 is, used to be
6 Did you use to like, find

51B

1 'll (will) always lend   4 'd (would) often
2 'd (would) never throw   spend
3 'll (will) carry on   5 'will go

51C

1 used to/would   4 used to/would
2 used to   5 used to
3 used to/would   6 used to

52A

1 the window wouldn't open
2 she won't marry
3 it wouldn't work
4 she won't listen
5 he won't help
6 my parents wouldn't let

53A

1 'll (will) pay, a promise
2 'll (will) leave, a threat
3 won't tell, a promise
4 won't do, a promise
5 'll (will) throw, a threat
6 won't speak, a threat

54A

1 We may as well walk to the station.
2 You might as well cancel the hotel bookings.
3 We might as well stay at home today.
4 I might as well clear the table.
5 I might as well apply for the job.

55A

1 She suggested (that) I should apply for the job.
2 The doctor recommended (that) he should stay in bed for a few days.
3 He insisted (that) I should help him.
4 They suggested (that) we should go to the cinema.

55B

1 should give up
2 should pass
3 should come
4 should feel

56A

1 I didn't get embarrassed so quickly
2 I weren't/wasn't so serious
3 I didn't find it so difficult to make friends
4 I were/was good-looking
5 my ears weren't so big

56B

1 would do their homework on time
2 would clean the bath after they've used it
3 wouldn't pick the flowers
4 would take their litter home
5 would keep together on a tour

56C

1 She wishes she hadn't stayed in the sun so long.
2 He wishes he'd (he had) eaten less.
3 He wishes he'd (he had) driven more carefully.
4 She wishes she hadn't tried to lift a heavy table on her own.

57A

1 'd (would) rather stay
2 would you rather go
3 'd (would) rather listen
4 would you rather do

57B

1 I'd rather you didn't open
2 I'd rather you phoned
3 I'd rather you didn't turn on
4 I'd rather you came

58A (Risposte possibili)

1 it's time you paid it?
2 it's time I started studying for the exam.
3 it's time you phoned Mike?
4 it's time I took my car to the garage.

59A

1 The road is being repaired.
2 The fence is being painted.
3 The cows are being milked.
4 The windows are being cleaned.
5 The cats are being fed.
6 The money is being counted.

59B

1 The window has been repaired.
2 The carpet has been cleaned.
3 The walls have been painted/repaired.
4 The light has been repaired.
5 Some posters have been put up.
6 The old fireplace has been taken out.

59C

(i)
1 is played
2 are exported
3 is used
4 are spoken

(ii)
1 was built
2 was played
3 was television invented
4 were built

(iii)
1 had been stolen
2 was being repaired
3 had all been sold
4 hadn't been invited

59D

1 created
2 was discussed
3 won, was assassinated
4 arrived, was interviewed
5 have been given, was announced

60A

1 The room will be cleaned.
2 The tree had to be cut down.
3 Sally should be told what happened.
4 A new hospital is going to be built.
5 The problem can be solved.

60B

1 have been delayed
2 have been thrown away
3 have been sold
4 have been killed
5 have been stolen

60C

1 I don't like being stared at.
2 I can't stand being told what to do.
3 I don't like being interrupted.
4 I don't like being joked about.
5 I enjoy being praised.

61A

1 got stuck
2 got bitten
3 got hit
4 didn't get caught
5 got arrested
6 got sentenced

62A

1 Sarah was shown the photographs.
2 Normally, I am paid my salary every month.
3 I think that we have been sent the wrong tickets.
4 I hope that Sally will be given the message.
5 I wasn't asked for my address.
6 I thought that you had been told about the meeting.

63A

1 was discovered by
2 was directed by
3 was composed and sung by
4 was invented by
5 was painted by

63B

1 with
2 by
3 with
4 by
5 with
6 by

64A

1 It is said that the monument is over 2000 years old.
  The monument is said to be over 2000 years old.
2 It is expected that the President will resign.
  The President is expected to resign.
3 It is thought that the fire started at about 8 o'clock.
  The fire is thought to have started at about 8 o'clock.
4 It was reported that seven people had been injured in the fire.
  Seven people were reported to have been injured in the fire.

64B

1 The new film is supposed to be very violent.
2 Those cars are supposed to be rather unreliable.
3 He is supposed to have moved to New York last year.
4 The new restaurant is supposed to be very expensive.
5 The concert is supposed to have been very good.

65A

1 They're having their flat decorated.
2 He's having a suit made.
3 She's having her hair done.
4 He's having a tooth taken out.
5 She's having her windows cleaned.
6 They're having a photograph taken.

65B

1 have these shoes repaired
2 having an extension built
3 have my glasses mended
4 have your hair done
5 had four new tyres fitted
6 had my suit dry-cleaned

65C

1 had his flat burgled
2 had the roof of their house damaged
3 had the radio stolen
4 had his nose broken

66A

1 when
2 When
3 if
4 when
5 If
6 If

68A

1 'll (will) enjoy, see
2 leave, won't be
3 miss, 'll (will) take
4 will she do, fails
5 need, will you tell
6 doesn't apologize, won't speak

68B

1 can lend
2 have finished
3 may go
4 should need
5 should phone
6 are feeling

69A

1 knew, would write
2 would buy, weren't
3 wouldn't buy, were
4 was/were, wouldn't live
5 would you live, could

70A

1 'll (will) switch
2 would you do
3 has
4 were
5 Would you buy
6 is

71A

1 hadn't been
2 would have enjoyed
3 had had
4 wouldn't have had

71B

1 If she hadn't been ill, she would have gone to work.
2 If it hadn't rained all morning, we would have gone out.

3 If she'd had enough money, she could have bought the shoes.
4 If I'd been hungry, I would have had breakfast.

72A

1 If I get a headache, I usually take some aspirin.
2 I feel terrible if I don't get 8 hours' sleep a night.
3 If I drink too much coffee, it makes me feel nervous.
4 If flowers don't get any water, they die.
5 You put on weight if you don't get enough exercise.

73A

1 Unless you wear your coat, you'll be cold.
2 I'll phone you unless you phone me first.
3 He won't receive the letter tomorrow unless you post it before 1 o'clock today.
4 I won't go to school tomorrow unless I feel better.
5 I can't write to you unless you give me your address.
6 Your cough won't get better unless you stop smoking.

73B

| 1 Provided | 3 unless | 5 as long as |
| 2 providing | 4 Unless | |

73C

1 Stop making that noise or I'll hit you.
2 Take this umbrella and you won't get wet.
3 Drive more carefully or else you'll have an accident.
4 Help me and I'll help you.

73D

| 1 should I need | 3 should I change |
| 2 should he fail | 4 should she miss |

73E

1 Suppose/Supposing I moved to Scotland, would you come and visit me?
2 Suppose/Supposing someone finds my wallet, do you think they will take it to the police?
3 Suppose/Supposing they had stayed at our house, where would they have slept?
4 Suppose/Supposing they had offered you the job, would you have taken it?
5 Suppose/Supposing you had won the competition, what would the prize have been?

74A

1 would wear	8 makes
2 wouldn't have had	9 weren't/wasn't
3 had	10 wouldn't have left
4 wait	11 gets
5 had known	12 will catch
6 would like	13 had asked
7 will speak	14 would you do

76A

| 1 tell | 3 said | 5 tell |
| 2 telling | 4 said | 6 say |

77A

1 I told her (that) I couldn't swim very well.
2 The secretary told me (that) Mr Mason had gone out.
3 Andrew said (that) he didn't want to go swimming.
4 We said (that) we were leaving on Friday.

5 They said (that) they had had lunch in Luigi's restaurant./They said (that) they had lunch in Luigi's restaurant.
6 Sarah told Simon (that) she would phone him later.

77B

1 (that) there was nothing wrong with my
2 didn't need to wear
3 had driven/drove very well
4 was making
5 would like a big family
6 wanted at least five
7 would get a pay rise later in the year
8 had done the shopping
9 would be home at about

78A

1 I asked the mechanic if it would take long to repair the car.
2 I asked the policeman if I could park my car in West Street.
3 I asked the cinema attendant what time the film finished.
4 I asked the hotel receptionist if he/she/they had a double room.
5 I asked the doctor how many times a day I should take the medicine.
6 I asked the waiter what the soup of the day was.

78B

1 what I was doing there
2 why I was carrying a camera
3 if I had seen the signs warning people not to enter the area
4 if I had been taking photos of the army base
5 what my name was
6 if he could see some proof of my identity

79A

1 I offered to do the washing up.
2 She threatened to phone the police.
3 The doctor advised my brother to stop smoking.
4 He asked me to change a light bulb for him.
5 She told me not to be stupid.
6 He invited her to come to his party.
7 I promised not to forget the shopping.
8 She warned them not to leave the door unlocked.

80A

1 I told them (that) I couldn't type.
2 They asked me if I was English.
3 I asked her where she was going.
4 They said (that) they were going into town.
5 He told me (that) he didn't have any money./He told me (that) he hadn't got any money.
6 He asked her if she could speak more slowly./He asked her to speak more slowly.
7 He warned me not to touch the wire.
8 He told her (that) he had been on holiday in July./He told her (that) he was on holiday in July.
9 They asked him what time he had got home./They asked him what time he got home.
10 She asked me if I could do her a favour./She asked me to do her a favour.
11 We told them (that) we wouldn't be home late.
12 I said (that) I had posted the letters.
13 He said (that) his sister didn't know.
14 She said (that) her parents had gone to bed.

15 She told him (that) he should go to the doctor./She told him to go to the doctor.
16 They promised (that) they would do the dishes./They promised to do the dishes.
17 I asked her where she worked.
18 She asked him if he could phone the doctor for her./She asked him to phone the doctor for her.
19 He told his boss (that) he had passed his driving test in 1986./He told his boss (that) he passed his driving test in 1986.
20 I said (that) I didn't know what to do.

83A

1 reading	6 doing
2 swimming	7 going
3 having	8 not making
4 playing	9 borrowing
5 robbing	10 being

84A

1 to be	5 to pay	9 to be
2 to test-drive	6 to accept	10 to accept
3 to buy	7 to get	11 to sell
4 not to like	8 to try	12 to give

85A

1 what to wear	4 how to make
2 how to spell	5 what to do
3 whether to stay	

86A

1 I expected him to pass easily.
2 … but her parents told her to go to bed at 9 o'clock.
3 He invited her to go to a party on Saturday.
4 … but a friend of mine persuaded me to change my mind.
5 I don't want her to know.

86B

1 Andrew to close the door
2 her to help me
3 us to go to a party
4 Sally not to be late home
5 the woman to get out of her car
6 me not to be late for work again

86C

| 1 talking | 3 to see | 5 to do |
| 2 to have | 4 driving | 6 telling |

87A

1 to listen	6 to visit
2 cooking/to cook	7 having to/to have to
3 windsurfing, sailing	8 playing/to play
4 to walk, go	9 to take (cfr. 87.2a)
5 going/to go	10 to play (cfr. 87.4a)

88A

| 1 saying | 3 to buy |
| 2 visiting | 4 to turn off |

88B

| 1 to come | 3 to be |
| 2 drinking, holding | 4 putting |

88C

| 1 making | 3 to ask |
| 2 to tell | 4 not learning |

89A

1 to working	4 to living
2 to live	5 to staying
3 to eating	6 to work, to getting up

90A

1 renewing/to be renewed
2 to practise
3 adjusting/to be adjusted
4 feeding/to be fed
5 to buy
6 to ask

91A

1 wear
2 lend
3 cry
4 sit
5 tell, promise
6 eat, wait
7 hurry
8 type, use

91B

1 let *me* go
2 makes *me* feel
3 let *him* have
4 make *him* understand

92A

1 to seeing
2 in learning
3 After having
4 to eating
5 for being
6 of hearing
7 for giving
8 at painting, drawing

93A

1 (i) you borrowing
  (ii) your borrowing
2 (i) me switching on
  (ii) my switching on
3 (i) us staying
  (ii) our staying
4 (i) them getting
  (ii) their getting
5 (i) her going
  (ii) her going
6 (i) Sue forgetting
  (ii) Sue's forgetting

94A

1 Babysitting is a big responsibility, especially with very young children.
2 Swimming is a very good way of keeping fit.
3 Watching late night horror films can give you nightmares.
4 Living on your own is quite difficult if you are used to being with a lot of people.
5 Reading English is much easier than speaking it.
6 Smoking can cause lung cancer.

94B

1 It is very strange to see yourself on video.
2 It isn't necessary to have your car serviced every month.
3 It can be dangerous to leave medicine lying around.
4 It doesn't have to be expensive to eat well.
5 It is difficult for old people to live on a pension.

95A

1 I went to the chemist's to buy some medicine.
2 I went to the post office to post some letters.
3 I went to the cinema to see a film.
4 I went to the hairdresser's to have a haircut.
5 I went to the car rental agency to hire a car.
6 I went to the park to play tennis.

95B

1 (i) He drank lots of black coffee in order to keep awake.
  (ii) He drank lots of black coffee so as to keep awake.
2 (i) I often write things down in order not to forget them.
  (ii) I often write things down so as not to forget them.
3 (i) She took an umbrella in order not to get wet.
  (ii) She took an umbrella so as not to get wet.
4 (i) We'll use the computer in order to save time.
  (ii) We'll use the computer so as to save time.
5 (i) I want to pass the exams in order to get a better job.
  (ii) I want to pass the exams so as to get a better job.

6 (i) We turned down the music in order not to disturb the neighbours.
  (ii) We turned down the music so as not to disturb the neighbours.

96A

1 to unlock
2 to tell
3 to write
4 to say
5 to wear
6 to catch

96B

1 easy to use
2 safe to go
3 pleased to hear
4 interesting to plan
5 impossible to finish

96C

1 It was nice of her to send me a birthday card.
2 It was wrong of him to open your letter.
3 It was clever of you to find the answer.
4 It was careless of me to leave my keys at home.

96D

1 It's unnecessary for you to pay me back the money.
2 It's essential for us to leave immediately.
3 It's important for everyone to try to keep calm.
4 It's unusual for him to complain.

97A

1 arguing
2 building
3 break
4 climb
5 post
6 repairing

98A

1 working/to work
2 to come
3 move/to move
4 to see, get
5 making, to sleep
6 to drink
7 try, driving
8 to think, making
9 to leave, to catch
10 to be
11 to work
12 skiing, ice-skating
13 walking
14 to be
15 to explain
16 not to walk
17 meeting
18 to make, show, to use
19 not doing
20 seeing
21 forget, to phone
22 empty
23 Eating
24 not to go
25 working, to have, to eat

98B

1 to lend
2 travelling
3 repairing
4 shopping
5 opening
6 to switch off
7 sunbathing
8 to fall
9 going
10 to have

99A

1 interested
2 shocked
3 amusing
4 worried
5 surprising

99B

1 embarrassing
2 depressing
3 interested
4 relaxing
5 interesting
6 annoyed
7 frightened

100A

1 That woman wearing the green coat is Kate Robinson.
2 That boy sitting over there is Sally's brother.
3 Who is that girl looking at us?
4 All those people waiting outside want to see you.

100B

1 He fell off a ladder changing a light bulb.
2 He burnt himself cooking his dinner.
3 He ran out of petrol driving to work.
4 He lost his keys getting out of his car.
5 He broke a cup doing the washing-up.

100C

1 The woman was driving along listening to her car radio.
2 I arrived at the examination hall feeling very nervous.
3 He came into the room carrying a suitcase.
4 They were walking down the street holding hands.

100D

1 Having typed the letters, he put them all in envelopes.
2 Having done all the housework, I went out for a walk.
3 Having got out of bed, he had a shower.
4 Having locked all the doors, she went to bed.

100E

1 Being a little deaf, she wears a hearing aid.
2 Not liking classical music, I didn't go to the concert.
3 Being rich, she can afford expensive holidays.
4 Having finished the book, I decided to take it back to the library.
5 Having gone to bed so late the night before, they felt quite tired the next day.

101A

1 children, girls, boys
2 restaurants, theatres, cinemas, discos
3 teeth
4 plates, knives, forks
5 countries, days
6 cats, mice
7 people
8 shoes, feet
9 eggs, tomatoes, potatoes
10 leaves, trees

102A

1 is
2 have, them
3 isn't
4 live/lives
5 was
6 Are these, they are
7 isn't, is it
8 is, It needs

103A

1 alarm clock
2 T-shirts
3 crossroads
4 clothes-hangers
5 bottle opener
6 hole punch
7 lawn mower
8 corkscrew
9 screwdriver
10 track-suit

104A

1 Gloria is Chris and Linda's mother.
2 Linda is Chris's sister.
3 George is Chris and Linda's father.
4 Chris is George and Gloria's son.
5 Charles is Ken's father-in-law.
6 Daisy is Linda and Chris's grandmother.
7 Kate is Chris and Linda's aunt.
8 Sally, Simon and Andrew are Chris and Linda's cousins.

104B

1 's
2 's
3 '
4 's
5 '
6 's

105A

1 the end of the film
2 Sarah's party
3 the top floor of the house
4 the back of my car
5 a friend of the woman who works in the post office
6 the end of this road
7 the girls' parents
8 the manager of the Black Cat Club

106A

1 Robert visited a relative of his.
2 A neighbour of ours is going to babysit for us.
3 Sally is going on holiday with some friends of hers.
4 Simon has borrowed some records of Sarah's.
5 Two colleagues of mine are ill at the moment.

107A

(i)

1 No 3 Nu 5 No 7 No 9 Nu
2 No 4 Nu 6 Nu 8 Nu 10 No

(ii)

Some cheese, a banana, some wine, some bread, an egg, some tomatoes, some water, an orange, some rice, some carrots, some apples, some meat.

107B

1 hair
2 journey
3 advice
4 some bread
5 a paper
6 is, traffic
7 job, isn't, work
8 Is, accommodation

108A

A

clock, university, sandwich, dog, game, house, hospital, school

B

orange, envelope, aunt, old car, hour, onion, umbrella, examination, ice-cream

108B

1 a
2 an, a
3 ——— , ———
4 ———
5 a
6 a

108C

1 the, the
2 a, an
3 the
4 the, the
5 a, the
6 the
7 the
8 an

109A

1 ———
2 the
3 ——— , ———
4 the, the
5 ——— , ———
6 the, the, the
7 ———
8 ——— , ———

109B

1 A florist sells flowers.
2 A child needs love.
3 A corkscrew takes corks out of bottles.
4 A large car is expensive to run.
5 A teetotaller doesn't drink alcohol.

110A

1 The swan
2 the radio
3 the country
4 The tulip
5 the piano
6 the sea

110B

1 the dead
2 the unemployed
3 the blind
4 the sick

110C

1 the British
2 the Australians
3 the Spanish (o 'the Spaniards')
4 the French
5 the Greeks

111A

1 ———
2 the
3 ———
4 the
5 ——— , ———
6 ——— , ——— , ———
7 the
8 ———
9 the
10 ———

112A

1 Canberra
2 China
3 Mexico City
4 the Sahara
5 California
6 Lake Superior
7 the Pacific
8 Mount Everest
9 the Alps

112B

1 ——— , ——— , the
2 ——— , the, ——— . ———
3 ——— , ——— , the, the

113A

1 The, the, the
2 ——— , ———
3 The, the, a
4 a, ——— , a
5 the
6 the
7 ———
8 ——— , ———
9 the, ———
10 ———
11 the
12 the
13 ———
14 ——— , ——— , ———
15 The
16 a, a, The, a, the, an
17 ——— , the,
18 ———
19 The, the
20 ——— , ———
21 ———
22 the, the

114A

1 all
2 each
3 some of, all of
4 any, any
5 Most
6 Neither of
7 Neither of
8 much, a lot
9 A few of, many
10 many
11 every one of
12 most of
13 every
14 each
15 either of
16 half of
17 each one

115A

1 some
2 some
3 some (cfr. 115.5), any
4 some (cfr. 115.5)
5 any, some (cfr. 115.5)
6 some/any
7 any
8 some
9 Some
10 some/any

116A

1 a few
2 a little
3 a lot of
4 a lot of, a few
5 a little
6 many/a lot of/a few
7 much
8 much, many, much/a lot of

116B

1 little
2 few
3 a few
4 few, little
5 a little, a little
6 little
7 a few
8 little

117A

1 None
2 no
3 no
4 no
5 None
6 none
7 none

118A

1 every
2 Everybody
3 All
4 everything
5 all/everything
6 everybody
7 all
8 every
9 everything
10 all/everything

118B

1 All the/The whole
2 all the
3 all/the whole
4 all the

118C

1 every
2 all
3 every
4 all

119A

1 neither of
2 both
3 either
4 either of
5 Neither
6 both/both of

119B

1 eat now or wait until later
2 read Arabic nor write it
3 nor Kate knew the address
4 his sister or his brother
5 and Sarah passed the exam easily
6 very comfortable nor very interesting
7 larger than my old flat and closer to my office

120A

1 her
2 me, he, I
3 Me
4 I, him, He
5 They, me, them

120B

1 We, us
2 them, they
3 It
4 I, it
5 It
6 They, they
7 You, you
8 they
9 it
10 she, I

121A

1 their, ours
2 My, hers
3 your, yours
4 her, her, theirs
5 Our, theirs, ours

121B

1 her own
2 your own
3 your own
4 their own
5 my own
6 his own

122A

1 themselves
2 itself
3 herself
4 myself
5 himself
6 yourselves
7 ourselves

122B

1 by myself
2 by herself
3 by yourself
4 by themselves

122C

1 ———
2 myself
3 ———
4 myself
5 ———
6 myself
7 ———
8 ———

122D

1 myself
2 ourselves
3 yourself
4 themselves
5 himself

122E

1 each other
2 each other
3 ourselves
4 themselves

123A

PRONOME PERSONALE		AGGETTIVO POSSESSIVO	PRONOME POSSESSIVO	PRONOME RIFLESSIVO
SOGGETTO	COMPLEMENTO			
I	me	my	mine	myself
you	you	your	yours	yourself
he	him	his	his	himself
she	her	her	hers	herself
it	it	its	———	itself
we	us	our	ours	ourselves
you	you	your	yours	yourselves
they	them	their	theirs	themselves

123B

1 Their, ours
2 yours, mine
3 her, she, herself
4 they, us
5 yourself, it, your
6 I, myself
7 He, me, I, his
8 you, you, I, them, you
9 your, we, ourselves
10 It, his, hers

124A

1 one (= a drink)
2 ones (= glasses)
3 one (= woman)
4 one (= film)

125A

1 nothing
2 somewhere
3 somebody
4 nowhere
5 anybody
6 everything
7 Everyone
8 something (cfr. 125.2b), anything
9 Nobody
10 everywhere, anywhere

126A

1 a two-hour concert
2 a fifty-year-old man
3 a twenty-minute delay
4 a ten-page letter
5 a two-hour meeting

126B

1 long, boring
2 late
3 sad, wrong
4 angry
5 shy, embarrassed

126C

1 Are the children asleep?
2 Sydney is a very modern city.
3 That building is over 500 years old.
4 You don't sound very happy.
5 He looks a very healthy man.
6 The bridge is 1.55 kilometres long.
7 Have you seen my blue T-shirt?

126D

Opinione	Dimensione	Età
horrible beautiful ugly	short small large	old middle-aged young

Forma	Colore	Provenienza
round square curly	grey red white	English Italian German

Materiale	Scopo
glass plastic leather	shopping sports writing

126E

1 a short fat man
2 a tall middle-aged woman
3 two small white paper cups
4 some tiny Japanese TV sets
5 a handsome young doctor
6 a cheap red plastic raincoat
7 an attractive long blue coat
8 a pair of expensive black leather shoes

127A

1 colder than
2 more comfortable than
3 better than
4 taller than
5 more interesting than

127B

1 worse
2 better
3 a lot easier than
4 much simpler
5 a little more advanced
6 a lot more complicated
7 rather bigger
8 more comprehensive

127C

1 bigger and bigger
2 worse and worse
3 more and more polluted
4 more and more automated

127D

1 The bigger a car is, the more expensive it is to run.
2 The worse the weather, the more dangerous it is to drive on the roads.
3 The older he gets, the more thoughtful he becomes.
4 The more complicated the problem, the harder it is to find a solution.

127E

1 the best
2 the cheapest
3 the most reliable
4 the most expensive
5 the largest
6 the most stupid
7 The oldest
8 the worst
9 the most famous

128A

1 as tall as
2 as clever as
3 as interesting as
4 as cheap as

128B

1 An elephant isn't as tall as a giraffe.
  A giraffe isn't as strong as an elephant.
  An elephant isn't as fast as a giraffe.
2 Gold isn't as strong as iron.
  Iron isn't as valuable as gold.
3 A gorilla isn't as intelligent as a human!
  A human isn't as strong as a gorilla.
4 A bicycle isn't as expensive as a car.
  A bicycle isn't as fast as a car.
  A car isn't as easy to park as a bicycle.

129A

1 the most popular
2 more serious than
3 friendly as
4 the best
5 more generous than
6 clever as
7 the hottest
8 more self-confident than
9 the strangest
10 the tallest
11 cheaper than
12 most enjoyable

130A

1 easily
2 fast
3 slowly
4 well
5 hard
6 badly
7 delicious, good
8 serious, carefully

131A

1 tennis very well now.
2 your letters in the town centre early this morning.
3 football in the park this afternoon.
4 heavily in the north of Scotland yesterday evening.
5 the map carefully later on in the day.
6 angrily out of the room at the end of the meeting.
7 the guitar beautifully at the concert last night.

132A

1 They've probably been trying to contact us.
2 She probably went to the meeting last week.
3 They normally take their summer holidays in May.
4 Have you ever lived in a foreign country?
5 I've never eaten Indian food.
6 Do you still live in the same flat?
7 He only wants to borrow the money.
8 I probably won't see Martin again until next weekend.

9 We've almost finished painting the outside of the house.
10 I always try to go jogging at least three times a week.
11 We certainly haven't got any time to lose.
12 I can certainly lend you some money until next week.
13 He's always complaining about something.
14 I don't usually watch this TV programme.

133A

1 already
2 still, yet
3 still
4 still
5 already
6 yet, yet

133B

1 You needn't clean the kitchen; I've already done it./I've done it already.
2 You don't need to tell me; I already know what to do./I know what to do already.
3 Haven't you received your invitation to the party yet?
4 I still can't decide what to do this evening.
5 I can still remember the first time I flew in a plane.
6 Robert still works for the same company in London.

134A

1 Sue no longer works for the same company in London.
2 My brother isn't a young child any more.
3 Her father is no longer unemployed.
4 There is no longer a large ship-building industry in Britain.

135A

all the time	(1)	always
	(2)	normally, usually
	(3)	often, frequently
	(4)	sometimes
	(5)	seldom, rarely
	(6)	hardly ever
at no time	(7)	never, not ever

135B

1 I've never seen that TV programme.
2 He's hardly ever late for appointments.
3 They rarely go to the cinema nowadays.
4 Is he often bad-tempered?/Is he bad-tempered often?
5 They listen to the radio every morning./Every morning they listen to the radio.
6 I'm seldom at home before 8 o'clock.
7 Have you ever had a really serious illness?
8 I'll never forget our holiday together.
9 She's always been interested in music.
10 I always brush my teeth three times a day.

136A

1 Simon is probably at Sarah's house at the moment.
2 There will probably be an election early next year.
3 Perhaps we'll play tennis later this afternoon.
4 They obviously enjoyed the film very much.
5 You should definitely go and see the doctor.
6 I definitely don't want to be home late tonight.
7 Computers are certainly becoming more and more important in our lives.
8 The bridge has probably been repaired by now.

137A

1 rather
2 quite
3 pretty/rather
4 quite
5 rather
6 quite
7 quite/pretty
8 rather

137B

1 quite different
2 quite useless
3 quite original
4 quite sure
5 quite impossible

138A

1 too dark
2 too quietly
3 early enough
4 too loud
5 warm enough

138B

1 enough
2 too much
3 too much
4 too many
5 enough

138C

1 I'm too tired to go to the cinema this evening.
2 The table was too heavy for me to move.
3 The children aren't tall enough to reach that shelf.
4 They arrived too late to see the beginning of the film.
5 Our old flat was much too small for us to live in.
6 He spoke too quietly for the people at the back of the room to hear.

139A

1 so
2 so
3 such, so
4 so
5 so
6 such
7 so
8 such

140A

1 earlier than
2 worse than
3 the longest
4 more efficiently than
5 fluently as
6 faster, faster
7 better than
8 harder than

141A

1 I don't like travelling by train.
2 He wasn't late for the appointment.
3 We haven't got a lot of time.
4 I'm not enjoying myself very much.
5 Robert doesn't work for a company in Manchester.
6 The weather isn't very nice today.
7 She can't come to the party on Saturday.
8 I haven't been working too hard recently.
9 She hasn't got a very interesting job.
10 They may not have gone home.
11 We didn't see you at school yesterday.
12 The bank doesn't open on Saturday afternoons.
13 My sister isn't going to work tomorrow.
14 The telephone hasn't been repaired.
15 We don't play tennis every weekend.
16 I won't be seeing Martin tomorrow.

142A

1 Did they play tennis yesterday?
2 Is he doing his homework?
3 Has she got a lot to do today?
4 Have they bought a new car?
5 Do you know Simon Robinson?
6 Can he play the piano and the guitar?
7 Does the shop close at 6 o'clock?
8 Would you like to go swimming?
9 Will the job be finished soon?

142B

1 Did they visit
2 Did she buy
3 Has she got
4 Do you speak
5 Have they gone
6 Can you play
7 Does he work
8 Are you going

143A

1 are you going
2 are you
3 were you reading
4 does he visit

5 will they do
6 has she been waiting
7 do you come
8 have you got
9 did you buy
10 does she like
11 did you see
12 was she talking

144A

1 Who did you tell?
2 Who wrote to you?
3 Who did you write to?
4 What is making that noise?
5 What is he making?
6 Who makes the decisions?
7 Who did they help?
8 Who helped them?
9 Who was she looking for?
10 Who was looking for her?
11 What moved?
12 Who gave you the book?

145A

1 What
2 Where
3 How long
4 How many
5 Who
6 When
7 How often
8 How much
9 Whose
10 How
11 Which
12 Why

146A

1 Don't you like it?
2 Isn't that your brother over there?
3 Can't you stay a little longer?
4 Isn't she a pretty child!
5 Haven't I met you somewhere before?
6 Isn't she going to work today?
7 Don't you want to come to the concert tonight?

147A

1 You don't like this music, do you?
2 Robert isn't at work today, is he?
3 I'm too late, aren't I?
4 You haven't seen the newspaper, have you?
5 Lynne speaks French and German, doesn't she?
6 They didn't go to the concert, did they?
7 You'd like to have something to eat, wouldn't you?
8 We're leaving tomorrow, aren't we?
9 You couldn't do me a favour, could you?
10 You don't know where Sarah is, do you?
11 Switch on the light for me, will/would/can/could you?
12 Don't forget to lock the door, will you?
13 Nobody was watching the TV, were they?
14 Everyone will be here soon, won't they?
15 Nothing terrible has happened, has it?
16 There's plenty of time, isn't there?
17 Pass me that magazine. will/would/can/could you?
18 Let's have a cup of tea, shall we?

148A

1 Were you?
2 Did you?
3 Didn't they?
4 Are you?
5 Do you?
6 Are you?
7 Have you?
8 have you?
9 Haven't you?
10 Would you?

149A

1 Can you tell me when the last bus leaves?
2 Do you know if he is over 18?
3 Do you know if she can speak French?
4 Can you explain how this machine works?
5 Have you decided where you are going on holiday?
6 Do you remember exactly what he told you?
7 Do you know if you will be here tomorrow?
8 Have you got any idea if she likes horse riding?

9 Can you remember if you switched off all the lights?
10 Do you know if everyone has gone home?

150A

1 I can't
2 I am
3 he did
4 I don't
5 she does
6 I haven't
7 he isn't
8 I was
9 I will
10 they haven't
11 she hasn't
12 he does

150B

1 No, they can't.
2 Yes, it does.
3 No, he wasn't.
4 Yes, it is.
5 No, it didn't.
6 No, it doesn't.

151A

1 Neither am I.
2 So do I.
3 Neither have I.
4 So would I.
5 Neither have I.
6 Neither have I.
7 So do I.
8 So did I.
9 So should I.
10 So do I.
11 So would I.
12 Neither did I.

152A

1 Yes, I think so.
2 Yes, I suppose so.
3 No, I don't think so. ('No, I think not.' è possibile, ma è meno frequente.)
4 No, I'm afraid not.
5 Yes, I imagine so.
6 No, I don't expect so./No, I expect not.
7 Yes, I'm afraid so.
8 No, I don't suppose so./No, I suppose not.
9 Yes, I expect so.
10 Yes, I imagine so.

153A

1 He's the man who painted my house.
2 What's the name of the boy who telephoned you?
3 What's happened to the money that was on my desk?
4 They're the people who offered Sue a job.
5 The car that was stolen has now been found.
6 She's the person who gives me a lift to work every day.
7 The lock that was broken has now been repaired.
8 Most of the people who work in Peter's office are very nice.

154A

1 who
2 (who)
3 (that)
4 (that)
5 who
6 (who)
7 that
8 (that)
9 who
10 that

155A

1 She's the woman whose husband teaches at Annie's school.
2 He's the man whose flat was broken into.
3 They're the couple whose children were injured in the accident.
4 That's the girl whose friend lent me the money.
5 I'm the person whose credit cards were stolen.
6 Are you the one whose mother phoned the police?

155B

1 why/that
2 where
3 when
4 where
5 why/that
6 when

156A

1 The people who live next door helped us to move the furniture.
2 Have you still got the money that I gave you?
3 Sydney, which has a population of more than three million, is Australia's largest city.

4 Peter's sister, who I've known for years, is a very nice person.
5 We saw Sue last night with that man who works in the library.
6 The chair that was broken has now been repaired.

156B

1	who	5	that/which
2	——	6	who
3	who	7	which
4	——		

157A

1 where	3 whose	5 whose
2 who/whom	4 where	6 when

158A

1 The man I introduced you to is Sue's cousin.
2 The hotel we stayed at overlooked the sea.
3 The shop I bought the shoes from is closed.
4 The people he works with like him very much.

158B

1 (i) Peter's party, which we are all invited to, is next Saturday evening.
  (ii) Peter's party, to which we are all invited, is next Saturday evening.
2 (i) Mr Mason, who we complained to, apologized for the mistake.
  (ii) Mr Mason, to whom we complained, apologized for the mistake.
3 (i) The film *Family Life*, which I've heard good reports about, is showing next week.
  (ii) The film *Family Life*, about which I've heard good reports, is showing next week.

158C

1 most of whom	4 neither of whom
2 many of which	5 none of which
3 all of whom	6 both of which

159A

1 She lent me the money, which was very generous of her.
2 They had to wait for over an hour, which annoyed them very much.
3 There was a lot of snow on the roads, which made driving dangerous.
4 I knew you didn't want to go to the concert, which is why I didn't buy you a ticket.
5 There was a bus strike, which meant I had to take a taxi.
6 There was a delicious smell coming from the kitchen, which made us all feel very hungry.

160A

1 When	4 until	7 when
2 while	5 as soon as	8 when
3 until, before	6 just as	

161A

1 Though they have a car, they rarely use it.
2 Although he was innocent, he was sent to prison.
3 Even though he has a number of relatives living nearby, he never visits them.
4 Even though she never takes any kind of exercise, she is quite fit and healthy.

161B

1 All the trains were on time despite the heavy snow.
2 Our coach didn't arrive late in spite of the terrible traffic.
3 A lot of people buy those houses despite the high prices.

161C

1 (i) I didn't buy the car despite having enough money.
  (ii) I didn't buy the car despite the fact (that) I had enough money.
2 (i) He stayed outside in the cold weather despite feeling ill.
  (ii) He stayed outside in the cold weather despite the fact (that) he felt ill.
3 (i) People continue to smoke in spite of knowing the dangers.
  (ii) People continue to smoke in spite of the fact (that) they know the dangers.

161D

1 She likes hard work while/whereas he's quite lazy.
2 She likes jazz and pop music while/whereas he prefers classical music.
3 She likes going out a lot while/whereas he prefers staying at home.
4 She's very practical while/whereas he's quite idealistic.
5 She's very generous while/whereas he can be rather mean.

162A

1 He phoned the police because he'd lost his wallet.
2 I didn't have any lunch because I wasn't hungry.
3 Our plane was delayed because of the fog.
4 He went to Paris because he wanted to learn French.
5 I took an umbrella because I thought it might rain.
6 He couldn't run very fast because of his bad leg.

162B

1 As	4 as a result	7 therefore
2 so	5 so	
3 Since	6 because	

162C

1 It was such a warm evening (that) we had dinner outside in the garden.
2 He was so nervous (that) he couldn't eat anything.
3 Our neighbours' party was so noisy (that) we couldn't sleep.
4 The restaurant was so crowded (that) they couldn't find anywhere to sit down.
5 We were all having such a good time (that) we didn't want to stop.

163A

1 I'm going to the library to return a book.
2 She's gone to the greengrocer's for some potatoes.
3 He's taking the car to the garage to have it serviced.
4 He phoned me to invite me to his party.
5 I get up early every day to go jogging.
6 They've gone to the pub for a drink.

163B

1 It's used for taking corks out of bottles.
2 It's used for cutting grass.
3 It's used for making holes in paper.
4 It's used for measuring temperature.

163C

1 He's started walking to work so as to get more exercise.

2 The government are going to increase taxes in order to raise more money.
3 We took a map with us on the journey so as not to get lost.
4 They stopped work at 1 o'clock in order to have lunch.

163D

1 He switched on the light so that he could see what he was doing.
2 I turned down the music so that I wouldn't disturb the neighbours.
3 She repeated everything so that we would remember it.
4 She's saving money so that she can buy a new car.

164A

1 You'd better hurry up in case you miss your train.
2 Take a book on the journey in case you get bored.
3 Put on some suncream in case you get sunburnt.
4 Wear a coat when you go out in case you catch a cold.
5 You should lock the car in case someone tries to steal it.

164B

1 if	3 in case	5 in case
2 if	4 if	

165A

1 on, in	5 at (o 'in')	9 on (o 'an'), at
2 at (o 'in')	6 in, in	10 at/in, in, on
3 at/in, in	7 at (o 'in'), in	
4 in, on	8 on	

166A

1 off	6 in
2 on	7 onto/on
3 in/inside, out of	8 off, into
4 outside	9 out of, into/in
5 out of, on/onto	

167A

1 above	3 over	5 under
2 under	4 on top of	6 underneath

168A (*Risposte possibili*)

1 behind	10 opposite/in front of/
2 in front of	behind/next to
3 between	11 through/in
4 up, down	12 along (anche 'down'
5 at	o 'up')
6 across	13 across/over (o 'along')
7 next to, in	14 over (o 'from')
8 from, to, in/at	15 past
9 to	16 towards/to

169A

1 at, ——	5 in, on	9 at, on
2 ——, in	6 at, in	10 in, in
3 on	7 in	11 in
4 ——, on	8 at	

170A

1 on time	3 on time	5 in time
2 in time	4 in time	

171A

1 in the end	3 in the end	5 at the end
2 at the end	4 in the end	6 at the end

172A

1 during | 4 for, during/in | 7 while
2 for | 5 during | 8 during/for
3 during/in | 6 for, during/in

173A

1 from, until/to | 3 from, until/to | 5 by
2 by | 4 until/to | 6 until

174A

1 for, before | 3 for, before
2 for, ago | 4 ago, since

175A

1 on, by | 3 in, by | 5 by, by
2 by, on | 4 on

176A

1 as
2 like
3 like
4 as (anche 'like' nello stile informale)
5 like
6 like
7 as (anche 'like' nello stile informale)

176B

1 They look as if they're having fun.
2 They look as if they're in love.
3 She looks as if she's just had some good news.
4 They look as if they've been running.
5 He looks as if he's going to fall.

176C

1 She's 50 years old, but she looks as if she was/
were 30.
2 He's only a receptionist, but he acts as if he
owned the hotel.
3 They're quite rich, but they behave as if they
were poor.
4 He's only got a cold, but he acts as if he was/
were dying.
5 It's my car, but he treats it as if it belonged to
him.

177A

1 with | 3 with | 5 in, with
2 in | 4 with

178A (*Risposte possibili*)

1 of | 6 of | 11 with | 16 at
2 to | 7 about | 12 of | 17 of
3 about | 8 in | 13 at/by | 18 from/to
4 at | 9 on | 14 of | 19 to
5 for | 10 of | 15 of | 20 with, for

179A

1 with | 5 of | 9 to/towards
2 to | 6 in | 10 for
3 between | 7 between | 11 for
4 to | 8 in | 12 of

180A

1 for | 3 by | 5 by, in | 7 By
2 on | 4 by | 6 on | 8 in, with

181A

1 at | 9 of | 17 in
2 to | 10 of/about | 18 of
3 about | 11 about | 19 about
4 to, about | 12 of | 20 for
5 on | 13 of | 21 on
6 to, for | 14 of | 22 into
7 to, for | 15 for
8 from | 16 after

182A

1 for | 5 from
2 of | 6 of
3 about | 7 to
4 on | 8 about

183A

1 out of | 8 up | 15 at
2 inside | 9 into | 16 near
3 Next to | 10 down | 17 in front of
4 off | 11 across | 18 on
5 outside | 12 towards | 19 opposite
6 Behind | 13 along | 20 round
7 onto | 14 past

183B

1 at, in, at | 16 at
2 in, on | 17 on, on
3 of/about, to, on, in | 18 in/at, for, at
4 at (o 'in'), in, for | 19 with
5 in, in | 20 for, about
6 at, on | 21 from/to, to
7 during, to | 22 for, with
8 In, on | 23 of
9 on, at | 24 of
10 at (o 'in'), in, since, in | 25 with, in, on
11 from, since | 26 between
12 in | 27 of
13 as, in, for, in/during | 28 about, in
14 on, under, in | 29 to, about, in
15 of | 30 to, for, in

184A

1 Have you sent your brother the letter?
2 I'll get Sally a present.
3 Have you told your parents the news?
4 I bought you some stamps.
5 She lent Peter her car.
6 I kept you a seat.
7 He's prepared us a meal.
8 Will you give Mrs Woods this message?

184B

1 They didn't offer me the job.
2 She bought a book for her son.
3 Can you pass me the salt?
4 Will you take this package to your parents?
5 They have ordered us a taxi.
6 He showed the photographs to all his friends.

185A

1 fill in | 4 speak up | 7 came across
2 kept on | 5 held up
3 gone up | 6 turned down

186A (*Risposte possibili*)

1 took off | 3 broke out
2 grows up | 4 getting up/to get up

186B

1 Would you like to try on this jacket?/Would
you like to try this jacket on?
2 I don't enjoy playing football any more. I
think I'll give it up.
3 My wife wants me to shave off my
moustache./My wife wants me to shave my
moustache off.
4 I have to speak to Mr Mason. I'd better ring
him up.
5 That music is rather loud. Would you turn it
down?

186C

1 look after | 3 came into
2 get over | 4 I ran into *an old friend*

186D

1 got rid of | 3 look back on
2 come up with | 4 put up with

186E

1 He's going to give it up.
2 I've thrown it away.
3 He's looking after her.
4 Are you looking forward to it?
5 Can you fill it in?
6 She takes after him.
7 He can't do without it.

187A

1 /ɪz/	2 /s/	3 /z/
washes	waits	opens
teaches	Mick's	cars
misses	stops	Sally's
dishes	admits	drives
Alice's	books	shows
watches	Bert's	studies
	hopes	brings

187B

1 /ɪd/	2 /t/	3 /d/
painted	passed	failed
ended	finished	loved
invented	hoped	opened
waited	danced	planned
admitted	worked	studied
	watched	lived
		remembered

188A

1 + -s	2 + -es	3 -y/ + -ies	4 -f/-fe + -ves
waits	catches	copies	shelves
plates	buzzes	worries	wives
runs	misses	flies	knives
pays	finishes	spies	
admits	tomatoes	marries	
discos	teaches		

188B

1 + -ing	2 -e/ + -ing	3 -ie/ + -ying	4 × 2 + -ing
drying	coming	dying	stopping
playing	making	tying	knitting
showing	writing		travelling
fixing	behaving		planning
offering	leaving		shopping
visiting			admitting
marrying			
staying			

188C

1 + -ed	2 -e/ + -ed	3 -y/ + -ied	4 × 2 + -ed
washed	arrived	applied	robbed
pulled	moved	emptied	trapped
discovered	phoned	carried	dropped
prayed	hoped	studied	travelled
showed	saved		admitted

188D

1 + -er/-est	2 -e/ + -er/-est
higher highest	nicer nicest
slower slowest	later latest
shorter shortest	simpler simplest
cheaper cheapest	wider widest
blacker blackest	whiter whitest

3
~~y~~ + -er/-est

happier happiest
busier busiest
easier easiest
funnier funniest

4
× 2 + -er/-est

bigger biggest
wetter wettest
fatter fattest
thinner thinnest
redder reddest

188E

1
+ -ly

lately
hopefully
really
quickly
beautifully
suddenly
definitely
politely

2
~~le~~ + -ly

gently
horribly
idly
probably

3
~~y~~ + -ily

happily
luckily
drily
heavily
temporarily

Risposte ai Progress Tests

1 i

1 has
2 'm (am) negotiating
3 rains, leave
4 'm (am) trying
5 is becoming
6 goes
7 are disappearing
8 falls
9 're (are) staying
10 is moving, are repairing

1 ii

1 A 2 B 3 A 4 A 5 B 6 B 7 B
8 A

2 i

1 The Titanic *was travelling* to New York...
2 The jumper *shrank* when I washed it.
3 ✓
4 I *broke* my toe...
5 The mouse *had* a heart attack...
6 The footballer *was running* towards the goal...
7 James Dean *was driving* a sports car when he *died*.

2 ii

1 While I was writing a letter the phone rang.
2 Did you read the newspaper as soon as it arrived?
3 She didn't lock the door when she left the office.
4 The train was going through the tunnel when it suddenly stopped.
5 Sally was washing her hair when the doorbell rang.
6 Did John Logie Baird invent the television or the telephone?
7 They cried when they heard the bad news.
8 The cat was lying on the sofa when the mouse came into the room.

3

1 been   4 been
2 been, been 5 gone
3 gone

4

1 It has just started to rain.
2 Have you finished that book yet?

3 I haven't seen that film yet.
4 The bus has just left.
5 Have you already done your shopping?/Have you done your shopping already?
6 Bob has already applied for several jobs./Bob has applied for several jobs already.

5 i

1 has grown
2 have been making
3 've (have) broken
4 've (have) been playing
5 've (have) lost
6 've (have) been putting up

5 ii

1 has he been losing, has he lost
2 have you looked, have you been looking
3 has she been doing, has she done
4 have they been playing, have they played

6

1 read *War and Peace* since 1980
2 studying Spanish for two years
3 directing films since the 1960s
4 raining since Monday
5 worked for ten years
6 skied since 1989
7 acting since the 1970s

7 i

1 ...I've lived...
2 Tolstoy *wrote*...
3 ✓
4 ...Someone *has stolen*...
5 Who *discovered*...
6 We *played* tennis...
7 When *did* you *pass*...
8 ✓
9 I've never *eaten*...
10 ...He's *grown* a beard.

7 ii

1 B 2 A 3 B 4 B 5 A 6 B 7 A
8 B 9 B 10 B

8

1 Carlo *has lived* in Rome *for* three years.
2 ✓
3 How long *have you been studying* English?
4 My parents *have been* married for thirty years.
5 ✓
6 Sarah *has known* Simon for a long time.
7 Those men *have been waiting* outside since 2.00.
8 ✓
9 My sister *has lived* in Brighton since 1980.
10 The Rolling Stones rock group *have been playing* together for over twenty years.

9 i

1 B 2 A 3 B 4 B 5 B

9 ii

1 When I visited the town last month, they'd (had) built a new hospital.
2 When we'd (had) had dinner, we went out for a walk.
3 When Sue looked in the fridge all the food had gone.
4 I didn't know the way to John's house because I hadn't been there before.
5 Mike got really exhausted in his first marathon because he hadn't run in such a long race before.

10

1 *We'd (had) been waiting* for an hour...
2 ✓
3 *We'd (had) been living* in Paris for ten years...
4 ✓
5 ...*I'd (had) been working* since early in the morning...

11

1 'll (will) meet
2 's (is) going to rain
3 'll (will) lend
4 'll (will) look
5 'll (will) teach
6 'm (am) going to take
7 're (are) going to live
8 'll (will) bite
9 'll (will) buy
10 's (is) going to have

12

1 ✓
2 *it's snowing* is a mistake
3 ✓
4 *are winning* is a mistake
5 ✓
6 *is passing* is a mistake

13

1 B 2 B 3 A 4 B 5 B 6 A

14

1 'll (will) have left, 'll (will) be driving
2 'll (will) have arrived, 'll (will) be checking-in
3 'll (will) be flying
4 'll (will) have arrived, 'll (will) be driving
5 'll (will) be having

15

1 Robert was going to watch the film on TV but he fell asleep.
2 I was going to visit you but I did not have enough time.
3 Sarah was going to change some traveller's cheques but the bank was closed.
4 We were going to go to the concert but it was cancelled.
5 I was going to finish work early but my boss asked me to work late.
6 My parents were going to fly to Scotland but they decided to go by train.

16

1 're (are) always complaining
2 always arrives
3 's (is) always looking
4 's (is) always helping
5 always have

17

1 B 2 A 3 A 4 B 5 B 6 A 7 B
8 B 9 B 10 B

18 i

I am writing to you in reply to your advertisement in last Monday's Evening Argus.

At the moment, *I am working* for Sun Travel, a company in London. *I have worked/I have been working* there for two years. Before *I joined* Sun Travel, *I worked* for a student travel company in Spain. *I worked* there for a year. Before that, *I worked* for Worldwide Travel in Brighton for a year. Now I would like to move back to Brighton and *I am looking* for a job with a travel company in the town.

18 ii *Suggested answers*

1 What is the most embarrassing thing that has ever happened to you in your life?
2 I had a terrible experience last Saturday.
3 This is what happened.

4 I left my flat at 2 o'clock and went into town to do some shopping.
5 I go shopping most Saturday afternoons.
6 By 4 o'clock, I had finished shopping and I went into a cafe for a cup of coffee.
7 While I was sitting in the cafe, I saw a friend called Julie Jones and she joined me.
8 At around 4.30 Julie and I paid the bill and left the cafe.
9 As we were leaving, I offered to give Julie a lift home in my car.
10 She said she would like a lift so we walked to the car park together.
11 I always put my car in the same car park near the town centre, but when we got to the car park, I had a big surprise.
12 My car was not there!
13 Of course, I immediately thought that someone had stolen it.
14 I was going to phone the police, but luckily I didn't.
15 I suddenly realised the truth!
16 I had not driven into town that day!
17 I had come on the bus instead.
18 Imagine how stupid I felt.
19 My face went so red.
20 Julie just smiled and said 'Don't worry. We can take the bus home together!'

18 iii   Suggested answers

1 was walking		10 started	
2 had been		11 took	
3 had spent		12 stabbed	
4 were walking		13 was passing	
5 stopped		14 stopped	
6 asked		15 helped	
7 had been drinking		16 visited	
8 was		17 got	
9 refused			

19

1 B 2 B 3 A 4 B 5 B 6 A 7 A
8 B 9 A 10 B

20 i

1 Boil 2 leave 3 add 4 stir 5 leave

20 ii

1 Let's hurry.   3 Let's not make
2 Let's not tell   4 Let's stay

21 i

1 's (is)	6 's (is)	11 are
2 's (is)	7 was	12 are
3 're (are)	8 was	13 Is
4 's (is)	9 was	14 were
5 'm (am)	10 's (is)	

21 ii

1 Is, is   5 Was, wasn't, was
2 Is, isn't, 's (is) 6 were, were
3 Is, 's (is)   7 Were, weren't
4 aren't, 're (are)

22

1 There's (is), It's (is)
2 There are, They're (are)
3 Is there, there is, It's (is)
4 Are there, there are, They're (are)
5 There was, It was
6 There will be, They'll (will), be

23

1 ✓
2 *I've got* a pain in my neck at the moment.
3 *Did you have* a good journey yesterday?

4 ✓
5 ✓
6 We usually *have* dinner at 7 o'clock.
7 'Have you got a car?' 'Yes, *I have.*'
8 ✓
9 *Did* Madonna *have* blonde hair in 1991?
10 *Have you got/Do you have* a driving licence?

24

1 B 2 C 3 B 4 A 5 C 6 C 7 B
8 A 9 C 10 B

25

1 'Yes, of course you *can/may.*'
2 The law says that you *can't/aren't allowed to* drive . . .
3 ✓
4 'Yes, of course you *can/may.*'
5 My brother *can/is allowed to* borrow . . .
6 ✓
7 My sister's daughter *was allowed to* stay up . . .

26 i

1 You don't have to be over 16 to get married.
2 I must pass the exam
3 You have to have an appointment to see the manager.
4 You don't have to apologise.
5 You mustn't drive without a seat belt.

26 ii

1 have to   3 must   5 having to
2 had to   4 have to   6 have to

27

1 C 2 C 3 A 4 B 5 C 6 B 7 A 8 C

28

1 ✓
2 Mike *didn't need to* go to work . . .
3 ✓
4 Sue *didn't need to* hurry home . . .
5 Kate *didn't need to* make . . .

29

1 B 2 A 3 B 4 C 5 A 6 C 7 B
8 A 9 B 10 C

30

1 It may rain tonight.
2 Peter could be in the Sports centre.
3 Sally might have written to the bank.
4 Ken may not have seen me.
5 I might not be here tomorrow.
6 The robbers may have had a key to the office.
7 The children might not be asleep.
8 People could be living on the moon in the year 2050.
9 Mike may not have received my letter.
10 Those people might be waving at us.

31

1 It may be very hot here tomorrow.
2 I may be wrong.
3 Anyone can be wrong.
4 Cats can live for 20 years.
5 Your cat may live for 20 years.

32

1 Simon should be in his room.
2 I ought to finish the book soon.
3 Maria should have received the letter yesterday.
4 We shouldn't be late home tonight.
5 My parents ought to have arrived at their hotel a few hours ago.

33

1 must be   5 can't have left
2 can't be   6 must be
3 must have gone   7 must have taken
4 can't be

34

1 B 2 A 3 C 4 B 5 C 6 A 7 B 8 C

35   Possible answers

1 Can I use your phone, please?
2 Could I have the menu, please?
3 Could you explain something to me, please?
4 Would you lend me some money?
5 Would you mind opening the door, please?
6 I'll give you a lift home in my car.
7 Shall I show you how to use the photocopier?
8 How about a walk in the park/having a walk in the park?
9 Would you like to go to the cinema this evening?
10 Where shall we meet tomorrow?
11 Let's go swimming this weekend.
12 Why don't we watch a video this evening?

36

1 *I go* swimming a lot nowadays.
2 ✓
3 *I don't get up* early these days.
4 My uncle *used to live* in San Francisco when he was younger.
5 Mike *lived* in Paris for a year.
6 Sarah *used to like* Madonna, but she doesn't any more.
7 ✓
8 When I was a student *I used to have* a beard.
9 Where did you *use to* live?
10 ✓

37 i   37 ii

1 wouldn't go   1 a refusal
2 'll (will) be   2 a promise
3 won't say   3 a refusal
4 'll (will) call 4 a threat
5 won't eat   5 a refusal

38

1 may as well apply   3 may as well sell
2 may as well clean   4 may as well give up

39 i

1 The doctor recommended that I should see a specialist.
2 I insisted that the shop assistant should give me my money back.
3 My teacher suggested that I should buy a larger dictionary.
4 The traffic warden insisted that we should move our car.

39 ii

1 I'm pleased that you should remember my birthday.
2 I was surprised that Sue should offer me a job.
3 I'm sorry that you should lose your wallet.
4 It was interesting that John should agree with me.

40

1 I had more money
2 I hadn't been rude to Jim's wife
3 Peter would listen to me
4 Annie hadn't eaten so much chocolate
5 I lived in the country
6 we could find a cure for cancer
7 it would stop raining

41

1 'd (would) rather have
2 'd (would) rather, didn't tell
3 'd (would) rather go
4 'd (would) rather not play
5 'd (would) rather, did

42

1 went   2 cleaned   3 asked   4 bought

43 i

1 have built a new motorway
2 keep the information on our computer
3 arrested a man late last night
4 should take the medicine after meals
5 'll (will) have to sell the hotel
6 criticizing him
7 'd (had) pulled down my old school
8 was following me

43 ii

1 The president is being interviewed on TV at the moment.
2 The post is delivered twice a day.
3 The old man was taken to hospital.
4 The traffic lights were being repaired yesterday.
5 This letter has been opened.
6 I remember being told the news.
7 Taxes should be reduced.
8 Ann must have been told about the accident.
9 The 9.15 train had been cancelled, so I took a later train.
10 The law is going to be changed soon.

43 iii

1 was robbed
2 was blown open
3 was stolen
4 took
5 are looking
6 were seen
7 also want
8 worked
9 disappeared
10 has not been seen

44

1 ... written *with* a typewriter.
2 ✓
3 ... made *with* three eggs.
4 ... painted *by* Leonardo da Vinci.

45

1 will be given the information later
2 was sent to me
3 was knocked over in the street
4 is expected that the president will visit Moscow
5 is said to have been invented in China
6 is thought that the Queen of England is one of the richest women in the world
7 are claimed to have visited the earth
8 to cause skin cancer

46

1 're (are) having our roof repaired at the moment
2 'm (am) having a stereo fitted in my car
3 has her flat cleaned once a week
4 had your eyes tested recently
5 had his briefcase stolen last week

47 i

1 B   2 B   3 B   4 C   5 A   6 C

47 ii

1 stops
2 were
3 'll (will) switch
4 'd (would) buy
5 won't be
6 wouldn't buy
7 lie
8 doesn't apologize
9 Would you stop
10 Will you phone

48

1 a) 'd (had) taken, wouldn't have got
  b) 'd (had) known, wouldn't have gone
  c) hadn't gone, wouldn't have caught
2 a) wouldn't have woken up, hadn't gone
  b) hadn't woken up, wouldn't have missed
  c) hadn't missed, wouldn't have been

49

1 Go now or I'll be very angry.
2 Provided you help me now, I'll help you later.
3 Give me your address and I'll write to you.
4 Unless they offer me a better job, I'll leave the company.
5 I'll stay up and watch the film as long as it isn't on too late.
6 Supposing you were in my place, what would you do?
7 Should I win the lottery, I'll give you half the money.

50 i

1 ... if *she fails* ...
2 ... *he wouldn't have broken* ...
3 ✓
4 If *I don't have* ...
5 ... *I wouldn't lend* ...
6 ✓
7 ... if *I didn't have to* work ...

50 ii

1 If we'd known the film was on TV, we would have recorded it on our video.
2 If I didn't go to bed late every night, I wouldn't always be tired.
3 If Janet had been in a hurry, she wouldn't have walked home.
4 If I had enough money, I could go skiing next week.
5 If we'd had an umbrella, we wouldn't have got wet.

51 i

1 I'm 25 years old.
2 I work in a bank.
3 I've been working there for a year.
4 I don't like my job very much.
5 I'm in Europe on holiday.
6 I'm having a great holiday.
7 I arrived in London last week.
8 I've been to Britain twice before.
9 I'm going to Italy next week.
10 I can't speak Italian very well.
11 I'll be in Italy for a week.

51 ii

1 (that) he had been working there for a year
2 her (that) he was looking for a better job
3 (that) he liked travelling
4 (that) he had been to the United States
5 her (that) he had been/went to New York last summer
6 (that) he would like to go to Australia one day
7 her (that) he had/had got one sister
8 (that) her name was Judy
9 her (that) his sister didn't live in England
10 (that) she lived in Spain

52 i

1 How old are you?
2 Where do you work now?
3 How long have you worked there?
4 Where did you go to school?
5 What exams did you take at school?
6 Can you drive a car?

52 i (cont.)

7 How long have you been driving?
8 Have you got/Do you have a car of your own?
9 What are your hobbies?
10 What do you like doing in your free time?
11 Do you want the job?
12 Can you start next month?

52 ii

1 They asked me where I worked.
2 They asked me how long I had been working there.
3 They asked me if I was on holiday in England.
4 They asked me when I had arrived/when I arrived there.
5 They asked me if I had been to Britain before.
6 They asked me how long I was going to stay there.
7 They asked me if I liked English food.
8 They asked me if I had/had got any brothers or sisters.
9 They asked me how long I had been studying English.
10 They asked me if I could speak any other languages.

53

1 She invited her friend to go to the cinema.
2 He offered to post the letter for her.
3 The doctor advised me to take more exercise.
4 I promised not to drive too fast.

54

1 Switch off your engine, please.
2 Where are you going?
3 I'm going home.
4 Where do you live?
5 Where have you just come from?
6 I've been at a friend's house all evening.
7 Can I see your driving licence, please?
8 Get out of the car, please.
9 Is it your car?
10 I bought it last year.
11 You can go home.

55 i

1 C   2 B   3 B   4 B   5 A   6 B   7 A
8 C   9 B   10 C   11 A   12 B   13 C
14 B   15 A   16 B   17 B   18 B   19 C
20 B   21 B   22 B

55 ii

1 I stopped *playing* ...
2 ✓
3 Thanks for letting me *borrow* ...
4 Would you like to *have* ...
5 *Walking* can be ...
6 It isn't easy *to learn* ...
7 I went to the station *to get* my train.
8 They wanted *me to go out* with them.
9 Everyone refused *to help* the old man.
10 ✓
11 How about *playing* tennis ...
12 ... I saw some men *building* ...
13 Have you finished *eating* ...
14 I'm used to *working* ...
15 ✓
16 We're thinking of *going* ...
17 Can you *come* ...
18 I'm looking forward to *seeing* ...
19 ✓
20 Do you feel like *listening* ...
21 Annie's mother made her *eat* her lunch.
22 Do you want *someone to help you move/someone to help you to move* the table?

56

1 the news surprising
2 shocked by the man's behaviour
3 travel interesting
4 bored by the tennis match
5 the sauna very relaxing

57

1 I dropped my bag running for a bus.
2 We got lost driving through Paris.
3 Having locked all the doors, I went to bed.
4 Having just had a drink, I wasn't thirsty.

58

1 ...and trousers?
2 ✓
3 The news isn't...
4 How many people...
5 Where are the scissors?
6 ...a new toothbrush.
7 ✓
8 How much are these blue Levi's jeans?
9 ...the children...
10 ✓
11 Your hair looks....... washed it?
12 Ten kilometres is a long way...
13 One of my brothers works in a shoe shop.
14 Physics was my favourite subject...
15 ✓
16 ✓
17 There was £30 in my wallet, but now it's gone.
18 Some passers-by...

59 i

1 this week's news
2 the thieves' stolen car
3 the roof of the hotel
4 the price of your meal
5 two weeks' vacation
6 the end of the film
7 the middle of our English lesson
8 the name of the girl who came to dinner
9 Jim's brother's girlfriend
10 the rising cost of petrol

59 ii

1 A friend of mine is having a party.
2 The town's only theatre is closed.
3 Some neighbours of ours have offered to help us.
4 Britain's rainfall has been light this year.
5 We've been visiting some relatives of ours.

60

1 ...has information about hotel accommodation.
2 ...your hair cut?
3 There is traffic news...
4 ...without a lot of luggage.
5 ...a loaf of bread/some bread... and some spaghetti.
6 Where is the money... Have you spent it...
7 We're having beautiful weather...
8 Some of our furniture was damaged...

61

1	a	7	a	13	the	19	the
2	the	8	a	14	a	20	The
3	an	9	a	15	an	21	the
4	The	10	the	16	the	22	an
5	the	11	an	17	the	23	the
6	the	12	the	18	the		

62

1	Noise	3	The water	5	money
2	the noise	4	Water	6	the money

63 i

1	⌐ , a	6	a, the
2	the, the, the	7	a, the
3	The ('A' is also possible), the, the	8	⌐, ⌐, ⌐
4	the, ⌐	9	the, the, ⌐
5	⌐ , ⌐	10	the

63 ii

1 Canberra is the capital of Australia.
2 San Diego is in Southern California.
3 Is the Amazon the longest river in Latin America?
4 Jamaica is an island in the Caribbean Sea.
5 Snowdon is the highest mountain in England and Wales.
6 Lake Michigan is in the United States.
7 The Gobi desert is in Asia.
8 The Uffizi is one of the most famous museums in the world.
9 The Statue of Liberty was made in France.
10 Macy's is a famous department store on 34th Street in New York.

64 i

1 B 2 D 3 A 4 D 5 A 6 C 7 B
8 D 9 B 10 D

64 ii

1 intelligent and charming
2 sing nor play the guitar
3 my girlfriend nor I enjoyed the party
4 people like Monday mornings
5 one of Steven Spielberg's films
6 she wanted was a cup of coffee for breakfast
7 much/a lot of French
8 houses have video phones
9 of my sisters are/is married
10 of my friends have/has failed their driving test

65 i

1 Look! There's Sally and her boyfriend! Can you see them?
2 My brother looks very young, but he's older than I am/me.
3 'Who's that outside?' 'It's me.'
4 My girlfriend and I phone each other every day.
5 Our flat was cheaper than theirs, but theirs is much smaller than ours.
6 Did the old man hurt himself when he fell out of his bed?
7 I woke up, got dressed and made myself some breakfast.
8 It's easy to cut yourself when you're shaving.
9 When we warned her not to walk home by herself, she just laughed at us.
10 We were very annoyed with ourselves for forgetting about your party.

65 ii

1	You ('One' is also possible)	5	yourself
2	herself	6	It
3	they, their	7	they
4	it	8	me, my

66

1 B 2 C 3 A 4 C

67 i

1 anything all day
2 anybody living in that house
3 nothing to do today
4 nowhere this week

67 ii Suggested answers

1 ✓
2 ...I've got nothing left.
3 There isn't anything good...
4 ...There's nobody living there.
5 We've looked everywhere..., but we can't find it anywhere.
6 ✓
7 ✓
8 There wasn't anywhere to sit down...

68

1 has got a powerful Japanese motorbike
2 looks beautiful this summer
3 seems a very cheerful woman
4 was wearing a long black leather coat
5 had lunch at an expensive French restaurant
6 are around 5,000 years old

69 i

1 Today is sunnier than yesterday.
2 My boyfriend isn't as clever as he thinks.
3 Ken is a much more careful driver than Simon.
4 You aren't taller than I am/me.
5 What was the happiest day of your life?
6 The older my grandmother gets, the more forgetful she becomes.
7 Camping isn't as comfortable as staying in a hotel, but it's much healthier.
8 The problem of world pollution is getting worse and worse.

69 ii

1 cheaper than playing golf
2 fastest animal in the world
3 best thing to wake you up in the morning
4 as big as Toyko
5 most talented footballer in the world
6 more exciting than listening to records

70

1	very slowly		
2	rather reckless driver	4	very good actor
3	very hard	5	angrily

71

1 My parents will be on holiday next week.
2 I walked confidently into the exam room.
3 We saw them in town on Saturday morning.
4 All the students worked hard last week.
5 The English like tea very much.
6 My grandmother went into hospital last week.
7 My brother never helps with the housework.
8 We always start school at 9.00.
9 My teacher is never late for class.
10 Robert no longer plays football.
11 I'll never forget the first time we met.
12 I always sleep 8 hours every night.
13 Carla probably hasn't finished working yet.
14 We have already been waiting for an hour and the bus still hasn't come.

72

1 A 2 C 3 B 4 C 5 A/B 6 B/C 7 A
8 A 9 B 10 C 11 A 12 C 13 B
14 C 15 A/C

73

1 as well as you do
2 more clearly than I do
3 more carelessly than I do
4 best of all the students in her school

74

1 I *don't think* politics is interesting.
2 *It isn't* (or *it's not*) *raining* at the moment.
3 *You haven't got* any brothers or sisters.
4 My sister *doesn't work* in London.
5 Liz *wouldn't like* to live in the country.
6 I *didn't work* yesterday.
7 Sue *won't be* here next weekend.
8 They *haven't been waiting* for us.

75

1 Is she going by car?
2 How often do you go swimming?
3 Which hotel did you stay at?
4 Aren't you hungry?
5 Can't you stay any longer?
6 Have you eaten Indian food?
7 How long has she been having piano lessons?
8 Doesn't he want to come out with us?
9 Who did you ask?
10 Who asked you?

76

1 didn't she?   5 shall we?
2 are you?   6 do you
3 doesn't it?   7 will/would/can/could you?
4 won't he?   8 wouldn't you?

77

1 Haven't you?   3 Did you?   5 Isn't he?
2 Does she?   4 Have you?

78

1 Can you tell me where the nearest bank *is*?
2 What time *do* you usually finish work?
3 ✓
4 Can you remember *where you put* my pen?
5 Have you decided what colour *you are* going to paint the flat?
6 Do you know if *the bridge has* been repaired yet?
7 When *did you start* to study English?

79

1 No, he didn't.   4 No, I don't think so.
2 Yes, I'm afraid it is.   5 Yes, I hope so.
3 Yes, I have.   6 Yes, I am.

80

1 You aren't hungry and neither is Jim.
2 Peter can drive and so can Sally.
3 I'm in a hurry and so are you.
4 I haven't seen the film and neither have you.
5 You saw what happened and so did we.

81 i

1 ✓
2 Have you seen the book *which was* on my desk?
3 ✓
4 The girl *who answered* the phone said you weren't at home.
5 Where's the newspaper *which I bought*/I bought this morning?
6 Is that the man *who* sold you the car?
7 She's the woman *whose briefcase* was stolen.
8 Steven Spielberg's new film, *which cost* more than $100 million to make, will be showing in British cinemas soon.
9 Albert Davis, *who* is only 25 years old, is the new manager of Acme Export Ltd.
10 ✓
11 John's father gave me the taxi fare, *which* was very nice of him.

81 ii

1 who   7 ——
2 ——   8 ——
3 who/that   9 ——
4 ——   10 who/whom
5 whose   11 whose
6 where   12 which

82

1 B   2 A   3 B   4 A   5 C   6 A   7 C
8 B   9 A   10 B   11 C   12 B   13 A
14 B   15 B   16 A   17 B   18 C   19 C
20 B

83

1 onto, next to
2 into, over
3 in, on, above
4 to, from, in, in
5 at, in, on, on, below
6 along, in front of, into
7 out of, onto, outside, round
8 inside, behind, off, into
9 under, down, on top of
10 past, through, up
11 into, behind, in
12 on, through, from
13 off, across, towards
14 at, in, between, opposite

84

1 My interview is *at* 2 o'clock *on* Monday.
2 We've been waiting here *for* ten minutes.

3 Are you leaving *on* Saturday morning?
4 I worked in a bank *for* five years.
5 Ken and Kate are on holiday *in* August.
6 I always visit my parents *at* Christmas.
7 Mike usually plays football *at* the weekend.
8 You've known me *for* ten years.
9 I was born *on* January 3rd *in* 1968.
10 Sarah was listening to the radio *while* she was taking a bath.
11 The doctors operated on the man just *in time* to save his life.
12 Are you doing anything *at the end* of next week?
13 I fell asleep in front of the TV *during* the football match.
14 The builders say they'll have finished the job *by* next weekend at the latest.
15 I found my new contact lenses strange at first, but I got used to them *in the end*.

85

1 with   4 in (or 'with')   7 as if (or 'like')
2 in   5 like   8 as (or 'like')
3 by, on   6 as

86

1 C   2 B   3 C   4 C   5 A   6 B   7 B
8 A   9 A   10 B   11 A   12 C   13 B
14 A   15 C   16 B   17 C   18 A   19 C
20 B

87

1 The company has given Kathy Cobuild the job.
2 My sister made me a cake on my last birthday.
3 The receptionist will order us a taxi.
4 I've promised someone these concert tickets.

88

1 I *turned down* their offer of a job.
2 We *kept on* working through our lunch break.
3 Robert *gave up* playing football years ago.
4 People say that I *take after* my father.
5 What time did you *set off* on your journey?
6 Unemployment has *gone up* by 10% since last year.
7 Our flight was *held up* by bad weather.
8 My grandfather never *went back on* a promise.
9 Mr and Mrs James may never *get over* the tragic death of their son.
10 The bank's computer *has broken down* six times this week already!